CORPORATE GOVERNANCE IN CENTRAL EUROPE AND RUSSIA

VOLUME 2

Insiders and the State

CORPORATE GOVERNANCE IN CENTRAL EUROPE AND RUSSIA

VOLUME 2

Insiders and the State

Edited by
ROMAN FRYDMAN
CHERYL W. GRAY
ANDRZEJ RAPACZYNSKI

CENTRAL EUROPEAN UNIVERSITY PRESS
Budapest   London   New York

First published in 1996 by
Central European University Press
1051 Budapest,
Nádor utca 9,
Hungary

Distributed by
Oxford University Press, Walton Street, Oxford OX2 6DP
Oxford New York Athens Auckland Bangkok Bombay Toronto
Calcutta Cape Town Dar es Salaam Delhi Florence Hong Kong
Istanbul Karachi Kuala Lumpur Madras Madrid Melbourne
Mexico City Nairobi Paris Singapore Taipei Tokyo Toronto
and associated companies in Berlin Ibadan
Distributed in the United States
by Oxford University Press Inc., New York

British Library Cataloguing in Publication Data
A CIP catalogue record for this book is available from the British Library

ISBN 1-85866-035-1 Hardback
ISBN 1-85866-036-X Paperback

Library of Congress Cataloging in Publication Data
A CIP catalog record for this book is available from the Library of Congress

Designed, typeset and produced by John Saunders Design & Production, Reading, UK
Printed and bound in Great Britain by Biddles of Guildford, UK

CONTENTS for volumes 1 and 2

Volume 2: Insiders and the State

ACKNOWLEDGMENTS

We are grateful to the World Bank and the Central European University Foundation for their support of our joint research project on Corporate Governance in Central Europe and Russia. The project culminated in the Conference on Corporate Governance in Central Europe and Russia, on December 15–16, 1994, in Washington, D.C. The chapters in these volumes are updated, revised, and edited versions of papers originally presented at the conference.

The editors

CONTRIBUTORS to Volumes 1 and 2

Roman Frydman, Professor of Economics, Department of Economics, New York University, and Co-Director, Central European University Privatization Project.

Cheryl W. Gray, Principal Economist, Policy Research Department, World Bank.

Andrzej Rapaczynski, Professor of Law, Columbia University School of Law, and Co-Director, Central European University Privatization Project.

Herbert L. Baer, formerly Financial Economist, Policy Research Department, World Bank. Tragically, Herb Baer died on February 27, 1995, from injuries sustained in a bicycle accident.

Bernard Black, Professor of Law, Columbia University School of Law.

Joseph Blasi, Professor, School of Management and Labor Relations, Rutgers University, and Fellow, Institute for Advanced Study, Princeton.

John C. Coffee, Jr., Adolf A. Berle Professor of Law, Columbia University School of Law.

Peter Dittus, Special Assistant to the General Manager, Bank for International Settlements (BIS).

John S. Earle, Associate Professor of Economics, Central European University; Center for International Security and Arms Control (CISAC), Stanford University; and Deputy Director, Central European University Privatization Project.

Saul Estrin, Professor of Economics, London Business School.

Jonathan Hay, Director, Harvard Institute for International Development Legal Reform Project, Moscow.

Bruce Kogut, Professor of Management, Wharton School, and Director, Emerging Economies Program, University of Pennsylvania.

Reinier Kraakman, Professor of Law, Harvard Law School.

Roland Michelitsch, Regional Economist, Sub-Saharan Africa Department, International Finance Corporation.

Katharina Pistor, Research Associate, Harvard Institute for International Development; formerly, Senior Research Fellow, Central European University Privatization Project.

Jane E. Prokop, graduate student, Harvard University, and Research Associate, Central European University Privatization Project.

Stephen Prowse, Senior Economist and Policy Advisor, Federal Reserve Bank of Dallas.

Charles F. Sabel, Professor of Law and Social Science, Columbia University School of Law.

Andrei Shleifer, Professor of Economics, Department of Economics, Harvard University.

David Stark, Associate Professor of Sociology and International Business, Department of Sociology, and Johnson Graduate School of Management, Cornell University.

Joel Turkewitz, Deputy Director, Central European University Privatization Project and Assistant Professor of Law and Economics, Central European University.

Dmitry Vasiliev, Deputy Chairman, Russian Federal Securities Exchange Commission.

Dimitri Vittas, Principal Financial Specialist, Financial Sector Development Department, World Bank.

1

EMPLOYEE OWNERSHIP
IN TRANSITION

JOHN S. EARLE and SAUL ESTRIN

The National Council for Soviet and East European Research provided support to John Earle early in the project. The authors would also like to thank Joseph Blasi, Roman Frydman, Cheryl Gray, Benedetto Gui, Derek Jones, Judit Karsai, Maria Lesi, Laurence Levin, Larisa Leshchenko, Peter Murrell, Tatiana Nemeth, Robert Oakeshott, Ugo Pagano, Bianca Pauna, Doina Rachita, Andrzej Rapaczynski, Nicusor Ruiu, Zuzana Sakova, Rebecca Schumann, and Lina Takla for assistance, comments, and discussions. Any errors of fact or interpretation remain entirely our own

Introduction

In this chapter we investigate the extent and likely impact of employee ownership on the transition process under way in Eastern Europe. Despite the fact that the political realities in most of the region imply that sales or transfers to employees often represent a significant privatization path, much of the literature on economic reform has been critical of the potential role of employee ownership in enterprise restructuring (for example, Blanchard *et al.* 1991), although the ownership form also has a few proponents (for instance, Ellerman 1990). The relative merits and differences in behavior of employee-owned firms compared with "conventional" capitalist firms in market economies have received considerable attention in Western literature (for example, Bonin and Putterman 1987; Bonin, Jones, and Putterman 1993; Hansmann 1990; Pencavel and Craig 1994). What is not yet well understood is the particular strengths and deficiencies brought by employee ownership to the process of transition itself. Our attempts to answer this question in this chapter provide the conceptual framework against which actual privatization proposals in various countries are evaluated and against which hypotheses about relative performance may be derived and tested.

We argue that a normative evaluation of the possible effects of employee ownership cannot be made in the abstract. Rather, it depends on the characteristics of the firm, on the market conditions under which it operates, and on the relative weights attached to the various objectives of economic policy. Despite its drawbacks compared with some other forms of corporate governance, employee ownership can contribute toward the development of a market economy, for example, when insider power is blocking alternative privatization paths. But the benefits would depend on the institutional form of employee ownership, the effectiveness and nature of employee control, as well as on external market conditions and the character of the restructuring problems to be solved. For example, privatization to employees should be carefully planned to include a guarantee that shares are freely tradable. Our analysis also suggests that the effects of employee ownership on firm behavior may depend on the company's profitability, especially on whether it is loss making. This leads us to propose such ownership arrangements to accelerate privatization of firms in declining sectors.

There are five further sections in the chapter. In the following section, the theoretical and empirical literature on employee ownership is briefly reviewed, to draw out implications about the situations in which employee ownership may be beneficial or damaging to enterprise performance both in the West and in the transitional economies. In the third section we offer a conceptual framework for evaluating the benefits and costs of employee ownership as a privatization strategy. Our evaluation of the potential impact of employee ownership is contingent on the alternative with which it is being compared and the conditions assumed to hold for the comparison. The attractions of employee ownership may be limited relative to an idealized form of external ownership based on a well-functioning legal system and competitive capital markets, but in some situations it may be superior to many of the options being discussed, and to the status quo. The nature and scope of employee ownership in Eastern Europe are outlined in the fourth section, which concentrates on the Czech Republic, Hungary, Poland, Romania, and Russia; except for the first, all of these are countries where the planned or actual privatization process is leading to a high degree of employee ownership. Some very preliminary evidence about the effects of employee ownership on company performance in Poland, relative to outside, managerial and state ownership forms, appears in the fifth section. Policy conclusions are drawn in the final section.

Effects on Enterprise Performance

There is an enormous literature on employee ownership and control, origi-
nating from theoretical work by Ward (1958), Domar (1966), and Vanek
(1970). In a brief section we cannot hope to do justice to this extensive
material, but we seek to summarize its principal conclusions and to apply
them to the transition context. We focus on theoretical results about the
effects of employee ownership derived from four strands of the literature,
each based on different assumptions about ownership structures and the
nature of corporate governance and ownership rights. These strands are the
agency approach, the self-management literature, the under-investment literature, and models of enterprise degeneration. We commence by highlighting
significant institutional and conceptual distinctions in the literature.

Assumptions and Institutional Arrangements

Disagreements in the literature about the impact of employee ownership
derive in no small part from ambiguity about what is meant by the term. We
will generally assume that ownership rights comprise the right to control the
firm and the right to a share of the surplus. Employee-owned firms are therefore controlled by their labor forces, who usually hold a majority of the
shares and determine the allocation of profits between wages and retentions.
In transitional economies, employee control mostly arises as a result of the
privatization process, rather than as the chosen ownership form for firms
founded *de novo*.[1]

Control without majority ownership is also possible, of course, especially
if ownership of the remaining shares is dispersed, and our analysis also
covers these cases. For example in one of the Polish firms analyzed below,
workers together own only 48 percent of the shares, but we classify this as
employee owned because the other holdings are dispersed among managers,
outside investors, and the state, none holding more than 30 percent. The
widespread application of privatization strategies that guarantee minority
stakes to workers as one element of the overall plan typically yields minority
employee holdings. For example, the mass privatization scheme in Poland
assigns workers up to a 20 percent shareholding, and Hungarian employees
of self-managed companies are able to acquire shares on a preferential basis,
the size of the discount not normally exceeding 10 percent of the total share

---

[1] One suspects that, as in the West (see Ben-Ner 1988), the proportion of firms formed *de
novo* as employee owned is negligible.

capital. Minority employee holdings, especially if held individually and therefore widely dispersed, may yield at best modest influence over corporate decision-making. This is an empirical question, which has been addressed in the West (see Conte and Svejnar 1990 for a survey of the American evidence) and which we also consider for the transitional economies below.

One can also have majority employee ownership without control over the enterprise. For example, current and past employees may in principle own a majority of the shares, but the institutional mechanisms for them to exercise their potential control (e.g. by electing employee representatives onto the board or by forming institutions enabling the labor force to vote as a block at stockholder meetings) may still be absent. Such firms we refer to as managerially controlled employee-owned firms (MCEOs). This organizational form is common in the West (e.g. the John Lewis Partnership in the UK; see Bradley, Estrin, and Taylor 1990) and perhaps also in transitional economies (see below). When employee ownership emerges via a plan to purchase shares by workers (Employee Stock Ownership Plans (ESOPs)) or managers and workers (Management Employee Buyouts (MEBOs)), the resulting employee shareholding often does not include mechanisms or arrangements for effective control to be exercised. This eventuality is sometimes institutionalized by the holding of employee shares in beneficial trusts controlled by the management.

The results in Western literature are sensitive to the way in which employee control is exercised, whether individually by employee owners with voting on the basis of the numbers of shares owned or "democratically" on the basis of one worker–one vote. Egalitarian voting arrangements of the type that characterize producer cooperatives and the "Illyrian firms" of the Yugoslav self-managed economy (see Estrin 1983; Bonin, Jones and Putterman 1993) are usually associated with ownership forms in which rights are associated with employment rather than with the holding of shares. Many of the negative results of employee ownership are derived from frameworks which assume nontradable ownership rights and collective modes of decision-making. But, democracy in decision-making could yield productivity benefits through worker solidarity that outweigh inefficiencies from other sources. Also relevant for these solidarity questions is the proportion of employees who own shares; many schemes have no explicit rules on this issue though a few require the involvement of a majority or even all workers. The bulk of employee ownership in the United States has arisen via ESOPs in which employee control is exercised individually if at all (e.g. Conte and Svejnar 1990) while collective ownership and control are the traditional form for employee ownership in Western Europe (see Estrin 1986; Bartlett *et al.* 1992). Both egalitarian and nonegalitarian voting arrangements exist in the transitional economies.

Additional significant institutional arrangements for employee-owned firms include the specification of property rights, for example, restrictions on the right to decumulate capital (as in the former Yugoslavia) or on the group eligible to buy and sell shares (such as current and former workers only). The latter is particularly significant because it may prevent the evolution of employee-owned firms into other organizational forms more conducive to coping with the evolving demands of the transition.

Incentives and Productivity

Incentives in employee-owned firms are addressed in the agency literature. This builds on pioneering work by Alchian and Demsetz (1972), which views employee ownership as a response to moral hazard problems in specifying employee contracts when labor effort is hard to monitor. Contracting and corporate governance under employee ownership have been analyzed by Williamson (1985) and Jensen and Meckling (1979), and the literature is well summarized by Hansmann (1990). The results are very mixed, with both forceful examples of the potential strengths of employee ownership as an organizational form, and dire warnings about the likely consequences of such arrangements for organizational efficiency.

There are a number of widely cited problems for corporate governance associated with employee ownership. Since the critical analysis by Beatrice and Sydney Webb (1926), who pointed out that managers may not be able to make effective decisions in situations where employees could remove them, many analysts have expressed severe reservations about the ability of democratically run organizations to deliver rational or speedy business decisions. Furthermore, managerial quality may be lower in such firms because employees often lack the appropriate experience and training, and managers, realizing this, will be wary of accepting a position in an organization where the managerial task is likely to be both more demanding and (if the employee owners are egalitarian in their sympathies) less rewarding.

Hansmann (1990) argues that forms of corporate governance in which employees are directly involved with the decision-making process have very high costs. These arise because employees are heterogeneous in skills, interests, and abilities. Employee-owned firms must put in place mechanisms to ensure that these conflicts are resolved. Potential gains are bought at a price: the time forgone in sitting in meetings that would not be necessary in outsider-owned firms, or the consequences of poor or slow decision-making. Examples of possible heterogeneity in the interest of different employee classes include different attitudes toward technical change between unskilled,

skilled, and white collar workers, and between younger and older workers about the benefits of internally financed investment. The greater the heterogeneity, the greater the costs of reaching agreement, and the greater the dangers of either failing to agree at all, or of taking decisions that represent economically inefficient compromises. These problems lead Hansmann to conclude that employee ownership would operate best in situations where employees are relatively homogeneous with respect to their skills, interests, and work and where firms are relatively small. Decision-making problems seem likely to be particularly severe when ownership is collective and voting procedures based on one worker–one vote. They will be less acute when employee shareholdings are owned individually, and perhaps are more concentrated.

Agency problems may be reduced if employee-owned firms are managerially controlled (MCEOs) and workers in practice have little ability to influence the decision-making structure. This may occur because of the absence of any formal mechanisms of employee control, such as representation on boards, or because of informal mechanisms, such as the continuation of highly hierarchical decision-making structures and a tradition of low employee participation. However, in the transitional context MCEOs may represent a continuation of the vacuum in property rights characteristic of the pre-reform period, because the formal transference of ownership has not brought in its train mechanisms of corporate governance. Thus, the emergence of MCEOs may not necessarily bode well for the evolution of the transition process, even if it does resolve immediate problems of decision-making.

One can, however, think of two situations in which employee ownership may act to enhance productivity. First, when labor marginal products are hard to monitor externally, a degree of employee ownership may encourage self-monitoring and peer group monitoring. Second, it may act as a general source of improved organizational efficiency, by improving the flow of communication of workers' preferences to managers, and thereby avoiding needless conflict; by locking workers into the firm, reducing the incentives for managerial opportunism against employees whose human capital has become enterprise specific; and by reducing the incentives for strategic behavior between managers and workers in wage bargaining. These benefits do not rely on majority employee stakes, let alone collective ownership or democratic decision-making, and hence may even flow from mass privatization combined with minority shareholdings for employees.

A practical example of these advantages, which is of relevance in transitional economies, concerns the turning around of bankrupt firms. There are many examples of this phenomenon in the West (e.g. Bradley and Gelb

1983), not least because employee ownership opens possibilities for wage concessions. But the underlying reason is that employee ownership increases the scope for cooperation between workers and managers, and reduces the domain for conflict. Cable (1984) modeled the bargaining process between mangers and workers over the range of company policy, especially innovation and the introduction of new technology, as a prisoners' dilemma game in which both could gain by cooperating, but each had short-term incentives to cheat on any agreed contract. Employee ownership, especially a majority or strategic holding, provided an institutional framework in which the cooperative outcome could be achieved. Specific indicators of improved productivity that have been found significant in the empirical literature include a reduction in working days lost through strikes, reduced labor turnover, increased employee "commitment" to the firm, and higher factor productivity and profitability (see Conte and Svejnar 1990; Kruse and Weitzman 1990; Bartlett *et al.* 1992).

While the productivity effects of employee ownership may hold equally well in transition economies, the nature of the transition process seems likely to magnify the inherent problems of workers in governance. State-owned enterprises were typically large, and their need to ensure input supplies under central planning implied a high degree of vertical integration. Coupled with the widespread need for drastic restructuring, this suggests that heterogeneous groups of workers must often make decisions concerning actions which affect them differentially. One has only to think of unbundling decisions involving profit-and-loss-making units that practice cross-subsidization to ensure wage equality between the units; or the even thornier question of employees working with the highly loss-making social assets of an otherwise profitable enterprise. This problem may be further aggravated because competitive product markets and other alternative corporate governance mechanisms (managerial labor markets, banking and financial markets) are largely absent in transitional economies.

Overmanning and Excessive Wages

The self-management literature has studied the effects of employee ownership on wages and employment, mainly focusing on collectively owned and democratically controlled institutional forms. These models assume that employee ownership does not cause agency problems, and (generally) that capital markets are competitive. In this framework, employee ownership can be seen as a form of monopoly power on the demand side of the labor market, an extreme situation of insider power. The consequences are that, relative to the outcomes under conventional firms, employee ownership

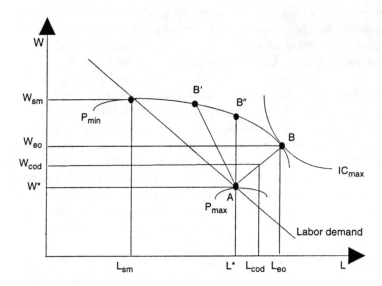

Fig. 1.1

leads to higher wages (and by implication lower retentions and investment) and to over- or under-employment depending on worker preferences between wages and employment and on the relative ownership stakes held by workers, managers, and owners.

Many of the results can be summarized by a simple diagram. An outsider-owned firm maximizing profits will hire labor until the marginal revenue product of labor equals the wage, a locus given by the labor demand curve in Figure 1.1. If we assume that the firm operates in a competitive labor market, at a wage W^*, then employment will be L^*. This provides a point of reference with equilibria under alternative ownership arrangements. Since workers absorb none of the firm-specific rents, their collective utility represented by the utility function is minimum available, while firms obtain the maximum level of profits represented by the isoprofit curve, P_{max}.

In the canonical model of self-management, it is assumed that self-managed firms maximize average earnings per worker (see Ward 1958; Vanek 1970) at the point in Figure 1.1 where the income per worker curve equals the marginal revenue product of labor, W_{sm}, L_{sm}. Since workers own the firm, they absorb all the surplus so the earnings curve is also the isoprofit curve for a profit level at zero, P_{min}. Self-management, therefore, leads firms to reduce employment in order to increase wages, with resulting output-reducing effects also emerging in the short run. The proposition relies on the assumption that the firm has rents or other sources of firm-specific surpluses; in a competitive situation W^* and W_{sm} coincide and the maximum profit that the firm can earn is zero.

While worker owners might give precedence to their earnings, it is hard to imagine that they would attach no weight to their prospects of continued employment, especially when a change in the economic circumstances of the firm throws up a trade-off between reductions in employment and increases in incomes for those who remain. This implies that collective preferences should be represented by a utility function in earnings and employment, so employee ownership may be analyzed as a special type of model of collective bargaining rather than as a case *sui generis*. Since workers are assumed to absorb all the surplus, the equilibrium must still lie on the zero profit isoprofit curve, P_{min}, at the point of tangency between the workers' utility function, IC_{max}, and the zero profit isoprofit curve, giving a wage-employment equilibrium (W_{eo}, L_{eo}). When workers attach some weight in their preferences to employment as well as earnings, the wage level is always less and the employment (and therefore in the short run the output) level is always more than that pertaining in an income-maximizing firm.

The comparison with the competitive capitalist firm is more complicated, however. Employee owners are absorbing the firm-specific rents, so the equilibrium is always off the labor demand curve. It is certain that the wage rate will always exceed that ruling under competition ($W_{eo} > W^*$). As we have drawn Figure 1.1, the employment level will also exceed that of the competitive firm. But this is in fact an assumption: namely, that the slope of the contract curve in wage-employment space given in Figure 1.1 by AB is positive. If the employees' preference function is assumed to take the form of an expected utility function with the two outcomes of W^* and W_{eo} weighted by the employment probabilities in the two situations, then a forward sloping contract curve implies that the workers are risk averse.[2]

One can also illustrate the impact of less than 100 percent employee stakes on wages and employment in the same framework. Let us suppose that a firm is owned by two groups, outside investors and workers, each with 50 percent of the shares. Further assume that outside investors are interested solely in profits.[3] As previously, equilibria will lie along the contract curve

---

[2] The contract curve will slope backwards, and hence employee-owned firms will hire fewer workers than competitive capitalist ones, though more than income-maximizing firms if workers are risk lovers. This possibility is illustrated by the contract curve AB' in Figure 1.1. Finally, contact curves are vertical with risk neutrality; employee ownership affects wages but not the level of employment compared with capitalist firms. This outcome is illustrated by contract curve AB" in Figure 1.1 (see Ben-Ner and Estrin 1991).

[3] The problem is more complicated when firms are owned or controlled by managers,

but now at a location determined by the relative bargaining power of the two groups. In the special case where equal shareholdings yield equal bargaining power in a Nash cooperative game, the equilibrium will be halfway along the contract curve at W_{cod}, L_{cod}.

An oft-noted curiosum in this literature is the result that two factor input income-maximizing firms in the short run respond to demand increases by reducing supply.[4] Meade (1972) established that income-maximizing firms always respond quantitatively less to changes in market situations, even if they do not always respond perversely. These conclusions are, however, contingent on assumptions about ownership and governance arrangements. Sertel (1982) and Dow (1993) have shown that the critical assumptions behind supply unresponsiveness are collective decision-making and the absence of tradable rights to the enterprise surplus. Employee-owned firms in which decisions are based on shareholdings rather than one worker–one vote, and most importantly, in which workers can freely buy and sell their shares in the firm on a competitive market should make output and employment decisions that are identical to those of investor-owned firms.

These theoretical results suggest that institutional forms including collective voting and restrictions on share tradability should be avoided, but they do not resolve the conundrum of "supply perversity" raised by employee ownership. Employee-owned shares are not generally traded on competitive markets, at least not if the organizations seek to maintain employee ownership as the predominant form for some time. Thus, in practice employee-owned firms that have individual shareholdings such as the West European

---

because the motivation of managerial owners is not well understood. Managerial theories of the firm in the West (for instance, Marris, 1966) focus on agency problems where managers have control but little or no ownership; they suggest that managers will be interested in size rather than profits. Ownership may diminish the agency problem, but it does not vanish unless one manager becomes the sole owner, and it may increase the difficulty of replacing an incompetent but entrenched manager. In the transitional context, managers may be interested in profits to establish their credentials on the emerging managerial market. However, if rent-maximizing behavior still predominates, they may instead be interested, for example, in maximizing employment to maintain the flow of employment-related subsidies.

[4] See Domar (1966) for an exhaustive examination of this result, and Bonin and Putterman (1987) for a survey of the succeeding literature. Drèze (1976) has established the equivalence of the general equilibrium allocation under self-management and under competitive capitalism. Differences in allocations outside equilibrium can only be maintained in the absence of entry by new employee-owned firms into profitable activities and exit by low-earning ones. If the economy is perfectly competitive in this sense of costless entry and exit, the resulting expansion of supply will eat away at the monopoly rents at the source of the misallocation until profits are eradicated and employee-owned firms make the same output and employment decisions as their investor-owned counterparts.

producer cooperatives allow only restricted trading, with prices often determined administratively rather than by the market (see Estrin, Jones, and Svejnar 1987; Bonin, Jones, and Putterman 1993). There has been insufficient analysis into the implications of these imperfect secondary share markets for the behavior of employee-owned firms.

There is patchy support for the view that employee ownership leads to restrictive employment and high wages relative to outsider owned firms; for example, for Yugoslavia, see Estrin (1983) and for British producer cooperatives, see Jones and Pliskin (1989). Ben-Ner and Estrin (1991) establish that high shares of surplus are allocated to labor in Israeli employee-owned firms. There is also evidence of low supply elasticities in employee-owned firms (e.g. Craig and Pencavel 1992).

The issue of adjustment flexibility takes on added importance for the restructuring and reorienting enterprises of East European economies. The relative inelasticities of output supply and labor demand functions are particularly worrying in the transition context because they may accentuate already existing deficiencies in the responsiveness of firms to the market. Not only is the internal restructuring of firms likely to proceed more slowly, but the lack of flexibility to market conditions implies that the crucial interfirm and intersectoral movements of resources may be inhibited.

Although, in self-management models, employee-owned firms deviate considerably from the equilibrium configurations of outsider-owned firms on the labor side, they do minimize nonlabor costs. This is, of course, a consequence of the assumption of earnings (or employee surplus) maximization. Incentives for the owners to minimize nonlabor costs may be a distinct improvement in transitional economies over continued state ownership, where managers may have the opposite motivation.[5]

Investment

Many analysts have argued that employee-owned firms will face problems in capital accumulation, though the reasons vary with the institutional form of employee ownership. We have already noted that employee-owned firms may absorb all profits as wages or overemployment. This was not assumed to cause investment problems in self-managed firms because capital markets were assumed to be perfect, so firms could borrow as much as they wanted at

---

[5] One can say more than this, however. When all factors vary and input markets are competitive, self-managed firms produce where the technology displays constant returns to scale. If we assume U-shaped long-run average cost curves, average earnings-maximizing employee-owned firms produce the level of output that, if the firm were capitalist, would minimize long-run average costs.

a market-determined interest rate. However, most analysts argue that employee-owned firms will invest less.

One important reason is that by their nature employee-owned firms cut themselves off from most sources of external finance. The fundamental problem for potential funders, whether via debt or equity, is that they open themselves to the threat of opportunistic behavior when governance is exercised by a factor of production other than capital. Minority equity holders in majority employee-owned firms do not have sufficient votes to prevent diversion of surplus from all owners to the employee owners alone via increases in wages. The problem is just as serious for lenders. For example, workers can decumulate the assets of the enterprise to increase their consumption by raising their remuneration above the level implied by the dividend per head. Hansmann suggests that employee owners may choose investment projects in which the upside gains accrue primarily to the owners, while the downside risks are borne primarily by the providers of capital. This phenomenon may in practice be accentuated by capital market discrimination against employee-owned firms on the grounds of unfamiliarity or via ideological suspicions. Avoiding the dangers inherent in worker opportunism and diversifying human and financial capital risks are probably the main reasons why capital typically hires labor rather than the other way round (see Meade 1972).[6]

If outside funds are rarely made available, employee-owned firms must rely disproportionately on their own resources. This may be somewhat less damaging in the transitional context, where capital markets are severely underdeveloped and employee ownership may make available to the enterprise a modest pool of savings that might not otherwise be available. These funds aside, employee-owned firms will have to rely exclusively on retained earnings to finance restructuring and investment. Furubotn and Pejovich (1970) have argued that employee-owned firms will invest less than outsider-owned firms. They assume democratic decision-making and no tradability of ownership rights, which derive solely from employment. The argument hinges on the proposition that worker owners would seek a higher rate of return from investment financed from retained earning than other types of owners because the principal that they had invested could not be recouped when the employee owner left the firm. This finding is not necessarily restricted to situations when workers' property rights are not tradable. As

---

[6] The conventional argument concerning the desirability of diversifying risks associated with human capital and with financial savings, however, ignores the point that human capital risk may be reduced if investing personal savings in the company also brings with it some control rights. Reducing the risks of layoff and loss of firm-specific rents is likely to be a principal motive for employees to become owners of their companies in Eastern Europe.

Ben-Ner (1992) points out, the conclusion that workers will require a higher return from investments may generalize to situations of individualistic ownership and tradability of shares if one believes that employees as owners will be more risk averse than outside investors because they do not have mechanisms to diversify their human and financial capital risks.

There is some evidence that employee-owned firms in the West are under-capitalized. For example, in a matched sample of private firms and cooperatives in Italy, Bartlett *et al.* (1992) found capital–labor ratios to be significantly lower in the employee-owned firms, a phenomenon confirmed for the United Kingdom, France, and Italy by Estrin, Jones, and Svejnar (1987) and for the American plywood cooperatives by Craig and Pencavel (1992). In their survey, Bonin, Jones, and Putterman (1993) report that Western producer cooperatives tend to rely disproportionately on internal funds and retained earnings, while the distribution of employee ownership across sectors confirms the very low penetration levels into capital intensive activities (see Estrin 1986).

The problems of employee-owned firms everywhere in raising capital grows in significance in the transition context. Because restructuring is expensive, the ability of firms to raise new capital and to generate retained earnings becomes critical to their ability to re-orient themselves toward markets. Moreover, a preponderance of employee ownership in the economy may also exacerbate problems in raising equity finance due to adverse selection problems in the market for corporate control. The informational advantages of insiders concerning the quality of the firm's assets imply that outsiders may be reluctant to acquire them at prices that the insiders claim are merited. Debt markets may also be weaker for employee-owned firms if bankruptcy institutions are poorly developed, because lenders cannot be sure of getting back even their principal.

The nature of the privatization process in Eastern Europe further exacerbates the potential for employee-owned firms to experience capital shortage. In situations where the state is seeking to sell its shareholdings rather than giving them away, the purchasers must raise sufficient money to buy the firm in addition to the money needed to finance investment, restructuring, and the other organizational and structural changes demanded by the transition. Hence the policy of selling state-owned enterprises to workers implies limiting the scope of this form of employee ownership to small and medium sized firms. In these cases, the upfront capital requirements can more easily be met from within the resources of the employee group, either from savings or by borrowing on the capital market, presumably against individual rather than enterprise collateral. A policy of privatizing to employees by sales will probably cause changes of ownership of this type to be concentrated in firms that are financially sound and, as a consequence, can pay for the purchase and necessary investments out of current cash flow. This is analogous to the way that ESOPs and MEBOs are formed in Western economies, in that sound cash flow is an important criterion in determining which enterprises are appropriate for such highly leveraged ownership structures.

Even when the state does not charge workers for its assets, the capital requirements argument suggests that employee ownership is less likely to be the appropriate method for privatization in capital intensive activities or in firms with major investment needs. One exception to this conclusion might be in situations when the capital is not sunk; if the assets purchased via an external loan are not firm specific, then the lender might be satisfied with a surety comprising the sale value itself. The problem for employee-owned firms on capital markets arises when the resale value of the asset is low relative to its price and to the return from its use in that particular firm.

Survival

The final set of issues discussed in the Western literature concerns the viability of employee ownership as a form of governance. There are few majority employee-owned firms in Western economies (and many of these exist to exploit the tax advantages of employee ownership (see Blinder 1990). One reason is that employee-owned firms are rarely formed, perhaps because of the difficulties in raising outside capital. Another is the tendency, more pronounced in North America than in the European cooperative sector, for employee-owned firms to revert to outside owner-ship.

The explanation developed by Ben-Ner (1984) is that (as we noted in Figure 1.1) if employee ownership exists in enterprises that generate surpluses for distribution to the employees, remuneration per worker must exceed the competitive market wage. Worker owners in these circumstances have an incentive to hire additional labor without offering them ownership rights. This is because an increase in employment would raise both output and surplus, provided that they could pay the new recruits less than existing employee owners. If the firm is profitable, the difference between dividend per worker and the wage means that employee owners will always have the incentive to hire nonowning employees rather than owners. As the original employee-owning cohort retires, the ownership form in successful producer cooperatives will gradually revert or "degenerate" to external investor control.

U.S. plywood cooperatives may degenerate in the manner predicted by the theory, with the proportion of workers who are members declining over time in successful firms (Ben-Ner 1984). However, in West European cooperatives where there are severe restrictions on the tradability of owner-ship rights there is no evidence of degeneration of this sort (see Bonin, Jones, and Putterman 1993). But degeneration is a far more general phenomenon than implied by cooperative life cycle models; in fact it includes all feasible forms of conversion from employee ownership to other ownership forms. Thus, a firm could be handed over to employee owner-ship to assist turnaround in situations when enterprise survival relies in no small part on improving employee–management relations. Once the turnaround has been achieved, the limitations of employee ownership, for example in the psychic costs of decision-making or in raising capital for new investment projects, might seem unnecessarily burdensome to the worker owners. They might prefer individually or as a group to liquidate their shares (presumably with a capital gain if the prospects of the firm have really improved) by selling either to outside interests or to a smaller insider group, such as managers.

The literature on degeneration generally presumes that ownership will ultimately end up in the hands of outsiders, namely retired workers and their heirs. But in transitional economies, there is the further possibility that employee-owned firms may degenerate back to state ownership. Consider the case noted above when privatization policies concentrate on selling firms to workers. The resulting private firms are highly leveraged, and in the East European context of highly imperfect capital markets, the bulk of the debt will probably have been provided by the state. It seems likely in cases of default on debt payments that the authorities might simply take the firm back into state ownership, especially if bankruptcy procedures are not yet in place or are operating imperfectly.

Declining Firms in Transition

The discussion in the foregoing sections suggests that the deficiencies of employee-owned firms in competitive market economies are not amelio-rated by the specific circumstances of transition; indeed they may be exacer-bated. However, there is one situation of some practical relevance in Eastern Europe where employee ownership can yield some benefits. Consider the case where workers want to accept pay reductions in exchange for job preservation, and this is implemented by the firm's becoming at least partly employee owned. Though the effects on productivity of employee owner-ship are likely to be dwarfed in the short term by the changes resulting from the re-organization of work and the adoption of superior technologies, such arrangements might play a valuable role in situations of previously poor industrial relations or when communication failures are a major cause of poor enterprise performance. Modest amounts of employee ownership might also reduce worker resistance to the sweeping changes that restructuring is likely to bring.

This suggests that employee ownership could be an institutional framework whereby workers in declining sectors could trade job security for pay. The case is strengthened when employee ownership is collective, provided such arrangements enhance employee solidarity and help to ensure the stability of the organization. This is because a major threat to the survival of such organizations comes from labor, as workers who are earning less than the market wage quit to earn higher wages in more conventional and better paying enterprises. The damaging impact of such departures on the incomes of those who remain will be amplified if there is a distribution of marginal products, with the more productive workers who quit first condemning the remainder to a downward spiral of declining productivity and pay. It is clear that the relevance of employee ownership in declining firms is related to the alternative sources of local employment and the costs of accepting employment in other locations. The welfare gains to be obtained from the survival of the enterprise under employee ownership will be greater when the loss-making firm is the major employer in a geographically isolated town or region.

A Conceptual Framework

The Western literature on worker participation and ownership, surveyed in the previous section, may be useful for forming predictions concerning some aspects of the behavior of firms privatized to their employees in Eastern Europe. But transition also introduces a number of special considerations which may be critical in evaluating the suitability of employees as new controlling owners of privatized companies. The Western approach assumes a starting point, and implicitly a history, different from that of the East European economies. As we have seen, employee ownership is generally analyzed in a first-best environment characterized by product and factor market competition, hard budget constraints, and clear property rights. The primary task in Western research has been to study the equilibrium properties and adjustments to perturbations of worker-controlled companies relative to capitalist firms. But the enterprises undergoing privatization in Eastern Europe have rather different origins, and both the evaluative criteria and the environmental conditions of employee ownership in the transition must be understood in this light. In this section we present our views on the objectives of the transition process and the peculiar nature of the transition environment and then proceed to a comparative evaluation of employee as against state, managerial, and investor ownership forms.

Criteria for Evaluating Ownership Forms in the Transition

We have previously reviewed Western literature on employee ownership, appraising its strengths and weaknesses according to conventional efficiency standards. In the transition context, however, such an evaluation requires a broader set of normative criteria, which should include the extent to which employee ownership, relative to other feasible ownership forms, facilitates the realization of the objectives of the transition process. The objectives we tentatively put forward here are not uncontroversial, and they contain inherently unscientific elements. Nevertheless, there does seem to be some agreement among students of the transition as to the goals of the process, and in the summary which follows we draw and elaborate on the large literature on transition, enterprise restructuring, and privatization.

A broad, fundamental objective for the new ownership structure is that it should promote the clarification of property rights. Communist systems placed little reliance on the rule of law, and private ownership of productive fixed assets was virtually unknown outside agriculture. Within the state sector, the authorities exercised control by giving orders, formally through the planning system and informally through extensive contacts, rather than by relying on the decentralized interactions of legally sovereign firms. State "ownership" under communism was not analogous to that found in utility companies in the West, but rather entailed a virtual vacuum in property rights, a vacuum which must be filled before any decentralized allocation mechanism can exist. The absence of property rights creates perverse incentives for individuals who control enterprises, leading them to misuse and appropriate assets, for instance by unbundling the enterprise in economically inefficient ways or by failing to invest and consuming the assets of the firm. However, property rights are not created merely by assigning titles of ownership to particular individuals but require the establishment of formal and informal mechanisms to enforce the ability of the putative new owners to use the assets as they choose. The development of such mechanisms in the transitional economies may depend in no small way upon the nature of the privatization process and the ownership configuration it generates.

An important corollary to the goal of clarifying property rights is establishing clear boundaries and new objectives of the firm, so that the new owners know what assets they possess and the scope of their rights over them, *vis-à-vis* other economic agents and the state. Founding a new relationship with the state includes not only ensuring the freedom of firms from arbitrary interference, but also radically re-orienting the goals of the firm, away from seeking rents from the state (or using its powers to create opportunities for rents) and toward satisfying the demands of the market. In the centrally managed economies, enterprise directors were rewarded for meeting plan targets and for pleasing their superiors in the plan hierarchy; success was rarely evaluated in terms of controlling costs, satisfying consumer demand, or making profits. Crucial managerial talents included the ability to obtain priority in the supply of raw material inputs and invest-ment funds, and to receive subsidies, success in the latter often being related to cost overruns of labor or investment. The re-orientation requires that managers devote their energies to the task of satisfying the demands of the market rather than pursuing subsidies and special concessions through their bureaucratic connections.

Lack of property rights and the associated absence of autonomy of decision-making at the enterprise level in socialist economies brought into question the very existence of firms as distinct entities in the standard Western sense. The boundaries of firms in a market economy are supposed to be determined by efficiency considerations: the costs and benefits of integration.[7] But in socialist economies, as emphasized by Kornai (1990), the relationship between the managers of firms and their superiors, whether the director of a trust or a branch minister, differed little from the relationship between managers and foremen or production supervisors under their direc-tion. A principal task of transition is, therefore, the reorganization of the productive units of the enterprise sector in the formerly socialist economies through vertical and horizontal disintegration and reintegration to form an industrial structure in which the boundaries of the firms ensure that costs are at a minimum.

The establishment of property rights and market orientation should be reflected in changes in the organization of firms. The structure of the organi-zation should adapt to be able to respond to the changing demands of customers, to ensure adequate mechanisms for managerial control, and to provide appropriate information for rational decision-making. Necessary changes will include the creation of functions and departments for sales, marketing, finance, human resources (in the Western sense), and product and technological development. Also significant might be the development of new internal organizational arrangements, for example a shift from "U" to "M" form structures (see Williamson 1985).

---

[7] See Coase (1937) for the seminal contribution on the boundaries between the firm and the market, and Grossman and Hart (1986) for a more contemporary approach to the issue.

A further, broad category of restructuring consists of the reallocation of resources of all types and at all levels of the economy and the associated changes in relative prices to ensure that inputs are used efficiently and that suppliers satisfy the new patterns of final demand. At a highly aggregated level, such changes include shifts from producer goods to consumer goods, from manufacturing to services, and from domestic or intra-Council of Mutual Economic Assistance (CMEA) trade to exporting to developed Western countries. Hare and Hughes (1991), for instance, indicate those sectors which might need to expand or contract in various countries. They also point out that considerable swaths of the socialist economies may have negative value added at world prices, and may, therefore, have to be closed down entirely once the economy is opened to international competition. The new ownership structure must facilitate significant downsizing in numerous activities while encouraging growth in others.

Considering the same phenomena at a more disaggregated level, the restructuring process demands that the newly privatized firms be responsive to market signals in the products they choose to supply and in their use of factor inputs. In firms for which the optimal level of output has fallen, the governance system must be able to effect large decreases in employment. Due to the inherited technologies and the production practices, which were wasteful in the use of inputs including energy and labor, new owners must have the incentives and the ability to ensure that costs are reduced, that the factor mix is rationalized, that productivity is raised, and that quality is improved. Much of this restructuring requires or would be accelerated by investment in new equipment; here enters the often noted importance of the ability of the new owners to raise capital and bring in new technologies.

Furthermore, transition includes dynamic adjustment by organizations to changed and changing economic circumstances. The outcome of the process may be path dependent, and the appropriate institutional arrangements may gradually change as the process unfolds. It may not be possible to specify *ex ante* the optimal ownership structure, for instance; this implies that whatever structure is selected should have the flexibility to evolve as the dynamic path of transformation proceeds. The lower the transaction costs, the less binding the initial allocation of ownership rights, for they would be quickly reallocated to achieve better matching of owners with assets. Institutions concerning property rights should, therefore, be designed to lower those transaction costs and to facilitate the development of financial markets. The new ownership configuration should minimize the probability of degeneration back to state ownership.

In addition to these objectives of the transition – clarifying property rights, redefining the scope of firms, re-orienting behavior toward the market, facilitating restructuring at all levels of the economy, and permitting further evolution to better matches and more appropriate ownership forms – social concerns should also be borne in mind when evaluating alternative ownership configurations. As we have noted, a significant portion of the capital stock inherited from the centrally-managed systems may be of such poor quality that it merits little or no maintenance expenditure or replacement investment. In a frictionless world, much of this equipment should be shut down immediately, and workers retrained for new jobs. But layoffs and retraining introduce social externalities, and the costs of reallocating a substantial part of the work force across industries, occupations, and geographic regions are likely to be immense. The policy questions are how to achieve the optimal rates of decline of firms, sectors, and regions, and how to internalize the losses of workers as stakeholders.

Any transition program faces the problem of resolving trade-offs in the attainment of these diverse objectives. For instance, there may often be conflicts between the restructuring and social goals. And even reallocating labor and increasing productivity may sometimes be incompatible; labor reallocation destroys the specific skills associated with long-term employment relationships. Increasing the flexibility of the ownership structure, so that it can readily evolve and adapt over time, risks lowering the incentives of workers to undertake new firm-specific investments because of their fear of expropriation.[8] If ownership is volatile, it may also reduce the willingness of workers to cooperate with internal changes, there may be a trade-off between voice and exit mechanisms in finding the best routes for restructuring and increasing efficiency. A feature of many trade-offs is that the costs and benefits associated with different objectives are realized over different lengths of time. A complete welfare evaluation would have to be sensitive not only to the weights placed on different objectives (and on the utility of different groups of the population), but also to the rate of discount applied over time.

Furthermore, the weights placed on alternative objectives and the evaluation of the degree to which different ownership forms may succeed in satisfying them will depend on the characteristics of individual firms and the environment in which they operate. Relevant characteristics of the firm include its size, capital requirements, prospects (expected future profitability), location, magnitude of internal restructuring problems, costs of monitoring effort, age structure of workers, and extent of heterogeneity of skills and interests among employees. For example, social considerations take

---

[8] Shleifer and Summers (1988) discuss this problem in the context of hostile takeovers in the United States, and Aoki (1994) analyzes the complementarity between various attributes of Japanese firms, including institutions of capital and labor markets.

on added importance when a firm requiring drastic downsizing is staffed largely by older workers and when it is geographically isolated, in the extreme case in a one-company town. Larger and more capital-intensive firms are likely to have more complex governance problems, as are firms facing enormous restructuring.

Environmental conditions include the local labor market and ease of migration, how well capital markets are functioning, the competitiveness of product markets, and the enforceability of property rights. Effective competition in product and factor markets can act to discipline firm behavior and thus function as an alternative governance mechanism. Functioning secondary markets may provide feedback from changes in share prices and allow the possibility of takeovers, and a better developed banking system would allow governance roles for banks to develop. The degree to which property rights can be readily enforced, through the legal system or otherwise, affects the ability of new owners to make the changes they deem desirable inside the firm and to make contracts with other firms. We will consider below the implications of serious imperfections in legal enforceability and in product and factor markets, especially the capital market.

Finally, a condition which is tremendously significant in transitional economies is the residual softness of budget constraints. If the budget constraints of firms continue to be soft, it seems unlikely that most feasible forms of ownership change would divert managerial behavior from the pursuit of government subsidies to the task of restructuring and making profits. For instance, when losses are almost automatically financed by preferential credits, firms neither reap the benefits nor bear the costs of their decisions. If budget softness is widespread, the macroeconomic effect of high inflation would also hinder effective enterprise decision-making.

Employee Ownership versus Other Organizational Forms

We now turn to a comparative analysis of four "ideal type" ownership forms – state ownership (the status quo), employee ownership, managerial ownership, and outside investor ownership. We define each type, consider the advantages of outside ownership compared with the other forms, compare the two categories of "insider privatization" – employee and managerial ownership – against continued state ownership, and evaluate alternative types of insider control.

Ownership Forms

We take the status quo of state ownership (SO) to be a situation in which property rights are not yet clearly defined, and the enterprise is drifting.

There may have been some restructuring as a consequence of the tightening of budget constraints, if they have been tightened, but profits remain minimal with the surplus absorbed by a coalition of workers, managers, and the local community. Spontaneous privatization of state property is probably under way through a variety of processes, creating private benefits for some parties. It may also sometimes result in social benefits through more productive utilization of assets, but the constraints on the open use and resale of assets acquired through illegal or questionable means imply that economically efficient unbundling, investment, retooling, productivity gains, and refocusing of activities are likely to have been very modest.

By employee ownership (EO), we mean a majority stake owned by nonmanagerial employees. Within this general type, we apply our previous analysis to delineate different institutional forms of employee ownership, according to the relationship of the new firms with the state and to the ways in which property rights are exercised. The relationship with the state takes on particular importance because employee buyouts are normally highly leveraged, and the state is the lender. Two different categories of property rights are especially relevant in the current context: control (voting) and disposal (tradability). At one extreme, the conventional producer cooperative is collectively owned and democratically controlled, with restrictions on tradability of shares. At the other, the open joint-stock company has majority employee ownership in individualistic form and tradability in shares. Mixtures of the two are possible and are quite common in Eastern Europe. In addition to these two polar types of employee-owned firms, a third type is what we have dubbed the "managerially controlled employee-owned firm" (MCEO), with the employees unable to convert their majority ownership into control; voting rights are in practice irrelevant, and there may or may not be share tradability.

Managerial ownership (MO) refers to majority managerial shareholding, possibly combined with a minority employee stake, while outside investor owned and controlled firms (OO) cover the range of standard Western enterprises. In both of these ownership forms we generally assume that companies follow the legal form of open joint-stock firms, so that ownership rights are freely tradable.

Outside Ownership

Under many conditions outside ownership would probably provide the strongest support for most of the goals of the transition: to clarify property rights and promote a profit orientation; to motivate restructuring, cost minimization, and the redefinition of the firm's boundaries; and to facilitate access to new investment and technologies. Even if the state has not been able to commit itself fully to hard budget constraints, investor-owned firms seem more likely than the other forms to reorient from rent seeking to profit maximization, not least because outside owners, at least if they were not part of the previous political order, would probably have more restricted access to subsidies. Widespread ownership by outsiders is likely to encourage the development of secondary markets and thus further the evolutionary process of matching and rematching assets with owners.

The advantages of outside ownership, however, are diminished under certain conditions. For instance, if alternative governance mechanisms, such as product market competition, function well, then they may serve to discipline the behavior of all types of firms facing hard budget constraints. Moreover, the ability of outside owners to implement restructuring programs may be inhibited in cases where shares are dispersed over a large number of small shareholders or in situations where there is poor development of court systems to enforce their rights. If insiders refuse or are slow to cooperate, outside ownership may display few benefits, even in the clarification of property rights. When evaluated by the social criterion, organizations controlled by outsiders are likely to be poor, because investor-owners of declining firms are unlikely to internalize the externalities for workers and their communities of plant closures or massive layoffs. Because these social costs are greatest in situations where the local labor market opportunities are few and migration is costly, outside ownership becomes less attractive under those conditions, a point to which we shall return below.

The privatization experiences of Eastern Europe reveal that investor ownership has rarely been a feasible option on a large scale. Even in the richer Visegrad countries (Hungary, Poland, and Czechoslovakia), there are few domestic agents willing to be an external owner, and the magnitude of the privatization problem alone is probably sufficient to rule out foreign capital as more than a relatively minor source of external ownership, even if widespread foreign involvement were to prove politically acceptable. Most importantly, insiders in several countries have acquired sufficient political power to prevent outside privatization. In many transitional economies, the only privatizations that have had an important impact on the share of output in the state sector reserve a large role for enterprise employees, whether managers or workers or both. Given these political constraints, the relevant policy question seems to be how managerial and employee ownership compare with each other, and against the status quo.

Insider Privatization

Firms that are owned and controlled by their employees, whether managers or workers, share some of the advantages of outside investor-owned firms compared with continued state ownership. Property rights may be clarified, although the extent of clarification of the firm's boundaries *vis-à-vis* the state may vary depending on the organization of the buyout, as discussed below. The agency problems and opportunities for opportunistic behavior of insiders against lenders may be modest compared with the status quo situation in which property rights are not defined at all, and stake holders have incentives to decumulate the assets of the firm. Most important, insider-owners will at least have more incentives to increase economic profits, to search out profitable investment opportunities, and to improve the boundaries of the firm than in the status quo.

However, there is one potential advantage of the status quo over all kinds of insider privatizations: it keeps open the possibility that the state could introduce outsider ownership. By privatizing to employees or managers, the state is foreclosing on the option of future outsider privatization. The value of the option arises from the fact that in many situations outsider privatization dominates insider privatization as a way to attain the objectives of transition. And while maintaining ownership, the state has at least two potential control mechanisms at its disposal, even if it fails to monitor its enterprises closely. The first is the threat over managers that if they are caught acting inappropriately, the firm will be privatized to outsiders (who will presumably get rid of the existing management). The second is the incentive (stressed by Pinto, Belka, and Krajewski 1993 and Aghion, Blanchard, and Burgess 1994, for example) for managers in state firms to restructure firms before privatization to establish their performance credentials to the new owners after privatization. If these arguments are correct, then insider privatization may not always be superior to state ownership. But, the option value of continued state ownership may not be very high, because of the limited credibility of the state's threat to punish malfeasance by imposing outsider ownership and because of empirical evidence (e.g. Estrin, Gelb, and Singh 1993) suggesting that the economic situation of the firms in the state-owned sector tends to deteriorate, in large part because of the absence of clear property rights. These arguments, therefore, fail to resolve the question of the extent to which employee ownership dominates state ownership; we will argue that this depends primarily on the precise institutional design of the employee-owned firm.

Compared with investor-owned firms, the lack of separation of ownership and control implies that insider-owned firms may have fewer governance problems of one type, but they will also experience greater difficulties in raising outside capital because of the agency problems faced by lenders and minority investors. For similar reasons, concentrated insider ownership will discourage the development of takeover markets, because the lack of liquidity in small numbers of shares implies that it may be very difficult in a takeover action to earn the control premium on minority stakes previously acquired; thus, rematching is inhibited. Employee owners are less likely to reorient the firm toward the market and away from the state than are outside investors, because of the insiders' problems in raising capital for restructuring and their ties with the state bureaucracy. But, if product markets are highly competitive, insiders may be forced to restructure and improve their efficiency to survive; more generally, if alternative governance mechanisms are improved, the disadvantages of insider ownership would be reduced.

Managerial and employee ownership are also significantly different from each other. While both may lead to cost reductions, the employee-controlled firm is likely to perpetuate inefficiencies in the allocation of labor, a very important difference in the overstaffed enterprises emerging from the socialist world of excess labor demand. Ownership by managers is also likely to dominate that of nonmanagerial employees in redefining the appropriate boundaries of the firm. As we argued above, employee ownership may be superior to the status quo because rearranging the boundaries of the firm will be possible if the gainers can compensate the losers. In principle even highly egalitarian employee-owned firms with high solidarity may, therefore, be able to undertake some restructuring and unbundling provided they offer a potential Pareto improvement, and some form of compensation package can be agreed upon. This is potentially an advance over the status quo.

In some situations this compensation will not be possible – potential Pareto improvements will not be convertible into actual Pareto improvements (for instance, because lump-sum transfers are infeasible). The biggest problems with the scenario in which everyone is made better off, however, are likely to arise from the difficulties of collective decision-making under uncertainty, particularly when some groups of workers are earning supracompetitive rents. Many enterprises have a large number of restructuring paths which they could potentially follow, for instance, changing product lines, reorganizing company divisions, or adopting different kinds of new technologies, but each of these paths has different implications for the value of the human capital of various groups of workers in the company. Given that the profit associated with each path is also uncertain, each group of workers will try to block paths which seem likely to downgrade their own skills. Thus, it may not be difficult for blocking coalitions to form, preventing desirable restructuring.

In resolving these agency problems, managerially owned firms have a clear advantage. They will be motivated to undertake any restructuring or rearrangements that increase profits. Supracompetitive wages may be reduced and workers laid off with little or no compensation. Managerial ownership can potentially yield restructuring benefits analogous to those of investor ownership and greater than those of employee ownership.[9]

The potential disadvantages of managerial compared with employee ownership are fourfold. First, under some conditions, a slower pace of restructuring may be desirable. Employee owners are more likely to internalize the social costs of layoffs than are managers. Second, the flip side of the argument that managerial owners would be able to shed workers more easily is that worker owners would be able to shed managers more easily. In cases where managerial turnover is a *sine qua non* for the firm to be turned around, managerial ownership has the disadvantage of entrenching bad managers.

Third, if employee shareholdings are widely dispersed, secondary markets may develop more easily than if shares are concentrated in the hands of a few managers. Although still difficult, it may be somewhat easier for outsiders to take over companies by buying up small numbers of shares than by negotiating with a single manager or a small group of managers. While there may be a collective interest of the insiders to keep out outsiders, individual employees may "free ride" by selling their small holdings to outsiders. Concentrated insider holdings are more likely to lead to entrenchment because of the informational advantage of insiders over outsiders. In an environment of great uncertainty over the prospects for any company and lack of financial markets functioning to provide estimates of value, the concentration of holdings together with the asymmetry of information may give rise to adverse selection in the market for corporate control.

Finally, managerial ownership suffers from the disadvantage that, compared with nonmanagerial employee owners, managers may be better not only at restructuring but also at rent seeking, so that under some conditions they may be less inclined to adopt a new market orientation. If budget constraints are soft, it is arguable that transfers of ownership to either managers or workers will have little or no effect on enterprise behavior because both sets of new owners will remain motivated to maximize rents rather than profits or earnings per worker. Insider privatization is, therefore, unlikely to bring many benefits until budget constraints are tightened. Under somewhat harder budget constraints, the net returns to the two activities will be determined by both the opportunity costs and the benefits, which are in turn affected by the prospects of the firm, its environment, the political situation, and so forth. However, there may be some differences between employee and managerial ownership in this respect. Employees represent a

[9] If supracompetitive wages are the result of firm-specific investments, however, reducing them may be unfair, and it may lower the willingness of employees to undertake such investments in the future.

new and more diffuse group of owners than managers, who as survivors from an earlier period maintain their good connections and bad habits. The costs to seek rents may be higher for employee-owned firms than those under managerial ownership because the former organization may have more diffuse and heterogeneous objectives. More importantly, the benefits to rent seeking may be lower in employee-owned firms because managers, given their long-standing connections under the previous regime, may be more effective at extracting subsidies. In such circumstances, privatization to employee owners, by weakening the old relationships, might be superior to managerial ownership.

Most of these points apply to a variety of employee ownership forms, but some important differences also arise. As discussed in the next section, most insider privatizations in Eastern Europe come about through highly leveraged buyouts in which employees borrow, implicitly or explicitly, from the state for long periods of time. Because the collateral for the debt is the company shares, defaulting on the loan could result in repossession of the shares, or renationalization. Often, the loan is made on highly preferential terms and accompanied by various restrictions on the firm's behavior, such as prohibiting layoffs or changes in production profile for the period of repayment. In such cases the firms may remain oriented toward bargaining with the state over these regulations, which arguably affect profitability and, therefore, the ability to repay the loan.

Disadvantages are also likely to accrue to institutional forms of employee ownership in which voting is not proportional to shareholdings and in which shares cannot be freely traded. If voting is on the basis of one member–one vote, decision-making is likely to remain hostage to the interests of the median worker. Even with proportional voting, restrictions on tradability may inhibit the formation of a dominant coalition inside the firm and will prevent outsiders from entering. Such forms of employee ownership are emphatically weaker in their capacity to evolve and convert into new organizational forms. In declining firms, this disadvantage may be offset by the ability of producer cooperatives to satisfy the social objectives of the transition process.

The evaluation of MCEOs turns on several factors. Like managerial ownerships (MOs), the MCEO should be able to avoid the agency problems of employee ownership (EO) and undertake some restructuring, but whether drastic forms of restructuring would be permitted by the employee owners is less clear. The scope of managerial authority may be limited to relatively minor decisions, particularly those which directly affect employees. Also like MOs, the MCEO may have an absolute advantage over EOs not only in making profits in the market, but also in lobbying the state; if there is a comparative advantage in rent seeking, the MCEO may offer more advantages compared with EOs if the firm is in a sound economic situation, but it may be inferior in poor economic conditions. Moreover, the MCEO (or any situation of managerial control in which the managers own significantly less than 100 percent of the shares) may have a standard agency problem due to the fact that the managers of such a firm have incentives to pursue their own interests at the expense of the other shareholders. Besides placing a higher weight on growth and personal perquisites, as in the standard managerial theory of the firm (see, for instance, Aoki 1984), in the transition context the danger is that the manager will continue to apply well-learned techniques for spontaneous privatization: asset stripping, transfer pricing, and the like. Compared with state ownership or even to outside ownership, the MCEO has the advantage that workers, who are in an excellent position to monitor such actions, will have a direct interest in preventing theft by managers. In contrast, the problem of managerial abuse does not afflict cases where employees have clear ownership and control.

In conclusion, employee ownership may dominate the status quo in transitional economies because it offers some elements of decentralization of decision-making to enterprises which could lead them toward market-related goals, and it may even dominate investor ownership in terms of political feasibility. When compared with managerial ownership, it has clear deficiencies where restructuring and especially rearranging the boundaries of the firm are concerned but may be superior at breaking down the rental relationships between former state-owned firms and the budget. If there are no decision-making costs, employee ownership can allow Pareto improving restructuring and unbundling to be implemented, and this can include the reduction of employment, provided that compensation arrangements have been agreed. Inferiority to managerial ownership arises because managers will be able to pay lower compensation to workers receiving supracompetitive wages, and because employee owners may be unable to agree on either the form of the unbundling or the compensation package if the labor force is heterogeneous. Any possible advantages of employee ownership over the status quo are heavily dependent on the particular institutional setup, and the particular forms usually adopted in East European privatizations are far from the most advantageous, as the next section will show.

Privatization Policies in the Creation of Employee-Owned Firms

The Czech and Slovak Republics aside, the vast majority of East European privatizations have involved transfers to employees of the formerly state-owned company. Table 1.1 provides an overview of the number of privatizations where all employees, including managers, have received majority stakes in the Czech Republic, Hungary, Poland, Romania, and Russia. Because of severe data limitations and comparability problems, these figures, which are discussed below for each country separately, should be taken as only rough approximations of the extent of "insider privatization." The estimates include

Table 1.1 Employee Ownership Resulting from Privatization (rough estimates)

Country (base group of co's. for estimations)	Companies with employee control	Privatizations (percentage)	Average % held by all employees	Estimated total employment in EOs
Czech Republic (voucher priv., 1st wave)	3	1	4.4	N.A.
Hungary (self-privatization)	187	43	42.0	36,000
Poland (priv. liquidation)	1,478	75	50.8	450,000
Romania (all large privatization)	600	98	95.0	150,000
Russia (all large privatization)	6,300	90	65.0	N.A.

Notes: "Employee" in this table includes managers, because of the difficulty in obtaining information on ownership by different categories of employees. The sources and calculation of the estimates in the table are described in detail below under the subsections for each country respectively. Note that the base for each country is different: Czech figures refer to companies privatized in the first wave of voucher privatization for which the approved privatization project granted more than 50 percent of shares to employees. Hungarian figures pertain only to the self-privatization program. Polish figures result from applying the proportion of employee-controlled firms in World Bank data on 23 firms in the liquidation program to the total of 1,999 Polish firms included in the program since 1991. The Romanian numbers refer to the results of a CEU survey of 66 privatized companies in the MEBO program. Those for Russia pertain to companies voucher privatized; the proportion of 90 percent comes from a survey conducted by Blasi (1994) on the ownership structures of 127 companies in the program; this figure applied to the approximately 7,000 companies in the program yields an estimate of 6,300 employee-controlled companies. The estimate of all employees' stake in each country is based on all privatized companies in the base group (not only those with dominant employee control). All estimates are preliminary.

managerial ownership, because separate figures for managers and nonmanagerial employees are usually unavailable in aggregate. Only legal transactions conducted through official government programs are counted, omitting most cases of "spontaneous" privatization, whereby assets are transferred either illegally or by exploiting legal loopholes and which necessarily involve at least the collusion of some insiders. The figures also exclude some cases where employees have become indirect shareholders through newly founded legal persons, because the latter normally appear in the statistics as outside investors. Moreover, they exclude the transfer of minority stakes to employees, which is a common feature of nearly all privatization programs in Eastern Europe. Nonetheless, the overwhelming preponderance of insider privatization is clear across the countries surveyed.

At the same time, both the policies by which employee-owned companies were created and the resulting institutional arrangements vary quite significantly across countries. As emphasized in previous sections, the different institutional forms may have quite different implications for firm behavior. The ways in which ownership rights are exercised, especially share tradability and voting rights, carry consequences both in terms of traditional issues of investment, output, employment, and wage determination and the particular transition problems of inter- and intrafirm restructuring. To these must be added the relationship with the state, which plays the roles of both the regulator of employee-owned firms and their founder through the privatization process. In practice the two roles of the state intermingle to a great degree, and privatization programs convey particular sets of property rights corresponding to various institutional forms. This section examines the policies of East European governments and their institutional consequences, focusing on those countries where emerging employee ownership seems to be most significant and on those aspects of the programs which bear upon the emerging corporate governance and behavior of employee-owned firms.

Romania

Romania represents one of the most interesting cases of emerging employee ownership in Eastern Europe. Management and Employee Buyouts (MEBOs) account for about 98 percent of all the privatizations of state-owned companies to date. The predominance of employee ownership forms was already established in the so-called "pilot privatization program," wherein 22 medium to large companies were privatized by the National Agency for Privatization (NAP), mostly in 1992. The purpose of the program was to experiment with alternative privatization techniques, and it was initially expected to be the vehicle for the privatization of a much larger number of companies (up to 350, according to the Privatization Law). Despite international financing and technical assistance, however, 15 of the 22 companies were privatized entirely, and 4 of the rest partially, through insider buyouts. The proportions of workers' shares in those four companies were 15, 29, 48, and 70 percent. The result of the experimentation thus seemed to be that only insider privatization was feasible.

Subsequently, privatization responsibilities shifted from the NAP to the State Ownership Fund (SOF), which became the 70 percent owner of all the corporatized enterprises (one of five so-called Private Ownership Funds, or POFs, received the other 30 percent), but it also failed to find outside buyers for state companies, as charged by the law.[10] Perhaps casting about for some way to accomplish at least some privatization and under the influence of British advisors, the SOF inaugurated an accelerated program for MEBOs in early 1993. As shown in Table 1.1, the program, at least in numbers of firms, has been quite successful: nearly 600 companies had been privatized as of June 1994, most of them 100 percent to their employees.[11] Other types of privatization, such as direct sales to foreigners and other outsiders, have been few; various plans for mass privatization and for public offerings have so far largely come to naught; and it seems likely that MEBOs will continue to represent the dominant privatization route in Romania for some time to come.

But employee ownership in Romania is also a particularly interesting case because of the institutional form of the newly privatized companies and their relationship with the state. The legal framework has left the employees much leeway to determine the precise institutional setup, and consequently MEBO firms exhibit a great deal of variety in terms of the tradability of shares and the voting rights of employee owners. The configurations of ownership rights typically put MEBO firms somewhere in the space between traditional producer cooperatives, majority ESOP firms, and open joint stock companies, with some of the characteristics of each. Their behavior, therefore, is also likely to represent composite influences.

The institutional peculiarity which determines the nature of each MEBO-privatized firm is an employees' association (known as the PAS, or Program for Shareholder-Employees), a legally and financially independent nonprofit form set up by a group of current and former employees to determine the distribution of shares, negotiate the acquisition of the firm, and arrange for

[10] A more comprehensive analysis of Romanian privatization, including a particular focus on the POFs as privatization intermediaries, may be found in Earle and Sapatoru (1994).

[11] Most were quite small: information on employment is available only for a limited sample of 200 companies, but of these, 90% had 500 employees or fewer.

Table 1.2 Ownership Structure in MEBO-Privatized Companies in Romania, August 1994

	EO	MO	Total
All current employees (%)	95.7	97.9	96.4
Managers	19.2	63.6	32.2
Nonmanagerial employees	76.5	34.4	64.1
Former employees (%)	1.6	1.9	1.8
Outside investors (%)	2.7	0.2	2.0
Number of firms	41	17	58
Employment in 1994	705	511	648
Profitability in 1994 (%)	8.4	8.4	8.4

Source: CEU Labor Research Project survey of 66 companies in the MEBO privatization program, September and October 1994. See Earle (1995) for a description of the survey and data. Several observations are omitted from this analysis because of a lack of comprehensive information.

credits to finance the purchase.[12] Concerning the distribution of shares within the firms, no comprehensive information on the results is available, but the results of a Central European University (CEU) survey of 66 companies that have passed through the program are reported in Table 1.2.[13] On average, all employees own 96 percent of the shares in the 58 companies for which comprehensive information is available, but the ownership distribution among employees shows significant variance: there are cases of dispersed and concentrated ownership, of clear managerial control, and of worker predominance. Even the principles for share distribution are left to the discretion of each PAS (although a recently passed law (August 1994) specifies them more fully), and it is well-nigh impossible to understand how the allocation is determined in the presence of the fixed overall price. Usually, somewhat arbitrary criteria such as firm tenure, salary level, and position are invoked, although possession of cash and Certificates of Ownership (for acquiring shares from the Private Ownership Fund or POF) must play roles.

In addition, the PAS plays a critical role in the governance of the company, at least until the debts associated with the privatization transaction are fully repaid (generally about five years). First, the PAS determines the tradability of shares both to outsiders and within the company. In most cases, it seems that outsiders are completely excluded from acquiring shares still held in the PAS,

[12] Unlike a typical ESOP, the board of the PAS is elected by its members and is not appointed by the company management, although it is possible that the distinction may not be great in practice.

[13] The survey was carried out by the CEU Labor Research Project. See Earle (1995).

and even transactions within the company and among PAS members require approval. The entry of outside expertise and capital and the possibility of increasing the concentration of ownership are both apt to be inhibited.

Second, in the shareholders' meeting, the PAS votes all shares that it holds; for a period of five or more years, 70 percent of the company shares could be voted by the PAS.[14] This takes on added significance when the regulation is followed (although it seems sometimes not to be) that voting within the PAS itself is based on a one member–one vote principle, thus independently of shareholding. Moreover, the CEU survey indicates that it is not uncommon for the board (Administration Council) of the PAS to have identical or nearly identical membership as the board of the company. In the extreme case, the additional layer in the structure of governance that is introduced by the PAS is essentially irrelevant, and the Romanian MEBO privatized firm could closely approximate the traditional producer cooperative with collective ownership and decision-making and little or no tradability of shares. In other cases it may more closely approach the characteristics associated with a 100 percent ESOP, including the possibility that managers control the company even when other employees own most shares: the case of the managerially controlled, employee-owned firm (MCEO). When the debt is fully repaid, all the shares are supposed to be distributed to employees who may then be able to trade them freely and to vote them in proportion to their holdings in the general meeting; in other words, the firms may become open joint stock companies.

As discussed earlier, these institutional setups have significantly different implications for such issues as governance, solidarity, evolution, and orientation to the market. We argued, for instance, that the chief advantage of producer cooperatives lies in achieving greater solidarity in declining firms, possibly increasing productivity and allowing layoffs to be avoided through general wage concessions. Compared with producer cooperatives, managerial control is probably worse in the firms with little chance to survive, insofar as their incentives will be to pursue subsidies rather than restructure, and the managers may be more successful in the former endeavor than the employees would have been. But, for firms with at least some chances of turning around, restructuring, and adapting to the market, managerial control and particularly the more flexible open form have significant benefits compared with the producer coop. Thus, the question of institutional choice turns at least partly on the types of firms in the program (i.e. whether they

---

[14] In some companies all shares purchased from the SOF are held by the PAS until the debt is fully repaid, while in others the shares are gradually distributed to individual members, who may then be able to vote them in the general meeting and to trade them more freely, although tradability seems to be often subject to continued restriction.

are hopeless or promising). We surmise that the privatized companies in Romania are mostly of the latter type: besides the fact that most Romanian observers and officials claim that these are "good firms without significant problems," it is notable that participation in the program has so far been entirely voluntary and requires a sufficiently large and steady cash flow to be able to finance the credit repayment schedule. Bankrupt firms have no reason to participate, as it is widely believed that all state support would be withdrawn at the moment of privatization. Under these conditions, it seems unfortunate that the state regulation of this privatization process has tended to encourage collective ownership and nontradability of shares, thereby diminishing the flexibility of decision-making and the possibilities for further evolution of the ownership structure.

In addition to regulating the institutional features of the privatized companies, the state has maintained an active role in their affairs in a number of other ways. To start, the privatization contracts stipulate significant restrictions on postprivatization behavior; most commonly, the restrictions prohibit changes in the level of employment and the main activity and severely constrain the prices that may be obtained from asset sales.[15] These restrictions can hold for periods as long as 10 years and obviously inhibit restructuring of many types: labor shedding, redirecting product lines, and unbundling of assets. The rationales for such restrictions include social and "fairness" criteria, but their fulfillment is difficult to monitor and to enforce, and they are determined by negotiation rather than stipulated across-the-board. The state remains involved in the operation of the companies, which then have fewer incentives to re-orient themselves away from the state and toward the market. Having lost the freedom to restructure at will, the companies may demand subsidies with the argument that they are in trouble because the restrictions have damaged their prospects.

The state also remains entangled through its role in financing the privatization transaction. The MEBO program is nominally a sales program, with the book value usually the price for small companies and a formal valuation required only for larger ones. But there is also a giveaway or preferential aspect in the form of the credit granted by the SOF to the PAS. The implicit real rate of interest is highly negative, and the repayment period is usually about five years.[16] This arrangement has a number of consequences. To

---

[15] If the price obtained from an asset sale exceeds the value paid to the SOF for that asset (generally, the book value), the company is obligated to pay the SOF the difference. Besides discouraging unbundling, this "clawback" provision renders the company less attractive to any potential outside investors and ensures that the price the employees could obtain in selling their controlling stake would be little more than the original price paid to the SOF.

[16] Interest rates from the CEU sample of firms ranged from 10 to 25%, while the rate of

begin, as long as the loan is not fully repaid, the PAS must remain in existence, and the negative real interest rates provide an incentive to extend this period as long as possible. Therefore, the institutional problems discussed above will tend to persist longer than they might otherwise. Furthermore, the companies become indebted to the state, and as creditor the state is a stakeholder with certain interests and rights. If the PAS fails to repay the loan, the implicit threat is that the SOF will repossess the unpaid shares. But this would amount to renationalization, and it is far from clear that the SOF has the willingness or ability, particularly in the face of widespread defaults, to carry out the threat. Once again, the companies may be likely to become embroiled in bargaining with the state over the terms of their repayment.

The debt burden resulting from these arrangements may be quite onerous, especially for the early installments before inflation has eroded their value. This carries important implications for company behavior because of the interrelationship of company and PAS balance sheets: although nominally independent, the PAS relies on dividends from the company to repay its debts. Profits will, therefore, tend to be siphoned off to pay the SOF rather than being at least partially retained and re-invested. Outside lenders are likely to be still shyer about providing credit to an organization under such constraints, a problem further exacerbated by the ineffective enforcement of bankruptcy.

The conditions under which the MEBO-privatized firms operate include a rather unstable macroeconomic environment, but in most cases they probably face hard budget constraints *vis-à-vis* the state budget. The firms are generally small and outside the favored, soft-budget sectors of heavy industry (Earle and Oprescu 1994). But in negotiations with the SOF, they may have some bargaining power due to the tangle of preferences and restrictions and the creditor–debtor relationship. As already noted, the absence of effective bankruptcy institutions implies exacerbated difficulties in raising capital.

Given this program design and set of conditions, the behavior of the companies is likely to be heterogeneous, depending on several factors. We have argued that most of them are likely to have some prospects of restructuring and surviving with a market orientation, but the probability that they will try to do so depends more particularly on the relative predominance of managerial and nonmanagerial owners, on the dispersion of ownership, and

consumer price inflation was 150 to 250% between 1992 and 1994. Typically, the SOF credit covers 49% of the shares, while 30% of them are obtained for Certificates of Ownership from the relevant Private Ownership Fund, and 21% are purchased from the SOF with cash either from the employees' personal savings or a loan from a commercial bank.

on the institutions of governance which they adopt. If the firms have little room to undertake massive restructuring, but much is to be gained from bargaining with the SOF[17] or other state bodies, then the firm will be directed toward lobbying efforts. If in addition, as previously argued, managers are better lobbyists, it may be desirable to have the weaker control of dispersed nonmanagerial employees. Probably most serious is the difficulties the firms face in evolving to more viable forms: the problem of the lack of secondary financial markets is exacerbated by institutional restrictions on share tradability, which present obstacles both to outsiders and to internal share concentration. Although the MEBO program must be judged as superior to the status quo of no privatization, it seems clear that the policy design and environment have also diminished the potential benefits which employee ownership could have been expected to achieve compared with continued state control.

Poland

Privatization to insiders has also dominated in Poland, where its primary vehicle of "privatization through liquidation" has been quantitatively much more important than trade sales or share flotations. During the 1980s, partial decision-making rights were granted to the workers' councils in state-owned enterprises, the legacy of which is the virtual veto of workers over privatization in the period since 1989. Even the "mass" privatization program is planned to include many fewer companies than already privatized through liquidation and will bestow large minority stakes on employees. As of the end of 1993, enterprises that had completed or were in the process of privatization through liquidation numbered 1,999 (Gomulka and Jasinki 1994).

Along this privatization path, a state enterprise is formally wound up, and a new company, in many cases founded by former enterprise employees, takes over the assets either by direct purchase or, more commonly, through a "leasing" arrangement essentially equivalent to a purchase by installments. Indeed, the participation of insiders is directly encouraged by a provision in the Privatization Law (1990) that grants special privileges to the new company only if a majority of the former employees are its shareholders. In an unknown number of cases, an outside investor has also been involved, providing necessary funds for the buyout. Unfortunately, no comprehensive information on the distribution of shares among employees and between managers and other employees is available, but we have constructed some

---

[17] The SOF currently engages in a great deal of cross-subsidization, taking 70% of dividends in all of the 6,500-odd commercial companies in its portfolio and redistributing them as it sees fit.

tentative estimates, reported in Table 1.1 above, based on a small sample of firms. Of the 23 firms in our sample, 6 were outsider owned, while the other 17 were predominantly owned by their employees. Applying the ratio 17:23 to the total of 1,999 firms yields an estimate of 1,478 for the number of employee-owned firms created by privatization through liquidation.[18] Of the 17 insider-controlled firms, there were 13 cases where nonmanagerial employees had a dominant share, and there were 4 cases of managerial control.[19]

Legal forms for the 17 firms in our sample included both limited liability and joint stock companies, but we have no reason to believe that this is a representative result. As discussed in the previous section, limited liability companies suffer from the disadvantage that tradability is likely to be inhibited. But ESOP-like trusts or associations seem not to be used, and ownership is individual, rather than collective, which may ameliorate the related governance problems.

The privatization procedure for viable firms is specified in the Privatization Law, while that for nonviable ones is in the Law on State Enterprises. Because roughly half the total number of privatizations fall under each, one might conclude that the method is being applied to enterprises in good condition as well as to those near bankruptcy. In practice, however, there may be little difference between the methods, with insiders in control of the firms under either law.[20]

As in Romania, the interest rate implicit in the installment payments is usually negative in real terms. The new company becomes indebted to the treasury, with all the potential consequences already discussed. Unlike Romania, however, the debt relation is direct, rather than through an employees' association; the survival of the entire company as a private entity is, therefore, at risk in case of default. It seems not uncommon for there to be real concern over the ability of the company to repay.[21]

[18] According to the OECD (1994), "about 90% of the more than 1,000 transactions of this type [liquidation privatization] have involved management and/or employee buyers."

[19] Of course, these data tell us nothing about share concentration within the managerial and nonmanagerial groups. It could well be the case in a particular company that a single manager accounts for 40% of the shares, while the remaining 60% are divided equally among hundreds of employees. In such a situation, our limited information would lead to a misclassification of the firm as employee owned, although it is plausible that the manager really has effective control.

[20] According to Gomulka and Jasinki (1994), only 87 out of 1,082 liquidations through the Law on State-Owned Enterprises were actually handled by the courts by the end of 1993, and only 172 had been removed from the state-owned enterprise register.

[21] Careful projections of cash flow are necessary to determine whether the company can be reasonably sure of meeting the repayment obligations. See, for instance, the case study of Drops (Belka and Estrin 1993). At the same time, our examination of a small sample of firms,

Despite these caveats, it seems likely that the liquidation privatizations contribute significantly to the development of a market economy in Poland. There are none of the restrictions on restructuring applied to MEBOs in Romania. The economic environment in which most of the new companies operate is probably much more competitive, due to the more rapid growth of the new private sector. And perhaps most importantly, the institutional characteristics of the companies allow for evolution through the formation of dominant coalitions inside the firm or through sale to outsiders.

The Czech Republic

The country which has granted by far the fewest concessions to insiders in privatization is the Czech Republic. No special price reductions, credit facilities, or pre-emptive rights in the privatization process have been made available to employees or, indeed, any other group.[22] Managers of state-owned companies in the large privatization program, however, did receive a special procedural role in the privatization process: they could submit the "basic privatization project" for their company which contained a business plan and proposal for the method(s) of privatization to be applied. Although these were subject to competition from outside proposals, the access to information probably gave the managers a distinct advantage, and despite the fact that the competing privatization projects outnumbered the basic by about four to one, the Privatization Ministry eventually approved basic over competing projects in nearly the reverse of this ratio (see Earle, Frydman, and Rapaczynski 1993a).

The informational and procedural advantages did not, however, translate into many cases of majority ownership by employees. As shown in Table 1.1 above, only 3 of the 988 projects approved for the first wave of voucher privatization contained the provision that employees would receive more than 50 percent of the shares; 7 companies had employee holdings of more than 30 percent, and the average employee stake across all firms in the program was 4.4 percent.[23] Information on the concentration of these shares among the employees is unfortunately unavailable. We are also unable to

reported below, shows that companies privatized to their employees in Poland have remarkably good financial health and liquidity. Thus, there seem to be large selection effects into the program.

[22] The one exception concerns advantages Czechs receive over foreigners: eligibility for restitution, participation in the first round of small privatization auctions, and receipt of vouchers for the first and second waves of large privatization. See Earle, Frydman, Rapaczynski, and Turkewitz (1994) for further discussion of all the issues in this paragraph.

[23] This is based on an analysis of unpublished data from the Czech Ministry of Privatization.

determine how many companies not included in voucher privatization have dominant employee stakes; this group might reasonably be supposed to contain more such examples. According to the OECD (1994), "the number of buyouts in the first wave of mass privatization amounted to only some 6 percent of all privatized units . . .." Nonetheless, our information is sufficient to justify the conclusion that employee ownership is not a significant property form emerging from the privatization process in the Czech Republic.[24]

Hungary

Although Hungarian privatization has been dominated from the start by insiders, whether exploiting legal loopholes in the 1988 to 1990 period of "spontaneous privatization" or initiating transactions to be approved by the State Property Agency (SPA) thereafter, most observers agree that it is managers who have been the prime beneficiaries of the process, and not other employees. The decentralization associated with partial reforms in Hungary from the 1960s onwards, accelerating in the late 1980s, provided enterprise directors with considerable autonomy in decision-making concerning the use of assets and profits and, ultimately, with regard to the disposal of the assets themselves. The legacy of this history has been the inability of the government in the post-1989 period to reclaim full owner-ship rights from the enterprises, to implement any mass or centrally organized privatization program, or even to sell to outsiders without insider cooperation.[25] The regulatory efforts of the SPA, after it was established in early 1990, probably halted the worst abuses in "losses of state property," but managers continued by-and-large to dictate the nature of transactions, even finding it convenient to bring in various outsiders who allowed them to maintain control. For instance, it was striking that in 1990–91, a large proportion of foreign investments containing state assets (joint ventures) entailed minority stakeholdings by the foreigners; indeed, the average invest-ment was less than 50 percent.[26]

[24] This conclusion does not apply to small privatization where, despite a complete absence of formal preferences for insiders, employees were able to purchase an estimated nearly half the shops and service establishments sold in open auctions (Earle *et al.* 1994). Moreover, the Czech Republic has adopted some German-style institutions of co-determination, with employee representatives on the company supervisory boards.

[25] Stark (1992) and the Introductory Essay in Earle, Frydman, and Rapaczynski (1993b) discuss the constraints placed on Hungarian privatization attempts by the history of partial reforms.

[26] According to the Hungarian Central Statistical Office (cited in Lesi 1994), the average proportion of foreign ownership in the founding capital of all joint ventures rose over the

Buyouts including nonmanagerial employees, however, have also been common in Hungarian privatization. Probably the most important vehicle creating opportunities for all employees, and not just managers, to acquire large stakes was the Law No. XLIV "on the Employee Stock Ownership Plan" (MRP in Hungarian), passed in June 1992. According to the MRP *Newsletter* (1994), a total of 184 MRP privatizations had been carried out by the end of September 1994; we discuss some of their characteristics below. Some data are also available for those privatization transactions accomplished under the rubric of the "Self-Privatization Program." Table 1.1, above, shows our estimates of the number of companies in this program with dominant employee ownership (sufficient to establish corporate control) as of November 10, 1994.[27] Of the 435 privatizations in the program, we estimate that 187, or 43 percent, resulted in dominant employee stakes. These include firms with dominant MRPs as well as those where direct employee shareholders are dominant.[28]

These estimates have several limitations. First, only about half of MRP privatizations have taken place through self-privatization, the other half through other privatization routes. Our data for the self-privatization program show 92 MRPs had completed transactions in the program by early November 1994, but this is only half of the total number of MRPs, as we noted above. Unfortunately, it seems to be impossible to know the number of companies privatized outside the self-privatization program where the employees became dominant direct shareholders, in other words, without using an MRP; nor is it easy to obtain reliable estimates on the extent of Hungarian privatization more generally. Thus, we provide estimates only using the base of the self-privatization program. Second, some MRPs account for only a minority of shares in the company: in our data there are

post-1989 period as follows: 1989, 24%; 1990, 34%; 1991, 45.2%; 1992, 56%; for 1993 the newly founded joint ventures were 70.1% foreign owned. Thus, in the founding of joint ventures, foreigners have been receiving ever higher shares. We speculate that this may reflect a declining influence of managers on the privatization process and its outcomes.

[27] These results are taken from an analysis of unpublished SPA data by the CEU Labor Research Program. We thank Gabriella Pal for help in obtaining the data. For further analysis of the self-privatization program, see Earle, Frydman, Rapaczynski, and Turkewitz (1994).

[28] In order to determine the "control type" for the purposes of estimating the extent to which employees have acquired controlling interests in their companies, we classified the companies using the following procedure. After calculating the proportion of shares held by the SPA and local governments, domestic investors, foreign investors, employees (both directly and through the MRP), and unclassified owners, respectively, we defined the "dominant owner" as the owner with the largest proportion of shares among those four groups. We then further subdivided the dominant employee shareholder group into those in which the MRP proportion was larger and those in which the proportion of directly held shares predominated.

dominant MRPs in 67 of the 92 companies with MRPs, and only these are counted as "EOs" in the table. Third, we have pointed out that employee ownership is also coming about through direct shareholding, not only by means of an MRP. In the self-privatization program, there were 120 companies where direct employee shareholders were the dominant new owner group, nearly twice the number with dominant MRPs. We conjecture that these direct shareholder employees are likely to be managers interested in voting and trading shares immediately, because the MRP requires the participation of 40 percent of employees, and the terms of the credits granted to MRPs are so highly preferential (as discussed below) that it seems likely that the employees would take advantage of them if they were available. Fourth, it is possible that in some cases "domestic investors" may actually be insiders, most likely managers. Analysts of the Hungarian transformation process (for instance, Mora 1991; Stark 1992; or Voszka 1993b) have observed that managers frequently set up new companies through which they become indirect owners in the original firm. Because these companies would be counted as outsiders in the data (indeed, there is generally no way to ascertain their ownership), our estimate of the proportion of firms privatized to insiders may be downward biased.[29]

Table 1.3 contains a detailed analysis of ownership structure for the companies in the self-privatization program classified according to their controlling owner. The designation SO refers to companies where either the SPA or local governments have retained more shares than acquired by any new group of owners; FO denotes foreign owner-controlled; DO outside domestic owner-controlled; EDO employee-controlled through direct shareholdings; and MRP employee-controlled through an MRP. DO is the most common type in the table, with 226 cases, and employee control is not far behind, with a total of 187 divided between 120 EDOs and 67 MRPs. The figures in the first seven rows of numbers contain the (unweighted) average structure of ownership (in percentages) for each ownership type. In the total 435 firms, domestic investors have 46 percent on average, while employees have an average of 42 percent. In the 14 firms controlled by foreign investors, their holdings are an average of 84 percent of all shares, and insider ownership is negligible. Interestingly, the MRP seems to be a substitute for direct employee shareholding rather than a complement: where direct shareholding predominates, the MRP is insignificant, and vice versa.

The table also provides information on the relationship of the price paid (including special discounts) by the controlling owner and the "nominal

---

[29] But, the special preferences provided to employees would not be made available, so there is also a disincentive for them to acquire shares in this fashion.

Table 1.3 Ownership Structure by Control Types; Self-Privatization in Hungary, 10 November, 1994

(percentage)	Control types					
	SO	FO	DO	EDO	MRP	Total
SPA	52.7	0.6	2.2	1.6	2.8	2.6
Local govts.	20.9	3.7	6.1	5.1	4.7	5.6
Foreign investors	0.0	83.9	0.4	0.3	0.0	3.0
Domestic investors	17.4	6.4	84.0	4.3	4.0	46.1
Direct employees	3.9	5.4	4.9	87.8	5.0	27.9
MRP (ESOP)	0.0	0.0	2.1	0.5	83.5	14.1
Unspecified owner	5.0	0.0	0.4	0.4	0.1	0.7
Price/nominal value	—	87.0	87.8	76.1	75.7	82.6
Credit/price	—	0.0	28.3	31.3	57.5	32.7
Av. employment	315	330	255	156	231	231
No. of firms	5	14	226	120	67	435

Note: Unpublished data from the SPA. The classification by ownership types in the table omits three companies for which the dominant owner could not be determined: one case had equal shares of domestic investors and direct employee shareholdings, and two cases had a dominant owner who was unspecified. Variables are defined in the text.

value," as determined by a valuation procedure.[30] Although the valuation of enterprises in the transition environment is at best highly uncertain, it is taken quite seriously by SPA officials anxious to avoid accusations of "giving away the country" to foreigners or to former nomenklatura. For our purposes, therefore, this price ratio functions as a kind of partial indicator of the preference shown by the SPA toward different kinds of new owners. Indeed, it seems that all new owners receive some discount off the nominal value, but insiders receive the largest – 25 percent – on average, and it does not differ appreciably between direct shareholdings and MRPs. The extension of credit, however, does vary significantly, as shown in the next row of the table. MRPs receive an average of nearly 60 percent of the price as a credit from the bank or deferred installments from the SPA.[31] EDOs receive only slightly more credit than do DOs, and FOs receive no credit. The credit arrangements and their implications for corporate governance, which are especially important in MRP companies, are analyzed further below.

The institutional features of the MRP companies share much in common with those of the Romanian MEBO-privatized companies, including the existence of a trust-like association, the MRP, functioning like the PAS to take on the debt associated with the leveraged buyout, to control share trading, and to exercise governance on the part of at least those shares for which a debt is still owed. On average it seems that the role of the MRP is potentially even greater than that of the PAS, because the MRP holds up to 97–98 percent of all shares purchased in the privatization transaction, much more than the 49 percent typical in Romania. In our data set from the self-privatization program, MRPs had purchased an average of 83.5 percent of the shares in companies in which the MRP was the dominant owner.

As in Romania, the ways in which shareholder employees are permitted to exercise property rights seem to vary widely across firms.[32] For instance, the MRP has the power to decide whether to distribute shares to employees as they are gradually paid off to the creditor, and thus how the shares are voted

---

[30] The row "price/nominal value" is defined as the average of the variable (price-discounts)/nominal value for the new owner with the largest stake among the owners in the control type category. Nominal value is sometimes simply the book value, but the peculiarity of the Hungarian self-privatization program is that the valuation is performed by an ostensibly independent consulting firm engaged by the enterprise.

[31] The row "credit/price" is defined as the average for each control type of the variable (credit + installment)/(price - discounts) for the new owner with the largest stake among the owners in the control type category.

[32] One aspect of dividend policy is legislated and does not vary across firms: all dividends due to shares held in the MRP must be used for debt repayment and may not be distributed to employee owners.

in general meeting; in some companies, all shares may be retained by the MRP indefinitely, and in all companies, the 2–3 year grace and 10–15 year payback periods imply that the MRP will play a role in company governance for a significant period of time. In the general meeting of shareholders, the MRP representatives vote the shares still held in the MRP. Within the MRP, voting rules are determined by the individual MRP statute, for example, they may be proportional to share holding, or they may follow the principle of one member–one vote.

In general, tradability is highly restricted in all MRP companies, although the nature of the restrictions varies across companies and across types of shares, as in Romania. In the case of joint stock companies, which accounted for 18 of the 67 MRP-dominant shareholder companies in our analysis of the self-privatization program, shares bought outright (without a credit) from the SPA are freely tradable according to the MRP Law. But shares initially bought with cash may account for as little as 2–3 percent of all shares, and the MRP Law states that the rest of the shares remaining in the MRP, even in those companies where voting rights on the shares are gradually distributed as payments on the debt are made, are permitted to be sold only in the event of death or retirement; indeed, they must be offered in this case to the MRP, which has the right of first refusal. If the employee quits the company, is laid off, or wishes to leave the MRP, the MRP has the right to purchase these shares, but if it does not, they nonetheless remain untradable as part of the collateral within the MRP. Joint stock companies acquired by their employees directly (without an MRP), of which there were 33 in the self-privatization program, are not subject to any of these tradability restrictions,[33] but a different and permanent restriction holds for the 10 percent or so of shares that are issued as "workers' shares," and which are tradable only among employees. Of course in the case of limited-liability companies, trading of shares ("quotas") is permitted only with the permission of the quotaholders' meeting. Our data on the self-privatization program shows 346 limited-liability companies, of which 105 had dominant direct employee shareholding and 49 were dominant MRPs. Thus, tradability seems to be highly restricted in most varieties of employee buyouts, the exceptions being the small number of joint stock companies with predominantly direct employee ownership.

The Hungarian MRP program also includes a complicated role for the state. The state promotes MRPs heavily, providing credits or credit guarantees for the buyout with highly advantageous implicit interest rates and

---

[33] If the shares were acquired with an E-credit, then they may not be sold until the credit is fully repaid (usually three years) without the approval of the creditor.

deferred payment schedules.[34] Table 1.3 provided evidence on the preferential prices paid and credits received by employees buying their firms through MRPs in the self-privatization program. Tax preferences come in several forms, including the possibility for the company to transfer 20 percent of its profit to the MRP every year tax free, which may further exacerbate capital shortage problems. The state lends up to 98 percent (85 percent in larger companies) of the estimated value of the firm. The dangers of the credit arrangement are the same in kind as, but potentially still greater in magnitude (because the amount borrowed is larger, and the terms of repayment are longer) than, those in Romania. As principal creditor to the MRP, the state remains an important stakeholder, if not shareholder, in the company, and the possibility of default leading to renationalization, which cannot be desirable from anyone's point of view, implies that the companies may become embroiled in renegotiating their debt schedule with the SPA rather than reorienting toward the market. Indeed, there are already widespread rumors of the difficulties the companies may face in meeting their future payment schedules.[35] Moreover, the process of privatization is not entirely transparent, relying heavily on bargaining with the SPA; Voszka (1993a), for instance, asserts the important role played by informal channels of the consulting firms that organize the transactions. Unlike Romania there are no across-the-board restrictions on restructuring, but the SPA often takes factors other than price into account when evaluating tenders, and it is possible that employment changes and investment promises are included in the contracts.

There is little information available concerning the characteristics of employee-owned firms in Hungary. Table 1.3 showed the average employment of firms in the self-privatization program according to their different ownership types; in general the firms in this program are quite small. Firms

---

[34] These preferences are over-and-above the standard preferences offered to employees, which include up to 50% price discounts, only 15% required as down payment, and three years of installments. MRP financing is still much more advantageous. Before January 1994 the loan was bank financed but guaranteed by the SPA, the grace period (on both interest and principal) was only 2 years rather than 3, and the payback period was 10 years rather than 15. Subsequently, the SPA has offered what it calls "payment by installment" rather than a direct loan, although they differ from one another largely in name. In both cases the original MRP shares remain the collateral for the loan until it is fully repaid, with important implications for tradability, as discussed above. It is also possible that banks may have been partially motivated to offer loans by the possibility of debt-equity swaps when the grace period expires, leading to their eventual participation as owners.

[35] However, Privinfo (1994) asserts that the firms have excellent liquidity, implying again that selection effects may be very important in comparing companies undergoing such buyouts compared with others. Whether this is indeed the case may become more apparent in 1995, when the grace periods begin to expire.

directly bought out by their employees (the EDOs) had significantly smaller employment than average, while FOs were significantly larger, but MRPs had exactly average employment. A reasonable inference is that the advantageous credits extended to MRPs have made it possible for employees to acquire larger firms. Data is collected by the MRP Foundation (1994) only for MRPs. Their analysis of 168 MRP buyouts finds the companies tend to be preponderantly in manufacturing, have a small number of employees, and "on a national economic comparison, have performed well to average." But this may well be a selection effect, rather than, as inferred by the authors of that study, the result of the advantages of employee owners. Given their influence over the privatization process, it should not be surprising that insiders tend to acquire relatively good firms.

Unfortunately, our data do not permit us to disaggregate employee ownership in Hungary among different types of employees, in particular between managers and workers, and only very limited evidence on this issue is available from a few case studies. Karsai (1994) presents the results of case studies of nine firms privatized to their employees; within this group, there are four cases where "middle and high-level management" have more than do "workers," while there are five cases with the opposite. Her conclusion and the nearly unanimous view among Hungarian observers, however, is that most MRPs and other employee buyouts lead to managerial ownership or at least strong managerial control, despite the possibilities for nonmanagerial ownership and influence inherent in the MRP method. Because the MRP required the participation of 40 percent of employees, it probably leads to quite dispersed ownership, which could lessen the power of workers *vis-à-vis* managers. Indeed, according to the MRP Foundation (1994), the average membership of MRPs is about 300 persons, or 68 percent of all employees in the companies (this also includes minority MRPs). Furthermore, regarding the distribution between managers and workers in the case of non-MRP employee ownership, we hazarded the conjecture above that "direct employee shareholdings" seem more likely to represent managerial holdings in view of the huge preferences granted for MRPs; but this remains only a conjecture.

Notwithstanding the conviction of many observers and the self-confidence of many managers, we question whether the widespread perception that managers do have a free hand, even when other employees own most of the shares (the case of the MCEO), constitutes sufficient evidence that managers really are in control. Particularly when decisions concern drastic restructuring, it is not difficult to imagine the normally quiescent work force intervening to prevent, for instance, a layoff of half their number or a shutdown of most of the plant. Of course these observations hold for MCEOs more generally and could be applied to some of the privatized companies in Poland, Romania, and Russia. Empirically, the issue comes down to determining whether the objectives of the firm, as demonstrated through observable actions, follow more closely those of managers or of workers. Given that these objectives of the different parties are themselves unknown (for instance, the relative weights of employment, wages, and benefits for workers; and the relative weights of profits, growth, salary, and nonpecuniary benefits for managers), the difficulty is distinguishing whether differences in observed outcomes result from differences in preferences or from differences in relative bargaining power. The discussion of the previous section suggests that in transitional economies the main variables for which employee ownership might lead to different behavior than managerial ownership are in the unbundling of the firm, in reducing employment and wages (the surplus allocated to labor), and in the balance of advantage between rent-seeking and market-oriented behavior.

Russia

Although the employees of state enterprises in most of the countries of Eastern Europe have received some form of special preferences – whether as procedural advantages or through special discounts or pre-emptive rights in acquiring their firms – direct, large-scale giveaways to insiders have been most widespread in the former republics of the Soviet Union, and particularly in Russia. Under the circumstances faced by reformers at the beginning of the 1990s, in which managers had accumulated tremendous political influence and enterprises had gained significant autonomy and *de facto* property rights, it is generally argued that no politically feasible alternative form of privatization was available. Early methods of ownership decentralization during the *perestroika* period already emphasized leasing arrangements, eventually resulting in insider buyouts at highly preferential prices. The voucher privatization program, beginning in late 1992, has transferred controlling stakes to insiders in an overwhelming number of cases.

Many of the same issues which we have discussed for other countries can be addressed in the Russian context. How is ownership distributed between outsiders and insiders and among insiders? Are the firms worker controlled, manager owned, or MCEO? How do institutional features of the newly privatized firms affect their ability to cope with the demands of the transition? Even if legally feasible, is trading, in particular selling to outsiders, blocked by informal barriers and/or transaction costs? Does the fact that practically every large firm in the Russian economy is dominated by its employees affect their ability to raise capital and to evolve into what may be more effective ownership forms? Finally, if budget constraints are still somewhat soft, does the change of ownership title have any consequences whatsoever for the firms' behavior?

Unfortunately, information sufficient to answer most of these questions is unavailable. In this section we review the existing evidence in order to arrive at a preliminary and partial assessment of some aspects of the outcome of Russian privatization. More comprehensive answers must await more complete information.[36]

Although no official data on the ownership structure of the newly privatized companies seem to be available, several surveys have attempted to obtain some of this information. Pistor (1995) reports on a sample of 36 companies privatized in late 1992 and early 1993, finding that all employees together received an average of 61.8 percent of all shares (57 percent of voting shares), while outsiders had 19 percent on average, and the State Property Fund retained 19.3 percent. While insider control is evidently quite strong in her sample, unfortunately there are only anecdotal data on the distribution of ownership among insiders. She concludes that the program has "facilitated entrenchment by managers."

Results of surveys of Russian firms are also reported in Blasi (1994). In a study of 127 privatized firms, 90 percent had majority employee ownership, an outcome that was essentially independent of the privatization option in the state program. On average, all insiders had 65 percent of shares in his sample, with a median of 60 percent; thus the distribution is positively skewed, implying that there were few firms that had a small proportion of insider ownership. Outsiders had an average of 21.5 percent of the shares, and the state retained 13 percent on average. Blasi also provides information on the division of shareholdings between top managers and all other employees: top managers had an average of 8.6 percent of all shares (the median was 5 percent).

What do these data on the structure of ownership imply for the ownership form of the typical privatized enterprise in Russia: EO, MO, or MCEO? Despite the small proportion of managerial ownership, most observers believe that managers have remained firmly in control. Blasi, for instance, cites the weakness of trade unions, the relative lack of nonmanagerial employees (indeed, many fewer than of outsiders) on boards, and the general view of managers that workers are passive and do not interfere with management determination of wages and employment, as evidence that the firms

---

[36] The purpose of this section is also not to provide a complete description of Russian privatization, for which there is a sizable literature, unlike the Hungarian and Romanian programs already discussed. More comprehensive and detailed analyses of Russian privatization may be found in Frydman *et al.* (1993b) and in Boycko, Shleifer, and Vishny (1993).

are what we have called MCEOs. Boycko, Shleifer, and Vishny (1993) argue that the nonpresence of significant outside blockholders itself indicates substantial independence of managers. We believe, however, as indicated in our discussion of this issue in Hungary, that the appropriate variables for deciding the question of who has control are behavioral: that is, one should test explicitly whether the behavior of firms is influenced by the objectives of worker owners. The existence of employment cuts in the privatized companies may be cited as indicating the freedom of managerial decision-making from worker interference, although it is not clear whether these resulted from layoffs or attrition. In practice it is of course a difficult task to ascertain the different objectives of managers and workers and to test the extent to which behavior conforms with each, controlling also for other factors affecting behavior, but it seems to us that this is what is required.

An examination of the real workings of the institutions of privatized companies provides more reason to believe that they may be MCEOs with little possibility for evolving into outsider owned, at least in the short run. From a legal point of view, the institutional features of the Russian companies are more straightforward than in Hungary or Romania. The legal form is normally an open, individually owned joint stock company, without the complicated governance of either the majority ESOP or the limited-liability form. One of the more obscure ways in which workers were able to acquire shares did involve a kind of ESOP, the FARP (Fund of Workers' Shares), but on average this seems to hold only a minor fraction of shares. In principle, shares are fully tradable, and voting rights (of voting shares) freely and equally exercised.

But most observers question the degree to which these institutions function in practice. For instance, there seems to be some evidence of ESOP-like trusts forming with the motivation of stifling worker influence. Many managers in Blasi's sample intended to form a trust for the employees' shares in order to control how those shares were voted. Moreover, voting rights may not always be so freely exercised. Managers have often postponed the first general meeting of shareholders after privatization, and voting is often neither by secret ballot nor proportional to shareholdings.

There also seem to be many constraints on the tradability of shares, partly resulting from attempts by insiders to prevent the entry of outside investors and partly due to the poor development of secondary markets. Probably the best evidence for the poor possibilities for share trading was the extremely low cash value of vouchers and implied low value of company shares. According to Boycko, Shleifer, and Vishny (1993), imputing the value of the entire Russian capital stock on the basis of the cash value of vouchers would result in a figure around the net worth of one large U.S. company. Because the cash value of vouchers was determined, for the most part, by transactions involving minority investors, it seems likely that the control premium in this case is simply enormous: outsiders have little willingness to pay for minority stakes in insider-controlled firms.

Further evidence may be found in Pistor (1995), who claims for her sample of recently privatized companies that in the summer of 1993 "trading volumes were low, and usually occurred among employees and former employees." Moreover, the prices on the secondary markets were reportedly still much lower than in the original voucher auctions, again implying extreme shyness on the part of outsiders. But Radygin (1994) finds that secondary trading has been quite extensive among employees, with managerial holdings rising from 15 to 25 percent as a result. Moreover, outsiders are allegedly acquiring blocks of shares through secondary transactions and new share issues. He points out the important problem of underdevelopment of interregional trading arrangements.

Finally, we come to the issue of residual softness of budget constraints. We have argued in previous sections that little change in behavior can be expected to result from ownership changes in situations where firms do not bear the costs or win the benefits of their actions. It is often assumed that subsidy reductions are necessarily associated with privatization, but in Russia this need not be true. Indeed, shortly after the voucher privatization process began in fall 1992, and no doubt intended to encourage that process to move forward, Yeltsin signed a state decree "On Not Permitting Discrimination Against Privatized Enterprises in the Provision of State Financial Support" (November 27, 1992). Nonetheless, there seems to be agreement that subsidies and money creation have generally been declining in 1993 and 1994, so that the "nondiscrimination" may be starting to apply in hard budget constraints for all. If true, then privatization could begin affecting behavior in Russia.

Conclusions

While insider ownership is clearly becoming a predominant property form in much of Eastern Europe and the former Soviet Union, the particular institutional manifestations vary considerably across countries. We have argued that understanding these institutional features – especially how control and tradability rights may be exercised and how the new relationship with the state is able to develop – is critical to an assessment of the ability of employee-owned firms to contribute to the objectives of the transition process. But we also maintained that such an assessment requires consideration of characteristics of the firm and of the environment in which it operates, for the comparative analysis of alternative ownership forms often hinges on such conditions.

Ideally, a privatization program should provide a mechanism to match particular kinds of firms with particular sets of new owners, assuming trans-action costs are sufficiently large to prevent a rapid reallocation. Because the characteristics of firms differ quite significantly within countries, in general the matching would include a variety of ownership forms. In this light it is interesting to note the stark contrast between the privatization strategies adopted in the Czech and Slovak Republics, Romania, and Russia on the one hand, and Hungary and Poland on the other. In the former group, one ownership form predominates – either almost total rejection of employee ownership in the Czech and Slovak Republics, or a conscious policy decision to embrace it in Romania and Russia. The specific legislative framework and policies encouraging employee ownership may or may not have been well designed, and we have argued that they often were not, but in these countries the balance of advantage of insiders versus outsiders as new owners for specific companies did not play a role in the choice of ownership form.

In the latter group of countries, however, the privatization process is leading to much more heterogeneous outcomes. Both Hungary and Poland have a number of different privatization paths that enterprises can follow, and the approach is in general much more case-by-case. This raises the possibility that different firms are being selected for different methods of privatization and for different types of new owners. Whether the particular selection mechanisms in these two countries are leading to relatively efficient or inefficient matches is difficult to judge, especially so inasmuch as the outcome of negotiations and tenders may often be based on political factors. But the possibility that firms may not be randomly distributed across new ownership forms does suggest that it may not be straightforward to infer the effect of different types of owners on firm performance. The next section grapples with this issue using data on enterprises in Poland.

Empirical Investigations

In this section we offer some very preliminary evidence from Poland about the relative performance of different ownership forms. We find confirma-tion of the view that employee-owned firms perform well in comparison with state-owned ones. However, they also compare favorably with mana-gerially and outsider-owned firms. We hypothesize that this is likely to be a consequence of the Polish privatization procedure, which in effect gave workers a power of veto over the method of privatization. As a result, the

Table 1.4 **Ownership Structure and Financial Indicators for Polish Companies** means (standard deviations)

	SO	EO	MO	OO	POE
No. of companies	122	13	4	15	19
Av. no. of employees	785 (764)	487 (368)	203 (173)	460 (392)	160 (213)
Ownership structure (percentage)					
State	99.863 (1.509)	0.0 (0.0)	22.25 (25.953)	17.473 (18.119)	0.0 (0.0)
Outsider ownership	0.0 (0.0)	5.061 (8.645)	6.5 (13.0)	71.306 (15.355)	60.168 (43.16)
Employee ownership	0.0 (0.0)	73.238 (18.281)	9.75 (14.5)	8.346 (14.65)	10.25 (27.39)
Managerial ownership	0.1366 (1.509)	18.238 (13.442)	58.5 (28.053)	2.776 (4.604)	25.837 (35.612)
Other	0.0 (0.0)	3.461 (12.489)	0.75 (1.5)	0.0 (0.0)	3.736 (12.328)
Financial indicators (1993)					
Profit/income	−0.0923 (0.333)	0.1086 (0.0415)	−0.0036 (0.1661)	−0.067 (0.208)	0.0321 (0.0948)
Receivables/Payables	0.7881 (0.7842)	0.4844 (0.2145)	0.0844 (0.0)	1.154 (0.786)	0.9721 (0.782)
Receivables/total assets	0.1875 (0.0951)	0.2596 (0.1107)	0.0655 (0.0068)	0.2859 (0.2835)	0.2247 (0.1148)
Payables/total liabilities	0.4326 (0.4155)	0.6325 (0.0904)	0.7194 (0.0)	0.2854 (0.2047)	0.3282 (0.2105)
Classified as uncreditworthy	0.3852 (0.4887)	0.0 (0.0)	0.5 (0.5774)	0.0667 (0.258)	0.0526 (0.229)
Refused bank credit	0.3852 (0.4887)	0.0769 (0.277)	0.75 (0.5)	0.0667 (0.2582)	0.1579 (0.376)
% machinery older than 15 yrs.	48.85 (30.341)	29.23 (21.871)	36.0 (38.6)	37.46 (27.67)	6.052 (22.88)

Source: Data come from a World Bank survey described in Belka, Estrin, Schaffer, and Singh (1994).

actual ownership structure chosen was selected by the workers themselves in the light of the financial situation of the firm, with outsiders being only permitted an ownership stake in firms where economic prospects of the firm were too poor to support the debt required in an employee buyout.

The empirical work draws upon a survey of Polish firms. The data, described in Belka *et al.* (1994), cover 80 state enterprises, 40 state-owned commercialized companies, 40 privatized companies, and 40 new private firms. The sample is not random, and the proportions are not representative, but our purpose is only to compare different ownership forms, and not to establish the characteristics of the Polish economy. We have reclassified 2 of the privatized firms as state, because the state remains the largest share-holder, and eliminated 21 new private and 6 privatized companies for which the ownership information is unclear. The remaining 32 privatized companies are divided into three categories – employee owned, managerially owned, and outsider owned – according to which type of owner predominates. All state-owned firms, including state enterprises and commercialized companies, are lumped together in one group, because it is not the purpose of this chapter to investigate the effects of corporatization when ownership remains unchanged. The final sample contains 13 firms with predominantly nonmanagerial employee ownership (abbreviated as EO), 4 managerially owned (MO), 15 outsider owned (OO), 122 state owned (SO), and 19 new private companies (POE). Thus, we have five categories distinguished along the ownership dimension, and as to whether the firm is old (state or privatized) or new (newly established private company). This is convenient because the problems of old firms in transition are quite significantly different from those of the new.[37]

In Table 1.4, we report the average employment, ownership structure, and some financial indicators for the 173 companies in the five ownership categories. The new private firms are unsurprisingly on average much smaller than the three categories of privatized firms and all the private firms are significantly smaller than SOs. In the case of EOs, this latter point may be due to the difficulties faced by employees of larger firms (which are also presumably more capital-intensive) in raising the capital necessary for the buyout. It may also be the result of a self-selection mechanism, whereby the ownership form tends to be chosen by workers in smaller firms due to fewer problems with governance and smaller needs for external sources to finance investment. That MOs are smaller than EOs may again result from the greater difficulties faced by a single manager, or small group of managers, in

[37] Unfortunately, the data do not allow us to measure the extent of concentration within ownership groups, so it is possible, for instance, that the majority stakes of employees in EOs are often widely dispersed and may not imply any strong influence of them on firm behavior.

Table 1.5 Restructuring Indicators for Polish Companies
means (standard deviations)

	SO	EO	MO	OO	POE
Major investment in two years (proportion)	0.688 (0.465)	0.923 (0.277)	0.5 (0.577)	0.8 (0.414)	0.894 (0.315)
Total investment outlay over total income	0.057 (0.052)	0.127 (0.0)	0.041 (0.0)	0.068 (0.071)	0.135 (0.085)
Asset disposals over total income	0.117 (0.155)	N.A.	N.A.	N.A.	N.A.
Sales force growth	0.293 (0.558)	0.754 (0.810)	−0.029 (0.694)	0.702 (1.34)	0.888 (1.49)
Advertisement expenditure growth	2.072 (6.03)	0.986 (1.32)	2 (1.41)	3.649 (4.99)	0.650 (1.44)
Involuntary layoffs (1991–93) employment	0.352 (0.261)	0.195 (0.204)	0.395 (0.145)	0.192 (0.187)	0.367 (0.331)
Exceeding of wage norm 1993	5.172 (8.18)	2.14 (3.37)	0.0 (0.0)	4.00 (10.5)	N.A.
Exceeding of wage norm 1992	3.92 (7.08)	1.69 (4.25)	0.0 (0.0)	1.13 (4.38)	N.A.
Exceeding of wage norm 1991	5.54 (9.56)	0.0 (0.0)	0.0 (0.0)	0.0 (0.0)	N.A.
Trade union members (percentage)	47.28 (21.7)	37.76 (15.1)	15 (30)	34.16 (24.0)	0.0 (0.0)

Source: Data come from a World Bank survey described in Belka, Estrin, Schaffer, and Singh (1994).

raising the down payment. OOs are on average about the same size as EOs.

Turning to the ownership structure, we note that the EOs represent 100 percent privatizations, while the MOs and OOs do not: the state retains a 22 and 17 percent stake respectively. Outsiders, as we would expect, are found to have little interest in either type of insider-controlled firm, as shown by their average 5 and 6.5 percent stakes in EOs and MOs respectively. The ownership structure of the EOs is totally dominated by the employees, who own 73 percent of the shares, but the MOs are somewhat less dominated, with only 59 percent for managers. The second shareholder in MOs is the state, with employees holding less than 10 percent. POEs are owned mostly by outsiders (60 percent of shares on average), but managers also have large stakes (25 percent) and employees a not inconsiderable amount (10 percent). It is interesting that POEs have the most diversified set of owners on average and the greatest variation in ownership structure (as evidenced by the size of the standard errors).

According to these data, EOs have the best financial health of any of the organizations. Their profit margins are higher, their receivables are lower, they are never classified by banks as "uncreditworthy," they are seldom refused bank credit, and they have the newest capital stock (measured as the smallest proportion older than 15 years). Particularly in contrast with the state firms, employee-owned firms are in remarkably good condition. But even compared with OOs and POEs, the EOs look remarkably good. However, given the short length of time since the privatization, not to mention the theory outlined in the previous sections, it seems unlikely that this is evidence for outright superiority of employee ownership in transitional economies. Rather, the causality is probably reversed, with workers only being able to obtain majority control under the Privatization Law where the balance sheet and projected cash flow were solid enough to support the repayment of the privatization loans from current profits. Such firms would require even better returns than in the *de novo* private sector because privatization would leave the firm so highly leveraged. Workers would only accept managerial ownership when the economic outlook for the firm was much worse, preventing them from borrowing the money to purchase the company themselves, and even then the state retained a significant shareholding. Finally, one can speculate that outsiders were only allowed to purchase the firm when the economic situation was very poor, with large losses and poor liquidity.

Table 1.5 shows the means by ownership category of some indicators of restructuring. The top two variables indicate the extent of new investments: the first is a dummy variable for whether there was any major investment whatsoever, and the second relates total investment spending to total income.

In both cases employee ownership is far superior to state ownership. We cannot distinguish, however, whether this reflects differences in objectives or in opportunities: if employees have bought the best assets, EOs will have better investment opportunities than do the SOs. EO is also superior to SO in terms of the growth of the sales force and wage discipline (measured inversely as the proportion by which wages exceed the Popiwek norm).

Table 1.6 displays some qualitative indicators of attitudes and behavior in the five categories of firms. Quite striking is the much greater preservation of social benefits by EOs compared with all other forms; the cuts are greatest in MOs. The EOs also tend, much more than the other firms, to believe that their employment levels are approximately optimal, while a majority of cases of the other old forms anticipate employment drops. Finally, the main objective of EOs is, compared with the others, least often profit maximization: only 15 percent of EOs as against 50 percent of MOs and 47 percent of OOs see increasing profits as the main objective of the company.

Table 1.6 Qualitative Indicators for Polish Companies

	SO	EO	MO	OO	POE
Change in social benefits over last 2 years (percentage)					
Increased a lot	4.9	7.7	0.0	0.0	10.5
Stayed the same	34.4	69.2	25.0	46.7	78.9
Cut a little	23.8	23.1	50.0	33.3	5.3
Cut a great deal	36.1	0.0	25.0	20.0	5.3
Current employment compared with optimal employment (percentage)					
Too high by more than 20%	8.2	7.7	25.0	0.0	0.0
Too high by 10–20%	20.5	0.0	25.0	6.7	5.3
Too high by 5–10%	25.4	23.1	50.0	40.0	15.8
Employment level about right	42.6	69.2	0.0	46.7	63.2
Employment level too low	3.3	0.0	0.0	0.7	15.8
Main objective of company (percentage)					
Increase or maintain output	66.4	69.2	50.0	53.3	57.9
Increase or maintain employment	1.6	0.0	0.0	0.0	0.0
Prevent social conflict	0.0	0.0	0.0	0.0	0.0
Increase workers' incomes	1.7	0.0	0.0	0.0	0.0
Increase profit	21.3	15.4	50.0	46.6	36.8
Prepare privatization	5.7	0.0	0.0	0.0	0.0
Other	3.3	15.4	0.0	0.0	5.3

Source: Data come from a World Bank survey described in Belka, Estrin, Schaffer, and Singh (1994).

Summary

The theoretical and empirical Western literature on employee ownership suggests that while such arrangements may bring both advantages and disadvantages for the performance of the firm, on balance in most circumstances the disadvantages probably outweigh the advantages. This view is probably explained by both the limited scope and specific characteristics of the employee-owned sector in Western economies. Moreover, at an abstract level an evaluation of this balance is altered toward the disadvantages by transferring the context of the discussion from Western market to transitional economies.

However, this conclusion fails to reflect either the institutional realities or the political imperatives of the transitional economies. We have argued that when privatization is stalled for political reasons or because of effective employee control at the workplace level, there is a strong case for a systematic government policy for privatization to employee ownership in firms where social considerations in the maintenance of employment over the short to medium term predominate. Such firms would be in declining sectors and regions, probably geographically isolated, and the predominant source of local employment. They should also not require significant unbundling. In this situation the firms should be given to workers at zero cost so that such funds as could be raised by the labor force can be used for restructuring and investment. The state should avoid retaining either a formal or an informal stake in the new organization and should not place any restrictions on the nature of the restructuring process. It is also important that the employee shareholding should be resalable in the future, so that if the new employee owners manage to turn the company around, it can evolve into new and more appropriate ownership forms.

Even if outsider privatization is not available and the option value of continued state ownership is low, it is less clear whether the state should privatize successful or clearly potentially successful firms to workers when the alternative is to privatize them to managers. Managerial ownership probably dominates when the major task is restructuring on the labor side or changing the boundaries of the firm. But even for successful firms, employee ownership may be preferable to managerial when managers are specialized in rent seeking, and thereby able to obtain better returns from that than from more market-oriented behavior, or when managerial stakes are not sufficient to prevent perverse behavior such as transfer pricing and "spontaneous privatization" of the assets.

We have seen that there exists considerable variation among countries in the amount of employee ownership that is coming into being through privatization. In some cases this is a direct consequence of an explicit policy, but where there is some degree of choice and diversity in the outcomes, it is possible that the selection of majority employee ownership may reflect the evaluation by insiders of the advantage of this ownership form. Our empirical work suggests that an important factor for prospective employee owners is a sound financial position, a selection effect which renders more complex any evaluation of the impact of employee ownership on performance.

References

Aghion, Philippe, Olivier Blanchard, and Robin Burgess. 1994. "The Behavior of State Firms in Eastern Europe." *European Economic Review.* 38:1327–49.

Alchian, A., and H. Demsetz. 1972. "Production, Information Costs, and Economic Organization." *American Economic Review* 62, no. 5: 777–95 (December).

Aoki, Masahiko 1984. *The Cooperative Game Theory of the Firm.* Cambridge,UK: Cambridge University Press.

——. 1986. "Horizontal vs. Vertical Information Structure of the Firm." *American Economic Review* 76(5): 971–83.

——. 1994. "The Japanese Firm as a System of Attributes: A Survey and Research Agenda," In *The Japanese Firm: Sources of Competitive Strength,* edited by M. Aoki and R. Dore. Oxford: Clarendon Press.

Bartlett, W., J. Cable, S. Estrin, D. Jones, and S. Smith. 1992. "Labor Managed vs. Private Firms: An Empirical Comparison of Cooperatives and Private Firms in Central Italy." *Industrial and Labor Relations Review* 46, no.1: 103–68.

Belka, Marek, and Saul Estrin. 1993. "Poland Case Studies." Discussion Paper No. 2, CIS-Middle Europe Centre, London Business School.

Belka, Marek, Saul Estrin, Mark Schaffer, and Inderjit Singh. 1994. "Enterprise Adjustment in Poland: Evidence from a Survey of 200 Private, Privatized, and State-Owned Firms." Center for Economic Performance Working Paper 658.

Ben-Ner, A. 1984. "On the Stability of the Cooperative Type of Organization." *Journal of Comparative Economics* 8, no. 3: 247–60.

——. 1988. "Comparative Empirical Observations on Worker-Owned and Capitalist Firms." *International Journal of Industrial Organization* 6, no. 1: 7–31.

——. 1992. "Organizational Reform in Central and Eastern Europe: A Comparative Perspective." Leuven Institute for Central and Eastern Europe Working Paper (August).

Ben-Ner, A., and S. Estrin. 1991. "What Happens When Unions Run Firms? Unions as Employee Representatives and as Employers." *Journal of Comparative Economics* 15, no. 1: 65–87.

Blanchard, Olivier, Rudiger Dornbusch, Paul Krugman, Richard Layard, and Lawrence Summers. 1991. *Reforms in Eastern Europe.* Cambridge, Mass. and London, Eng.: MIT.

Blasi, Joseph. 1994. "Ownership, Governance, and Restructuring." In *Russia: Creating Private Enterprises and Efficient Markets,* by I. Lieberman and J. Nellis. Washington, D.C.: World Bank.

Blinder, A.S., ed. 1990. *Paying for Productivity: A Look at the Evidence.* Washington, D.C.: Brookings Institution.

Bonin, J., and L. Putterman. 1987. *Economics of Cooperation and the Labor-managed Economy.* Fundamentals of Pure and Applied Economics, no. 14. New York: Harwood Academic Pub.

Bonin, J., D. Jones, and L. Putterman. 1993. "Theoretical and Empirical Studies of Producer Cooperatives – Will Ever the Twain Meet?" *Journal of Economic Literature* 31, no. 3: 1290–320.

Boycko, Maxim, Andrei Shleifer, and Robert Vishny. 1993. "Privatizing Russia," Brookings Papers on Economic Activity. The Brookings Institution, Washington, D.C.

Bradley, K., and A. Gelb. 1983. *Cooperation at Work: The Mondragon Experience.* London: Heinemann.

Bradley, K., S. Estrin, and S. Taylor. 1990. "Employee Ownership and Company Performance." *Industrial Relations* 29, no. 3: 385–402.

Cable, J. 1984. "Employee Participation and Firm Performance: A Prisoners' Dilemma Framework." EUI Working Papers. No. 84/126, European University Institute, Florence.

Coase, R. 1937. "The Nature of the Firm." *Economica* 4: 386–405.

Conte, M. A., and J. Svejnar. 1990. "The Performance Effects of Employee Ownership Plans." In *Paying for Productivity: A Look at the Evidence,* edited by A. S. Blinder. Center for Economic Progress and Employment Series, pp. 143–72. Washington, D.C.: Brookings Institution.

Craig, B., and J. Pencavel. 1992. "The Behavior of Worker Cooperatives: The Plywood Companies of the Pacific Northwest" *American Economic Review* 82: 1083–1105.

Domar, E. D. 1966. "The Soviet Collective Farm as a Producers' Cooperative." *American Economic Review* 56, no. 4: 734–57.

Dow, G.K. 1993. "Why Capital Hires Labor: A Bargaining Perspective." *American Economic Review* 83, no. 1: 118–34.

Drèze, J. 1976. "Some Theories of Labor-Management and Participation." *Econometrica* November 1976, 44, no. 6: 1125–39.

Earle, John S. 1995. "After MEBO Privatization: Property Rights and Corporate Control in Employee-Owned Companies in Romania." Central European University Economics Department, draft.

Earle, John S., and G. Oprescu. 1994. "Aggregate Labor Markets in the Restructuring of the Romanian Economy." In *Unemployment, Restructuring, and the Labor Market.* Washington, D.C.: World Bank.

Earle, John S., and D. Sapatoru. 1994. "Incentive Contracts, Corporate Governance, and Privatization Funds in Romania." *Atlantic Economic Journal* 22, no. 2.

Earle, John S., Roman Frydman, and Andrzej Rapaczynski. 1993a. "Notes on Voucher Privatization in Eastern Europe. In *The New Europe: Evolving Economic and Financial Systems in East and West,* edited by D. Fair and R. Raymond. Dordrecht, The Neth.: Kluwer Academic Publishers.

——. 1993b. "Privatization Policies in Eastern Europe: Diverse Routes to a Market Economy." In *Privatization in the Transition to a Market Economy: Studies of Policies and Preconditions in Eastern Europe.* Edited by John S. Earle, Roman Frydman, and Andrzej Rapaczynski. London: Pinter Publishers and St. Martin's Press.

Earle, John S., Roman Frydman, and Andrzej Rapaczynski, and Joel Turkewitz. 1994. *Small Privatization: The Transformation of Retail Trade and Consumer Services in the Czech Republic, Hungary, and Poland.* Budapest: Central European University Press.

Ellerman, D.P. 1990. *The Democratic Worker-Owned Firm.* Boston, Mass.: Unwin-Hyman.

Estrin, Saul. 1983. *Self-Management: Economic Theory and Yugoslav Practice.* Cambridge, Eng.: Cambridge University Press.

—— 1986. "Long-Run Supply Responses under Self-Management." *Journal of Comparative Economics* 10, no. 3: 342–45.

Estrin, Saul, A. Gelb, and I. J. Singh. 1993. "Restructuring, Viability and Privatization: A Comparative Study on Enterprise Adjustment in Transition." World Bank. Mimeographed.

Estrin, Saul, D. Jones, and J. Svejnar. 1987. "The Productivity Effects of Worker Participation: Producer Cooperatives in Western Economies." *Journal of Comparative Economics* 11, no. 1: 40–61.

Estrin, Saul, ed. 1994. *Privatization in Central and Eastern Europe.* London: Longman.

Frydman, Roman, Andrzej Rapaczynski, John S. Earle *et al.* 1993. *The Privatization Process in Russia, Ukraine, and the Baltic Republics.* Central European University Press.

Furubotn, E.G., and S. Pejovich. 1970. "Property Rights and the Behavior of the Firm in a Socialist State: The Example of Yugoslavia." *Z. Nationalokon* 30, nos. 3–4: 431–54.

Gomulka, S., and P. Jasinki. 1994. "Privatization in Poland 1989–1993: Policies, Methods, and Results." In *Privatization in Central and Eastern Europe*, edited by S. Estrin. London: Longman.

Grossman, Sanford J., and Oliver D. Hart. 1986. "The Costs and Benefits of Ownership: A Theory of Vertical and Lateral Integration." *Journal of Political Economy* 94, no. 4: 691–719.

Hansmann, H. 1990. "When Does Worker Ownership Work? ESOPs, Law, Firms, Codetermination, and Economic Democracy." *Yale Law Journal* 99, no. 8: 1751–816.

Hare, P., and G. Hughes. 1991. "Competitiveness and Industrial Restructuring in Czechoslovakia, Hungary and Poland." Center for Economic Policy, Research Discussion Paper 543, Heriot-Watt University, Edinburgh.

Jensen, Michael C., and William H. Meckling. 1979. "Rights and Production Functions: An Application to Labor-Managed Firms and Codetermination." *Journal of Business* 52, no. 4: 469–506.

Jones, D., and J. Pliskin. 1989. "British Evidence on the Employment Effects of Profit-Sharing." *Industrial Relations* 28, no. 2: 276–98.

Karsai, Judit. 1994. "Management Buyouts in Hungary." Mimeographed (January).

Kornai, J. 1990. *The Road to a Free Economy: Shifting from a Socialist System: The Example of Hungary.* New York and London: Norton.

——. 1992. *The Socialist System.* Princeton, N.J.: Princeton University Press.

Kruse, D.L., and M.L. Weitzman. 1990. "Profit-Sharing and Productivity." In *Paying for Productivity: A Look at the Evidence*, edited by A.S. Blinder. Washington, D.C.: Brookings Institution.

Lesi, M. 1994. "The Effects of Foreign Direct Investment on the Hungarian Economy,"

Central European University, Economics Department, unpublished M.A. thesis (August).

Marris, R. 1966. *The Managerial Theory of the Firm.* London: Macmillan.

Meade, J.E. 1972. "The Theory of Labor-Managed Firms and of Profit Sharing." *Economic Journal* 82, no. 325, supplement: 402–28 .

Mora, M. 1991. "The (Pseudo)-Privatization of State-Owned Enterprises (Changes in Organizational and Proprietary Forms, 1987-1990)." *Acta Oeconomica* 43.

MRP (Employee Stock Ownership Plan, Hungary). 1994. Foundation and National Alliance of MRPs, *Newsletter*, no. 3.

Organization for Economic Cooperation and Development (OECD). 1994. *Trends and Policies in Privatization* 1, no. 3. Special Feature on Management and Employee Buyouts in the Context of Privatization. Paris.

Pencavel, J., and B. Craig 1994. "The Empirical Performance of Orthodox Models of the Firm: Conventional Firms and Worker Cooperatives." *Journal of Political Economy* 102, no. 4: 718–44.

Pinto, Brian, Marek Belka, and Stefan Krajewski. 1993. "Transforming State Enterprises in Poland: Evidence on Adjustment by Manufacturing Firms." *Brookings Papers on Economic Activity* 1: 213–70. Brookings Institution, Washington, D.C.

Pistor, Katharina 1995. "Privatization and Corporate Governance in Russia: An Empirical Study." In *Privatization, Conversion and Enterprise Reform in Russia,* edited by M. McFaul and T. Perlmutter. Boulder, Colo.: Westfield Press.

Privinfo. 1994. "ESOP: A Successful Privatization Technique – SPA [State Property Agency]." Budapest State Property Agency (January). Mimeographed.

Radygin, A. D. 1994. "Privatization and Investment in Russia: Why the Model Needs Revision." *Studies on Russian Economic Development* 5, no. 5.

Sertel, M.R. 1982. *Workers and Incentives.* Amsterdam, The Neth.: North-Holland.

Shleifer, Andrei, and L. Summers. 1988. "Breach of Trust in Hostile Takeovers." In *Corporate Takeovers: Causes and Consequences,* edited by A.J. Auerbach. Chicago, Ill.: University of Chicago Press.

Stark, David 1992. "Path Dependence and Privatization Strategies in East-Central Europe." *East European Politics and Societies* 6: 17–51.

Vanek, J. 1970. *The General Theory of Labor-Managed Market Economies.* Ithaca, NY: Cornell University Press.

Voszka, E. 1993a. "Servant of Two Masters." *Közgazdasági Szemle* 40, no. 5.

———. 1993b. "Spontaneous Privatization in Hungary." In *Privatization in the Transition to a Market Economy: Studies of Policies and Preconditions in Eastern Europe.* edited by J. Earle, R. Frydman, and A. Rapaczynski. London: Pinter Publishers.

Ward, B.M. 1958. "The Firm in Illyria: Market Syndicalism." *American Economic Review* 48: 566–89.

Webb, Sydney and Beatrice. 1926. *Industrial Democracy.* London: Longman, Green.

Williamson, Oliver. 1985. *The Economic Institutions of Capitalism: Firms, Markets, Relational Contracting.* New York: Free Press.

MANAGEMENT OWNERSHIP
AND RUSSIAN
PRIVATIZATION

ANDREI SHLEIFER and DMITRY VASILIEV

Introduction

Between December 1992 and June 1994, Russia went through an extraordinary mass privatization program at the end of which over 14,000 medium and large-scale enterprises, employing two-thirds of the industrial labor force, had been privatized. This privatization program has succeeded in part because of the generous benefits it offered enterprise insiders, both the workers and managers, in exchange for their agreeing to privatize. As a consequence, enterprise managers in Russia have emerged from the privatization program with a substantial amount of equity ownership and a very high degree of control. An evaluation of the economic success of Russian privatization will, therefore, inevitably depend on how one views high levels of management ownership and control.

In this chapter, we discuss management ownership in Russia in order to evaluate the privatization program. We begin by discussing both theoretical and empirical research on management ownership that has recently been conducted in the West. We then turn to the role of management ownership in the Russian privatization program and present some empirical evidence, obtained by Joseph Blasi, on the emerging ownership structures in Russia. Lastly, we assess the implications of management ownership and control in Russia for the probability of restructuring. While we see some reasons for concern over the degree of management entrenchment in Russia, there are also signs of emerging market mechanisms aimed at addressing the need for higher management turnover.

Western Research on Management Ownership

Theoretical Studies

Economic theory has generated a variety of hypotheses concerning both the costs and benefits of high management ownership of shares in their own companies. The classical argument for the benefits of high management ownership revolves around incentives. When managers become shareholders, they bear the financial consequences of their decisions, and hence their interests are aligned more closely with those of other shareholders. The informal argument along these lines goes back to Berle and Means (1932), who complained that in a modern corporation ownership is separated from control. As a result, managers (who have control rights) do not bear the consequences of their actions, whereas the shareholders (who have cash flow rights) do.

There are two modern approaches to this issue. Jensen and Meckling (1976) held that managers want to consume perquisites or pursue projects that benefit them personally. When managers owns 100 percent of the company, they pay for a dollar of perquisites with a dollar of their own forgone profits. But, when managers own only 10 percent of the company, they pay for a dollar of perquisites with only 10 cents of their own forgone profits, and hence will overconsume perquisites. Of course, there may be other mechanisms for keeping down the consumption of perquisites, such as oversight by boards of directors, the managerial labor market, takeovers, and so on, but the basic problem remains, namely, that as long as there are outside investors, managers on the margin do not pay for the so-called benefits of control.

The literature offers a variety of examples of what the benefits of control are. Some of these benefits are simply consumption items that could not be obtained easily without running a company. These include luxurious offices, company airplanes, newspaper interviews, and invitations to the White House available only to captains of industry. These, however, are probably not that expensive to shareholders relative to the capital of large corporations. The more costly activities that managers pursue involve shaping the company according to their own preferences, which may entail excessive growth, diversification, or expansion in lines of business in which managers have a personal interest or skill. Various studies have shown that such managerial behavior can be enormously expensive to shareholders. Lastly, the benefits of control sometimes include the ability to stay in control when the manager is no longer the best person to run the firm.

A second approach to the agency problem, presented by Holmström

(1979), Shavell (1979), and others, is to focus on unobservable managerial effort and the moral hazard problem arising from it. When shareholders do not know how hard managers work, managers may slack off. To elicit higher effort, shareholders provide managers with incentives to work harder, in part through share ownership. If managers are risk neutral, then in general it is optimal for them to own 100 percent of equity in the companies they run. However, if managers are risk averse, then the optimal management ownership is below 100 percent, and in general, a fully efficient level of effort cannot be extracted. In moral hazard models, excessive risk bearing by managers is one of the costs of high management ownership of shares. Risk aversion reduces the optimal management ownership to below 100 percent but in the process also reduces the effort that managers supply.

The implication of both agency models is that, when management ownership is high, managers will take actions that are closer to maximizing shareholder wealth than when management ownership is low. These actions include working hard, forgoing the consumption of perquisites, making positive rather than negative net present value investment decisions (such as diversification), and so forth. They also include quitting and agreeing to be replaced by another manager when the current manager is no longer the best person for the job. When incentives are strong enough, the managers are prepared to do what's right for shareholders even when that means losing their job. Thus the effort problem is solved together with the allocation of human capital problem, in that inferior managers are willing to yield their positions to superior managers.

Given the benefits of high management ownership, why are not public corporations wholly owned by their managers? We have already begun to answer this question by noting that 100 percent management ownership puts too much consumption risk on the managers. Also, when firms need to raise money, they have to go to an external capital market, which again makes 100 percent insider ownership infeasible. Firms could, of course, raise money through debt, but debt also has costs, such as bankruptcy and agency problems between shareholders and debtholders. A similar argument explains why the best manager cannot simply buy the firm and become a 100 percent owner.

There is another potentially important cost of high management ownership, namely, the cost of management entrenchment. When managers own a high percentage of a firm's equity, they not only have high-powered incentives, but control as well. As a result, they cannot be thrown out by shareholders or by external raiders who are hoping to become shareholders. Furthermore, managers with high equity ownership of their firms are typically very rich, particularly in the case of large public firms. As a result, they may have little interest in further maximization of the market value of their firms (the marginal utility of consumption is low) relative to their interest in the consumption of various perquisites.

As an example, when Ford Motor Company became extremely successful, Henry Ford instituted a five dollar day, which gave his employees much higher wages than were common at that time in the United States. Some people have interpreted this as a thoughtful "efficiency wage" policy by Ford, although a fair amount of circumstantial evidence suggests that Ford simply wished to overpay his workers and could afford to do it. Tycoons do strange things just because they are tycoons. In the traditional model, Henry Ford's behavior is not inefficient. After all, he owns the whole company and can do with it anything he wants, since he pays for any spending out of his own pocket. Ford's wage policies are then efficient just like the burning of a house by a person who owns it solely for amusement value is efficient.

Another example of the same problem would be a manager clearly unqualified to run a company who runs it simply because he owns it. This too is not inefficient in a standard model because the owner pays for the mismanagement of corporate assets. In fact, when this owner issues equity to the public, the public recognizes his ability and willingness to take such actions, and pays correspondingly less for the stock – again consistent with efficiency. As we argue later, however, this argument does not apply to entrenched managers who got their shares through privatization, where the entrenchment of unqualified managers does constitute a social cost.

Empirical Evidence

We turn now to reviewing some of the highlights of recent Western work on the efficiency of management ownership. Until the mid-1980s, the conventional wisdom in the United States was informed more by the Berle–Means (1932) theory of insufficient management ownership than by any empirical evidence. Starting in the mid-1980s, however, several empirical studies began to shed light on the relationship between management ownership and performance.

One of the first studies was by Demsetz and Lehn (1985), who argued theoretically that for each company the optimum level of management ownership may be different, but that market forces will assure that managers own the efficient amount at which the costs of higher ownership exactly offset the benefits. In support of their theory, Demsetz and Lehn looked at the relationship between management ownership and measures of performance, such as profitability and Tobin's Q, in a sample of large U.S. industrial corporations, the Fortune 500. Demsetz and Lehn performed a variety of tests and found no relationship between management ownership and performance. They concluded that there is no presumption that performance can be improved through higher management ownership. On the contrary, the evidence indicated that the existing ownership structures were optimal.

Looking independently at the same data set, Morck, Shleifer, and Vishny (1988) reached a very different conclusion. They reasoned that, to a first approximation, management ownership is given by historical accident, including such factors as the company's age, its need for external funds, and the founder's preference for control. Hence it can be viewed as exogenous. Looking at the relationship between management ownership and performance, particularly as measured by Tobin's Qs, Morck, Shleifer, and Vishny found that performance generally improves as management ownership rises from zero to about 5 percent, and deteriorates thereafter. Thus, they concluded that the incentive effect dominates at low levels of management ownership, whereas the entrenchment effect dominates at higher levels of ownership. Empirically, the finding of a roof-shaped relationship between management ownership and performance has since been documented by several other authors, using larger samples and better data. The Demsetz–Lehn results thus appear to be a fluke of their linear specification. The evidence shows clearly that high management ownership is not unequivocally good, a result that turns out to be quite relevant to the analysis of privatization.

There are two additional research areas that bear on the question of managerial incentives. The first is the analysis of the relationship between executive pay and performance. Perhaps the best known study in this area is that of Jensen and Murphy (1990), who found that management pay is not sensitive to stock price performance. Management ownership remains the most significant component of managerial compensation that is responsive to performance, but ownership is, in general, too low to make a huge difference. Jensen and Murphy have estimated that in their sample of large U.S. corporations, a top executive's wealth rises by about $3 for each $1,000 gain in shareholders' wealth once all components of compensation are taken into account. They conclude that this is far too little sensitivity, although given the size of the companies, the fluctuations in executive wealth implied by their estimates are still very substantial. Jensen and Murphy thus bring us back to Berle and Means' problem that ownership is really separated from control. Kaplan (1994) finds similar estimates of sensitivity of pay to performance in a sample of large Japanese corporations.

The studies of Morck, Shleifer, and Vishny and of Jensen and Murphy are consistent with each other. The former says that at least over the range of low levels of ownership, performance improves with higher ownership; the latter that most large American corporations were in the range of management ownership where performance improves with higher ownership. The fact that at a very high level of ownership, performance deteriorates does not preclude the need for higher management ownership for the largest companies in the United States. Optimum management ownership appears to be between 5 and 10 percent.

The second, enormous literature bearing on managerial incentives is on mechanisms of controlling managers, other than direct ownership and incentive contracts. We can here only touch on some of the arguments. Some authors have argued that boards of directors monitor managers and make sure that they serve shareholders. While this argument has some merit, the empirical literature suggests that boards are often captured by the managers themselves. Other authors have argued that debt and the resulting threat of bankruptcy keep managers on their toes, although many large corporations are relatively debt free, and managers often succeed in financing expansion with profits rather than with a high level of external borrowing. Still other studies have focused on the managerial labor market, holding that managers will be rewarded with better jobs if they maximize shareholder wealth and, perhaps, even fired if they do not. Unfortunately, for the vast majority of American CEOs, the job they hold is the last one they are going to have, and so their concerns about subsequent employment are probably minimal. Lastly, there is an enormous literature arguing that takeovers and proxy fights – the most hostile corporate governance mechanisms – play a key role in ensuring maximization of shareholder wealth. While there are periods in U.S. corporate history when takeovers seem very important, the political mechanism usually keeps them in check, and takeovers are probably as often an expression of managerial preference for growth as they are an effective control device. In sum, there are multiple mechanisms of controlling managers along with management ownership. Some are more effective than others, and together they guarantee reasonably effective, though far from perfect, corporate governance in the West.

Corporate Governance in Russia

Managers as Owners

From the start, authorities in charge of Russian privatization recognized that moderate management ownership had to be part of the privatization program. This recognition came from both political and economic considerations. On the political side, enterprise managers emerged from the Gorbachev era with a great deal of economic and political power. Gorbachev's reforms and the collapse of the Communist Party sharply reduced, though did not eliminate, ministerial oversight of enterprises. As a consequence, managers gained a very high degree of control over firms, including most production, employment, and sales decisions. Unlike Eastern Europe where legitimate and independent labor unions sprang up, workers collectives in Russia were relatively weak, and in most cases were dominated by managers. Although managers gained a lot of control over enterprises, cash flows remained publicly owned. The only way in which managers could capitalize on their power was by stripping firms' assets through spontaneous privatization, which they proceeded to do. In part, this caused the extraordinary decline of the Russian economy at the end of socialism.

Politically, managers translated their control over firms into enormous political power in the Russian Parliament. Many deputies in 1991 were controlled by the managerial lobby, and this lobby's leader, Arkady Volsky, was viewed as a serious power broker in national politics. Managers used their control of the Parliament to extract vast subsidies from the government, and to assure that their control was not challenged too much. If the Russian privatization program was to proceed, the political and economic power of managers had to be recognized.

Importantly, the goal of reform was not to get rid of the managers, but of the ministries. The principal objective of Russian privatization, as argued by Boycko, Shleifer, and Vishny (1993, 1995), was depoliticization of firms, which meant the elimination of political control over their decisions. Given this objective, the reformers were quite willing to compromise with managers, as well as with workers' collectives, as long as that compromise could lead to a sharp reduction of ministerial and other political interference with business. In fact, co-optation of managers through high equity ownership was the explicit agenda of the privatizers dictated by political necessity.

At the same time, following the arguments above, the organizers of Russian privatization understood the incentive benefits of moderate management ownership. If managers were to be interested in restructuring, they had to become owners of equity. Moreover, equity ownership was viewed as a potentially important device for stopping asset stripping. However, the Russian privatizers also feared that excessively high management ownership could lead to full entrenchment of incompetent managers, and as a result slow down restructuring.

The turnover problem is much more important in transition economies than in market economies. In market economies, managers are selected over time based on their performance in tasks similar to the ones they will perform as top executives. As a result, boards of directors and shareholders have relatively good estimates of the relevant skills of the potential top executives. In transition economies, in contrast, top managers got their jobs because they excelled at lobbying the government for credits, jawboning suppliers into delivering the inputs, and so on. These managers did not have to care about selling the products, cutting costs, and other issues central to restructuring. As a result, managers of privatizing firms were in many cases incapable of overseeing a restructuring program, and hence the need for management turnover was much greater than in market economies.

The problem of entrenchment of unqualified managers in transition economies, such as Russia, is exacerbated by the weakness of other corporate governance mechanisms. Boards of directors are usually dominated by the appointees of the managers or by government officials sympathetic to them. The managerial labor market is not developed, and the managers' interest in subsequent jobs is probably even weaker than in the West. Debt mechanisms are also ineffective, since bankruptcy procedures are usually undeveloped, and even developed ones are vastly more sympathetic to managers, and less sympathetic to creditors, than they are in the West. Finally, takeovers and proxy fights are very rare and are often stopped by politicians, who are influenced by the managers even more easily than in the West. Thus, given the weakness of alternative corporate governance devices (to which we return below), the need to get management ownership to provide incentives rather than to guarantee entrenchment is much greater in transition economies than in the West.

Of course, the Russian managers recognized these issues extremely well and understood that the allocation of equity would determine the extent of their control. In particular, they recognized that equity in the hands of outsiders would lead to the most direct challenge to their control, whereas equity in their own hands, and perhaps in the hands of the workers, would bring them the best protection. Because of the political power of the managers, any program that the Russian reformers had any hope of passing had to give incumbent managers a reasonable amount of job security, at least in the short run, through equity ownership. Not surprisingly, the program that was eventually accepted was quite manager friendly.

It is not our goal in this chapter to present the Russian privatization program in great detail. A short description of the program is contained in Boycko, Shleifer, and Vishny (1993) and a longer description in Frydman, Rapaczynski, and Earle *et al.* (1993). Some aspects of the program, however, are highly relevant. First, managers generally got about 5 percent of the shares at highly subsidized prices, as well as some additional cheap shares available for purchase through pension plans. In addition, employees of the enterprises had a choice of receiving either 25 percent of nonvoting shares free or 51 percent (including the managers) of voting shares at a substantial discount. Over 80 percent of the firms chose the second variant. In both cases, employees got some additional shares through a pension plan allocation. The shares remaining after worker and manager benefits were divided between those sold for vouchers to the public in general and those set aside for future investment tenders. Between 20 and 30 percent of the shares of most privatizing firms were sold for vouchers. Importantly, both the managers and the workers could buy additional shares in voucher auctions, and in fact many managers did.

Subsidized share allocations were not the only benefit that enterprise managers received in Russian privatization. In addition, they got a substantial amount of influence over the writing of privatization plans, which specified how the shares, other than those sold to the workers and managers, were to be allocated. Most voucher auctions were conducted locally, so even though outside investors participated, managers of many companies had an opportunity to discourage undesirable investors. Finally, enterprise managers received an extraordinary amount of control over the conduct of investment tenders, whereby potential core investors were given an opportunity to buy large blocks of shares in exchange for commitments of future investment. In short, managers received an opportunity to influence, if not completely control, all stages of their companies' progress through privatization.

This package of privileges was attractive enough that the vast majority of enterprise managers eventually supported the privatization program and took their companies through it. In fact, the managers of the worst performing military and other enterprises who opposed the program were left behind, and the Volsky lobby effectively disappeared from the political landscape.

Implementing Privatization

Over the 19 months of the mass privatization program, between December 1992 and June 1994, Russia privatized over 14,000 enterprises by means of voucher auctions, bringing two-thirds of industrial workers into the private labor force. One of the principal reasons for the wide participation in the program was the large benefits it offered to enterprise managers.

As we already mentioned, managers of Russian enterprises got both substantial subsidized equity stakes and the right to buy additional shares in voucher auctions, which many of them did. In addition, following privatization, many managers began buying shares from individual workers to supplement their stakes, while workers began actively selling their shares not only to managers, but to outside investors.

Although we cannot yet predict where this process will converge and do not have official data on management ownership at any given time, we do have the results of a survey of 143 privatized medium and large Russian firms conducted by Joseph Blasi (1994) of Rutgers University between March 1993 and April 1994. Blasi's survey offers some information on the emerging ownership structures of Russian firms *before substantial selling by the workers had taken place* and thus gives us a glimpse of where management ownership was headed. His results have also been consistent with other survey evidence, such as that collected by Katharina Pistor for the Russian Privatization Agency (GKI). We can, therefore, view his evidence as reasonably representative.

At the time Blasi surveyed it, a privatized firm had an average of 65 percent of its shares owned by insiders (workers and managers), 22 percent owned by outsiders, and 13 percent owned by the government in anticipation of a pension fund purchase or investment tender. The median insider ownership was 60 percent, the median outsider ownership was 20 percent, and the median government ownership was 12 percent. The average top management ownership was 8.6 percent, and the median was 5 percent.

Because managers often had substantial influence over workers' collectives, the degree of managerial control is understated by managerial share ownership. Managers, as we mentioned, were actively buying worker shares, and in many companies were developing formal trust agreements with the workers, whereby managers would get voting control over workers' shares. In contrast, outsiders owned only 22 percent on average, of which only 11 percent on average was owned by blockholders (investors with over 5 percent of the shares). Some blockholders, incidentally, were related enterprises friendly with the managers, and some were equally friendly investment funds. In most cases, therefore, managers at the end of privatization controlled more shares than the concentrated outsiders who might have presented a credible control threat.

Interestingly, managers did not regard their ownership as sufficient. An average manager in the Blasi sample presented the following as an "optimal" ownership structure from his viewpoint: insiders should control 72 percent, of which employees control 32 percent and top management 40 percent; all outsiders should control 27 percent; and the government should control none. Of the 40 percent insider ownership, general directors on average believed that they should personally own 31 percent, with the rest of the top management team owning 9 percent. This evidence confirms the point that the privatization program effectively separated the managers from their ministries. However, it also shows that general directors are quite determined to increase their degree of control *vis-à-vis* both the workers and the other top managers.

What do we make of this ownership structure in light of the theoretical and empirical discussion at the start of this chapter? The current levels of top management ownership are not far from those found in Western firms. To the extent that the ownership levels in the West are not far from optimal from the incentive point of view, management ownership in Russia after privatization may not be far from efficient. This, however, is only part of the story. Since managers are buying up shares from the workers and since they often have some control over workers votes, the true amount of voting control that Russian managers have is much higher than in the West. Add to this the fact that corporate governance mechanisms – including board of directors oversight, proxy fights, takeovers, and bank lending – are not nearly as well developed in Russia as they are in the West, and the conclusion is that the Russian managers are far too entrenched. This is not so much a consequence of excessive direct ownership as of the absence of external governance mechanisms that are available in the West.

As we mentioned, managerial entrenchment in Russia might be much costlier than it is in the West, since most managers have skills that are very different from those needed to restructure privatized firms. This evidence, therefore, raises perhaps the most important question for the analysis of management ownership in Russia. Specifically, what external forces will prevent managers from exercising complete control over firms?

Developments in Governance

Nonmanagerial Shareholders

The most direct challenge to entrenched managers in Russia is likely to come from large outside shareholders, who are interested in maximizing the value of their shares. Although the privatization program did not insist on introducing core investors from the start, vouchers were made tradable, which gave outside investors an opportunity to accumulate blocks of vouchers and to use them to buy blocks of shares. Many in fact did, and as a result, many Russian companies have acquired core investors. Blasi's research provides some evidence about these investors.

In the Blasi sample, an average of about 21.5 percent of the shares were owned by outside investors. Of those whom managers were willing to identify to the interviewer, about 11 percent of the shares were owned by holders of blocks larger than 5 percent. The remaining shares held by outsiders were owned by individuals (4 percent) and investors, such as voucher funds, with blocks of less than 5 percent. Evidence from the largest companies suggests an even greater incidence of blockholders. Of the 30 percent of shares offered in a voucher auction of the truck maker ZIL, about 28 percent were bought by seven large investors, many of whom turned out to be affiliated with Mikrodin, a private computer trading firm. A private conglomerate called Bioprocess bought an 18 percent stake in Uralmash, a huge Siberian machine builder, as well as in dozens of other industrial firms. The investment fund Alpha Capital bought a 10 percent stake in the Bolshevik Cake Factory. The investment bank First Boston bought large stakes in several companies, including LOMO, a well-known optical firm in St. Petersburg. Indeed, a core investor seems to have emerged in nearly every one of the most promising privatizations.

This evidence underscores the importance of voucher tradability for the formation of blockholdings in Russia. To acquire large stakes in firms, investors needed to accumulate blocks of vouchers and then bid them in voucher auctions. Without voucher tradability, only investment funds would have been able to build large stakes before the after-market developed. The liquid voucher market has enabled Russian privatization to do what for political reasons it could not do directly: to create core investors for many major companies.

Who are these large investors in Russia? They appear to be of three types. The first is private voucher investment funds which were created following the Czech model, and which, as we mentioned, collected 45 million vouchers. Although most Russian funds so far appear to be uninterested in corporate governance, some of the largest funds have acquired large stakes in several companies and have actively challenged management.

The second type of large investors is wealthy individuals and private firms, such as Bioprocess and Mikrodin, which made their fortunes in the last few years in trade and other commercial activities. These investors often have the financial muscle to stand up to the managers. While managers try to discourage these investors, they typically do not just go away.

The third category of large investors is foreigners. To them, the low prices in voucher auctions had a powerful attraction. At the same time, they did not often openly challenge the managers, for fear of a political reaction. Foreign participation in the voucher auctions played a relatively minor role until May 1994, but in the last two months of mass privatization and shortly afterwards, over $2 billion in foreign portfolio investment entered Russia.

Anecdotal evidence suggests that large shareholders often try to use their votes to change company policies. Alpha Capital, for example, has campaigned to force firms it invested in to pay dividends. An outside investor in Vladimir Tractor Works eventually gained control of the company and installed his own management. Mikrodin succeeded in replacing the general directors of both Permsky Motors, the largest jet engine maker in Russia, and the Moscow truck maker ZIL. First Voucher, the largest voucher fund, has its representatives appointed to chair the boards of the companies in which it holds large stakes. In other cases, such as that of Uralmash, Bioprocess cooperated with the management in an aggressive restructuring program.

Large shareholder activism is beginning to show up in statistics as well. In Vladimir, Yaroslavl, and Rostov, three large Russian cities for which GKI collected data, 10 percent of the general directors were removed at the first shareholder meeting by coalitions of outside investors and employees. While Russia sorely needs even faster turnover of the old guard directors, the existing pace is already impressive. Large shareholders are clearly pushing companies toward efficient ownership structures in which cash flow and control rights are effectively lined up.

Not all managers have acquiesced. In some cases where workers are talking and selling shares to outsiders, managers threaten them with dismissal. Some managers physically threaten challengers at shareholder meetings, rig shareholder votes, illegally change corporate charters (from one-share-one-vote to one-shareholder-one-vote), refuse to record share trades in corporate share registers, and so on. The current situation is best described as a stalemate: large outside shareholders are challenging the existing managers, who in turn use worker support to resist the challenges, often effectively.

The key question is whether large shareholders will be able to play their role without being stopped by politicians. Many managers are appealing to local governments (and to the central government) to restrain large investors. Right after the voucher auction, the manager of Bolshevik Cake Factory unsuccessfully lobbied GKI to force Alpha Capital, the large investor, to sell its shares. Several local governments have intervened to force block-holders to sell their shares. And in perhaps the most extraordinary action so far, the director of ZIL, who was subsequently removed, publicly appealed to Russia's President Yeltsin to maintain the government's control of the company through a so-called "golden share," thus eliminating the controlling influence of Mikrodin. Yet despite these attempts, political interference in most cases has failed to prevent outside investors from exercising meaningful control.

Over time, the role of the large shareholders in corporate governance is likely to increase. In the summer and fall of 1994, as the market values of shares of privatized firms began to rise, workers sharply accelerated the pace of selling their shares. Outside (and sometimes inside) the gates of many companies, it is common to see a bus which serves as a buying point for workers' shares. In most cases, these shares are bought by brokers for large investors. Managers are buying shares from the workers as well, but in many cases outsiders are getting more. By some estimates, workers have already sold a quarter of the shares that were distributed to them. If outsiders succeed in getting a significant fraction of workers' shares, their role in corporate governance will increase dramatically.

The other substantial opportunity for outside investors to gain more control is investment tenders, in which the government sells its residual 15 to 20 percent equity stake in exchange for a commitment to future investment in the company. Despite a slow start in 1994, the pace of investment tenders had accelerated by the time privatization ended, largely because subsidized credits got harder to come by and firms needed funds. Many of these investment tenders have been tainted, as the managers accepted less capital from investors who did not challenge their control. For example, the winner of the investment tender for Lada carmaker VAZ was AVVA, the dubious financial group controlled by VAZ itself. Not surprisingly, AVVA received the stake for the reserve price, and there were no competitors. Despite the common occurrence of rigged investment tenders many managers choose to give up some control in exchange for capital and know-how, which bodes well for the future of corporate governance. In market economies as well, managers typically give up control only in exchange for capital.

In sum, the ownership structure of Russian firms has taken a giant leap toward efficiency as a result of privatization. The government has sold most of its shares in the process, and most of the remaining government stakes have been allocated to workers and to investment tenders. Political control through share ownership has largely disappeared. The managers emerged from privatization with large share ownership, which gave them considerable interest in maximizing profits. Many large companies have obtained block investors, who are in many cases pushing the managers toward restructuring, or even replacing the managers. At the same time, managers often have control rights out of proportion to their cash flow claims and use these rights to keep themselves at the helm, a policy that is usually inconsistent with efficiency. These managers are also tied to politicians through a system of subsidies and government orders. The evidence from shareholdings suggests that the ownership structure in Russia is not fully efficient but is moving in the right direction.

The Role of Financial Markets

What about other developments in corporate governance, that might serve to offset the effects of managerial entrenchment? In some areas, progress has been very slow. The present bankruptcy procedure gives too much power to the government agency in charge of it, and too little power to the creditors. As a result, debt is unlikely to become an effective control device in Russia in the near future. The securities markets – while developing extremely rapidly – are not yet sufficiently liquid to sustain an active takeover market. And, as we mentioned, boards of directors are dominated by the insiders.

Nonetheless, it is important to remember that one of the principal ways in which managers lose control in the West is when they access external markets for capital. Outside providers of capital usually insist on control rights, and actually get them. The fact that most Russian companies severely need capital to restructure opens critical opportunities for the development of corporate governance. Managers would in fact be willing to give up some of their control rights in exchange for sorely needed capital, since the alternative is to remain at the helm of a rapidly declining firm.

In all likelihood, since the corporate voting procedure with all its imperfections works better than the bankruptcy procedure, Russian companies will be raising capital in the near future through the equity market. To do that, they will need to accommodate the desires of providers of equity capital – unless of course they succeed in running pyramid style schemes in which small individual investors simply part with their cash in exchange for vague promises. The development of a securities market that accommodates the need by firms to raise capital presents new opportunities for progress on corporate governance. Specifically, outside investors will insist on transparent share registers, freer trading of shares, recognition of their voting rights, some transparency in accounting and disclosure, and so on. All of this has already begun to happen. These developments will be critical for corporate governance in Russia and for the necessary reduction of managerial control over firms.

Conclusion

In sum, we have presented some evidence on the emerging ownership structures of the Russian companies. These structures have been to a large extent determined by the political imperative of accommodating managerial preferences in the privatization program, since without manager support firms would have remained under political control. We believe that the ownership structures emerging from Russian privatization, while far superior to state ownership, still give managers too much control relative to what is needed to speed up efficient restructuring, since such restructuring depends to a significant degree on fast management turnover. At the same time, the growth of large shareholders and the development of financial markets in Russia is likely to play a key role in restraining the misconduct of the existing managers and bringing better managers to the Russian companies. Privatization is only a first step in the development of efficient ownership structures in the Russian economy.

References

Berle, Adolf A., and Gardiner Means. 1932. *The Modern Corporation and Private Property*. New York: Macmillan.

Blasi, Joseph 1994. "Ownership, Governance, and Restructuring". Rutgers University School of Management and Labor Relations, New Jersey, unpublished manuscript.

Boycko, Maxim, Andrei Shleifer, and Robert Vishny. 1993. "Privatizing Russia." Brookings Papers on Economic Activity II: 139–181. The Brookings Institution, Washington, D.C.

——. 1995, *Privatizing Russia*. Cambridge, Mass.: Massachusetts Institute of Technology (MIT) Press.

Demsetz, Harold, and Kenneth Lehn. 1985. "The Structure of Corporate Ownership: Causes and Consequences." *Journal of Political Economy* 93: 1155–77.

Frydman, Roman, Andrzej Rapacyznski, John S. Earle, *et al*. 1993. *The Privatization Process in Central Europe*. London/ Budapest: Central European University Press.

Holström, Bengt. 1979. "Moral Hazard and Observability." *Bell Journal of Economics* 10: 74–91.

Jensen, Michael C., and William H. Meckling. 1976. "Theory of the Firm: Managerial Behavior, Agency Costs and the Ownership Structure." *Journal of Financial Economics* 3: 305–60.

Jensen, Michael C., and Kevin J. Murphy. 1990. "Executive Pay and Top Management Performance." *Journal of Political Economy* 98.

Kaplan, Steven N. 1994. "Top Executive Rewards and Firm Performance: A Comparison of Japan and the United States." *Journal of Political Economy* 102: 510–46.

Morck, Randall, Andrei Shleifer, and Robert Vishny. 1988. "Management Ownership and Market Valuation: An Empirical Analysis." *Journal of Financial Economics* 20: 293–315.

Shavell, Steven. 1979. "Risk Sharing and Incentives in the Principal and Agent Relationship." *Bell Journal of Economics* 10: 55–73.

Russia
P21   L33
P34   632

3

CORPORATE GOVERNANCE IN RUSSIA
An Initial Look

JOSEPH BLASI and ANDREI SHLEIFER

The research reported here was conducted with the assistance of Daria Panina, Katerina Grachova, Alexander Kalinin, and Maya Kroumova, and is funded by the Eurasia Foundation of Washington, D.C. We wish to thank Maxim Boycko of the Russian Privatization Center, Dmitri Vasiliev of the Russian Federation Commission on Securities and Stock Exchanges, the Russian Federation State Committee for State Property, and Jonathan Hay of the Harvard Institute for International Development Legal Reform Project without whose support this research would not have been possible. We wish to thank Joanne Mangels for her administrative support and Cheryl Gray who provided helpful comments.

Introduction

Corporate governance is a key determinant of enterprise restructuring (see Boycko and Shleifer 1993; Boycko, Shleifer, and Vishny 1993; Corbo, Coricelli, and Bossak 1991; Kikeri, Nellis, and Shirley 1992; Monks and Minow 1995, Oxford Analytica, 1992). One goal of Russia's privatization program has been to encourage responsible corporate governance. (See Frydman, Rapaczynski, Earle *et al.* 1993; Boycko, Shleifer, and Vishny 1995). This chapter updates the corporate governance data presented at the World Bank conference on Russian privatization in June of 1994 and reported elsewhere (Blasi 1994 and Blasi, with Panina and Grachova 1994; Lieberman and Nellis 1994). It is based on three surveys.

The first survey was conducted between August 1992 and December 1993, by interviews with 170 enterprises in 36 oblasts (regions) during the initial stages of the privatization program and immediately thereafter (see also

Webster *et al.* 1994). The second set of interviews was conducted at 40 postprivatized enterprises in 14 oblasts (regions) between February and April of 1994; its purpose was to ascertain trends in compliance with Russian government decrees on corporate governance during annual shareholder meetings, which were supposed to take place between 1 January and 30 April 1994. The third and most recent set of interviews were conducted at an additional 61 postprivatized enterprises in 19 oblasts from May to December 1994. The third set of interviews are mainly revisits of the enterprises in the first survey, which had been studied about a year earlier. All of these interviews are conducted with general directors or their deputies. The enterprises are medium and large firms that have participated in Russia's mass privatization program. The appendix provides more detail about the interviews and the sample.

First Survey, 1992–1993

After one year of privatization in Russia, our data indicated that most of the boards of directors were solidly controlled by insiders. These insiders were generally other senior managers who reported directly to the general director (Blasi 1994). Up to the end of 1993, senior management indicated in interviews that they opposed outsiders on their boards of directors. They intended to operate the boards mainly as councils of experts who were already specialists of the firm. Some noted that they might support occasional board seats for large investors. Senior managers wanted to dominate the ownership and the control of their enterprises by continuing management-dominated boards and reducing rank-and-file employee ownership while increasing management ownership. Table 3.1 summarizes the average and median ownership percentages for different groups and Table 3.2 examines the figures for blockholders (which are nonstate holders of more than 5 percent of stock) in the first survey.

At the outset of privatization, most of the firms were majority employee owned. As noted in the table, at the median, insiders owned 60 percent of the stock. As noted in an initial analysis of the privatization program in 1993, over 60 percent of the firms chose Option 2 (51 percent employee ownership) (Boycko, Shleifer, and Vishny 1993). This first survey indicates that most of those firms where workers were originally capable of buying only a minority stake under Option 1 eventually became majority employee owned by purchasing additional shares through the voucher auctions, investment tenders, and the secondary market. Majority employee ownership was typically the initial outcome of the entire privatization program. According

Table 3.1 Equity Holdings in Privatized Enterprises in the Russian Federation, December 1993 (in percentages)

	Average	Median
All insiders	65	60
Top management	8.6	5
All outsiders (non State)	21.5	20
State	12.9	12

Source: Russian Privatization Research Project, 1994.
Notes: Sample consists of 142 enterprises in 32 oblasts; average no. of employees, 2,776; median no. of employees, 1,200. Of the enterprises, 91% were majority employee owned; 9% minority employee owned.

Table 3.2 Equity Holdings in Privatized Enterprises in the Russian Federation: Distribution and the Role of Blockholders, December 1993 (in percentages)

	Average	Median
All blockholders [a]	11	6
Blockholders present[b]	20	15
All individual citizens	4	1
Individual citizens present	7.2	5.7

Source: Russian Privatization Research Project, 1994.
Notes: Sample consists of 142 enterprises in 32 oblasts; average no. of employees, 2,776; median no. of employees, 1,200. Blockholders are holders with more than 5% equity. Of the enterprises, 57% had blockholder stakes; 43% did not.
[a] This number averages the blockholder stakes among the entire sample, including the firms that have no blockholder stakes.
[b] This number averages *only* the enterprises that have blockholder stakes.

to this first survey, only 9 percent of firms did not obtain majority employee ownership through these various methods. As a consequence at the end of 1993, the senior managers were determined to operate their boards of directors according to the maxim that the "majority holder elects the entire board."

At this early stage in the privatization effort, government policymakers were concerned about public perceptions of fairness in the new corporate structure of these formerly state-owned enterprises. Thus, in the corporatization stage of privatization, the Russian Federation State Committee for State Property (GKI) required all firms to provide rank-and-file employees with one board representative out of a total number of five members on the board. Nevertheless, after the enterprises privatized, there was very little evidence of *any* rank-and-file worker board representation in these firms.

The rank-and-file board member was dropped from most boards by management. Worker control did not exist in these firms before privatization, and it did not emerge after privatization despite the fact that workers in 91 percent of the enterprises could have theoretically voted rank-and-file members to the entire board. Trade unions had little power, and individual employee shareholders had no influence in most firms.

The situation of corporate governance at the beginning of 1994 was nevertheless fluid given developments in several key areas:

1. Contrary to the initial wishes of many senior managers, outsider ownership had already reached an average of 21.5 percent, and 20 percent at the median, in the privatized firms. Many of these outside shareholders had an incentive to expand outside shareholder rights because they had significant investments to protect. Many outside shareholders were blockholders, who had a concentrated equity holding of more than 5 percent of all outstanding common stock. The average blockholder stake across all firms in the sample, including those firms without blockholders, is 11 percent, and 6 percent at the median. When one examines only the 57 percent of the firms with blockholders, blockholders have 20 percent average stakes and 15 percent stakes at the median. One can focus on the other 43 percent of enterprises without blockholders and the high insider ownership as a poor outcome of privatization. But, given the political struggle on the part of the managers against *any* significant outsider ownership in the constitution of the privatization program, the early result of 57 percent of firms with blockholders represented some movement toward the development of corporate governance.

2. Most senior managers reported in the first survey that they had generally exhausted the financial resources of themselves and their work force to purchase the initial stock ownership stakes. Thus, it was likely that the earlier reported residual state ownership stakes of 12.9 percent on average and 12 percent at the median would also later be sold to outsiders. If this assumption proved to be correct, these sales *could* potentially create outsider stakes approaching 30 percent. The expectation of this event could only increase pressure for action on outsider and minority shareholder rights.

3. Neither the top managers and workers with their individual savings nor the firms themselves with retained earnings could finance the capital investment necessary for restructuring. Rational outside investors would view this as an invitation to an expanded corporate governance role for themselves in postprivatized enterprises. Few investors would risk providing capital to restructure firms whose boards would be completely

controlled by insiders. Thus, some accommodation of outside investors was likely to emerge.

4. The political struggle over privatization somewhat stabilized at the beginning of 1994 after the showdown between the Supreme Soviet and President Boris Yeltsin. Contrary to alarmist predictions, the regions accelerated the privatization of state-owned industry after a brief pause, and citizens, voucher investment funds, and commercial firms continued to participate actively in the sell-off.

In the beginning of 1994, all of these factors set the stage for a further push for corporate governance. The Russian president issued a decree on minority shareholder rights that mandated that no more than one-third of the members of the board of directors could be employees of an enterprise. It also stipulated that each enterprise had to have a new shareholder meeting within 120 days of 1 January 1994 to choose a new board of directors using cumulative voting as the required method of voting. Obviously, cumulative voting is a very different mechanism of choosing a board than that practiced by most Russian enterprises before 1 January 1994. Under the old method, slates of directors were nominated for the board and each share of stock had one vote. Whoever controlled at least 51 percent of the shares could elect their entire slate to the board.

In theory, cumulative voting was designed to introduce some measure of influence over corporate governance by outside shareholders. Despite insider control of the majority of ownership, cumulative voting would allow a minority shareholder to elect some members to the board. Under cumulative voting each share of stock had the same number of votes as persons to be elected to the board. The top vote winners among all individual board nominees – not slates – would be elected. A minority shareholder could target all votes toward one or more particular nominee in order to elect at least some outsiders to the board. A minority shareholder could also join with other minority shareholders to accomplish the same end, as could groups of employee shareholders theoretically join with outsiders or form coalitions. Furthermore, the additional limit on insider board membership to one-third of a board would theoretically force management to select outside representatives with whom their authority relationship was perhaps more tenuous than their supervisory relationship with directors who were also management employees. Despite these possibilities, it is also true that cumulative voting has been successfully kept out of the legal systems of most Western capitalist economies by managers interested in their own entrenchment.

Second Survey, Second Quarter 1994

An examination of the evidence of whether or not these two decrees were implemented by 1 April 1994 would provide a preliminary indication of how the corporate governance question was evolving in the Russian Federation at that time. From February to April 1994, the authors surveyed 40 enterprises in 14 oblasts on these and other issues in a series of long interviews. This research provided observers with immediate feedback on the impact of the government's new regulations. The percent of enterprises that implemented cumulative voting at a meeting before 30 April 1994 was 7.5 percent (3 firms). The percent that were planning to implement cumulative voting at a shareholder meeting soon was 2.5 percent (1 firm). The percent that said they would implement cumulative voting in one to two years at a future board election was 5 percent (2 firms). Table 3.3 shows the characteristics of the firms that implemented cumulative voting.

While most firms did not implement the cumulative voting decree, Table 3.3 shows that those that did implement the decree had large individual blockholder stakes and larger than average total blockholder stakes when compared with the Federation-wide sample described in Table 3.2. The firms that implemented the decree also had large total outsider stakes, which were far in excess of the average outsider stakes of 21.5 percent on average and 20 percent at the median reported in the first study.

Table 3.3 Characteristics of the Postprivatized Firms That Have Implemented or Intend to Implement the Cumulative Voting Decree of the Russian Federation, April 1994.

	No. of employees	Blockholder stakes (%)	Total outsider stakes (%)	Outsider board seats as a % of the total board
Implemented				
Firm 1	5,500	27.5, 10[a]	37.5	57
Firm 2	1,940	20	48.2	55.5
Firm 3	650	47	47	60
Will implement[b]				
Firm 1	3,796	21	21	
Firm 2	1,850	0	27.62	
Firm 3	4,873	9, 7.8[a]	28	

Source: Russian Privatization Research Project, 1994.
Notes: Sample consists of 40 enterprises in 14 oblasts; average no. of employees 2,223. Implementers' total blockholder stakes averaged 34.8%; total outside ownership averaged 44.2%.
[a] Percentage for each of two blockholders.
[b] Firms that said they would implement it now or in one to two years.

The other key part of the decree required corporate boards to conduct an election by 30 April 1994 so that no more than one-third of the members were insiders. From our sample (40 enterprises in 14 oblasts with 2,223 employees on average) only 5 percent or two firms implemented the decree and had two-thirds or more outsider board members; the other 95 percent or 38 firms had more than 33 percent insider board members. The characteristics of the two firms that implemented the decree were as follows:

Outsider stakes in each firm	66.6% and 71%
Use of cumulative voting	0
Total outsider stake in each firm	73% and 95%
Stake of biggest outsider in each firm	63% and 95%
Number of workers in each firm	620 and 500
Average size of the blockholder stakes in both firms	56%

The second part of the decree was not followed except in a few small firms (5 percent or two firms in our sample) with very large outsider stakes, very large total blockholder stakes and very large average blockholder stakes. Evidently, these outsiders were able to compel management to follow the decree. Certainly, a very tentative pattern in this very small sample is emerging, namely, that larger outsider stakes seem to be accompanied by outside board members.

What about the firms that did not implement cumulative voting? What was the incidence of outside board membership in these firms? Before considering the data, two words of caution are in order. First, the definition of an "outside board member" for the purpose of this research is a nonstate outsider. Thus, state-appointed representatives were excluded from these calculations. Second, one cannot automatically presume that an outside board member is truly independent of management. Corporate governance depends on many other factors in addition to the number of outside directors, such as the terms of outside directors, whom they represent, the stakes of the owners they may represent, the quality of company information to which they have access, and the legal environment in which they operate.

Indeed, the lack of compliance with cumulative voting was not the end of the story. The majority of the enterprises in this entire second sample had some nongovernmental outside representatives on their corporate boards or were planning to add such outside representatives very soon. Why would a group of senior managers with majority insider ownership and boards made up of management employees who were their subordinates accept outside directors? Of the firms in the sample that did not implement the decree on cumulative voting (to allow outside directors), 32.5 percent had nevertheless added outside directors to their boards by some other method. This finding was a bit surprising because the change had occurred and been measured in just the four month period between January and April 1994 when the directors were to implement cumulative voting! This finding had to be viewed as preliminary until further investigation.

What could explain this change in the 40 enterprises observed? What are the characteristics of this 32.5 percent of firms that did not implement the President's decree but added some outsiders to their boards? Our research examined the percentage of total outside ownership, the percentage of blockholder ownership, the size of blockholder stakes, and the size of firms. From our survey (40 firms in 14 oblasts from February to April 1994 with an average of 2,223 employees) 40 percent had outside directors on their boards (the sum of 7.5 % that implemented cumulative voting and 32.5% that added directors without implementing cumulative voting). Thirteen firms or 32.5 percent had some nongovernmental board representation without having used cumulative voting to achieve it.. The characteristics of these firms that now have outside directors on their board included:

Average number of	
employees	1,983
outside directors	2
outside directors excluding former employees	1.8
Average percentage of	
total outsider ownership	32 (22 at the median)
blockholder ownership (averaging all total ownership of those with more than 5% across all firms)	26.7 (21 at the median)
each blockholder's stake (averaging all individual blockholders across all firms)	27.4 (at the median 14)
Percentage that have nongovernmental board representation, excluding those in which the only outside board representatives are former employees	27.5 (in 2 of 13 firms only the director is a former employee)

Again, these preliminary data show the presence of high average individual blockholder stakes and high average total blockholder stakes in the firms that added outside directors. In these cases, the average total outsider ownership is 32 percent compared with the Federation-wide average of 21 percent (Table 3.1), the average total blockholder ownership is 26.7 percent compared with the Federation-wide average of 11 percent (Table 3.2), and the average size of each blockholder that is present is 27.4 percent compared with the Federation-wide average of 20 percent. Note, however, that total *outsider* ownership (as opposed to blockholder ownership) does not seem to be a clear-cut indicator of outsider directors. An average outsider ownership among firms that add outside directors is 32 percent, and it is only 21.5 percent among the entire sample of postprivatized enterprises. But the median outsider ownership among firms that add outside directors is 22 percent, compared with 20 percent for the sample as a whole.

To get further insight on the role of total outsider ownership, consider enterprises where the managers said they have an intent to add outside directors in the near future. Our survey of postprivatized enterprises in the Russian Federation that reported the intent to add outsiders to their boards of directors very soon but did not implement the cumulative voting decree resulted in the following characteristics (out of 40 firms in 14 oblasts from February to April 1994 with an average of 2,223 employees):

Number of firms	10
Average number of employees	3,589 (at the median 2,476)
Average percentage of	
total outsider ownership	25.3 (at the median 26.5)
blockholder (more than 5 %) ownership	19.4 (at the median 15.9)
each blockholder's stake	10.9 (at the median 9.5)

The data further strengthened the notion that large average total blockholder ownership and large average individual blockholder stakes influence the readiness of senior managers to bring outsiders on corporate boards. The *average individual blockholder stake* of 10.9 percent was much less than in the firms that actually already put outsiders on their boards. There it was 27.4 percent. But the *average total outside blockholder ownership* across those firms that have already put outsiders on their boards (26.7 percent) is comparable to that number in the firms that only intend to put outsiders on their boards in the near future (25.3 percent).

These preliminary data suggest several working conclusions:

1. These data reflect an acceptance by senior managers that outsiders will play a role in restructuring firms. Upon follow-up questioning in the firms that added outsiders to their boards, we found that the mechanism for introducing outsiders to all of these boards was a negotiation between the senior managers and the outside shareholder rather than a confrontation at the shareholder meeting or some unpredictable event which surprised senior management. Senior managers may be accepting the fact that they will not be successful at increasing their own ownership of the firms substantially in order to further consolidate their control.

2. The privatized enterprises that did not implement the cumulative voting decree and did not exhibit senior management negotiation for greater

outside board representation had one of the following characteristics: (1) they had very low outsider stock ownership; (2) they had high outsider stock ownership which was spread between small diffuse holdings such as individual citizen holdings; (3) they had large outsider stock holdings that were in the hands of a business partner who wanted no seats; and (4) they were voucher investment funds which held the stock and did not want to make significant efforts for board seats or have substantial involvement in the firms.

3. The Russian government's major initiatives on corporate governance were formally ignored. An analysis of the narrative parts of the interviews indicates that the problem was neither lack of knowledge of the regulations nor lack of understanding of them. They were often rejected with an attitude of arrogance and defiance.

Next we examine all three phenomena together, namely, those firms that added outside directors as a result of complying with cumulative voting, those that added outside directors as a result of voluntary negotiation, and those who intend to add outside directors as a result of either behavior in the near future. The survey results are as follows:

Percentage of firms in survey
   that *now* have outside directors on their board: 40
   with more than one outside director: 22.5
   that *plan to add* outside directors to their board either by implementing cumulative voting in the future or negotiating with outside shareholders: 25
   that have outside directors on their board of directors or plan to add outside directors very soon: 65

This evidence suggests that the main engine driving corporate governance reform in Russia will be market relations between investors with significant outsider holdings organized in large blockholder stakes and managers of firms (see Shleifer and Vishny 1986; Phelps *et al.* 1993). Corporate governance will not be mainly determined in Russia by what is in the heads of experts but by investors seeking to protect the risk of their investment in real companies. Finally, the general directors indicated that they expected the number of firms with outsider board representation to increase in the near term.

Third Survey, December 1994

More recent interviews with an additional 61 postprivatized enterprises in 19 oblasts were conducted from May to December 1994. Three of these enterprises were separately visited in the 40 enterprise sample cited above. The rest were privatized enterprises that were not visited in the second survey. Thus, the third survey provides a separate opportunity to examine the findings of the second survey. Most of the third survey consisted of follow-up visits to the postprivatized enterprises in the sample of firms visited in the first survey, which comprised firms visited between August 1992 and April 1994. While all regions have not yet been revisited, the number of employees of the firms in this subsample is similar to the original sample, that is, the first survey. The average number of employees is 2,360 and 1,327 at the median. One goal of this new survey is to take a longitudinal look at the enterprises studied earlier with a more extensive and detailed survey: share ownership distribution, managerial attitudes towards optimal ownership, corporate governance, restructuring plans, involvement in debt and equity markets, labor–management relations, and employment trends. This study also looks at many other corporate governance issues in addition to outside board membership.

This particular review of the third survey will focus on five questions relating mainly to corporate governance: (1) To what extent are the above findings of an increase in outside directors and corporate governance supported in the new survey? (2) What is the size of the blockholder stake and the size of the company when outside directors are present and absent? (3) What is the current structure of ownership in the privatized sector and how does it help us explain trends in corporate governance? (4) What are some of the specific dynamics of the tug for power between insiders and outsiders in the corporate governance arena? (5) What evidence do we have of the positive or negative effects of employee ownership?

Role of Outside Directors

According to the new survey presented in Table 3.4, 76 percent of firms have some outsider (nonstate) board representation compared with 40 percent of firms in the last survey that said they had outside board representation and 65 percent of firms that said that they had or were planning to add such outsiders to their board in the near future. According to the recent survey, 36 percent of the firms now have more than one outside board representative compared with 22.5 percent in the last survey. The average board membership is 6.7 members, with 6 at the median. The typical board has 1 outsider, 1 state representative, and 4 insiders. In almost all cases the insiders are the general director and other senior managers who are subordinates of the general director. There seems to be a slight increase in nonmanagement employee representatives on the boards.

Table 3.4 Board Membership in Postprivatized Enterprises in Russia,
December 1994

	Average	Median
Number of		
Board members	6.7	6
Managers	3.0	4
Nonmanagement employee representatives	0.2	0
Nonstate outsiders	1.2	1
State representatives	1.0	1
Firms with	%	
Any outsider board members	76	
No outsider board members	24	
More than one outsider	36	
Firms in which		
Outsider is former employee	6	
Former ministry official is outsider	4	

Source: Russian Privatization Research Project Survey.
Note: From a sample of 61 enterprises in 19 oblasts with an average of 2,360 employees; median of
1,321 employees.

Our earlier studies found almost no nonmanagement employee representatives on boards. In the third survey, we became suspicious about reports of
employee representatives on boards, because there are indications that the
general directors are self-conscious about reporting boards made up entirely
of their immediate subordinates. As a precaution, the research assistants
were instructed to review each board member in great detail. They have now
observed that managers often attempt to present other top management
members who serve on the board as rank-and-file board representatives. As a
result, the apparent slight increase in rank-and-file employee representation
may actually be lower.

While earlier findings on the growth of outside board representation are
confirmed, the influence of outsiders on boards should be put in perspective.
First, the average and median quorum for board decisions in these firms is
four members, so board meetings can be convened, in theory, without the
presence of the outside board representative. Second, the board can *also* be
convened without the presence of the one board member representing the
state *and* the one board member representing outsiders. Third, the lack of
rank-and-file employee representation by an independent outsider or an
independent trade union official and the constitution of the rest of the board
by senior managers who are subordinates to the general director leave no
independent representative of the employees at these meetings. Of course,
employees can potentially police insiders for all shareholders.

Outside Directors and Company Characteristics

Are there any clear-cut differences between companies with outside directors and companies without outside directors in terms of the size of the company and the size of the blockholders owning its stock? Our survey results indicate that the presence of outsider directors is accompanied by the presence of blockholders while the absence of outsider directors is not accompanied by the absence of blockholders When companies have outsiders on their board, they have quite large average and median blockholder stakes for all blockholders (15–17 percent) as well as for the dominant blockholder (19–21 percent). Nevertheless, two companies do have outside board members without the obvious presence of blockholders. They have an average employment of 738 employees. In these two cases, an aggregate of individual citizens owned 10 percent and 29 percent respectively of the stock. A pensioner on the board was the probable blockholder among individual citizens in one case. And a general director from a parallel company was the board representative in the other case.

The exception to the general pattern is the evidence that 16.2 percent of the firms with blockholders did not have any outsider board representation. Companies that do not have outsiders on their board have smaller average and median blockholder stakes for all blockholders (12–14 percent) as well as for the dominant blockholders (16 percent). Clearly, some holders choose not to assert their governance rights or they have trouble doing so. An examination of the actual cases clarifies that the companies with no outside board representation and blockholders have nine different blockholders. Five of the nine are investment funds, one is a friendly supplier, two are unrelated commercial firms, and one is a foreign investor. The proportion which the blockholding represents of the total outside ownership does not present itself as an explanation for the lack of board seats of these blockholders. For example, in companies with blockholders and outside board representation, blockholders have 70.69 percent on average of total outsider ownership (71.33 percent at the median). In companies with blockholders and with no outside board representation, blockholders have 74.57 percent on average of total outsider ownership (74.71 percent at the median). Finally, the firms with no blockholding and no outsider board seats have very low outsider ownership. Also, size is not a strong determinant of the absence of board seats. Companies with and without blockholding that had no outsiders on their board had median (average) employment of 1,104 (4,652) and 1,314 (1,314) respectively.

The following descriptive data from the December 1994 survey examines whether companies with outsiders on their boards have or do not have blockholders present and whether companies without outsiders on their boards have or do not have blockholders present. This provides some preliminary indication of the association of outsider ownership and block-holding. Then the characteristics of each of the four possible types of firms are presented: firms with outsiders on the board and blockholders, firms with outsiders on the board and no blockholders, firms with no outsiders on the board and blockholders, and finally, firms with no outsiders on the board and no blockholders. The numbers in parentheses in the list of the four types of firms that follows are the averages and median percentages of ownership of the dominant blockholders in each group. (The findings tend to underestimate the presence of blockholders because aggregate stakes held by individual citizens could not be reliably disaggregated into block-holders and small shareholders.)

The following data show whether blockholders are present or absent when companies have or do not have outsiders on their board:

Percentage of companies with outsiders on board
   83.8 (blockholders present)   22.3 (blockholders absent)
Percentage of companies with no outsiders on board
   16.2 (blockholders present)   77.7 (blockholders absent)

The evidence shows that 83.8 percent of companies with blockholders had outsiders on their board, while only 16.2 percent of the companies with blockholders had no outsiders on their board. Conversely, it indicates that 22.3 percent of the companies without blockholders had outsiders on their board, while 77.7 percent of the companies without blockholders had no outsiders on their board.

The characteristics of firms that have outsiders on the board and block-holders are:

Average percentage of blockholder stake 17.36 (median 20.96)
Median percentage of blockholder stake 15.5 (median 19)
Average number of employees 2,311 (median no. of employees: 1,586)

The characteristics of firms that have outsiders on the board and *no* block-holders are (small number of cases raises questions about this finding):

Percentage of average total outsider stake 19.5
Median percentage of total outsider stake 19.5
Average number of employees 738 (median no. of employees: 738)

The characteristics of firms that have *no* outsiders on the board and block-holders are:

Average percentage of blockholder stake 14.05 (median 16.28)
Median percentage of blockholder stake 12 (median 16)
Average number of employees 4,652 (median no. of employees: 1,104)

The characteristics of firms that have *no* outsiders on the board and no blockholders are:

Average percentage of outsider stake 4.8
Median percentage of outsider stake 3
Average number of employees 2,069 (median no. of employees: 1,314)

These descriptive data suggest that blockholding and outsider ownership may explain outsider board representation. How are outsider ownership and blockholding correlated with outsider board representation in this sample? Are they the key factors in explaining the appearance of outsider board representation? In other words, can the influence of company size and other characteristics be excluded from explaining this relationship? The results of a preliminary correlation analysis follow.

Total outside ownership and outsider board representation are correlated. The total percentage of outsider ownership has a significant positive relationship to the presence of outside board representation ($r = 0.37$, $p = 0.01$). The total percentage of outsider ownership has a significant positive relationship with the total number of outsider directors on a company's board ($r = 0.29$, $p = 0.03$) and outsider board seats as a percentage of total board seats ($r = 0.32$, $p = 0.03$).

Blockholder ownership and outsider board representation are also correlated. A significant positive relationship was found between the sum of blockholder stakes and the number of outsiders on a company's board ($r = 0.33$, $p = 0.03$). The actual number of blockholders itself is not significantly related to outside board representation. Regarding the relationship between the presence or absence of blockholders and outsider board representation, more companies than expected had blockholders in the group of companies with outside board representation, and fewer companies than expected had no blockholders in the group of companies without outsider board representation. The relationship was not significant due to a small sample subgroup size. But the direction of the relationship is clear. The presence or absence of a blockholder is not sufficient to predict outsider board representation. Rather the total percentage of outsider ownership and the sum of blockholder stakes determine whether outsider ownership and blockholder stakes are associated with board representation.

Neither company size as measured by the number of employees nor a simple measure of financial performance explains outside board representation. There is no significant relationship between company size as measured by the number of employees and outsider board representation. There is no significant relationship between a measure of whether company cash flows cover operating costs or not and outsider board representation.

Developments in the Structure of Ownership

The structure of ownership in privatized enterprises has continued to change since the first and second surveys. The sales of shares from privatized enterprises in Russia and their main buyers in 1994 according to the Russian Privatization Research Project (1994) survey had the following characteristics:

Average % sold by employees	4	(at the median 0)
Average % sold by voucher funds	1	(at the median 0)
Main buyers as a % of all buyers mentioned:		
insiders	25	
top managers	12.5	
other workers	12.5	
outsiders	75	
firms and investors	50	
voucher funds	25	

Our data show that workers sold an average of 4 percent of the company's shares and the main buyers (75 percent) were outsiders and individual citizens. These data on sales of shares by workers do not exactly match the slightly larger declines on insider ownership reported by the senior managers in Table 3.5. Senior managers may be presenting their current estimates of a set of changes that could be pinned down exactly if the shareholder register were completely audited on that day. Perhaps senior managers are underestimating the amount employees have sold. There were also a large number of missing answers on this question. Thus, the data are useful mainly because they are one indication of the direction of the ownership changes: in general, the role of insiders is decreasing and the role of outsiders is increasing. The data suggest that outsiders are the main buyers of shares. Between the December 1993 survey of the structure of ownership (Table 3.1) and the December 1994 survey (Table 3.5), the major goal of the privatization program was to encourage the sale of the state-owned shares to outside investors for cash. In the survey, senior managers indicate that outsiders not insiders are the main buyers of these shares. Table 3.5 provides more detail about these changes.

When compared with the ownership figures in the first survey, the figures in Table 3.5 indicate that insider ownership dropped by an average of 6 percent (2 percent at the median), outsider ownership increased by an average of 8.8 percent (9 percent at the median), and state ownership dropped by an average of 2.9 percent (12 percent at the median). Thus, average and median state ownership continued to fall in every stage of postprivatization ownership.

Table 3.5 Structure of Ownership in Privatized Enterprises in the Russian Federation, December 1994 (in percentages)

	Average	Median
General ownership structure[a]		
All employees	59	58
All outsiders	29	30
The state	10	0
Insider ownership structure		
Nonmgt. employees	42	43
All managers	17	15
Top managers	9	6
General director	3	1
Middle managers[b]	8	N.A.

Source: Russian Privatization Research Project, 1994.
Note: Employees owned a majority of the firm in 63% of the cases and a minority in 37%.
[a] Figures do not add up to 100% because of missing values.
[b] Estimated from data shown. Median cannot be estimated.

The major news, however, is hidden within these numbers: *37 percent of the firms are no longer majority employee-owned, up from 9 percent at the outset of privatization according to the first survey.* The reformers who designed the privatization program believed that increasing outsider ownership would be one sign of restructuring in these firms. The significant decrease in the number of firms that are majority employee owned is a step in this direction.

The next task is to examine this emerging trend toward greater outsider ownership in more detail. Tables 3.6 and 3.7 examine the structure of outside ownership by category of outsider and the structure of a particular kind of outside ownership especially important to corporate governance, namely, blockholder ownership.

The presence or absence of blockholders cannot be explained by company size or financial performance. There is no significant relationship between the presence or absence of blockholders, the number of blockholders, or the total percent of shares which blockholders own and company size as measured by the total number of employees. There is also no significant relationship between the presence or absence of a blockholder and a measure of whether company cash flows cover operating costs or not. And outside board representation has the same chance of appearing in majority employee-owned companies as in minority employee-owned companies.

The following patterns of blockholder ownership (more than 5%) in December 1994 emerged from the Russian Privatization Research Project:

Percentage of all firms with:

outsider nonstate owners	78.6
no outsider nonstate ownership	21.4
one or more blockholder owners	57.3
no blockholder owners or no outsider nonstate owners	42.7
outsider nonstate ownership with one or more blockholder owners	72.9
outsider nonstate ownership without one or more blockholder owners	27.1

Percentages of outsider ownership and blockholder ownership in the entire sample:

nonstate outsider ownership where outsider ownership exists average	32	(at the median 31)
blockholder ownership across all firms with any blockholders average	16.7	(at the median 15)
Average number of blockholders per firm	1.1	(at the median 1).

Several preliminary conclusions emerge from these data:

1. When outsider and blockholder ownership are compared from the first survey (Table 3.1) with recent results, average outsider ownership has increased from 21.5 percent (20 percent at the median) to 29 percent (and 30 percent at the median), but the average size of blockholder stakes has gone down slightly from 20 percent(15 percent at the median) to 16.7 percent (15 percent at the median.) There has been no change in the proportion of firms with blockholders. Thus, blockholding is remaining stable, and its role in this short period has not significantly expanded. Outside ownership is increasing, but there is no preliminary evidence that more blockholding emerged in this period.

2. When the entire sample is examined (i.e. for all cases, in Tables 3.6 and 3.7), voucher investment funds, individual citizens, and commercial firms are the main outsiders, but their average and median ownership is quite small (4–5 percent) across all companies. If these trends held up upon closer examination of the cases *where only outside ownership is present*, they would be very bad news indeed. They would also not be consistent with the moderate increase in the corporate governance role of outsiders that has been identified. On the contrary, commercial firms, voucher investment funds, and individual citizens do have more sizable average stakes (9–13 percent) when the firms with only outsider ownership are examined. The process of developing focal equity holdings has begun, but it is still relatively slow in a large proportion of firms.

Table 3.6 The Structure of Outsider Ownership, December 1994 (in percentages)

Type of outsider entity[a]	Ownership of all firms in sample		Ownership of only firms in sample with outsider ownership present[b]		% of all firms in sample with this category of outsider ownership[b]	% of all firms with outsider ownership in sample with this category of outsider ownership[c]
	Average	Median	Average	Median		
Commercial firms	5.0	0	13.7	12.5	41	52
Individual citizens	5.5	2.9	9.32	6.8	61	77
Investment funds	4.29	0	9.04	6	61	77
Banks	1.9	0	8.8	2	13	16
Holding co's.	1	0	14.6	13	5	6
Suppliers	0.97	0	24.6	28.2	3	4
Customers	0.19	0	3.5	3.5	3	4
Foreign firms	0.93	0	19.9	20	5	6
Insurance co's.	0.01	0	0.8	0.8	1.6	2

Source: Russian Privatization Research Project, 1994.

Note: Figures do not add up to average for entire sample because of missing values. Because the first column of figures includes firms without outsider ownership, it understates the size of stakes in those firms. This is adjusted in the second column where the category of outsider ownership is analyzed only where it is present.

a In rank order of the most significant outsider entities according to the size of the average percentage of ownership and the incidence of outsider entity.

b This is the percentage of the total sample that has each particular category of outsider ownership, for example, 41% of all firms have outside ownership by commercial firms.

c This is the percentage of the firms with outsider ownership present that has each particular category of outsider ownership (i.e. the incidence of the outsider entity), for example, 52% of firms with outside ownership present have outside ownership by commercial firms.

Table 3.7 Average and Median Blockholder Stakes of Different Types in All Firms with Blockholder Ownership, December 1994 (in percentages)

Type of blockholder[a]	Average	Median	% of all firms in sample with this category of blockholder ownership[b]	% of all firms with outsider ownership in sample with this category of blockholder ownership[c]	% of all firms with blockholder ownership in sample with this category of blockholder ownership[d]
Commercial firms	16.7	15	26	33	45
Investment Funds	12.9	9	38	48	66
Banks	21.5	23.1	3	4	6
Foreign firms	19.9	20	5	6	9
Holding companies	14.6	13	5	6	9
Related supplier firms	24.6	28.2	3	4	6
Related customer firms	0	0	0	0	0
Insurance companies	0	0	0	0	0
Individual citizens[e]	9.32	6.8	0	0	0

Source: Russian Privatization Research Project, 1994.

[a] In rank order of most important blockholders by size of average blockholder stake and incidence of this kind of blockholder ownership among all blockholders.

[b] This is the percentage of the entire sample having each particular category of blockholder ownership, for example, 26% of the firms have commercial firm blockholder ownership.

[c] This is the percentage of firms with outsider ownership having each particular category of blockholder ownership, for example, 33% of the firms with outsider ownership have commercial firm blockholder ownership.

[d] This is the percentage of firms with blockholder ownership having each particular category of blockholder ownership, for example, 45% of the firms with blockholder ownership have commercial firm blockholder ownership. This column adds up to more than 100% because some firms have more than one blockholder.

[e] This level of analysis of the data did not allow us to disaggregate the individual citizen stakes in order to identify blockholder persons who were individual citizens. We do not know which of these individual citizens are blockholders, and they are not counted as blockholders in this research.

3. Unrelated commercial firms and voucher investment funds make up 45 to 66 percent of all blockholders (see table 3.7). As corporate ownership evolves in Russia, it will be interesting to track changes in the different categories of blockholders in privatized firms.

4. Both tables indicate that other shareholders, such as banks, insurance companies, and foreign firms, are still playing a minor part in the overall structure of outside ownership, although, surprisingly, banks and foreign firms (see Table 3.6) are playing a much stronger role than holding companies, and related supplier and customer firms. This is further evidence that some initial gains were made in the serious political struggle with the nomenklatura over its moves to preserve the ties between firms organized by the former ministries. Many of these ministries were to be recreated as holding companies to keep their related firms intact and unchanged in terms of governance and ownership. In the earliest interviews before the implementation of the privatization program, many senior managers said they desired holding companies and supplier and consumer firms as their preferred investors. There is no evidence that this actually happened.

5. Do the outside blockholders and their designated directors represent "friends" of the senior managers? Very few blockholders were identified as being holding companies or related supplier and consumer enterprises. Indeed, an analysis of the narrative sections of the interviews suggests that top managers have developed a lot of hostility to members of former ministries and related firms that want to have a connection with them but have no new resources to offer their company. Also, it is unlikely that voucher investment funds represent "old friends" of management. However, we did not exhaustively trace every commercial firm to figure out whether they had a previous tie with management or not.

6. There are still a sizable number of firms, 21.4 percent, without any outside nonstate owners. And 42.7 percent of the firms are without any blockholder ownership. This is almost exactly the number of firms without blockholder ownership in the first survey (43 percent). Clearly, no Federation-wide progress was made between the first survey and this survey in changing either the rate of blockholder emergence or the number of firms where blockholders have emerged.

7. Foreign firms are taking high average stakes (19–20 percent) in 5 percent of enterprises, but foreign firms represent almost 10 percent of all blockholder ownership. Presumably, foreign firms only want sizable equity stakes.

8. The incidence of banks and insurance companies in both overall outsider ownership and blockholder ownership is low. The privatization program specifically created and energized voucher investment funds,

individual citizens, and commercial firms as bidders when banks and insurance companies were just getting organized. Their future role remains uncertain.

The emerging structure of outside ownership helps explain the broader trends in corporate governance observed earlier. While there is little evidence that blockholding has significantly expanded, it plays a role in the evolving structure of ownership in privatized firms. This fact helps explain why outsiders on boards became more common. It demonstrates the specific economic self-interest of the takers of those board seats.

Dynamics of Corporate Governance

One should not exaggerate the importance of the preliminary signs of corpo rate governance activities in privatized firms. Let's examine both the "glass half-empty" and the "glass half-full" perspectives.

Glass Half-Empty

1. Two Presidential decrees on corporate governance – cumulative voting and limitation on insider board members to one-third – have been largely ignored. If these decrees were carefully followed by the 61 firms in the third survey, given a median number of six board members, median outsider ownership of 30 percent, and, the assumption of full organization on the part of the outside shareholders, one would expect corporate boards to look as follows:

Two outsiders representing the 30 percent of shareholders
Two insiders representing management and employees
Two outsiders representing management and employees in compliance with the decree limiting the number of insiders on the board.

2. A six-person board with outsiders representing insiders (since insiders cannot have more than one-third of the board representing them) and with four outsiders is potentially more independent than a board of six insiders or four insiders, but the current average and median quorum (for conducting board meetings) of four board members theoretically still allows the insiders and *their* two outsider representatives to dominate the company under this hypothetical scenario.

Glass Half-Full

1. Senior management has not been able to continue to use clear-cut majority employee ownership as a defense against outsider influence.

Average and median employee ownership is falling. Senior management has not been able to buy substantial amounts of shares themselves. The holding company defense has collapsed. Average and median outsider ownership is increasing. The state buffer is disappearing. And the absolute number of firms that are majority employee owned is shrinking from 91 percent of firms in the first survey to 63 percent in this survey.

2. One or more blockholders exists in 57.3 percent of the firms. The average and median number of blockholders per firm is only one and, likewise, the average number of outside board members per firm is one. Thus, if 76 percent of the firms have an average of one outside director, the proportion of firms with outside directors is greater than the proportion of firms with blockholders. From this perspective, blockholders may be achieving through negotiation one of the results envisioned by the cumulative voting law.

3. Some observers of Russian privatization predicted that *rank-and-file employees* would control corporate boards and establish a conservative form of worker control based on protecting collective property. The total insignificance of employee representation on corporate boards indicates that the problem is the more conventional corporate governance problem of managerial control and not the emergence of a different and unique form of entrenchment in Russia. If anything, Russian rank-and-file employees in their role as large investors deserve some independent activist board representation by outsiders who have the skills to help protect the workers' investment.

A closer examination of the details of corporate governance sheds light on which of these perspectives is more plausible. Our survey found that a quorum of 4 members with an insider-dominated board that averages 4 insiders favors management insiders. Noncompliance with cumulative voting is almost 86 percent. Blockholders only managed to get management to comply with the decree limiting insiders on boards in 1.6 percent (only one) of the firms. But the noncompliance with the cumulative voting decree must be put in perspective. Activist corporate governance is an uphill battle in most modern capitalist societies. American shareholder activists would be thrilled if they got as many outside directors representing investors, elected by any method in the past year, as outside investors achieved in the Russian Federation. This is not to say that outsider directors in Russia represent "shareholder activism."

The large number of firms with outsiders as nominees must be discounted because the data do not tell us whether these nominees are state or nonstate outsiders. The low average and median percent of outside shareholders who came to the shareholder meeting (30 and 3 respectively) may reflect either shareholder passivity and resignation or practical difficulties in getting to the meeting or both. But, shareholder absenteeism certainly enhances management's ability to manipulate the meeting. The issue of employee shareholders will be discussed below. Finally, the use of confidential voting in only 34 percent of the companies and use of a special registrar for the shares in only 58 percent of firms put two very important parts of the governance machinery in management's hands.

Now we turn to management's actions toward the employee shareholders. Despite the increase in outside ownership and outsider directors in the enterprises, rank-and-file employees still own an average of 42 percent of the stock (43 percent at the median, see Table 3.5). To control insider ownership, managers must design a mechanism to influence the voting of these shares. One way management can influence employee shareholders is to organize a trust or other collective entity that collects employee shares under managerial control. Another way management can control employee shareholders is to organize the proxy voting to collect employee proxies before the shareholder meeting. Managers can attempt to influence their vote by having the employees' supervisors oversee the process of proxy collection and voting.

The data show that management kept majority ownership and control out of the hands of outsiders in 63 percent of the firms so far. Regarding managerial control of employee shareholding, top managers seem to believe that it is one thing to dominate employee shareholding through the subtle and not-so-subtle authority of the employer–employee relationship, but quite another to formally compel each employee to put their shares in a legal trust controlled by the general director. This might provoke a backlash and make the general director the target of accusations of formal and obvious domination. Also, perhaps the success of informal controls over employee shareholding has eliminated the need to formalize it. The centerpiece of that informal control of employee shareholding is the lack of confidential voting noted above, which creates enormous risks for subordinates who decide to come to a shareholder meeting and vote against their superior, who is after all the provider of their job, salary, perks, and so forth.

The average 28 percent employee attendance (only 12.5 percent at the median) at the shareholder meeting is not simply a result of employee passivity. Many top managers report that they stage-managed the meetings beforehand in the following ways:

> They spread the word that it will be inconvenient to find a room big enough for all employees and shareholders.
> They instructed middle managers to organize "bush meetings" in their

departments throughout the plant to "prediscuss" issues of the share-holder meeting, elect delegates, and sign up proxies.

They refused to mail the government-required individual shareholder information to individual employees and made only one copy available on a bulletin board or in an office.

On the subject of employee voting, managers report that an average of 58 percent of employees (62 percent at the median) gave proxies to others to represent them at the last shareholder meeting and chose mainly (65 percent) management representatives to vote their shares. Managers in various parts of the country provided the interviewers with a number of very clear descriptions of the bush meeting/proxy voting method of collecting employee votes. The similarity of the mechanisms used in regions quite distant from each other was quite striking for a research assistant traveling a few thousand miles! The percentage of employees, as reported by managers, who come to the shareholder meeting is 28 percent on average and 12.5 percent at the median. Those employee *representatives* who come to the meeting are mainly managers themselves. Remember that these managers on average own 17 percent of the firm's stock in addition to the stock for which they have gained proxies. Thus, employee proxies in the 60 percent range present a fairly clear picture of management restriction of an employee's individual shareholder rights. Finally, management control of the share-holder register creates an employer supervision of employee sales that threatens the ultimate employee right to "exit" as an investor. These mechanisms of managerial control of employee voting help explain why only 4 percent of managers report the use of an employee trust for this purpose. Only 3 percent say they have plans to establish such a trust. But, as a reflection of potential tension with employees, only 17 percent of managers say the establishment of such a trust would be very easy.

Further Evidence of Insider Ownership

Tables 3.8 and 3.9 examine employment declines and the relationship between majority employee ownership and outside board representation. Table 3.8 examines employment declines since the beginning of reform, which have been substantial, although they have slowed over time. Despite the slowdown in employment declines, managers report that more jobs need to be cut. Table 3.9 shows that majority employee ownership does not explain the presence or absence of outsiders on boards of directors.

What then are the possibilities in these firms regarding the loss of executive control by the existing management and the loss of control over both the board and the equity holdings? Our research indicates that more broadly

Table 3.8 Declines in Employment in Privatized Enterprises in the Russian Federation since the Beginning of Reform, January 1991 through December 1994 (in percentages)

	Average	Median
1/91–12/94	24.03	20.45
1/92–12/94	21.3	15.9
1/93–12/94	15.1	10.4
1/94–12/94	12.29	6.65
1/95–6/95 (planned)	4.72	0
Added % gen. director would cut if no social considerations	9.7	0

Source: Russian Privatization Research Project, 1994.

Table 3.9 Employee Ownership and Outsiders on Boards in Privatized Firms in the Russian Federation, December 1994
(in percentages)

	Firms with majority employee ownership	Firms with minority employee ownership
Outsiders on board	71	83
No outsiders on board	29	17
Total	100	100

Source: Russian Privatization Research Project, 1994.
Note: Numbers are rounded.

based shifts in control beyond the introduction of modest numbers of outside directors on the boards are under way. In the sample, 15 percent of the managers have already been replaced. Preliminary data, however, indicate that most have been replaced by their deputies. Almost a third of the general directors would agree to give majority control of the firm to an outside investor who would provide the necessary capital for restructuring, 13 percent have received such an offer, and 42 percent believe that they can persuade employees to go along with such an offer if they received one. When combined with the trend toward a grudging but real acceptance of outsiders on boards, this additional evidence suggests that senior managers are beginning to come to terms with the realities of future restructuring and the role of outside investors.

Conclusions

The findings of our research suggest the following policy recommendations:

1. The creation of blockholder stakes must be accelerated. The size of the blockholder stakes must be increased by moving rapidly to make all remaining state stakes available for sale and to make it easier for existing shareholders to trade stakes and agglomerate shares to become block-holders.
2. While blockholders often take board seats, their governance role remains difficult. Management manipulation of the investor–company relationship must be directly addressed through coordinated introduction of a strong company law, strict corporate governance provisions that remove the machinery from management control, disclosure regulations, and strict enforcement of independent registrars for shareholders. The experience with cumulative voting suggests that it is a combination of both aggressive civic norms and the desire by an investor to protect an investment that will lead to a restructuring of the investor–company relationship. Indeed, work is moving forward on a draft corporate law that addresses many of these problems (see Black, Kraakman, and Hay in this volume).
3. The "worker control" bogeyman must be put to rest by a two-pronged approach. First, hard budget constraints and the elimination of subsidies will eliminate the ability of workers to take refuge in state support or of management to lean on the state for bailouts. Second, the protection of employee shareholder rights must be viewed as a priority in protecting the integrity of the investor–company relationship because employees are and will be an important class of shareholders in Russia. U.S. experience with employee shareholder rights suggests that it would be unrealistic to assume that employee shareholder rights and outside directors repre-senting insiders could quickly be either a cornerstone or an important feature of corporate governance. But, at a minimum, corporate law should at least protect the right of employee shareholders to take decisions confidentially as individuals. One benefit of this protection is that workers can sell their shares without fear (see Blasi and Kruse 1991).

Appendix: The Surveys

Following are some details about how the sample of enterprises was constructed. The sample is not random, although the researchers have attempted to insure that it is representative. The first survey is of 170 enterprises in 36 oblasts or regions of the Russian Federation. This survey began in August 1992 after the privatization program passed the Supreme Soviet and was signed into law but before it was implemented. Implementation began later that fall and went into full force in the winter and spring of 1993. Twenty-three interviews were conducted before implementation in order to identify key issues and problems. In winter 1993 we began conducting the first interviews of firms that were nearing the end of the first phase of the privatization process. The main objective was to have a sample that would fairly represent Russian Federation-wide trends in newly privatized enterprises. Because most firms had not yet privatized and because only a few oblasts had begun to implement the privatization program in earnest, it was decided that a national random sample was impractical. The next best approach was to conduct interviews in many regions of the country, in a large number of enterprises, and over a long period of time.

The oblasts for visits were chosen on the basis of the following criteria:

1. The oblasts that had begun implementing the privatization program first and had a larger number of enterprises undergoing voucher auctions relative to other oblasts were visited first. As more and more oblasts initiated privatization, the research team initiated research in these additional oblasts.
2. With the exception of Far Eastern Siberia, oblasts of all regions of the Russian Federation were visited, although the city of Moscow and the Moscow region were de-emphasized in the postprivatization part of the survey. The researchers made an early judgment that too many students of privatization were focusing their attention on visits in the city of Moscow or the Moscow region (oblast). Subsequently, the city of Moscow did not fully participate in the privatization program and this vindicated our earlier decision to exclude it. On a monthly basis, researchers attempted to choose oblasts in all regions of the country. The rule-of-thumb was to chose a region within a reasonable train ride from Moscow one week and one further away the next week.

Once the team arrived at an oblast, enterprises were chosen for participation based on the following criteria:

1. Local privatization authorities were asked to provide a list of all enterprises that had completed corporatization, closed subscription, and voucher auctions. Frequently, the research team also had access before the trip to a (less updated) list and summary oblast-level data on the number of voucher auctions completed. The research team would go down the list of enterprises and look for enterprises that fitted their criteria and begin scheduling visits immediately. The single most important criterion that they applied was to choose enterprises of the largest size. The team was instructed to veto almost every suggestion not leading to a prospective interviewing group meeting this criterion. The reason for this instruction should be clear: we wanted to be sure that this entire research effort did not focus on small-scale privatization or medium-sized enterprises that were easier for local officials to get to agree to interviews.

2. The research team was instructed to choose the largest enterprises and to work to achieve as much as possible an equal balance between industrial and service firms. The effect of this criterion was to achieve some balance, since a larger proportion of the firms were industrial.

3. The research team was instructed to indicate to local privatization authorities that they specifically did not wish to visit only enterprises that were in favor of privatization or were having positive experiences and that the goal of the research was to reach as objective an understanding of what people really felt and were doing as was possible. The goal of this criterion was to put the local officials at ease so that they would assist us in visiting a wide range of enterprises. If the level of harsh criticism of the privatization program and blunt talk of the interviews is to be believed, we succeeded beyond our expectations in avoiding such bias.

4. Occasionally, local officials would strongly recommend that a particular firm be included in the visits. Typically, this would be a large and important enterprise where the general director heard of the team's visit and wished to have an opportunity to express his or her views or where the general director was seeking government assistance and perceived (incorrectly as the team was instructed to explain) that the research team was capable of communicating his message.

There is no question but that this research is biased toward larger enterprises, which are among the most important enterprises in a particular region. That is what the team was looking for and in general that is what comprises the sample. There is no question that the sample is biased in favor of enterprises and oblasts that entered the privatization program first. It is also biased toward enterprises within a two hour drive of the capital city of the oblast visited because of the practical requirements of a research team that arrived for a two to three day visit. It also under-represents the Moscow region. Nevertheless, it is our opinion that several features of this research helped ensure its representative nature:

1. The large number of oblasts visited forced the team to move frequently around the country and not emphasize "friendly" oblasts.
2. The large number of enterprises included in the sample and the long period over which the interviews were conducted allowed us to sample opinions during periods where moods and attitudes about privatization and the government varied widely.
3. Each interview included a lengthy unstructured free-flowing interview along with a more organized defined survey questionnaire. Our analysis of the unstructured interviews provides data that strongly parallels our analysis of the structured questions and statistical data. These interviews are quite blunt.
4. Each research team conducted both an informal and formal interview with officials from the local privatization agency in the oblast about oblast-wide trends in the areas we were studying. One goal of these interviews was to identify information which would suggest that the interviews and the surveys were yielding misinformation. These officials were often aware of the details of the enterprises with which they worked. With the exception of one subject area, which was the unwillingness of the general directors to discuss serious labor problems at their enterprise, we have been unable to identify any serious patterns of misinformation.

The oblasts and enterprises for the second survey were chosen in the same way as for the first survey. The oblasts and enterprises for the third survey were chosen in the following manner:

> The research team began revisiting all oblast and enterprises, in general, in the order in which they were originally visited in the first survey and second survey.
>
> If an enterprise refused to have a second visit, the team used the same criteria of the first survey to choose a different enterprise.

This chapter is based mainly on data from the third survey when it was about one fifth completed. For the purposes of this chapter, this data has not been analyzed by focusing on the changes that have taken place within each enterprise since the last visit. When the third survey is completed, a longitudinal analysis will be implemented. The third survey in this study is looked at as aggregate data on a Russian Federation-wide sample.

References

Blasi, Joseph R. 1994. "Privatizing Russia – A Success Story." *New York Times*, 30 June.

Blasi, Joseph R., and Douglas Kruse. 1991. *The New Owners: The Mass Emergence of Employee Ownership in Public Companies and What It Means to American Business.* New York: HarperCollins.

Blasi, Joseph R., with Darya Panina and Katerina Grachova. 1994. "Russian Privatization: Ownership, Governance, and Restructuring." In *Russia: Creating Private Enterprises and Efficient Markets*, edited by Ira Lieberman and John Nellis. Washington, D.C. World Bank, Private Sector Development Department.

Boycko, Maxim, and Andrei Shleifer. 1993. "The Politics of Russian Privatization," in *Post-Communist Reform: Pain and Progress*, by Oliver Blanchard, Maxim Boycko, Marek Dabrowski, Richard Layard, and Andrei Shleifer. Cambridge, Mass.: Massachusetts Institute of Technology (MIT) Press.

Boycko, Maxim, Andrei Shleifer, and Robert W. Vishny. 1993. "Privatizing Russia." *Brookings Paper on Economic Activity*, pp. 139–92. The Brookings Institution, Washington, D.C..

——. 1995. *Privatizing Russia*. Cambridge, Mass.: MIT Press.

Corbo, Vittorio, Fabrizio Coricelli, and Jan Bossak, editors. 1991. *Reforming Central and Eastern European Economies: Initial Results and Challenges: A World Bank Symposium.* Washington, D.C.: World Bank.

Frydman, Roman, Andrzej Rapaczynski, John S. Earle *et al.* 1993. *The Privatization Process in Russia, Ukraine and the Baltic States.* Budapest and New York: Central European University Press.

Kikeri, Sunita, John Nellis, and Mary Shirley. 1992. *Privatization: The Lesson of Experience.* Washington, D.C.: World Bank.

Lieberman, Ira, and John Nellis, editors. 1994. *Russia: Creating Private Enterprises and Efficient Markets.* Washington, D.C. World Bank, Private Sector Development Department.

Monks, Robert A.G., and Nell Minow. 1995. *Corporate Governance.* Cambridge, Mass., and Oxford: Basil Blackwell Ltd.

Oxford Analytica. 1992. "Board Directors and Corporate Governance: Trends in the G7 Countries over the Next Ten Years." Oxford, England (September).

Phelps, E.S., Roman Frydman, Andrzej Rapaczynski, and Andrei Shleifer. 1993. "Needed Mechanisms for Corporate Governance and Finance in Eastern Europe." *Economics of Transition* 1, No. 2: 171–207

Shleifer, Andrei, and Robert W. Vishny. 1986. "Large Shareholders and Corporate Control." *Journal of Political Economy* 94, No. 3: 461–88.

Webster, Leila, with Juergen Franz, Igor Artemiev, and Harold Wackman. 1994 "Newly Privatized Enterprises: A Survey," In *Russia: Creating Private Enterprises and Efficient Markets*, edited by Ira Lieberman and John Nellis. Washington, D.C. World Bank, Private Sector Development Department.

4

NETWORKS OF ASSETS, CHAINS OF DEBT

Recombinant Property in Hungary

DAVID STARK

This chapter is an expanded version of an article that appears in American Journal of Sociology, *vol. 101, no. 4 (January 1996) and is reprinted with the permission of the journal. Research for this paper was supported by grants from the National Council for Soviet and East European Research (NCSEER) and the Program on Institutional Reform and the Informal Sector (IRIS). My thanks to Ronald Breiger, Rogers Brubaker, László Bruszt, Christopher Clague, Ellen Comisso, Paul DiMaggio, Neil Fligstein, Geoff Fougere, Roman Frydman, István Gábor, Péter Gedeon, Gernot Grabher, Cheryl Gray, Elisabeth Hagen, Szabolcs Kemény, János Köllö, János Kornai, János Lukács, Peter Murrell, László Neumann, Claus Offe, Éva Polócz, Andrzej Rapaczynski, Ákos Róna-Tas, Éva Voszka, Andrew Walder and especially Monique Djokic Stark for their criticisms of an earlier draft.*

The Science of the Not Yet

How can mainstream economics explain the momentous transformation in Eastern Europe when it lacks a theory of change? The answer has been an undisguised borrowing of the *problematic of transition* from sociology, the discipline founded at the turn of century on studies of transition – whether from tradition to modernity, *Gemeinschaft* to *Gesellschaft*, rural to urban society, feudalism to capitalism, or mechanical to organic solidarity. For the founders of sociology, the crisis of European societies in the last decades of the nineteenth century was diagnosed as a normative and institutional vacuum. The old order regulated by tradition had passed, but a new moral order had not yet been established. The crumbling of the traditional structures, Durkheim wrote, had "swept away all the older forms of organization. One after another, these have disappeared either through the slow usury of time or through great disturbances, but without being replaced" (Durkheim 1897:446).

During our own *fin de siècle,* not the crumbling of traditional structures, but the collapse of communism gives new life to the transition problematic. Whereas Durkheim saw sociology as the science of morality that could guide society from the "state of mental confusion" to a stable moral order, today it is the science of choice that will guide the economies of Eastern Europe through the transition from socialism to capitalism. The difference between the transition that opened the century and the transition at its close is, of course, that this time, with almost a century of experience, we are no longer burdened by the ignorance of outcomes. Armed with this knowledge of destination, the marriage of economics with the transition problematic generates a new science of transition.

As a sociologist, I should, no doubt, be flattered that the more exalted specialization has chosen, at such a critical time, such an important concept from my own discipline. But I am not sanguine about this borrowing. Indeed, it is the starting premise of this chapter that the greatest obstacle to understanding change in contemporary Eastern Europe is the concept of transition.

As the science of the not yet, transitology is known to many for its engineering applications: blueprints, road maps, recipes, therapies, formulae, and marching orders for how to get from socialism to capitalism in six steps or sixty (Sachs 1989; Klaus 1992; Peck and Richardson 1992). Working away from the glare of publicity are the theoreticians of the science who aim to systemize a social embryology for the rigorous analysis of what is about to be. Common to both the theoretical and the applied sides is an underlying teleology in which concepts are driven by hypothesized end-states. As in all versions of modernization theory, transitology begins with a future that is not only desired but already known. The destination has been designated: Western Europe and North America hold the image of the East European future.

Although it begins with the future, transitology is not silent about past and present for this science holds a distinctive philosophy of history: the transition is undergone by a society as the passage through a liminal state suspended between one social order and another, each conceived as a stable equilibrium organized around a coherent and more or less unitary logic.

Such a view overstates the coherence of social forms both before and after the hypothesized transition and conversely exaggerates the degree of social disorganization in the presumed liminal period of "institutional vacuum." Difficult to assimilate within the transition problematic are the numerous studies from Eastern Europe documenting parallel and contradictory logics in which ordinary citizens were already experiencing, for a decade before 1989, a social world in which various domains were not integrated coherently (Gábor 1979, 1986; Stark 1989; Mirody 1992). Through survey research and ethnographic studies researchers have identified a multiplicity of social relations that did not conform to officially prescribed hierarchical patterns. These relations of reciprocity and market-like transactions were widespread inside the socialist sector as well as in the "second economy" and stemmed from the contradictions of attempting to "scientifically manage" an entire national economy. At the shop-floor level, shortages and supply bottlenecks led to bargaining between supervisors and informal groups; at the managerial level, the task of meeting plan targets required a dense network of informal ties that cut across enterprises and local organizations; and the allocative distortions of central planning reproduced the conditions for the predominantly part-time entrepreneurship of the second economies that differed in scope, density of network connections, and conditions of legality across the region (Kornai 1980; Gábor 1979; Laky 1979; Sabel and Stark 1982).

The existence of parallel structures (however contradictory and fragmentary) in these informal and interfirm networks means that the collapse of the formal structures of the socialist regime did not result in an institutional vacuum. Instead, we find the persistence of routines and practices, organizational forms and social ties that can become assets, resources, and the basis for credible commitments and coordinated actions in the postsocialist period.[1] In short, in place of the disorientation expected in the transition problematic (Bunce and Csanadi 1993), we find the metamorphosis of *sub rosa* organizational forms and the activation of pre-existing networks of affiliation.

By the 1980s, the societies of Eastern Europe were decidedly not systems organized around a single logic; nor are they likely to become, any more or less than our own, societies with a single system identity.[2] A modern society is not a unitary social order but a multiplicity of orders, a plurality of ordering principles for reaching agreement, a polyphony of accounts of work, value, and justice (Boltanski and Thévenot 1991; White 1992a; Stark

---

[1] On the importance of routines and habits, see especially, Bourdieu (1990) and Nelson and Winter (1982).

[2] I don't live in a market economy in the United States but in an economy in which markets are but one of the coordinating mechanisms. The idea that Eastern Europe should be in transit to *a market economy* mistakes the triumph of capitalism for the triumph of the market and – like the introduction of socialism, which sought to impose a single coordinating mechanism – risks destroying the organizational diversity required for flexible adaptation. On the distinction between market *orientation* and market *coordination*, see Bresser (1993). For analyses of the broad range of nonmarket coordinating mechanisms consistent with market orientation, see Schmitter (n.d.); Boyer (1991).

1990a; Padgett and Ansell 1993). Change, even fundamental change, of the social world is not the passage from one order to another but rearrangements in the patterns of how multiple orders are interwoven.

Thus, instead of *transition* we examine *transformation,* in which new elements emerge through adaptations, rearrangements, permutations, and reconfigurations of existing organizational forms. Instead of *institutional vacuum* we examine *institutional legacies,* rethinking the metaphor of collapse to ask whether differences in how the pieces fell apart have consequences for rebuilding new institutions. Instead of examining country cases according to the degree to which they conform to or depart from a pre-established model, we see differences in kind and ask how different paths of extrication from state socialism shape different possibilities of transformation. Instead of building *tabula rasa on the ruins* of communism, we examine how actors in particular locales and settings are rebuilding organizations and institutions *with the ruins* of communism. Instead of paralysis and disorientation we should expect to see actors, already accustomed to negotiating the ambiguity of contradictory social forms, adjust to new uncertainties by improvising on practiced routines. Instead of grand schemes of architecture, social engineering, and designer capitalism, we examine transformative processes of bricolage.

Most importantly, instead of thinking about institutional or organizational innovation as *replacement,* we see it as the disassemblage and reassemblage of existing institutional configurations. In short, we think of organizational innovation as *recombination* (Schumpeter 1934; Nelson and Winter 1982; White 1992b; Kogut and Zander 1992; Sabel and Zeitlin forthcoming).

To survive in a rapidly changing environment, actors redefine and recombine resources. These resources include organizational forms (that are likely to migrate across domains), habituated practices, and social ties, whether official or informal. Thus, transformation will resemble innovative adaptations that combine seemingly discrepant elements – bricolage – more than architectural design. In this perspective, actors do not set out to create "a market economy." They are not motivated to pursue particular strategies by "systemic requirements" but by the urgency of their immediate practical dilemmas. Instead of designating a future that shapes the present, we should examine how the future is being shaped by the pragmatics of the present. This pragmatics – redeploying available resources to survive – may yet result in private property and competitive markets. More likely, it will render property boundaries more ambiguous and create new forms of coordination that are neither market nor hierarchy.

Postsocialist societies can be seen as an extraordinary laboratory to test existing social theories. This chapter does not formulate such a test – not because the changes examined are not extraordinary, but because momentous changes are not likely to leave existing theories intact for simple testing. The efforts of this chapter are less grandiose than elaborating a "new theory of social change" and more ambitious than testing old ones. Its task is to craft analytic concepts capable of registering and translating the specific insights and patterned learning being generated in this new social experiment. In developing a perspective of transformation as recombination in the specifically postsocialist setting, it provides concepts for rethinking property, organizational change, and the relationship between adaptability and accountability. Outside the tired dualism of deductive versus inductive approaches (Peirce 1934; Hodgson 1993) it sees merit, at this critical juncture, in a research strategy that formulates concepts with an eye to theory while being closely grounded in empirical contexts. The arguments presented here are thus based on data collected by the author during an 11 month stay in Budapest in 1993–94. That research includes: (1) Field research in six Hungarian enterprises. Three of these firms are among the 20 largest firms in Hungary and are at the core of Hungarian manufacturing in metallurgy, electronics, and rubber products. Three are small and medium-size firms in plastics, machining, and industrial engineering.[3] (2) Compilation of a data set on the ownership structure of the 200 largest Hungarian corporations (ranked by sales) and the top 25 Hungarian banks.[4] These data were augmented by ownership data drawn from the files of some 800 firms under the portfolio management of the State Property Agency (SPA). (3) Interviews with leading actors in banks, agencies, parties, and ministries.[5]

---

[3] This field research, conducted in collaboration with László Neumann, involved longitudinal analysis of the same firms in which we had earlier studied an organizational innovation of internal subcontracting inside the socialist enterprise during the mid-1980s (Stark 1986, 1989, 1990a; Neumann 1991).

[4] Such data collection is not a simple matter where capital markets are poorly developed. There is no Hungarian *Moody's* and certainly no corporate directory equivalent to *Industrial Groupings in Japan* or *Keiretsu no Kenkyu* (see, for example, Gerlach and Lincoln 1993). The labor-intensive solution has been to gather that data directly from the Hungarian Courts of Registry. Corporate files at the registry include not only information on officers and members of the board of directors but also a complete list of the company's owners at the most recent shareholders meeting. My thanks to Lajos Vékás, Professor of Law, ELTE, and Rector of the Institute for Advanced Study, Collegium Budapest, for his interventions to secure access to these data and to Szabolcs Kemény and Jonathan Uphoff for assistance in data collection.

[5] A partial list of interviewees includes: the former president of the National Bank; the former deputy minister of the Ministry of Finance; executives of the four largest commercial banks and two leading investment banks; the former president of the State Holding Corporation; directors, advisors, and officials of the State Property Agency; senior officials of the World Bank's Hungarian Mission; the chief economic advisors of the two major liberal parties; the president of the Federation of Hungarian Trade Unions; and leading officials of the Hungarian Socialist Party (who later ascended to high-level positions in the new Socialist-Liberal coalition government).

In the sections that follow we shall see that property transformation is not a transition from public to private but a blurring of their boundaries. Recombinant property is a form of organizational hedging, or portfolio management, in which actors are responding to extraordinary uncertainty in the organizational environment by diversifying their assets, redefining and recombining resources. It is an attempt to have resources in more than one organizational form, or similarly, to produce hybrid organizational forms that can be justified or assessed by more than one standard of measure. As we shall see, parallel to the decentralized reorganization of assets is a centralization of liabilities, and these twinned moments blur the boundaries of public and private: On the one hand, privatization produces the crisscrossing lines of recombinant property; on the other, debt consolidation transforms private debt into public liabilities. The clash of competing organizational principles that characterizes postsocialist societies produces new organizational forms, and this organizational diversity can form a basis for greater adaptability. At the same time, however, this multiplicity of ordering principles creates acute problems of accountability.

Property Transformation in Hungary: The Policy Debate

Our point of departure is a question that stands at the center of contemporary debates in the societies of Eastern Europe and the former Soviet Union. By what means can private property become the typical form of property relations in economies overwhelmingly dominated by state ownership of productive assets?

Much of that debate can be organized around two fundamental policy strategies. According to the first strategy, the institutionalization of private property can best be established by transferring assets from public to private hands. Despite differences in the specific methods designated for such privatization (e.g. sale versus free distribution, etc.), the various proposals within this radical perspective share the assumption that the creation of a private sector begins with the existing state-owned enterprises. That is, the basic organizational units of the emergent market economy will be the pre-existing but newly privatized enterprises.

The alternative policy strategy argues from the perspective of institutional (and specifically, evolutionary) economics that, although slower, the more reliable road to institutionalizing private property rests in the development of a class of private proprietors. Instead of transferring the assets of a given organizational unit from one ownership form to another, public policy should lower barriers to entry for small and medium scale genuinely private ventures. Instead of focusing on the existing state-owned enterprise, this perspective typically looks to the existing second economy entrepreneurs as the basic organizational building blocks of an emergent market economy.

Recent evidence suggests that Hungary is adopting neither a Big Bang approach nor the policy prescriptions of evolutionary economics. Contrary to the optimistic scenarios of domestic politicians and Western economists who foresaw a rapid transfer of assets from state-owned enterprises to private ownership, the overwhelming bulk of the Hungarian economy remains state property. Two years after Prime Minister Jozsef Antall confidently announced that his new government would privatize more than 50 percent of state property by 1995, the director of the Privatization Research Institute functioning alongside the State Property Agency (SPA) estimated that only about 3 percent of the state-owned productive capital had been privatized (Mellár 1992). By mid 1994, the SPA (the agency responsible for privatizing the state's assets) had only sold about 11 percent of the value of its original portfolio (Pistor and Turkewitz, see their chapter in this volume).

Contrary as well to the hopes of many observers that the new government might adopt a policy of stimulating new entrants to a dynamic private sector based on the proto-entrepreneurial experiences of "second economy" producers, the evidence on Hungary's private sector is similarly discouraging. Although the number of registered private ventures has skyrocketed, Hungarian researchers advise caution in interpreting the numbers. Some firms exist only in the courts' registries having never produced any income, and a significant number are "dummy firms" set up to help intellectuals and professionals write off expenses such as rent, telephone, and heating for their apartments (Laky 1992). A considerable body of evidence now suggests that the second economy has not become a dynamic, legitimate private sector: many entrepreneurs (a majority in some categories) still engage in private ventures only as a second job (Laky 1992; Gábor 1992, 1996); tax evasion is pervasive; and although employment is slowly increasing in the sector, most researchers agree that the proportion of unregistered work (for which the state receives no social security payments and the employee receives no benefits) is increasing faster (see Kornai 1992:13).

These observations by Hungarian researchers suggest skepticism about the confident assertions (in ever more excited and breathless tones) of the type "*x* percent of the GNP of Poland (Hungary, Russia, or the Czech Republic) is now generated in the private sector."[6] These are bold statements when one

---

[6] See, for example, the special section of *The Economist,* 13 March 1993. Much of the current literature on the "private sector" in Eastern Europe starts from the assumption that all forms of economic activity outside "the public sector" should be counted as taking place

considers the tenuous validity of statistics of this kind in contemporary Eastern Europe where statistical agencies face enormous technical problems. For example, constructing even so basic an instrument as the representative sample (finding the part that stands for the whole) is difficult where the shape and contours of the economy are still unknown. Such measurement problems are compounded, moreover, by political pressures to show higher and higher levels of "private sector" activity in order to represent better the government's case to international lending institutions, potential foreign investors, and the domestic electorate. The race among Hungary, Poland, and the Czech Republic to show the highest private sector statistics to the International Monetary Fund (IMF) recalls, of course, an earlier race during the period of "building socialism" (especially immediately following the ouster of Tito's Yugoslavia from the Comintern) when the parties and governments of these countries competed for the right to claim the highest proportion of collectivized or state property in their national statistics. Indeed, it is an open secret in Budapest that high government officials urged the use of different statistical cut-offs and measures upon returning from international conferences where Polish officials proudly displayed figures showing that the Hungarians no longer deserved the yellow jersey as first place in the statistical race to capitalism.

These tendencies together with new forms of corruption, extortion, and exploitation have prompted one researcher to label the transition as one "from second economy to informal economy" arguing that it is now, under these new conditions, that Latin American comparisons are more applicable to the Hungarian setting (Sik 1992). When private entrepreneurs look to government policy they see only burdensome taxation, lack of credits, virtually no programs to encourage regional or local development, and inordinate delays in payments for orders delivered to public sector firms (see Kornai 1992). Through violations of tax codes, off-the-books payments to workers, and reluctance to engage in capital investment (Gábor 1992), much of the private sector is responding in kind. Such government policies and private sector responses are clearly not a recipe for the development of a legitimate private sector as a dynamic engine of economic growth.

---

within the private sector. But should our criteria for designating a private sector be so inclusive as to include the kinds of primitive trade in household articles in the "Polish markets" that one can encounter on street corners, vacant lots, and under the shelter of elevated roadways across the region? Is this the vaunted free market capitalism, or is it just flea market capitalism? Journalists and politicians can call it what they like, but as scholars our classifications should be more rigorous and this kiosk capitalism should not be included in our more restrictive category of private sector.

Decentralized Reorganization of Assets

But although they fail to correspond to the policy prescriptions of either Big Bang or evolutionary economics, significant property transformations are taking place in Hungary. Actors within the formerly state sector of large public enterprises are not waiting for the economists or policymakers to resolve the debate over transferring assets versus encouraging private proprietors. Instead, they are acting to modify and transform property relations at the enterprise level. The results, however, are not well-defined rights of private property, yet neither are they a continuation or reproduction of old forms of state ownership. For these reasons, instead of mixed (or hybrid) or intermediate property, I use the term *recombinant property*.

Since 1989, there has been an explosion of new economic units in Hungary. In Table 4.1 we see that:

- the number of state enterprises declined by about 60 percent from the end of 1988 to the middle of 1994;
- the number of incorporated shareholding companies (RT) increased by more than 20 fold (from 116 to 2,679); and
- the number of limited liability companies (KFT) increased most dramatically from only 450 units in 1988 to over 79,000 by the middle of 1994.

Table 4.1 clearly indicates the sudden proliferation of new units in the Hungarian economy. But does the table provide a reliable map of property relations in contemporary Hungary? No, at least not if the data are forced into the dichotomous public/private categories that structure the discussion about property transformation in the postsocialist countries.

Table 4.1 Main Enterprise Forms in Hungary, 1988–1994

Organizational form	Dec. 1988	Dec. 1989	Dec. 1990	Dec. 1991	Dec. 1992	Dec. 1993	May 1994
State enterprises	2,378	2,400	2,363	2,233	1,733	1,130	892
Shareholding companies (RT)	116	307	646	1,072	1,712	2,375	2,679
Limited liability companies (KFT)	450	4,464	18,317	41,206	57,262	72,897	79,395

Source: National Bank of Hungary, *Monthly Report* 1994/2, and Hungarian Central Statistical Office, *Monthly Bulletin of Statistics* 1994/5.

New Forms Of State Ownership

Take first the shareholding companies (RTs) on line two of the table. Some of these corporations are private ventures newly established after the "system change." But many are the legal successors of the state-owned enterprises that would have been enumerated in the previous year on line one of the table. Through a mandatory process of "corporatization," (the deadline for which has been repeatedly extended) the formerly state-owned enterprise changes its legal organizational form as it is transformed into a shareholding company.

The question, of course, is who is holding the shares? In almost all cases of such transformation, the majority of shares in these corporatized firms is held by the State Property Agency (SPA) or the newly created State Holding Corporation (Av. Rt.). That is, as "public" and "private" actors co-participate in the new recombinant property forms, the nature and instruments of the "public" dimension are undergoing change: whereas "state ownership" in socialism meant unmediated and indivisible ownership by a state ministry (e.g. Ministry of Industry), corporatization in postcommunism entails share ownership by one or another government agency responsible for state property.

Such corporatization mandated by a privatization agency in the current context has some distinctive features of renationalization. In the 1980s, managers in Hungary (and workers in Poland) exercised *de facto* property rights. Although they enjoyed no rights over disposal of property, they did exercise rights of residual control as well as rights over residual income streams. In the 1990s, corporatization paradoxically includes efforts by the state to reclaim the actual exercise of the property rights that had devolved to enterprise-level actors. The irony, of course, is that it is precisely the agencies responsible for privatization that are acting as the agents of *étatization* by providing the instruments for the exercise of control through share owner- ship (Voszka 1992a, 1992b).

The effective exercise of such centralized control, however, varies inversely with the scope and the degree of direct intervention (the trap of centraliza- tion already well known in the region). Thus, simultaneously with this move toward centralization, one encounters proposals for privatizing the asset management function. In such programs, the state (through its property agencies, the SPA and the Av. Rt.) retains the right to dispose of the property while engaging "private" actors (e.g. consulting firms, portfolio management teams) to exercise the agency's rights as shareholder regarding daily opera- tions and strategic decisions through various kinds of subcontracting/ commission schemes.

Inter-Enterprise Ownership

But the state is seldom the sole shareholder of the corporatized firms. Who are the other shareholders of the RTs enumerated on line two of Table 4.1? The straightforward answer is that the typical owners of large shareholding companies are other large shareholding companies. This conclusion is drawn from an analysis of the ownership structure in 1993 of Hungary's largest 200 enterprises and 25 largest banks (virtually the entire financial sector).[7] These firms are major players in the Hungarian economy employing an estimated 21 percent of the labor force and accounting for 37 percent of total net sales and 42 percent of export revenues (*Figyelö* 1993). "Ownership structure" in this analysis is limited to the top 20 owners of a given corporation. Because only 37 firms are traded on the Budapest stock exchange, and because even in these cases shareholding is not widely dispersed among hundreds of small investors, this restriction, reasonable in itself because it limits the analysis to owners who "count," still allows us to account for at least 90 percent of the shares held in virtually every company.

In the Budapest Court of Registry and the 19 county registries we were able to locate ownership data for 195 of the "top 200" enterprises and for all of the 25 banks. Some form of state ownership – whether by the Av. Rt., the SPA, or the institutions of local government (who had typically exchanged their real estate holdings for enterprise shares) – is present in the overwhelming majority of these enterprises and banks; 36 companies are in majority foreign ownership. Hungarian private individuals (summed down the top 20 owners) hold at least 25 percent of the shares of only 12 of the largest enterprises and banks. Most interesting from the perspective of this paper are 87 cases in which another Hungarian company is among the top 20 owners. In 42 of these cases the other Hungarian companies together hold a clear majority (50 percent plus 1 share). Thus, by the most restrictive definition, almost 20 percent of our 220 companies (enterprises and banks) are unambiguous cases of inter-enterprise ownership, with evidence of some degree of inter-enterprise ownership in almost 40 percent of these large companies.

Figure 4.1 presents two discrete networks formed through such inter-enterprise ownership. Arrows indicate directionality in which a given firm holds shares in another large enterprise. Weak ties (shareholdings with other firms that do not have at least one other tie, whether as owner or

---

[7] The lists of firms and banks are drawn from the Hungarian business weekly's *Figyelö*'s "Top 200," the Hungarian counterpart of the Fortune 500. Several firms were dropped and several added after discussions with *Figyelö*'s editors about their selection criteria.

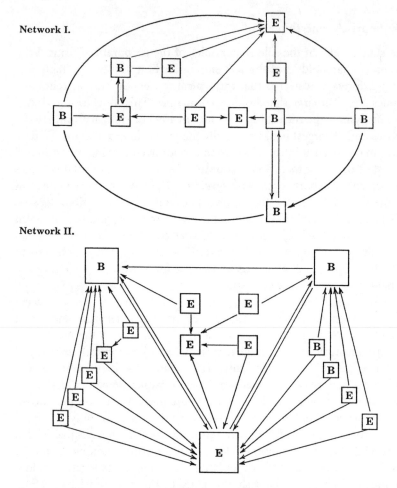

Fig. 4.1 Two inter-enterprise ownership networks among large Hungarian firms. B: financial institution (bank or insurance); E: enterprise.

Source: Corporate files of the largest 200 enterprises and top 25 banks in the Hungarian Courts of Registry.

owned, to any other firm in the network) are not displayed.[8] The relations depicted in Figure 4.1, it should be emphasized are the direct horizontal ties among the very largest enterprises – the superhighways, so to speak, of Hungarian corporate networks. The diagrams presented in Figure 4.1

---

[8] The total pattern of strong and weak ties will be examined in a later study using block-model analysis, testing for bank centrality, and assessing the relationship between ownership ties and director interlocks. The purpose of that study will be to identify the major corporate groupings in the Hungarian economy.

indicate a dramatically different way of mapping the social space of property transformation from that suggested in Table 4.1: in place of counting entities grouped by legal categories as we saw in the groupings by corporate forms in Table 4.1, here we register patterns of relations. We examine not the distribution of attributes but the construction of social connections.

In analyzing the relational dynamics of recombinant property, we now shift our focus from the corporate thoroughfares linking the large enterprises to examine the local byways linking spin-off properties within the gravitational field of large enterprises.

Corporate Satellites

Thus, we turn to the form with the most dramatic growth during the post-socialist period, the newly established limited liability companies (KFT), enumerated on line three of Table 4.1. Some of these KFTs are genuinely private entrepreneurial ventures. But many of these limited liability companies are not entirely distinct from the transformed shareholding companies examined above. In fact, the formerly socialist enterprises have been active founders and continue as current owners of the newly incorporated units.

The basic process of this property transformation is one of decentralized reorganization: under the pressure of enormous debt, declining sales, and threats of bankruptcy, or in the cases of more prosperous enterprises, to forestall takeovers as well as attempt to increase autonomy from state ministries, directors of many large public enterprises are taking advantage of several important pieces of legislation that allow state enterprises to establish joint stock companies (RTs) and limited liability companies (KFTs). In the typical cases, the managers of these enterprises are breaking up the organization (along divisional, factory, departmental, or even workshop lines) into numerous corporations. It is not uncommon to find virtually all of the activities of a large public enterprise distributed among 15–20 such satellites orbiting around the corporate headquarters.

As newly incorporated entities with legal identities, these new units are nominally independent – registered separately, with their own directors and separate balance sheets. But on closer inspection, their status in practice is semi-autonomous. An examination of the computerized records of the Budapest Court of Registry indicates, for example, that the controlling shares of these corporate satellites are typically held by the public enterprises themselves (Stark 1992). This pattern is exemplified by the case of one of Hungary's largest metallurgy firms represented in Figure 4.2. As we see in that figure, "Heavy Metal," an enormous shareholding company in the

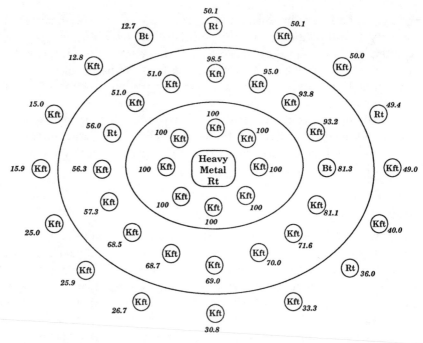

Fig. 4.2 Corporate satellites at Heavy Metal. Rt: shareholding company; Kft: limited liability company; Bt: partnerships; numerals in italics indicate Heavy Metal's owner-ship stake in a given satellite.
Source: Internal company documents at Heavy Metal.

portfolio of the State Holding Corporation, is the majority shareholder of 26 of its 40 corporate satellites.

Like Saturn's rings, Heavy Metal's satellites revolve around the giant corporate planet in concentric orbits. Near the center are the core metallurgy units, hot-rolling mills, energy, maintenance, and strategic planning units held in a kind of geo-synchronous orbit by no less than 100 percent owner-ship. In the next ring, where the corporate headquarters holds roughly 50–99 percent of the shares, are the cold-rolling mills, wire and cable production, oxygen facility, galvanizing and other finishing treatments, specialized castings, and quality control and marketing units. As this listing suggests, these satellites are linked to each other and to the core units by ties of technological dependence. Like the inner ring, they are kept in geo-synchro-nous orbits by the headquarters' majority ownership as well as by their technological dependence. Relations between the satellites of this middle ring and the company center are marked, on one hand, by the center's recurrent efforts to introduce stricter accounting procedures and tighter financial controls countered and, on the other hand, by the units' efforts to increase their autonomy – coordinated through personal ties and formalized in the bi-weekly meetings of the "Club of KFT Managing Directors." The satellites of the outer ring are even more heterogeneous in their production profiles (construction, industrial services, computing, ceramics, machining) and are usually of lower levels of capitalization. Units of this outer ring are less fixed in Heavy Metal's gravitational field: some have recently entered and some seem about to leave. Among the new entrants are some of Heavy Metal's domestic customers. Unable to collect receivables, Heavy Metal exchanged inter-enterprise debt for equity in its clients, preferring that these meteors be swept into an orbit rather than disintegrate in liquidation. Among those satellites launched from the old state enterprise are some for which Heavy Metal augments its less than majority ownership with leasing arrangements to keep centrifugal forces in check.

The corporate satellites among the limited liability companies enumerated on line three of Table 4.1 are, thus, far from unambiguously "private" ventures; yet neither are they unmistakably "statist" residues of the socialist past. Property shares in most corporate satellites are not limited to the founding enterprise. Top and mid-level managers, professionals, and other staff can be found on the lists of founding partners and current owners. Such private persons rarely acquire complete ownership of the corporate satellite, preferring to use their insider knowledge to exploit the ambiguities of institutional co-ownership. Not uncommonly, these individuals are joined in mixed ownership by other joint stock companies and limited liability companies – sometimes by independent companies, often by other KFTs in a similar orbit around the *same* enterprise, and frequently by shareholding companies or KFTs spinning around some *other* enterprise with lines of purchase or supply to the corporate unit (Voszka 1990, 1991a; Stark 1992). Banks also participate in this form of recombinant property. In many cases, the establishment of KFTs and other new corporate forms is triggered by enterprise debt. In the reorganization of the insolvent firms, the commercial banks (whose shares as joint stock companies are still predominantly state owned) become shareholders of the corporate satellites by exchanging debt for equity.

We have used the term, corporate satellite, to designate this form of recombinant property. A more exacting terminology is cumbersome, but it reflects the complex, intertwined character of property relations in Hungary: a limited liability company owned by private persons, by private ventures, and by other limited liability companies owned by joint stock companies, banks, and large public enterprises owned by the state. The new property forms thus find horizontal ties of cross-ownership intertwined with vertical ties of nested holdings.

Recombinets

The recombinant character of Hungarian property is a function not only of
the direct (horizontal) ownership ties among the largest firms and of their
direct (vertical) ties to their corporate satellites, but also of the network
properties of the full ensemble of direct and indirect ties linking entities,
irrespective of their attributes (large, small, or of various legal forms) in a
given configuration. The available data do not allow us to present a
comprehensive map of these complex relations. Records in the Courts of
Registry include documents on the owners of a particular firm; but enterprises are not required to report the companies in which they hold a stake.
However, on the basis of the enterprise-level field research, examination of
public records at the State Property Agency, and interviews with bankers
and with consultants (who make it their business to know not just single
firms but networks of firms), we have been able to reconstruct at least
partial networks. Figure 4.3 is a stylized representation of such a reconstruction.

For orientation in this graphic space, we position Figure 4.3 in relation to
the representations in Figures 4.1 and 4.2. Figure 4.1 presented inter-enterprise ownership networks formed through horizontal ties directly linking

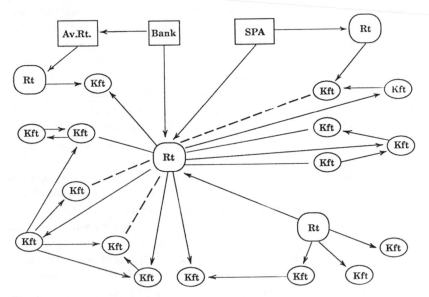

Fig. 4.3 A Hungarian recombinet.
Source: Internal company documents; State Property Agency files; Corporate files,
  Budapest Court of Registry.

large enterprises. Figure 4.2 presented the corporate satellites arrayed around a single large holding. With Figure 4.3 we zoom in on a fragment of an inter-enterprise ownership network bringing into focus the ties that link corporate satellites to each other and that form the indirect ties among heterogeneous units in a more loosely coupled network. The contrast to the patterns at Heavy Metal (from Figure 4.2) is immediately apparent. Whereas the concentric rings around Heavy Metal indicated a tightly integrated holding, simple even in its gigantism, here we see much greater complexity twisting into a different configuration.

We label this emergent form a *recombinet*, an appropriately hybrid term designating the hybrid phenomenon of a *network of recombinant property*. Here we see that the limited liability companies that began as corporate spin-offs are oriented through ownership ties at times to more than one shareholding company, and significantly, often to other limited liability companies. The recombinet is not a simple summation of the set of horizontal and vertical ties: to categorically label the ties between a given KFT and a given RT as "vertical" would be to ignore the ways the KFTs are recombining properties. To the extent that genuinely network properties are emergent in the recombinet, the language of horizontal and vertical should give place to more appropriate descriptors such as extensivity, density, tight or loose coupling, strong or weak ties, structural holes, and the like (Granovetter 1973; White and Breiger 1975; Breiger and Pattison 1986; Burt 1992).

The existence of pervasive inter-enterprise ownership and the emergence of the recombinet organizational form suggests, moreover, that *the proper analytic unit*, because it is the actual (*de facto*) economic unit of the Hungarian economy, is not the individual firm but a *network of firms*. The real units of entrepreneurship and of restructuring are not the individual personality or the isolated firm, but the social networks in which previously unidentified resources are recognized and recombined. Property is already being reorganized along such lines; but such networks are not acknowledged in public policy. So long as the policy of privatization is based on getting the highest price for a set of assets already bundled in a given enterprise, and so long as the policies of restructuring and debt consolidation operate on a strictly firm by firm basis, so long will the network properties of the Hungarian economy be continually underutilized. Networks will remain shady as long as they remain in the shadows of official policy.

An East European Capitalism?

As we have seen, there has been considerable property transformation in Hungary – but little of it has resulted in decisive boundaries clearly separating public from private.[9] The fundamental analytic question at stake is not where to draw the boundaries of the private sector, but whether the postsocialist economies can be adequately represented in a two-sector model. Almost every analytic stance and every policy position in the privatization debate share this dualistic representation of public sector and private sector. Those schema are not only inadequate but misleading, and policies based on them will yield distorted results. This analytic shortcoming cannot be remedied by more precise specification of the boundary between public and private: the old property divide has been so eroded that what once might have been a boundary is now a zone.

Perhaps the most ironic legacy of state socialism is that at precisely the time that political and economic actors are trying to free the economy from the grip of state ownership, our thinking about property remains essentially Marxist: everywhere policy advisors are looking for *the owner*. But, as developments throughout the industrial countries suggest, property can be productively dis-integrated in ways such that different actors can legitimately claim rights to different aspects and capacities of the same thing (see, especially, Grey 1980; Hart 1988, Barzel 1989; Comisso 1991; Walder 1994). In such a view, transforming property rights is about renegotiating relations among a wide set of actors to resolve their claims over *different kinds of property rights*.

We should not be surprised, therefore, that reorganization in Eastern Europe is yielding new property forms that are neither statist nor private. The economies of Eastern Europe are evolving in forms that are neither state capitalist nor market socialist. These are mixed economies not because there are state-owned firms and privately owned firms, but because the typical firm is itself a combination of public and private property relations. What we find are new forms of property in which the properties of private and public are dissolved, interwoven, and recombined. Property in East European capitalism is *recombinant property* and its analysis suggests the emergence of a distinctively East European capitalism that will differ as much from West European capitalism as do contemporary East Asian variants.

---

[9] For a compatible view of blurred boundaries and interwoven property relations in China, see Nee (1992); Walder (1994); Cui (1994 and forthcoming); on recombinant property in the Czech Republic, see McDermott (1996); Stark and Bruszt (1994).

From Destruction to Diversity

How are we to understand these unorthodox forms, these organizational "monsters" regrouping the seemingly incongruous? What are their causes and their consequences? Will they contribute to economic development or will they inhibit it? And what might we learn from them that would enrich and deepen more generally our understanding of economic change?

One starting point, ready-at-hand from the burgeoning literature on the "transitional" economies, would be to ask, "Do they contribute to creative destruction?" That litmus test is based on a widely held assumption that economic development will be best promoted by "allowing the selection mechanism to work" through bankruptcies of underperforming enterprises. Recombinant property would not receive an unambiguously positive score measured by this standard. Indeed, the kinds of inter-enterprise ownership described above are classic risk-spreading and risk-sharing devices that mitigate differences across firms. By dampening the performance of the stronger and facilitating the survival of the weaker firms in the inter-enterprise recombinet, they might even impede creative destruction in the conventional sense.

But there is some question that a tidal wave of mass bankruptcies is a long-term cure for the postsocialist economies. With the catastrophic loss of markets to the east and with the stagnation of the economies of potentially new trading partners to the west, the depth and length of the transformational crisis in Central Europe now exceeds that of the Great Depression of the interwar period (see Kornai 1993; Szelenyi 1993). In such circumstances, an absolute hardening of firms' budget constraints not only drives poorly performing firms into bankruptcy, but also destroys enterprises that would otherwise be quite capable of making a high performance adjustment (see especially, Cui 1994). Wanton destruction is not creative destruction, goes this reasoning; and recombinant property might save some of these struggling but capable firms through risk-sharing networks that do not require massive state bailouts (see below). Moreover, extraordinarily high uncertainties of the kind we see now in the postsocialist economies can lead to low levels of investment with negative strategic complementarities (as when firms forgo investments because they expect a sluggish economy based on the lack of investments by others). By mitigating disinclinations to invest, risk spreading might be one means to break out of otherwise low-level equilibrium traps.[10] Firms in the postsocialist transformational crisis are like

---

[10] On strategic complementaries in the postsocialist economies, see especially, Litwack

mountain climbers assaulting a treacherous face, and the networks of inter-enterprise ownership are the ropes lashing them together. Neoliberals who bemoan a retarded bankruptcy rate fail to acknowledge how this mutual binding is a precondition for attempting a difficult ascent.

Economic development in Eastern Europe does require more exit (some, indeed many, firms must perish) and more entry as well. But for destruction to be *creative,* these deaths must be accompanied by births not simply of new organizations but of *new organizational forms.* Socialism failed not only because it lacked a selection mechanism to eliminate organizations that performed poorly, but also because it put all its economic resources in a single organizational form – the state enterprise. Socialism drastically reduced organizational diversity and in so doing prohibited a broad repertoire of organized solutions to problems of collective action. Organizational forms are specific bundles of routines and the reduction of their diversity means the loss of organized information that might be of value when the environment changes (Hannan 1986; Boyer 1991; Stark 1989, 1992). The relative paucity of organizational diversity in Eastern Europe gives added urgency to the question: where do (new) organizational forms come from?

Economic sociology has three dominant answers to this question. The first might be called "imperfect reproduction" as, for example, when an existing organization (or its former personnel) attempts to establish a new venture by reproducing a successful form but fails to perfectly encode the various bundles of routines that make up an organizational form. The resulting organizational mutant is quite likely to fail; but if it survives, a new organizational form might take hold in the ecology of organizations (Hannan and Freeman 1986). The second answer is diffusion from outside a given sector or perhaps from outside the economy entirely. In the more sophisticated variant of this answer, organizational isomorphism occurs through mimetic processes when organizations imitate successful organizations in their field (DiMaggio and Powell 1983). The third answer is "de-institutionalization." When legal or other rules that maintain boundaries between previously discrete populations of organizations are relaxed, the blurring of organizational boundaries engenders new organizational forms (Powell and DiMaggio 1991; Hannan and Freeman 1986).

All three processes are at play in contemporary Eastern Europe. Imperfect reproduction, no doubt, occurs. But the slow rate at which it can contribute to change makes it of negligible importance in comparison with the second

(1994). On low-level equilibrium traps and the importance of risk spreading for economic development, see Hirschman (1958).

and third processes. As for diffusion, Western multinationals are entering the region in force, directly bringing new managerial practices that have strong indirect demonstration effects (Kogut 1994). But the multinationals' contribution to organizational diversity should not be overemphasized. The danger that they will, like a foreign species that invades a fragile ecology, eliminate organizational diversity is possible only in the very long run since foreign direct investment is still only a small fraction of business activity even in Hungary, which remains the leader in the region. More worrisome is that foreign direct investment can fit too neatly into the existing monopolistic structure inherited from state socialism. Many Western multinationals are all too eager to privatize state-owned enterprises because of the inordinate market share that they command. Cigarette manufacturers, for example, are notorious for paying top price in exchange for state concessions that virtually guarantee monopolistic markets (Kasriel 1993), and automobile manufacturers seek state subsidies, preferential credits, and strict import restrictions to reduce competition (Volvey 1993). The new multinational's foot slips easily into the boot of the old socialist enterprise.

De-institutionalization, the third type of process of generating new organizational forms, is also at work in contemporary Eastern Europe: the overlapping of previously well-bounded populations of organizations was, in fact, taking place in the Hungarian economy throughout the 1980s. Most important for the current debate over property transformation were the broad economic, legal, and social changes that eroded the boundaries between state and private property. Whereas the communist *policy* had been based on eliminating the boundary between public and private, the state socialist *economy* had been built on an absolute barrier separating public and private property, sanctified in a rigid hierarchy of collective, cooperative, and private property forms. These absolute barriers were crossed first in agriculture in the late 1970s with the blurring of boundaries between the property of the cooperatives and those of the household plots (Szelenyi 1988). By 1982, boundaries between state and private property were being eroded in even the most advanced sectors of Hungarian manufacturing. With this de-institutionalization came greater organizational diversity as the population of organizations in the "second economy" now overlapped with the population of socialist firms. The most prominent new organizational form was a hybrid property form, the intra-enterprise partnership (or VGMK), in which semi-autonomous subcontracting units used enterprise equipment to produce goods or services during the "off hours" (Stark 1986, 1989). Modified in their migration from agricultural to manufacturing, these "household plots of industry" had no rights to dispose of assets, but they did have a claim to the use of equipment during parts of the day/week. Moreover, the "partnerships" had captured significant rights over residual income (their "entrepreneurial fees" not uncommonly exceeded managerial earnings) and enjoyed significant rights of control ("From six to two we work for them; from two to six we work for ourselves," went the common expression).

Thus, as the partnerships spread to virtually every socialist enterprise and eventually included more than 10 percent of the industrial labor force, a good part of Hungary's managerial stratum had some practical experience with an organizational form of a hybrid property character. In fact, in the field research conducted for this study, I repeatedly encountered new corporate satellites (the KFTs) that are the literal organizational successors of the earlier subcontracting partnerships (the VGMKs).

Where they were not the direct organizational predecessors, the partnerships were, nonetheless, organizational precursors of the present recombinant forms. The partnership members were the consummate *bricoleurs*, making do with what was available. Within the VGMK, they regrouped resources from diverse parts of the shop floor and regrouped, as well, the informal norms of reciprocity with the technical norms of the professional. Because the intrapreneurial units were not hierarchically designated but left to self-organization, membership criteria attempted to combine within one unit personnel with different types of assets – political capital, social capital, technical skills, managerial capacities, and so forth – in such a way that the value of their collective capital exceeded the sum of their individual qualifications (for details, see Stark 1989). As such, they could bid for jobs across factory units. And the more fluid division of labor within the unit further made it possible for them to underbid the parent enterprise for contracts with outside partners.

Some of the partnerships were scarcely disguised rent-seeking schemes that privatized profit streams and left the expenses with the state-owned enterprise. Others would have been a surprise and perhaps delight to Schumpeter, who would have marveled at entrepreneurs *inside* a *socialist* firm. We might say that these partnerships "identified" new resources; but this would suggest that the resource was simply hidden or underutilized and only needed to be uncovered. In fact, before recombining resources, they first had to redefine resources – to see in a relation, an object, or a process, something of value (for examples, see Stark 1990a). Recombining property requires redefining the properties of things. This ability to see a resource where none was marked before, to see something in a different guise, to recognize new resources, was grounded in an acute organizational reflexivity.[11]

---

[11] See especially, Grabher (1994) for a discussion of how rivalry of coexisting organizational forms contributes to adaptability.

That reflexivity arose from the elemental fact that the partnership members lived, on a daily basis and within a single physical, technological, and social setting, in a multiplicity of organizational forms based on fundamentally different principles.

This brief overview of the partnership form together with our knowledge of the recombinant forms of the present transformation suggests another answer to the question "Where do (new) organizational forms come from?" We should expect to find new organizational forms being generated not only where routines mutate, where organizations interact, or where populations overlap, but also where social orders collide (White 1993).

Thus, if the hybrid organizational forms of late socialism result from the overlapping of once discrete *populations* of organizations, the recombinant property forms of postsocialism result from the overlap of *principles* of organization. If the members of the intra-enterprise partners were regrouping assets, the managers of the inter-enterprise recombinets are regrouping principles of association. Or, more accurately, both of these new types of hybrids include rearranging social ties and regrouping social forms. New organizational forms are new interweavings of social orders. In the world of recombinant property, organizing entails maneuvering not only through an ecology of organizations, but also through a complex ecology of orders.

The Multiple Accounts of Recombinant Property

Analysis of this maneuvering requires a distinction between *risk* – which is in principle calculable and can thus be expressed in the language of probability – and a more fundamental, though diffused, *uncertainty about the organizational environment* (for the classic statement, see Knight 1921). In transformative economies, firms have to worry not simply about whether there is demand for their products or about the rate of return on their investment or about the level of profitability, but also about the very principle of selection itself. Thus, the question is not only "Will I survive the *market test?*" – but also, under what conditions is proof of worth on market principles neither sufficient nor necessary to survive. Because there are multiple operative, mutually co-existent principles of justification according to which you can be called on to give accounts of your actions, you cannot be sure what counts. Transformative economies are acute cases of ambiguities of value, of evaluation, of worth (see Padgett and Ansell 1993 for an analysis of similar multivocality in another historical setting). By what proof and according to which principles of justification are you worthy to steward such and such resources?

Because of this uncertainty, actors will seek to diversify their assets, to hold resources in multiple accounts.

A possible candidate for a term to refer to this learned ability to glide among coexisting accounts in response to this kind of environmental uncertainty would be *organizational hedging*. But I have to emphasize that this is not the same kind of hedging to minimize risk exposure that we would find within a purely market logic – as, for example, when the shopkeeper who sells swimwear and sun lotion also devotes some floor space to umbrellas. Instead of acting within a single regime of evaluation, recombinant property is organizational hedging that crosses and combines disparate evaluative principles. Recombinant property is an attempt to have resources in more than one organizational form – or, similarly – to produce hybrid organizational forms that can be justified or assessed by more than one standard of measure. Thus, perhaps it is better if we think about recombinant property as a kind of *portfolio management*. And adopting this metaphor, we see actors clearly attuned to the first dictum of a good portfolio manager: *diversify your holdings!*

The adroit recombinant agent in the transformative economies of Central Europe differs from the diversifying fund manager in the West who with a known and single measure of value – money – puts that known and measurable resource here into stocks, there into treasury bills and money markets, there into bonds. Actors in these transformative economies diversify holdings in response to more fundamental uncertainties about what can constitute a resource. Under conditions not simply of market uncertainty but of organizational uncertainty, there can be multiple (and intertwined) strategies for survival – based in some cases on *profitability* but in others on *eligibility*. Where your success is judged, and the resources placed at your disposal determined, sometimes by your market share and sometimes by the number of workers you employ in a region; sometimes by your price–earnings ratio and sometimes by your "strategic importance"; and when even the absolute size of your losses can be transformed into an asset yielding an income stream, you might be wise to diversify your portfolio, to be able to shift your accounts, to be equally skilled in applying for loans as in applying for job creation subsidies, and to have a multilingual command of the grammar of credit worthiness and the syntax of debt forgiveness. To hold recombinant property is to have such a diversified portfolio.

The Centralized Management of Liabilities

Portfolio management, in the sense of maneuvering among multiple accounts as outlined above, must manage not only assets but also liabilities. This elemental concept that property embraces liabilities as well as assets has been almost entirely neglected in the now vast literature on privatization with its myopic focus on the distribution of rights and assets. In that debate, the worlds of the public and the private are lexically bounded. The realm of the private is a world of assets and rights; the realm of the public is a world of liabilities and obligations. This lexical separation has two causes. First, it is shaped by an intellectual division of labor in which one specialization – theorists of privatization and property rights – holds claims to one triad (private/assets/rights) while the analysis of the other triad (public/liabilities/obligations) is left to specialists in credit policy and public finance. Second, it reflects underlying processes in the postsocialist economies themselves. All too often privatization actually is an attempt to organizationally separate assets from liabilities. Moreover, this institutional separation of rights and obligations occurs not only at the moment of privatization but can continue well after the assignment of property rights. As Frydman and Rapaczynski (1994) persuasively demonstrate, privatization in itself provides no guarantee that private actors will not attempt to hold up the state.

The following section analyzes what happens in a postsocialist economy when actors are called to account for enterprise debt. As we shall see, these accountings bring into our focus a broader circle of actors including bankers, policymakers, and political parties as well as the enterprise directors whom we have already seen managing their assets in multiple accounts. To understand the intertwined strategies for managing liabilities we will need to explain how the Hungarian government, under the nationalist–conservative leadership of the Hungarian Democratic Forum launched a massive 300 billion forint ($3 billion) "debt consolidation" program amounting to 10 percent of Hungarian gross domestic product (GDP) and 18.3 percent of the 1994 national budget.[12] At the conclusion of that analysis we shall see how this governmental attempt at the centralized management of liabilities stimulated actors at the enterprise level to complement their strategies of recombinant risk spreading with new strategies of risk shedding.

[12] To put this figure in perspective, for the United States the $105 billion savings and loan bailout represents 1.6% of GNP and 7% of the projected 1995 federal budget. Venezuela's recent $6.1 billion bank bailout is on a magnitude with the Hungarian program, representing 11% of Venezuela's gross national product and 75% of the government's 1994 national budget (Brooke 1994).

Taking the Last Small Steps

The liabilities' management story begins in 1991 when the Hungarian government, within only a few months, fundamentally modified three important pieces of legislation regulating the accountings of assets and liabilities: the Law on Standard Accounting Practices, the Bankruptcy Act, and the Law on Banking were all brought into correspondence with Western practices. By 1991 the heady days of 1989, when communist regimes had toppled like dominoes across the region, seemed like the distant past. Now the young democracies of Eastern Europe were competing for foreign direct investment and support from the IMF and the World Bank. Actual levels of foreign direct investment were small when compared with the needs,[13] but the stakes for the future were big. And Hungary seemed the undisputed leader, garnishing as much foreign investment as the other countries in the region put together.

To maintain and perhaps even extend that lead, the government reasoned, Hungary should build on its comparative advantage. Hungary had not needed the shock therapy that brought Poland's hyperinflation under control (and brought Leszek Balcerowicz to the spotlight), and it lacked a charismatic figure such as the Czech Republic's Vaclav Klaus who captured attention when he lectured Western leaders on the virtues of free market liberalism. Hungary's advantage was the gradualism which across the decades of the 1970s and 1980s had brought it a full range of market-like institutions. These were admittedly not the institutions of a market economy, but they were close; and so, the government reasoned, why not take the last steps? To keep the lead in the regional competition, and to lead the nation to a fully fledged market economy, the government would rewrite the laws to conform with Western accounting and banking standards.

Thus, the new Accounting Law of 1991 (which took effect on 1 January 1992) required enterprises to switch to Western style accounting principles. A tough new Western style Bankruptcy Act (also implemented on 1 January 1992) contained stiff personal penalties for directors of enterprises who failed to file for bankruptcy after the accountants (using the new measuring instruments) sounded the alarm. Similarly, although with some gradualist steps built in, the new Act on Financial Institutions introduced in December

---

[13] In the first two years after the changes in the regime, approximately $3 billion in foreign direct investment flowed to Czechoslovakia, Hungary, and Poland. To put that figure in perspective, in the same period, the campaigns to *increase* the capital endowments of Harvard University, Stanford University, and Cornell University totaled approximately the same $3 billion figure. Harvard, Stanford, and Cornell are major universities, but about 64 million people lived in Czechoslovakia, Hungary, and Poland.

1991 was designed to put Hungary's commercial banks on a Western footing. In particular, the reserve requirements for measuring capital-adequacy ratios were modified, and the securities and other financial instruments for provisioning against qualified loans were respecified. According to international banking practices, banks must set aside funds to provision against outstanding loans that it suspects will not be paid in full. In the new Hungarian banking law, a loan is qualified as "bad" if in default for more than a year or if the debtor has filed for bankruptcy. In this categorization, "bad" is the worst, and the loan must be provisioned at 100 percent of its face value. "Doubtful" loans are those in default for more than 60 days, or where the debtor has reported losses for two consecutive years, and must be provisioned at 50 percent. Loans are qualified as "substandard" and require 20 percent provisions where the bank holds claims against companies in crisis sectors.

The last small steps proved to be a leap into the abyss. Already reeling from the collapse of the Council of Mutual Economic Assistance (CMEA) markets, enterprise directors now learned from their accountants that the new accounting practices were coloring the companies' books even redder than expected. By the end of 1992, over 10,000 bankruptcies and liquidation proceedings had been initiated – a figure 10 times higher than during the previous year when enterprises had experienced the worst shock of the collapsed Eastern markets (Bokros 1994).[14] With one-third to one-half of enterprises in the red (Piper, Ábel, and Király 1994) the loss-making firms began to stop payment on their bank credits. By the end of 1992, the overdue loan stock of the banking system was Ft 127 billion, up 90 percent from the previous year (National Bank of Hungary 1992:109).

With thousands of firms filing for bankruptcy, the banks were forced by the new banking law to reclassify loans from doubtful to bad. The subsequently dramatic increase in provisionings cut deeply into bank profits – reducing taxes from the financial sector and eliminating the dividends the state received from its shares in the large commercial banks. In 1990 the banks' profit margins had been high enough for taxes and dividends from the financial sector to constitute 7.6 percent of fiscal receipts (Ábel and

---

[14] Filings for bankruptcy and liquidation continued to pour in at a high rate in 1993 but have begun to turn down in 1994. Yet, although the number of new filings for bankruptcy is declining, the number of firms actually liquidated is increasing as the courts are beginning to make a dent in the huge backlog of filings from 1992-93. To understand the magnitude of 10,000 filings for bankruptcy and liquidation in a small economy such as Hungary's, in roughly the same period (mid-1992 to mid-1993) there were only 993 bankruptcy filings in the Czech Republic where policymakers had crafted a stringent bankruptcy law whose implementation has been twice postponed (Brom and Orenstein 1993).

Bonin 1993). These had been paper profits, to be sure, produced by the old accounting and financial standards; but to the state they had been real revenues all the same. Thus, fiscal planners were stunned when revenues and dividends from the banking sector for 1992 totaled only Ft 2 billion instead of the Ft 64 billion estimated a year earlier.[15]

The banks' scramble to improve their balance sheet structures and the state's scramble to finance its skyrocketing deficit interacted to cause further deterioration in the structure of lending: banks curtailed investment credits to enterprises in favor of buying Treasury bills and lending to the state.[16] Nonetheless, the banks continued to lend to their client-owners, the formerly state-owned enterprises that held shares in the banks – acquired in the days when the newly established commercial banks were looking for corporate shareholders that could offset the weight of the Ministry of Finance. For the enterprises, owning shares in a profitable bank promised high dividends and a steady flow of credit: a "no-lose" situation, especially in the many cases when the purchase of large amounts of bank equity were directly financed by credit from the same bank (Bokros 1994). Caught in the squeeze were the small and medium startup ventures upon whom many laid hopes for the revitalization of the economy: small entrepreneurs received less than 9 percent of total investment credits to the business sector in 1992 (National Bank of Hungary 1994:95, table IV/3). As the large commercial banks raised interest rates to cover an increasingly shaky loan portfolio, profitable Hungarian firms began to turn abroad (or to foreign-held banks) for investment financing. Their desertion of the Hungarian banks could only worsen the risk structure (Ábel and Bonin 1993). The banks responded by widening the spread between lending rates and deposit rates[17] – triggering more defaults and bankruptcies requiring, in turn, higher levels of provisioning in desperate attempts to keep capital-adequacy ratios from falling into the deep negatives. Spiraling away from its function of financial intermediation, the banking system was in crisis.

That crisis was announced, less than a year after Hungary's bold leadership in adopting Western-style accounting, bankruptcy, and banking practices, in the pages of the *Financial Times* (Denton 1993a and b). Hungary's three top

[15] Personal communication from László Antal, Hungarian Foreign Trade Bank.

[16] Whereas loans to the government were only 7.2% of the banks' total loan portfolio in January 1992, they rose to 22% by December 1992 and to over 30% by November 1993, with loans to enterprises falling from 74% to only 52% over the same period (National Bank of Hungary 1994:95, table IV/2).

[17] In January 1992, the spread was 6.6 (the difference between the average lending rate of 36.0% and average deposit rates of 29.4% to the business sector). By August of the same year lending rates had fallen to 32.0%, but deposit rates had dropped to 18.9% – for a spread of 13.1 (National Bank of Hungary 1994:99, table IV/7).

banks were technically insolvent: instead of capital-adequacy ratios of 4 percent or 8 percent that would put them within reach of international standards, these banks were in the –4 percent to –8 percent range.

From Small Steps to Big Bailouts

The same government that had launched an unintended financial shock now launched a bold plan to save the banks. In its 1992 loan consolidation program, the government bought Ft 104.9 billion (about $1 billion) of qualified debt (almost all in the "bad" debt classification) involving 14 banks and 1,885 companies.[18] In a related move in early 1993, the government also purchased the bank debt of 11 giant enterprises (the so-called "dirty dozen") for roughly $300 million. The loan consolidation and enterprise recapitalization programs, it seemed, had restored stability in the banking sector. Yet, by September 1993, only nine months later, financial experts were estimating that qualified loans (for the greater part, bad loans) had once again soared to 20 percent of total loan portfolios. And the 10 largest banks were again hovering at or below the zero percent capital-adequacy ratio (technical insolvency).[19]

What had happened? Banks had treated the government bonds as broad money. Instead of provisioning, many banks had used these funds to continue making loans to loss-making enterprises. Piper, Ábel, and Király (1994) provide a trenchant assessment: "The 1992 loan consolidation program did nothing to change the incentives that lead to the creation of bad debts in the first place. The same owners, the same governing boards, the same managers, and the same bankers had the same roles within the banks under the same operating constraints." We might go further. The precedent of a bank bailout in which the government bought only bad loans set up a perverse incentive to the banks for reclassifying doubtful and substandard loans.

The new accounting, bankruptcy, and banking rules had not caused the economic crisis – for that we can find straightforward explanations in the structural features of the state socialist economy – but they had shaped the particular forms in which that crisis was manifested (for example, that the

[18] In exchange for the debt, the banks received 20-year government bonds, and about 40% of the debt was transferred to the newly created Hungarian Investment and Development Bank, which, most analysts agreed, was unprepared for the difficult task of collecting the loans.

[19] By the end of 1993, these 10 banks, accounting for 90% of all credit extended, were expected to hold Ft 316 billion of poorly performing debts and other investments representing "roughly 35% of total loans to households and enterprises (compared to bad debts to total loans averaging 3% in the West)" (Piper, Ábel, and Király 1994).

crisis of the enterprises and the fiscal crisis of the state were immediately translated, within only a few months, into a massive crisis of the financial sector). The new accounting technologies, moreover, shaped the resources with which actors played their strategies during the crisis. New banking rules made new accountings possible, and there was no rule that the state could not bail out the banks again.

That is exactly what the government did when it announced a new bank recapitalization/debt consolidation program in the late fall of 1993. The new program was not, however, a simple replay of the 1992 bailout but included new methods and justifications. Whereas in the earlier program the government had bought the bad debt directly from the banks, in the new program it adopted a multiphase approach, first of recapitalizing the banks[20] and then later negotiating the workout of the particular loans that composed the qualified debt. The significance of these methods must be understood in terms of the new justifications offered for the new bailout. To justify the 1992 loan consolidation program, the government had argued that these were bad debts inherited from the old regime. But that justification had become untenable when, instead of getting better, the debt crisis worsened after the first bailout. By 1993, the financial crisis could no longer be blamed on past practices. Therefore, methods and justifications had to be adjusted to address current practices.

Instead of liberation from the past, the slogan of the new consolidation program became, "Assets liberated from liabilities can be more productive." If this was to be anything more than a truism, of course, the question was how to identify assets that could be performing from those that were worthless under any circumstances. The answer was to rely on the banks as the primary repository of information about the true health of Hungarian enterprises. Reliance on the banks, however, could not be unequivocal since it was the current practice – the imprudent lending – by those same banks that was pushing the crisis toward the precipice.

The two-stage strategy (recapitalization first, workouts later) was designed to harness the expertise of the banks to the service of the state. Because it was not buying debt, but injecting fresh funds into the banks, the new "investor" would acquire shares in the banks (already transformed into shareholding companies before the regime change). And because the sums were enormous, the new shares would yield a controlling interest. In this way, the Ministry of Finance became the dominant, even majority, shareholder of the

[20] Recapitalization was to occur in two waves, the first in late 1993 to bring capital-adequacy ratios to zero, the second in the spring of 1994 to raise these ratios to 4 and 8% for selected banks.

large commercial banks. The first stage of the strategy, then, could be summarized in a phrase: don't acquire the debt; acquire the banks. Or, less euphemistically, renationalize the banks. Because it was the banks, and not the state, that would be left holding the qualified debt, the banks would have an incentive to collect that debt, or at least the part they had not already written off their books. And they would do so this time, not with the state as their sometime partner, but with the state as their majority owner.

But efforts to exercise control through direct ownership do not equal more effective state capacity. If we need evidence for that we could turn to several decades of state socialism, or we can look at the second stage of the debt consolidation program in which the state and the banks were supposed to negotiate the workout of particular loans.

At the beginning of 1994, the government slated 55 firms for immediate workout just months before the parliamentary elections held in May. The firms were to draw up and submit business plans. The banks could accept the plans; but if they rejected them, the firm could still be saved from liquidation if the State Property Agency (SPA) elected to buy the debt. Most bankers agreed that the business plans – hurriedly thrown together, with only a few weeks of preparation – were of poor quality. In one revealing exchange, an official at the State Property Agency called a banker to inquire about the status of the business plans the bank had just received from six firms in the SPA's portfolio. The banker, who had just read the mountain of thick documents on his desk, responded that these weren't serious business plans. Each could have been summarized in one sentence, "Please forgive our debts." In that case, responded the privatization official, perhaps the bank could write up new business plans, adding that it was, after all, the creditor, and who could know more about the companies? The banker, expressing his reluctance to draw up one set of numbers in the morning and approve them in the afternoon, countered that perhaps the SPA should draw up the plans because, after all, who should know more about a company than its owner? The enterprise directors, meanwhile, were puzzled by all this fuss about business plans. The selection of the "55" just months before the election had been made on political grounds, and the decisions about them, it was thought, would be political as well.

In this way, through endless rounds of meetings, some small number of the plans were accepted by the banks, some small number were rejected by all and allowed to fail, and for the greater number, the banks entered negotiations with the SPA, which, we recall, had the option to buy the debt from the bank in cases where the bank refused to accept the firm's workout plan.

At what price should the SPA buy the debt? – clearly at a considerable discount since this was qualified debt already provisioned in proportion to its level of qualification (bad, doubtful, substandard) by the terms of the recapitalization program. To "apply" for that program, banks had been required to produce a list of qualified loans, the categorization of each (with the corresponding figure indicating the funds needed to provision that loan), and a bottom line summing the reserves it would set aside if accepted to participate in the program. This time, the government was determined both to avoid the perverse incentives created by buying only "bad" loans and to insure that recapitalization would restore banking health rather than further finance loss-making enterprises. Nonetheless, and despite the hundreds of billions of forints of taxpayers' money at stake, the Ministry of Finance and other state agencies saw only the bottom line of the application – accompanied by an auditor's certification that this figure was an accurate summation of the enumerated loans.

Thus, if a loan had been classified as "substandard" and provisioned through the recapitalization program at 20 percent of its face value, it would seem reasonable that it should not be sold to the SPA for more than 80 percent of its face value; "doubtful" debt at 50 percent; "bad debt" at next to nothing. But there was nothing to stop the bank, at this point, from modifying the classification of a particular loan – and so a loan categorized as bad when applying for recapitalization funds could become only doubtful when negotiating to sell it. That is, the bank could have a bad loan provisioned at 100 percent in the recapitalization program and then turn around and try to sell it as a doubtful loan for 50 percent of its face value. And when the SPA called the bank's hand, the bank responded that the interim upgrading was not arbitrary but based on "new information": the business plan – that the bank was rejecting.

In the end, and to the great relief of the World Bank officials overseeing it, the program was spared the expensive farce of the state paying for debt twice over (once through the recapitalization program, again through an SPA debt purchase): the SPA simply did not have the cash. During the nine months leading up to the May election, the SPA took in little revenue. As part of the government's electoral strategy, the agency began to favor domestic over foreign buyers, to extend cheap credit, to accept installment payments, and to actually give property away in the form of "compensation" vouchers. During the same time, funds flowed into the governing parties' "foundations," scarcely disguised campaign treasuries. But the Hungarian electorate was clearly looking for an alternative, voted Socialist, and got a new Socialist-Liberal coalition government. That government promises an enterprise restructuring program that "will rely more on the banks."

But, as the previous discussion has already suggested, the government might not find a very reliable partner in banks that are already sitting atop billions of fresh capital. With their balance sheets back in the black, the banks are not now disposed to develop creative solutions. First, provisioning has made the banks less than aggressive in pursuing liquidations. To be sure, too many liquidations all at once would hurt not only their balance sheets, but would also harm the national economy. In fact, however, the opposite problem is the more likely: with their reserve requirements (temporarily) secure, the banks will allow liquidation procedures to drag out for years through the bankruptcy courts as thousands of enterprises experience an agonizingly slow death, all the while making nothing but losses. Moreover, despite the assumption that the Ministry of Finance's ownership would yield control of the banks, the government has been almost entirely ineffective in monitoring how the banks use the recapitalization funds, and it is doubtful whether the new coalition government will be more successful. Thus, during the protracted liquidations, there is little to prevent the banks from extending loans to continued lossmakers.

Second, to date, the banks have shown almost no willingness to use the consolidation funds for actively restructuring firms. The institutionally youthful Hungarian banking community takes its cues from New York City: the "glamour" jobs are in bonds and securities. There is not yet an established career pattern for an ambitious and energetic young banker who would like to chalk up a track record of successful "turnarounds."[21] Yet this is exactly what must happen if the network properties of assets are to be recognized and creatively recombined in new configurations. Compared with the passive stance of waiting for a liquidation, restructuring is time consuming and difficult. It is also much riskier. The banks are unlikely to adopt such a strategy if left to their own devices.[22]

Returning to the present, what has happened to date with the second phase (debt consolidation at the enterprise level) of the 1993/94 program? While negotiations for the list of "55" were under way, the government

---

[21] The outlook is not entirely gloomy. One of the largest commercial banks has established a new workout unit. With solid leadership, the unit shows signs of attracting talented personnel with a strong commitment to active restructuring.

[22] One proposal currently being discussed is for the creation of a new "development agency" differentiated both from the "ownership" agencies (the soon to be recombined SPA and Av. Rt.) and from the banks. It would also differ from the already established Hungarian Investment and Development Bank (a misnomer since the institution is simply a glorified collection agency). The task of the new agency would be to work with banks to create incentives for restructuring. Implicit in the proposal is a reversal of the sequencing of the 1993/94 program: instead of receiving fresh funds first and then doing little by way of restructuring, banks and enterprises would have to demonstrate creative solutions before receiving any financial assistance in restructuring. To be successful, the new agency would have to tread the thin line between facilitating risk management and promoting risk shedding.

announced that the second round of debt resolution would not discriminate by property form: virtually any enterprise (under state, private, or mixed ownership) could apply to participate in the program. By the deadline at the end of June 1994, some 2,000 enterprises had submitted plans to the consolidation commission. The initial reaction by bank officers, government officials, and observers in the World Bank was puzzlement: tempted by the lure of a bailout of unprecedented proportions, why had so few enterprises applied?[23] The designers of the program cautiously offered an interpretation with a decidedly positive spin. Enterprise directors, they argued, had correctly read the signals being sent out about the negotiations for the list of 55, "Don't apply if you can't take the heat – this program is not a giveaway." But other interpretations can be provided to understand why so relatively few enterprises applied. We offer four such explanations, none of whose colors is particularly rosy.

1. Faced with an opportunity to workout debt and put their companies on a course toward more sound financial management, many enterprises simply lacked the basic knowledge, background, and competence to prepare even the most minimal business plan.
2. Faced with an uncertain process, some enterprises assessed the potential gains against the risk that the procedure would culminate in a decision to force the liquidation of the firm. Instead of formal application, they felt that the prospects for successful access to the state's deep pockets were better if they continued to use informal back channel bargaining ties to other ministries and agencies.

(The following explanations break with the assumption – implicit in the first two explanations – that, however incompetent or conniving, senior management identifies with the indebted enterprise.)

3. Some senior managers are simply not interested in the financial health of the enterprise that they currently manage. In fact, they have already adopted strategies to strip that firm of its assets (perhaps through leasing, pricing, or rental arrangements with KFTs in which they hold control) or to purposefully drive the firm into bankruptcy when they can then use their insider knowledge to acquire it on the cheap. Formal application to the debt consolidation program would ruin such strategies.
4. Some loans, perhaps many of the qualified loans to private enterprises in

---

[23] Although no official figures have been released, knowledgeable sources in the financial community estimate that only 15–25 % of the potential pool of qualified loans have made an application to the program.

the pool of potential applicants, were not taken out with the aim of investing in the enterprise named in the loan. Application for debt forgiveness was out of the question because it would bring the conditions of the loan and the uses of its funds under direct scrutiny.

Support for this fourth explanation comes from a recent internal analysis, by one of the large commercial banks, of the qualified loans in one of its divisions. The loans (most of them qualified as bad debt) totaled Ft 3.8 billion ($38 million) to some 45 companies. Remarkably, 33 of the named enterprises were no longer operating (and some perhaps never were), yet they had neither been liquidated nor had the bank initiated bankruptcy proceedings. The firms had simply stopped paying the loan and gone out of existence. Of the loans 39 had been made during 1990–91 (i.e. just after the regime change) and contained gaping irregularities. For example, the bank had secured no collateral for 24 of these loans, and many had been granted without authorization of the bank's Credit Committee.

What had happened to these funds? Some of these loans, no doubt, were taken out with no intended business purpose (consumption, "black" activities, etc.). Others, the bank's analysts suspect, were used to acquire state property through the privatization program. In some of these cases, the debtor might have taken out the loan with an intention to capitalize an independent venture but, after observing that a new startup is much more vulnerable than an already existing company, later used the money from the loan for the cash downpayment to acquire a state-owned firm in a related field. For others, the target of privatization had already been identified at the time of the loan application. But in both types of fraud, a loan used for privatization was not a liability on the books of the privatized company but was on the books of a bankrupted limited liability company with no assets that the banks could claim. This is looting, a Hungarian version of "bankruptcy for profit" (Akerlof and Romer 1993).

Adaptability and Accountability

Recombinant property is, thus, produced in two simultaneous processes. Accompanying the decentralized reorganization of assets is a centralization of liabilities. Both processes blur the boundaries between public and private. On the one hand, privatization produces the criss-crossing lines of recombinant property; on the other, debt consolidation transforms private debt into public liabilities. Together these twinned moments of property transformation create a new basis of paternalism in Hungary. Whereas in the state socialist economy, paternalism was based on the state's attempts at the centralized management of assets, in the first years of the postsocialist economy, paternalism is based on the state's attempts at the centralized management of liabilities.

In the highly uncertain organizational environment that is the post-socialist economy, relatively few actors (apart from institutional designers) set out with the aim to create a market economy. Many indeed would prefer if such were the outcome. But their immediate goals are more pragmatic: at best to thrive, at least to survive. And so they strive to use whatever resources are available. That task is not so simple because one must first identify the relevant system of accounting (the measuring instruments and the justificatory principles) in which something can exist as a resource. At the extreme, it is sometimes even difficult to distinguish a liability from an asset. If the liabilities of your organization (enterprise or bank) are big enough, perhaps they can be translated into qualifications for more resources. And what could be more worthless than a bankrupted limited liability company – except, of course, if you have shed the risk to the banks (and then to the state) and put the assets in another form. And so actors diversify their portfolios because they are not sure what counts; they measure in multiple units; they speak in many tongues. In so doing, they produce and reproduce the polyphonic discourse of worth that is postsocialism.

We can see that polyphony in the diverse ways that firms justify their claims for participation in the debt relief program. The following litany of justifications are stylized versions of claims encountered in discussions with bankers, property agency officials, and enterprise directors. The Hungarian reader will perhaps recognize specific firms:

> Our firm should be included in the debt relief program because we will forgive our debtors.[24]
> Our firm should be included in the debt relief program because we are truly credit worthy;[25]
> because we employ thousands;
> because our suppliers depend on us for a market;
> because we are in your election district;
> because our customers depend on our product inputs;
> because we can then be privatized;
> because we can never be privatized;

[24] I.e., our firm occupies a strategic place in a network of inter-enterprise debt.
[25] I.e., if our liabilities are separated from our assets, we will again be eligible for more bank financing. Explanations could be provided for each of the following justifications.

because *we* took big risks;

because we were prudent and did not take risks;

because we were planned in the past;

because we have a plan for the future;

because we export to the West;

because we export to the East;

because our product has been awarded an International Standards Quality Control Certificate;

because our product is part of the Hungarian national heritage;

because we are an employee buyout;

because we are a management buy-in;

because we are partly state owned;

because we are partly privately held;

because our creditors drove us into bankruptcy when they loaned to us at higher than market rates to artificially raise bank profits in order to pay dividends into a state treasury whose coffers had dwindled when corporations like ourselves effectively stopped paying taxes.

And so we must ask, into whose account and by which account will debt forgiveness flow? Or, in such a situation, is anyone accountable?

Should there then be only one accounting, perhaps with profitability as the single metric? Such was the attempt of communism – the imposition of a unitary justificatory principle, a strict hierarchy of property forms, and a reduction of all of human history to one grand narrative. It would be a tragedy beyond irony if East European capitalism would replicate such a monochrome with a different coloring. The vitality and exuberance of modernity stem precisely from the colorful interweaving of multiple ordering principles. It might be objected, of course, that multiple orders are fine – provided that each occupies a distinctly bounded domain. Such is the perspective of modernity in "modernization" theory: through differentiation, each domain of society would develop as a separate autonomous subsystem with its own distinctive logic. Complexity in this view was diversity, but only through the juxtaposition of otherwise clearly bounded rationalities. Marxism, of course, had its own view of complexity: the temporary overlap of mutually contradictory principles. Both modernization theory and Marxism were deeply grounded in the transition problematic. The noisy clash of orders is only temporary: the revolutionary moment for one, the passage to differentiated domains in the other.

If we break with this transition problem, we can escape from the impoverished conceptions of complexity in both Marxism and modernization theory. In an alternative conception, complexity is the interweaving of multiple accountings on the same domain space. The alternative view holds to this conception, not for the aesthetic reason that life is then more colorful or lively, but for good economic reasons. An economy's dynamic efficiency rests on diversity. Without diversity of organizational forms an economy cannot adapt to changes in the environment. Or it can do so only at extraordinary costs when organizations and institutions are replaced wholesale. Diversity is less expensive in the long run even if not every organizational form performs at some maximum allocative efficiency. Least expensive are organizations with enough reflexivity to reshape themselves. And both diversity (the emergence of new organizational forms) and reflexivity (the ability to redefine resources and arrange them in new combinations) are products of the clash of ordering principles within an economy and sometimes even within the same organization.[26] Thus, we might say that, as opposed to allocative efficiency, an economy's adaptive efficiency depends on a multiplicity of ordering principles within the economy itself.

The problem is that too many ordering principles – too many diverse accountings – can produce unaccountability. An actor who, within the same domain space, is accountable to every principle is accountable to none. Accountability, like diversity and adaptability, is a value not simply for moral reasons, but for good economic reasons: there is nothing of value outside of accounts. The difficult condition of modernity is to facilitate enough diversity to foster adaptability and enough boundedness of rationalities to foster accountability. It is not in finding the right mix of public and private, but in finding the right mix of adaptability and accountability that postsocialist societies face their greatest challenge.

[26] For similar argumentation based on different cases, see especially, Grabher (1994); and also Landau (1969); White (1993). For related views on adaptability and complexity, see especially, Morin (1974); Conrad (1983).

References

Ábel, István, and John Bonin. 1993. "State Desertion and Financial Market Failure: Is the Transition Stalled?" Budapest Bank Working Papers, no. 5

Akerlof, George A., and Paul M. Romer. 1993. "Looting: The Economic Underworld of Bankruptcy for Profit." Brookings Papers on Economic Activity, no. 2, pp. 1–73.

Barzel, Yoram. 1989. *Economic Analysis of Property Rights.* Cambridge, Eng.: Cambridge University Press.

Bokros, Lajos. 1994. "Privatization and the Banking System in Hungary." In *Privatization in the Transition Process: Recent Experiences in Eastern Europe,* edited by László Samuely. pp. 305–20. Geneva: United Nations Conference on Trade & Development and KOPINT-DATORG.

Boltanski, Luc, and Laurent Thévenot. 1991. *De la justification: Les économies de la grandeur*. Paris: Gallimard.

Bourdieu, Pierre. 1986. "Forms of Capital." In *Handbooks of Theory and Research for the Sociology of Education*, edited by John G. Richardson. pp. 241–58. Westport, Conn.: Greenwood Press.

———. 1990. *The Logic of Practice*. Stanford: Stanford University Press.

Boyer, Robert. 1991. "Markets within Alternative Coordinating Mechanisms: History, Theory, and Policy in the Light of the Nineties." Conference on the Comparative Governance of Sectors, Bigorio, Switzerland.

Breiger, Ronald L., and P.E. Pattison. 1986. "Cumulated Social Roles: The Duality of Persons and Their Algebras." *Social Networks* 8: 215–56.

Bresser Pereira, Luiz Carlos. 1993. "The Crisis of the State Approach to Latin America." Discussion Paper no. 1, Instituto Sul-Norte (November).

Brom, Karla, and Mitchell Orenstein. 1993. "The 'Privatized' Sector in the Czech Republic: Government and Bank Control in a Transitional Economy." *Europe-Asia Studies* 46, no. 6: 893–928.

Brooke, James. 1994. "Venezuela's Banks: A Catastrophe Awaiting Rescue." *International Herald Tribune*, May 17.

Bunce, Valerie, and Mária Csanadi. 1993. "Uncertainty in the Transition: Post-Communism in Hungary." *East European Politics and Societies* 7: 240–75.

Burt, Ronald. 1992. *Structural Holes*. Cambridge, Mass.: Harvard University Press.

Comisso, Ellen. 1991. "Property Rights, Liberalism, and the Transition from 'Actually Existing' Socialism." *East European Politics and Societies* 5, no. 1: 162–88.

Conrad, Michael. 1983. *Adaptability*. New York: Plenum Press.

Cui, Zhiyuan. 1994. "Epilogue: A Schumpeterian Perspective and Beyond." In *China: A Reformable Socialism?* edited by Yang Gan and Zhiyuan Cui. Hong Kong: Oxford University Press.

———. forthcoming. "Moebius-Strip Ownership and Its Prototype in Chinese Rural Industry." *Economy and Society*.

Denton, Nicholas. 1993a. "Two Hungarian Banks Said to Be Technically Insolvent." *Financial Times*, May 20.

———. 1993b. "The Hole in Hungary's Banking Heart." *Financial Times*, May 21.

DiMaggio, Paul, and Walter W. Powell. 1983. "The Iron Cage Revisited: Institutional Isomorphism and Collective Rationality in Organizational Fields." *American Sociological Review* 48: 147–60.

Durkheim, Emile. 1897. *Le suicide: étude de sociologie*. Paris: Presses Universitaires de France.

Figyelö. 1993. "Top 200 1993: a legnagyobb vàll alkozàsok a szàmok tükrében." Budapest (special issue).

Frydman, Roman, and Andrzej Rapaczynski. 1994. *Privatization in Eastern Europe: Is the State Withering Away?* Budapest: Central European University Press.

Gábor, István. 1979. "The Second (Secondary) Economy." *Acta Oeconomica* 22, no. 3–4: 91–311.

———. 1986. "Reformok másod gazdaság, államszocializmus. A 80-as évek tapasztalatainak feljödéstani és összehasonlító gazdaságtani tanulságairól" (Reforms, second economy, state socialism: Speculation on the evolutionary and comparative economic lessons of the Hungarian eighties). *Valóság*, no. 6: 32–48.

——. 1992. "A második gazdaság ma: az átalakulás kérdöjelei" (The second economy today). *Közgazdasági Szemle* 34: 946–53.

——. 1996. "Too Many, Too Small: Small Businesses in Postsocialist Hungary." In *Restructuring Networks: Legacies, Linkages, and Localities in Postsocialism*, edited by Gernot Grabher and David Stark. London and New York: Oxford University Press.

Gerlach, Michael L., and James R. Lincoln. 1993. "The Organization of Business Networks in the United States and Japan." In *Networks and Organizations*, edited by Nitin Nohria and Robert G. Eccles. pp. 491–520. Cambridge, Mass.: Harvard Business School Press.

Grabher, Gernot. 1994. *In Praise of Waste: Redundancy in Regional Development.* Berlin: Edition Sigma.

Granovetter, Mark. 1973. "The Strength of Weak Ties." *American Journal of Sociology* 78: 1360–80.

Grey, Thomas. 1980. "The Disintegration of Property." In *Property,* edited by J. Rolland Pennock and John W. Chapman. pp. 69–85. New York: New York University Press.

Hannan, Michael T. 1986. "Uncertainty, Diversity, and Organizational Change." In *Behavioral and Social Science: Fifty Years of Discovery.* pp. 73–94. Washington, DC: National Academy Press.

Hannan, Michael T., and John H. Freeman. 1986. "Where Do Organizational Forms Come From?" *Sociological Forum* 1, no. 1: 50–72.

Hart, Oliver. 1988. "Incomplete Contracts and Theory of the Firm." *Journal of Law, Economics, and Organization* 4, no. 1: 119–39

Hirschman, Albert. 1958. *The Strategy of Economic Development.* New Haven, Conn.: Yale University Press.

Hodgson, Geoffrey M. 1993. *Economics and Evolution.* Ann Arbor: University of Michigan Press.

Kasriel, Ken. 1993. "Nasty Habit." *Business Central Europe,* p. 28 (November).

Klaus, Vaclav. 1992. "Adam Smith's Legacy and Economic Transformation of Czechoslovakia." *Business Economics* 28, no. 1: 7–9.

Knight, Frank H. 1921. *Risk, Uncertainty, and Profit.* Boston: Houghton Mifflin.

Kogut, Bruce. 1994. "Foreign Direct Investment and Corporate Governance in Eastern Europe." Paper presented at the Workshop on Corporate Governance, The World Bank. School of Law, Columbia University (April).

Kogut, Bruce, and Udo Zander. 1992. "Knowledge of the Firm, Combinative Capabilities, and the Replication of Technology." *Organization Science* 3, no. 3: 383–97.

Kornai, János. 1980. *The Economics of Shortage.* Amsterdam: North Holland.

——. 1992. "The Post-Socialist Transition and the State: Reflections in the Light of Hungarian Fiscal Problems." *American Economic Review* 82, no. 2: 1–21.

——. 1993. "Transitional Recession." Institute for Advanced Study/Collegium Budapest, Discussion Paper Series.

Laky, Teréz. 1979. "Enterprises in Bargaining Position." *Acta Oeconomica* 22, no. 34: 226–41.

——. 1992. "Small and Medium-Size Enterprises in Hungary." Report for the European Commission. Institute for Labour Studies, Budapest.

Landau, Martin. 1969. "Redundancy, Rationality, and the Problem of Duplication and Overlap." *Public Administration Review* 29, no. 4: 346–58.

Litwack, John. 1994. "Strategic Complementarities and Economic Transition." Institute for Advanced Study/Collegium Budapest, Discussion Paper Series.

McDermott, Gerald A. 1996. "Rethinking the Ties that Bind: The Limits of Privatization in the Czech Republic." In *Restructuring Networks: Legacies, Linkages, and Localities in Postsocialism*, edited by Gernot Grabher and David Stark. London and New York: Oxford University Press.

Mellár, Tamás. 1992. "Two years of privatization." *Népszabadság*, May 22.

Mirody, Mira. 1992. "Contradictions in the Subconscious of the Poles." In *Polish Paradoxes*, edited by Stanislaw Gomulka and Antony Polonsky. pp. 227–36. London: Routledge.

Morin, Edgar. 1974. "Complexity." *International Social Science Journal* 26, no. 4: 555–82.

National Bank of Hungary. 1992. *Annual Report*. Budapest.

———. 1994. *Monthly Report* 2. Budapest.

Nee, Victor. 1992. "Organizational Dynamics of Market Transition: Hybrid Forms, Property Rights, and Mixed Economy in China." *Administrative Science Quarterly* 37: 1–27.

Nelson, Richard R., and Sidney G. Winter. 1982. *An Evolutionary Theory of Economic Change*. Cambridge, Eng.: Cambridge University Press.

Neumann, László. 1991. "Labour Conflicts of Privatization." *Acta Oeconomica* 43: 213–30.

Padgett, John F., and Christopher K. Ansell. 1993. "Robust Action and the Rise of the Medici, 1400-1434." *American Journal of Sociology* 98:1259–319.

Peck, Merton J., and Thomas J. Richardson, eds. 1992. *What Is To Be Done? Proposals for the Soviet Transition to the Market*. New Haven, Conn.: Yale University Press.

Peirce, Charles S. 1934. *Pragmatism and Pragmaticism*. vol. 5 of the *Collected Papers of Charles Sanders Peirce*, edited by C. Hartshorne and P. Weiss. Cambridge, Mass.: Harvard University Press.

Piper, Rosemary Pugh, István Ábel, and Júlia Király. 1994. "Transformation at a Crossroads: Financial Sector Reform in Hungary." Policy Study no. 5, Commissioned by the Joint Hungarian-International Blue Ribbon Commission.

Powell, Walter, and Paul DiMaggio, eds. 1991. *The New Institutionalism in Organizational Analysis*. Chicago: University of Chicago Press.

Sabel, Charles, and David Stark. 1982. "Planning, Politics, and Shop-Floor Power: Hidden Forms of Bargaining in Soviet-Imposed State-Socialist Societies." *Politics and Society* 11: 439–75.

Sabel, Charles, and Jonathan Zeitlin. forthcoming. "Stories, Strategies, Structures: Rethinking Historical Alternatives to Mass Production." In *Worlds of Possibility: Flexibility and Mass Production in Western Industrialization*, edited by Sabel and Zeitlin.

Sachs, Jeffrey. 1989. "My Plan for Poland." *The International Economy* 3: 24–9.

Schmitter, Philippe. n.d. Modes of Governance of Economic Sectors, unpublished manuscript, Stanford University.

Schumpeter, Joseph A. 1934. *The Theory of Economic Development*. Cambridge, Mass.: Harvard University Press.

Sik, Endre. 1992. "From Second Economy to Informal Economy." *Journal of Public Policy* 12, no. 2: 153–75.

Stark, David. 1986. "Rethinking Internal Labor Markets: New Insights from a Comparative Perspective." *American Sociological Review* 51: 492–504.

———. 1989. "Coexisting Organizational Forms in Hungary's Emerging Mixed Economy." In *Remaking the Economic Institutions of Socialism: China and Eastern Europe*, edited by Victor Nee and David Stark, pp. 137–68. Stanford, Calif.: Stanford University Press.

———. 1990a. "Work, Worth, and Justice in a Socialist Mixed Economy." Working Papers on Central and Eastern Europe, no. 5, Center for European Studies, Harvard University, Cambridge, Mass.

———. 1990b. "Privatization in Hungary: From Plan to Market or from Plan to Clan?" *East European Politics and Societies* 4: 351–92.

———. 1992. "Path Dependence and Privatization Strategies in East Central Europe." *East European Politics and Societies* 6: 17–51.

Stark, David, and László Bruszt. 1994. "Restructuring Networks in Postsocialist East Central Europe." Cornell Working Papers on Transitions from State Socialism, no. 94.6, Cornell University, Ithaca, N.Y.

Szelenyi, Ivan. 1988. *Socialist Entrepreneurs.* Madison: University of Wisconsin Press.

———. 1993. "Transformational Crisis." Paper presented at the Annual Meetings of the American Sociological Association, Miami (August).

Volvey, Anne. 1993. "La politique d'approvisionnement des entreprises localisées en Hongrie," Institute for Advanced Study/Collegium Budapest, Discussion Paper Series.

Voszka, Éva. 1990. "Ropewalking: Ganz Danubius Ship and Crane Factory Transformed into a Company." *Acta Oeconomica* 43, no. 1/2: 285–302.

———. 1991. *Tulajdon — reform* (Property — Reform). Budapest: Pénzügykutató Rt.

———. 1992a. "Escaping from the State, Escaping to the State." Paper presented at the Arne Ryde Symposium on the "Transition Problem," Rungsted, Denmark (June).

———. 1992b. "Az ellenkezöje sem igaz: a központositás és a decentralizáció szineváltozásai" (The contrary is untrue as well: changes of centralization and decentralization). *Kulgazdaság* 36, no. 6.

Walder, Andrew. 1994. "Corporate Organization and Local Government Property Rights in China." In *Changing Political Economies: Privatization in Post-Communist and Reforming Communist States,* edited by Vedat Milor. pp. 53–66. Boulder, Colo.: Lynne Rienner.

White, Harrison C. 1992a. *Identity and Control: A Structural Theory of Social Action.* Princeton, N.J.: Princeton University Press.

———. 1992b. "Agency as Control in Formal Networks." In *Networks and Organizations,* edited by Nitin Nohrira and Robert G. Eccles. pp. 92–117. Cambridge, Mass.: Harvard Business School Press.

———. 1993. "Values Come in Styles, Which Mate to Change." In *The Origins of Values,* edited by Michael Hechter, Lynn Nadel, and Richard E. Michod. pp. 63–91. New York: de Gruyter.

White, Harrison C., and Ronald L. Breiger. 1975. "Patterns from Networks." *Society* (July/August).

5

STABILIZATION THROUGH REORGANIZATION ?
Some Preliminary Implications of Russia's Entry into World Markets in the Age of Discursive Quality Standards

CHARLES F. SABEL and JANE E. PROKOP

Without the knowledgeable assistance of the Economic Committee for the Development of the Urals region, and particularly of Sergei Vozdvizhenskiy and Evgeniy Popov, we could not have conducted the discussions with factory managers on which this chapter is based. We are grateful for their help. The names of factories used in the chapter and some characterizations of their products have been altered to preserve the anonymity of our interlocutors. We also benefited greatly from discussions with Ron Gilson, Jeffrey Gordon, and Reinier Kraakman, and especially David Charny, who kept us all looking as we leapt.

Dissenting from the Common Sense of Economic Adjustment

The commonsense conversion of plan to market economies makes stabilization of prices and the creation of private-property relations the first steps to the reconstruction of firms and the rearrangement of production. The argument has the self-evidence that comes from endless repetition: unless domestic prices are stable and freed of distorting subsidies, tariffs, and taxes, no one can determine which combinations of labor and capital will result in products competitive on world markets. Unless property has not only been released from state tutelage, but also placed under the exclusive control of a private owner liable for the consequences of bad decisions but entitled to the rewards of good ones, no one has an incentive to make use of the information provided by stable, undistorted prices. Hence, the commonsense preoccupation of international creditors and the post-Soviet governments, who must respond to them, with plans to stabilize domestic prices and privatize property so as to create markets within which reconstruction takes care of itself.[1]

In its most general form, of course, the commonsense view is eminently sensible: absent information as to potentially competitive production arrangements and incentives to use such information as is available, there will surely be no conversion to world markets. But it is hardly self-evident that the only way to provide such information and incentives is through the price mechanism and apportionment of control to exclusive owners; still less is there warrant to assume that information and incentives provided this way are sufficient to assure restructuring. To the extent that there are efficient alternatives or necessary complements to these mechanisms, and these alternatives and complements can be encouraged by distinctive forms of public action, then current stabilization programs, in their haste to translate common sense into institutional blueprints, may do little to advance and may even obstruct realization of the ends to which they are addressed.

The purpose of this chapter is precisely to describe and present evidence of the increasing centrality to firms the world over subject to international competition of an adjustment mechanism in which price and property operate in the background, not the foreground, of decision-making, and to different effect from that in the standard understanding. In this alternative system, market prices set very general boundary conditions on the possibility of continuing exchange. International standards of a new kind provide finer-grained information about potential partners and their ability to make efficient use of factors of production. These standards do not directly specify features of products or even production processes. Rather, they measure the capacity of a firm to promise credibly to produce what its customers want and to detect and correct shortfalls in performance. Firms that learn what is required for certification under such standards signal their competence to discuss design, production, and continuous improvement of their products with their customers. We will refer to the type of production in which the parties know they depend on such discussion as collaborative, and the standards registering their capacity to engage in it as discursive.

The collaborative flow of information between consumers and firms and firms and their suppliers undermines, we argue, the current, broadly persua-

---

[1] For this view, see Blanchard *et al.* (1990); Dornbusch (1991); Lipton and Sachs (1990); Nuti (1991).

sive understanding of ownership of a firm as residual control over its (nonhuman) assets, where residual control means the owner's exclusive authority to determine the assets' use except as restricted by prior contractual or other obligations. As understood in the advanced countries, ownership as residual control rests on two assumptions: the complementarity of assets and the irreducible ambiguity of contracts (Hart 1988; Hart 1989). Because assets are complementary, their value depends crucially on the precise form in which they are combined; because contracts are in the end incomplete or ambiguous, parties can never specify fully in advance the optimal form of combination given all contingencies. Changes in circumstance or, more broadly, the sheer limits of human foresight mean, therefore, that during the life of an agreement, some party will likely have the opportunity to exploit contractual ambiguities so as to secure more favorable terms as the price of continued participation. This prospect dulls the incentives to enter such agreements in the first place. Ownership as residual control breaks the logjam. In acquiring property in the most complementary of the assets required for production of a certain type, the owner of a firm gains the right to resolve eventual ambiguities in arrangements as self-interest determines. Nonowners will go along for fear that they will be denied access to the use of the (predominantly physical) assets without which their own complementary (primarily human) assets have little value. Thus, the owner as claimant of residual control – responsible for the firm's losses, entitled to benefit from its gains, and correlatively empowered to direct its activities – responds to the need of post-Soviet transition economies to make the economic actors bear the consequences of their actions and the need in the advanced economies to overcome the paralysis that results when the actors assume each to be responsible only to itself.

But in a system of collaborative production, we will see, the notion of ownership of the firm as the right to residual control of its assets loses its purchase. Firms in collaborative production do not have a central, directing agent with the knowledge effectively to choose among ambiguous arrangements the means to a self-interested end, nor, for that matter, could such an agent define in isolation the self-interest of the firm with sufficient resolution to guide strategic choice. The power to decide unilaterally questions that one cannot decide alone is a power one does not have. Accordingly, a system of coordination and incentive that works primarily by creating owners with, and rewarding them for, effective use of a kind of control irrelevant to their actual purposes and possibilities is out of place.

The coordinating mechanism and system of incentives for good performance that do work in such a collaborative world are provided by a new and rapidly diffusing class of agreements among those who jointly control production that is inspired by, but no longer directly tied to, the innovations of postwar Japanese manufacturing. The central feature of these agreements is to link evaluation of performance and the fairness of the distribution of returns – monitoring – to discussion of the possibilities for improvement and the re-evaluation of goals generally – learning. I, therefore, refer to them, and the system of coordination they undergird, as learning by monitoring (Sabel 1994). These arrangements allow wary parties to establish provisional goals and organizational means for prosecuting them, and to refine both, even as they evaluate the advisability of collaborating with one another in the current of any other project. The institutional problem in such a setting is not – as commonly supposed in debates about the construction of transition economies or reform of corporate governance in the advanced ones – the exigent and perhaps insoluble task of transferring proprietary control from the state to entrepreneurs or corporate monitors motivated and capable to organize production or to pick managers who can. The task is rather the more forgiving one of encouraging creation of *de facto* productive partnerships or collaborations among groups within and among firms in which the distribution of returns to particular streams of projects are mutually fixed and jointly adjusted to changing circumstances through disciplined discussion, without need to determine initially or even eventually an owner of last resort for the ensemble of producers as a whole.

The operation of this alternative system in the former "plan" economies, we will argue further, can paradoxically reverse the sequence of development underlying the commonsense view of conversion. As restructuring is informed by the application of discursive standards and does not require determination of ownership in the conventional sense, restructuring in the ex-plan economies can precede and even contribute to stabilization. The more competitive firms become through restructuring, the better able they are to pay their debts to each other and to the state, as well as to pay lump-sum compensation to the parts of their work force or staff that do not find a place in the reorganizing entity. Reductions in debt and tax arrears then reduce inflationary pressures by making firms less dependent on an accommodating monetary policy and the state better able to service its debt. Compensation of losers allows firms to pledge an increasing share of their revenue streams to the remuneration of active participants in production and so allows them to draw boundaries around themselves that may have the form – but not, as we will see, the substance – of corporate entities that look conventional by traditional Western standards. But stable prices and the emergence of corporate entities are supposed to be the preconditions, not the result of, restructuring. More curiously, we will find that within certain limits indefinite monitoring arrangements actually encourage the formation of the managerial teams and structures required for successful adjustment, rather than hindering such progress as the common sense view suggests.

The particulars with which we illustrate and develop these general claims are drawn from current developments in Russia, and specifically from detailed discussions of restructuring projects in progress with managers from 10 leading firms, mostly large and mostly in the metalworking sector, centered on Ekaterinburg in the Urals. But although much of our evidence and the core of our discussion will thus be localized and limited, our claims concerning the growing importance of discursive standards and collaborative production claims are literally global in the sense of pertaining to the character of world markets as a whole.

Indeed, the changes in adjustment mechanisms we describe must be global in sweep, or nearly so, if they are to be of significance for new and less capable entrants to those markets, such as the former plan economies. Otherwise, it would be reasonable to assume, as the commonsense view routinely if silently does, that the ever more demanding conditions of competition in the advanced countries, whatever their effect on adjustment mechanisms there, leave space for less developed economies to compete by rules under which exclusive property arrangements and adjustment by price do make sense. Our argument, on the contrary, is that there is little or no such space, and that the fall of communism and the opening of markets have, under current conditions, created a single world economy where all, despite differences in their capacities, must respect the same new rules. We will, accordingly, refer to evidence from economies such as Brazil, India, Turkey, and Mexico that are also entering into world markets to corroborate the claim that there is indeed only one game in town.

For readers still possessed of their common sense, claims like the foregoing will likely appear implausible, if not simply unintelligible. To secure the suspension of disbelief that any novel argument, regardless of its eventual merits, requires for a reasonable hearing, we therefore examine at the outset two related and particularly plausible grounds for incredulity in the hope of inducing you to wonder about your own assumptions regarding the underpinnings of economic development in the way you may already be wondering about ours.

The first goes to the aptitude of any economy, post-Soviet or not, for advanced forms of cooperation, however these are best understood. In one form this concern expresses a familiar worry about the development capacities of "backward" economies. Surely, the argument goes, a precondition for mastering the most advanced form of capitalism is mastery of the more basic ones?[2] But then only as developing countries shake the habits of tradition or the central plan, as the case may be, can they acquire the experiences and beliefs – the economic culture – required for the next cooperative steps. Even if the institutional requirements for adjustment were different from and less exigent than those in the standard conception in the way we suggest, why assume that Russians, or anyone else in their place, could make use of the theoretically available opportunities?

In another form this concern expresses a more recent worry about the developmental capacities of the advanced countries themselves. Could it not be that the most advanced forms of cooperation – those exemplified, say, by the most successful Japanese firms – require as preconditions forms of sociability and, particularly, a disposition to forbearance and trust among economic actors that are simply given as an historical legacy to some cultures but not others? Taken together the two worries are mutually reinforcing and compel the despairing questions: how can transition economies, inexperienced in capitalism and divided by the struggle to adopt it, dream of mastering the most advanced forms of cooperation if many of the most experienced and consolidated capitalist economies doubt their own ability to do so?

The difficulty with these worries is that they have been an extremely poor guide to actual economic developments in the last century and particularly the postwar period. In the late nineteenth century "late" developers such as Germany and Italy caught up with and in many ways leapfrogged the pioneer of industrialization, Great Britain (Gerschenkron 1962). In the last two decades "late late" developers such as South Korea and Taiwan have shown that they can catch up with and perhaps surpass more developed competitors (Amsden 1989; Wade 1990); and we shall see that the list of the latest developers is longer still. There is, furthermore, good evidence that the advanced countries, despite differences in their cultural endowments are capable of substantial adjustment themselves. Ten years ago, for example, it was widely suspected that U.S. managers and workers could not learn Japanese production methods (the lineal ancestors of the production system described below), and this, ironically enough, because they had learned the capitalist lesson of individualism all too well to be suited for team work (Dore 1983). Today certain U.S. automobile makers have successfully adopted and perhaps even improved Japanese methods (Helper 1994; Nishiguchi 1994); the methods have been widely applied and further developed in many other industries as well; and the problems of

---

[2] In the United States such *marxisant* arguments draw on motifs found most clearly in Rostow (1960).

firms struggling to master them are widely regarded as company, not cultural, problems.

The coarse-grained lesson of these experiences is simply that religions, economies, and political systems contain vast repertoires of complex, often conflicting experiences and interpretations; that is why they have the where-withal to adapt to new environments, and the extinction of a whole society that has survived into the modern age is the rarest of events. Consider only the example of Confucianism: Thirty years ago, the Confucian ethic, with its emphasis on the fixed mutual responsibilities of particular social groups and its apotheosis of stability was regarded as an impediment to economic devel-opment in East Asia. Today it is regarded as encouraging growth, particularly by disciplining state officials to act in the public interest rather than their own, as they are otherwise inclined to do (Johnson 1982; Tai 1989). To assume cultural obstacles to learning is, therefore, to make strong assump-tions not just about what a "cultural" group does, but what it can imagine doing; and assumptions about the limits of a group's powers of imagination and self-reinterpretation more often than not reveal the limits of capacities of those doing the assuming.

A second source of incredulity concerns institutional rather than cultural backwardness. Surely, this objection goes, even in the unlikely case that collaboration in the advanced countries does proceed without the super-vision of a residual corporate owner, then this is only possible because so many experienced monitoring institutions, ranging from banks to financial markets, oversee company behavior in the background and punish mistakes before losses can be transferred to the economy as a whole. Together these institutions form a loosely defined but effective system of governance, which detects faults in the self-monitoring capacities of firms, alerts creditors and other partners to the potential risks, and imposes sanctions if appeals for redress are ignored. Developing countries – Russia, perhaps, first and foremost – lack such background institutions; unsupervised collaboration, however much it looks like advanced forms of cooperation, will thus certainly lead to disaster there.

There is truth in this argument, but of a kind that points as much to the limits of the commonsense understanding of restructuring as to the need for caution in the interpretation of our own findings. The valid core of the objection is that in the last instance firms in the advanced countries *are* held accountable for their mistakes, and the pressure of this accountability does drive them to restructure in distress, often with success. The disquieting admission accompanying the claim is that in the advanced countries the governance institutions, whose purpose is to detect and correct failed strate-gies before they lead firms to the brink of disaster, have proven to work much

158   *Sabel and Prokop*

less well than imagined; and no one has clear, systematic ideas of how pressures for reorganization arising inside and outside of firms combine in any country to actually encourage reconstruction. In the equity systems typical of the Anglo-Saxon countries, the problem is that the equity owners' portfolios are too diversified and their holdings of outstanding shares in individual companies too small for them to have, as a rule, the motive or capacity for informed, self-interested monitoring of particular firms (Gilson and Kraakman 1991). In the bank-monitoring systems typical of Germany and Japan, managers eventually escape the discipline of periodically refinancing bank debt by financing their projects from retained earnings, issuing corporate bonds, and in other ways; and banks, thus cut off from a steady flow of information about corporate performance, then lack the expertise to discipline managers by voting shares or proxies they hold.[3]

Nonetheless, even in the absence of effective supervisory governance substantial restructuring is occurring in both the advanced and developing countries.[4] What we know from horseback empiricism is that firms and groups of firms cut off from state aid and in distress will seek to reorganize themselves with the help of any external partners they find. The caricature-like extension of this observation is that governance does not matter at all. All that is required for successful performance is the pressure for adjustment provided by competitive product markets and some simple mechanism for making managers act in the interests of residual corporate owners (by, for example, giving them a sufficient ownership interest in their firms to benefit directly from appreciation in company value, but too little to entrench themselves against the influence of the actual owners).[5]

But this summary dismissal of governance questions is at once too optimistic and too resigned. It is too optimistic because not all firms or even national economies in dire situations succeed in equal measure; and surely there is a difference between duress in, say, Russia, and duress in the advanced countries. "Not to worry" would strike those who cannot take sanguine outcomes for granted as cavalier and "polyannaish" counsel. But it is too resigned because it assumes, without warrant, that no monitoring institutions will ever do better under the emergent conditions than the ones discredited by current adjustment. Still less does it entertain the possibility

[3] For a survey of bank monitoring systems that shows them to be ineffective when most needed – in financing startups and guiding major reorganizations, see Dittus and Prowse (in volume 1 of this book). See also Edwards and Fischer (1991); Sabel *et al.* (1994). For the shortcomings of bank monitoring in Japan in particular, see Ramseyer (1991).

[4] See, for examples close at hand, the discussion in Coffee (in volume 1 of this book); Stark (in this volume); Stern (1994).

[5] For discussion of an adjustment system of these lines, see Shleifer and Vasiliev (in this volume).

that developing country firms in distress could in their need pioneer these new governance methods or adopt them rapidly from advanced countries once their efficiency is demonstrated there. For the moment and for present purposes, our ignorance about the operation of governance mechanisms is finely balanced. Not having a system of background governance that is indeterminately effective in the current environment may or may not be an obstacle to creating a system better suited to a new one. At the least, adjustment in Russia should not be ruled out because Russian institutions do not provide an answer to a problem that, so far, puzzles our institutions as well.

The argument proceeds in three steps. (1) The first shows how changes in the conditions of competition are moving manufacturing firms to abandon vertical integration as an organizing principle in favor of a decentralized system of collaborative manufacturing. (2) This joint control, we argue, appears sufficient to guide reorganization under current conditions. (3) But it does not make governance structures in the standard sense of back-stopping supervision superfluous; nor is it immediately obvious how monitoring institutions might be designed both to learn from and to instruct collaborative producers.

We discuss what traditional forms of governance may be supplemented or replaced by the mutual monitoring of collaborators using discursive standards, to exercise joint control of production. Price becomes under these conditions a boundary condition on, rather than the most informative signal regarding, the possibilities of exchange. We then present circumstantial evidence for the claim that such an alternative system is coming to dominate transactions in the developing as well as the advanced countries, especially where it counts most – at the margin of activity where new investments are made. The next step is to show that these principles are indeed at work in restructuring in the Urals; but, as in any exploratory investigation, our intent is more to illustrate and establish the plausibility of our claims than to show how they trump all alternative explanations. An exploratory and speculative essay of this kind is by nature provocative, not conclusive. So by way of conclusion, we give a general formulation to our provocative findings and derive from them a counsel of caution for those presumed to be of counsel to the transition economies.

From Vertical Integration to Collaborative Production

A brief juxtaposition of the principles of industrial organization in the world of relatively stable international markets that prevailed roughly until 1975 with those in the world of fragmenting, fluctuating markets that have come to dominate the global economy thereafter indicates why relative prices recede into the background as a guiding principle of coordination within and among firms, and discursive standards come to the fore (Piore and Sabel 1984; Porter 1990). It also explains why this change goes hand in hand with a reconceptualization of the relation between property and actual control of the use of resources.

Two qualifications to our stylization of these changes are best entered here to avoid confusion later. First, for present purposes what matters is that such changes occurred, not why; and we will consequently pass over this latter, complex question by jumping from before to after. Readers who want to know more on this score can find ample, if inconclusive, treatments elsewhere (Boyer 1986). Second, partly as a result of compressing discussion into a lapidary contrast, what follows may suggest that the new model of organization is as consolidated and well understood as the old. Do not be misled. Although there is broad agreement on how the new differs from the old and on some of the general features of the new model organizations that take account of these differences, there is no agreement even in the advanced countries on how whole corporations singly and in collaborative association should be constructed and monitored in conformity with these organizational innovations. Although the style of exposition will temporally suggest otherwise, we will thus argue in this section not only that there is one, novel world economy for all the economic actors, but also that even those with the most experience of this novel order have not been able to make full institutional sense of what they are creating.

In a world of stable markets and product designs, design costs were a small fraction of total production costs because they could be amortized over long production runs. Design times were a matter of indifference because, however long, they were only a moment in very long product life cycles. This same stability also induced firms to produce key components on dedicated or special purpose machines, whose cost could likewise be amortized over the long production runs. As such capital equipment was good for producing any one make or model of a final product, the firm that manufactured the final product had strong incentives to own it. An outside owner, after all, might threaten to withhold production of an indispensable part unless the sale price were renegotiated in its favor. Hence, the vertical integration of production widely remarked as characteristic of this period and, concomitantly, an understanding of property as residual control. The reason firms owned so many of the units that supplied components of their final products was precisely to eliminate through exclusive ownership the possibility that an outsider could use gaps or ambiguities in contractual agreements to hold up the vulnerable customer.

By the same logic relations with suppliers not owned by the end producer were regulated primarily by price. Such suppliers worked to detailed specifications provided by the customers. The average quality of the output had to meet certain standards; but quality levels could vary around the average requirements without substantially inconveniencing the customer because with stable markets the costs of maintaining inventory reserves against defects were thought to be insubstantial. Large customers had no reason to prefer one potential supplier over another except for price – the cheaper the better. New entrants to world markets could thus find their footing by supplying less demanding components or products to firms in the advanced countries that designed, performed such assembly as was required, and then sold the final product. Firms that began in this way were thought to acquire through practice the capacity to take on more demanding and rewarding tasks. This view of economic apprenticeship as organized by price negotiations among residual owners continues, on our reading, to inform much of the common sense of reconversion, although it is seldom formulated explicitly.

In the world of fluctuating markets that prevails after 1975, design costs and times *do* matter, and in ways that undo the logic of special-purpose machines, vertical integration, coordination of supply through price, and apprenticeship through low-cost production. As demand fluctuates and differentiates, product life cycles become shorter and shorter, and products become more and more complex amid shifting combinations of rapidly changing technologies. Not even the largest firms can command the expertise and investment capital necessary to keep abreast of all the developments relevant to current and anticipated production needs. Under these circumstances large and small firms worldwide have begun to adopt a model of organization that grows out of, but is today no longer directly tied to, the efforts of Japanese manufacturers to improve the U.S. system of mass production while adopting it to the conditions of their own postwar economy (Shimokawa 1993; Wada 1991).

The solution with regard to design is codevelopment (Clark, Fujimoto, and Chew 1987). Instead of designing products as integral wholes, firms decompose them into discrete subsystems or modules, specify the performance requirements of each, and then entrust further elaboration of the specification and design to independent firms specializing in the respective lines of work. This economizes on development costs and times in several mutually reinforcing ways. First, the customer benefits from expertise the specialist has acquired solving related problems for other clients and pays, in effect, a pro-rated share of the costs of producing such knowledge, rather than assuming them all. Second, the concurrent efforts of all systems suppliers to master the tasks set them produce a steady flow of suggestions about how to modify the overall design or significant parts of it. This simultaneous problem solving directs attention to solutions that might have escaped notice if design work had proceeded sequentially from the most important component to the next and the next. By the same token, it reduces total design time. This is just a variant of the familiar idea that conception can often be expedited by execution, as in the low-budget film device of finishing an incomplete screen play by taking cues from each day's shooting.

Analogous changes reshape the organization of production (Shingo 1989). Because production runs are short, defects in design that affect manufacturability have to be detected before production is running, not afterwards. This means that module or part designers must exchange information about potential difficulties and ways of eliminating them with the shop floor just as they would exchange information on other aspects of design among themselves and with the designers responsible for the product as a whole. Again, because production runs are short, dedicated equipment is uneconomic. What is required instead are flexible machines or assembly layouts that can cheaply and quickly be converted from production of one part or module to another. Finally, when production runs are short and product changeovers frequent, the penalties for low or fluctuating quality levels become prohibitive. The cost of maintaining reserves against defects become intolerably high as modules proliferate and product life cycles shorten. To make matters worse, the chances and costs of missing a market entirely if supply of the product is disrupted by defective parts increase correspondingly. The solution is inventoryless or just-in-time production, where parts are made in effect one at a time so that defects are immediately detected and their causes eliminated as a work piece passes from station to station, ideally without ever entering inventory.

These changes lead away from vertical integration as a principle of industrial organization and toward the system of collaborative manufacturing sketched above (Nishiguchi 1989; Smitka 1991). In the fluctuating world system we have been describing, direct ownership of (most) design and production facilities by the end-product manufacturer is not a paying proposition. Firms want to reduce their pro-rated share of development costs by having module designers acquire expertise at the expense of other customers. A design firm that is not dependent on any single customer is *de facto* an independent firm; and the more large customers want their design partners to diversify their clientele, the less their (design related) motives for owning them outright. Moreover, the less predictable the direction of technological development – and such unpredictability is, of course, among the premises of the fluctuating economic world – the less willing a final producer will be to make a long-term investment in a particular area of technical expertise, diversification of the expert's market aside. Similarly, the switch from dedicated to flexible machines and from buffered to inventoryless production reduces the motives for designers to own (most) manufacturing facilities. Indeed, just as end-product producers want to benefit from the economies of scope – the greater the range of products, the cheaper the cost of extending the range – acquired by module designers through diversification, so module designers want to benefit from the economies of scope in manufacturing that their producers may gain in switching setups frequently to accumulate many and constantly changing clients.

The linchpin of this system is learning by monitoring as a principle of coordinating the decentralized parts by disciplined goal setting. Recall that it links discussion of actual performance by the cooperating parties to discussion of how to improve operations given that performance. Just-in-time production provides a particularly clear example because the organization of production itself directly embodies the principle of coordination. A defect introduced at one work station literally stops the flow of production, so discussion of improving the production setup by identifying and eliminating the disruption becomes a precondition for continuing production at all. Strictly analogous disciplines allow groups to set goals and metrics for assessing progress in achieving them in relation to design (value-added engineering) or production projects (statistical process controls, single-minute exchange of dies) undertaken jointly with other groups, and then jointly to revise both goals and metrics as the progress advances (Nishiguchi 1994; Smitka 1991).

Notice that learning by monitoring addresses the problems of ambiguity endemic to a volatile world by identifying and reducing them through explicit discussion rather than by assigning responsibility for their resolution to an owner with rights to residual control. In learning by monitoring, the normal gap between the promise to perform an action and performance is so reduced by the exchange of information that differences of perspective are detected before they harden into differences of interpretation and thence into disputes requiring arbitration. "Long-term supply agreements" of the kind now proliferating through U.S. industry, in fact, specify *only* the forms of information exchange and provide no separate machinery for dispute resolution (Esser 1993).[6]

---

[6] Notice further that learning by monitoring relations differ from and resolve problems associated with relational contracts, the form of coordination often said to be suited to regulating collaborative exchanges in volatile environments. Relational contracts go beyond standard or neoclassical contracts in that they acknowledge the impossibility of specifying all contingencies in complex joint efforts and provide rules for arbitrating disputes arising from conflicting interpretations of the agreement (Williamson 1986, pp. 104–5). But constant

There is, finally, the question of incentives. To participate in collaboration of the kind we are describing, individuals and groups must be assured, on the one hand, that the resulting flows of information will not be used to their disadvantage. Otherwise, they will obstruct such flows. On the other, they must be assured that extraordinary efforts at problem solving will be rewarded; otherwise, they have no incentive to exceed the ordinary. In the Japanese system, "lifetime" employment (defined as ending for practical purposes at age 55) and long-term, renewable contracts are the means for meeting the first condition for, respectively, employees and subcontractors who meet expectations of acceptable performance. Promotion to higher-level tasks – coordinating the problem solving of one or more work groups, coordinating the efforts of lower tiers of (sub-) subcontractors for suppliers – is the reward for superior performance (Koike 1988). Promotions are awarded by what Aoki (1988) calls a "ranking hierarchy," whose purpose is precisely to identify the individuals and groups best able to change the organization. But these institutions are merely particular cases – with distinctive problems[7] – of a general class of solutions whose boundaries and precise definition are being explored by firms the world over as they intro-duce the new methods of organization and coordination with experimental compensation mechanisms of their own devising.

Next we revisit the standard notions of ownership and residual control and price as the principle mechanisms of economic coordination to show how these are being transformed by the spread of collaborative production.

The Factor-Controlled Firm

It follows directly from the new logic of decentralization of production and the ensuing discussions among collaborators that the very idea of residual control has a ghostly significance in the emerging system.[8] What is at issue in the discussions between "customer" and "supplier" is precisely the joint regulation of "proprietary" control. We put the familiar terms of subcon-tracting arrangements in quotation marks to indicate how awkwardly they fit in the new setting. If one firm assesses the ability of another to exchange

arbitration produces a web of precedents and rules that so bind adjudication of disputes that, in a turbulent world, it becomes impossible to resolve fundamental disputes without threat-ening the understandings that maintain peace among the parties (Kolb 1983).

[7] See, for example, the discussion in Gao (1994); Ramseyer (1991); Sabel (1995).

[8] The notion of an interregnum between governance structures and the notion of a factor-controlled firm owe much to discussions with Reinier Kraakman and Ronald Gilson, who are, of course, not accountable for our debts.

information to produce results so novel that they influence the subsequent behavior of both in unpredictable ways, then surely neither supposes itself able to give definitive instructions to the other. Neither, on reflection, can know precisely what it will become as a result of the association. It is as natural to think of both as partners or collaborators as it would be artificial to declare one or the other in possession of ultimate control. Whereas in the standard corporation the equity owners buy or rent the factors of production and use them at their discretion, subject only to explicit terms of the purchases or leases, in the collaborative alternative it is, at the limit, the factors of production – suppliers of goods, labor, and capital – who jointly exercise residual control.

To see how the factor-controlled firm arises spontaneously from collaborative production, yet by its operation automatically neither creates the forms of self-monitoring required for governance nor adapts existing governance institutions to that task, consider a skeletal collaborative venture consisting of a manager-operator, a single supplier, and a single bank creditor. The manager-operator designs the product with the supplier's help, then finds financing for its production and markets it, being paid a small fixed salary and a large bonus that increases with revenues and the difference between revenues and costs. The supplier codesigns the product and manufactures it. It is guaranteed a fixed share (100 percent) of the production of the codesigned product at an agreed (but periodically decreasing) price, plus a fixed share of the proceeds of productivity gains in excess of those needed to meet the moving price target. The bank provides credit at a fixed rate of interest, but also efficiency-improving information such as advice about possible co-investments, the advantages and disadvantages of alternatives to proposed investments, and sources of low-cost finance. It is guaranteed a fixed, 100 percent share in all rounds of debt financing.

Thus, all benefit directly from decisions that increase the long-term output of the firm and directly or indirectly from decisions that reduce the cost of the input each supplies to the company. The manager and the supplier, for example, each stand to gain twice from a redesign of the product that cuts its cost of production and the cost of subsequent improvement – once because the new design may lead to increased revenues, and once again because costs decrease even if revenues remain constant. Similarly, the bank stands to benefit twice by providing information that reduces the risk of an investment along with the investment capital – once by increasing the firm's chances of successful, continual expansion, and again by reducing (via lower, risk-adjusted reserves) the cost to itself of providing funds to a customer. Imagine further that the nominal owner of the "final" producer is a family trust whose beneficiaries, the founders' heirs, are content to leave the manager-operator alone so long as they receive, as they do, returns on their investment at slightly above the risk-free rate. And for the sake of completeness, finally, imagine further that by agreement among the collaborators and the trust, any economic residual – the remainder of proceeds less all costs of production, new investment, dividends, and taxes – is set aside in a reserve fund to provide assistance to any of the collaborators in case of distress connected with the joint venture.

The paradox of such an entity, given current understandings of the well ordered corporation is this: the collaborators possess residual control of their activities, at least in whatever sense that term is still relevant in their situation. Periodic decisions to approve, redefine, or abandon projects as experience warrants reshape their economic identities; and what is residual control if not the power to determine which of the many economic interests at play in joint production shall determine action in the future? But, it is unclear how the factor-controlled firm might organize review of its normal collaborative practices so as to avoid the errors against which conventional governance structures would protect firms, if only they worked. Nor is it clear how conventional governance systems can be modified to supervise effectively the new forms of collaborative exchange.

Looked at from either perspective, the problem is the same. Collaborative production works because of the extraordinarily informative, mutual relations it creates; but the kinds of decisions typical of governance matters – whether to abandon a whole line of business, acquire a new firm, or sell the corporation to an outsider – are now normally made by entities disconnected from and, more fundamentally, operating by different forms of deliberation from, those engaged in the new collaborative relations. To monitor such relations, it seems that a governance structure would have to become in effect one of the collaborators, exchanging information on like terms with the others. There are, indeed, signs that this is occurring. Evaluation of performance and especially performance measures (and the accounting practices to which they are related) by work teams and production units is broadening into a more comprehensive and higher level review of corporate goals and performance (Kaplan and Norton 1992; 1993). In addition, pension funds and banks are being urged to participate more actively in the monitoring of corporations they own and fund; in acquiring and providing firms the kind of efficiency-improving information necessary to make such activism effective, they would by stages transform themselves from disciplinarian monitors to collaborators (Coffee, Gilson, and Lowenstein 1995).

But it is hard to see how to pass from such beginnings to a mechanism that addresses the hard questions of governance, such as the sale of jointly controlled assets or the purchase of new ones, without resorting to an exercise of authority inconsistent with the principles of day-to-day collaboration. For such matters are normally decided by vote, with votes weighted to reflect ownership of the firm's assets, whereas decisions made by the deliberative logic of learning-by-monitoring relations turn on the actors' knowledge of the situation and its possibilities, not on rights anterior to and independent of the questions at hand. Nor is it possible to reconcile this conflict by assimilating the factor-owned firm to the familiar form of the partnership as embodied in the law firm or the cooperatively owned dairy. These partnerships function, it has been observed, because the partners supply similar if not homogeneous inputs, and valuation of their contributions and hence their claims to carry a corresponding weight in constitutional decisions is (relatively) easy to assess (Hansmann 1988). This is precisely not the case for the factor-owned firm, which is defined by the heterogeneity of its *de facto* owners. Learning by monitoring renders this heterogeneity tractable day to day; whether it can be extended to constitutional questions is still an open question.

We may interpret the current situation, therefore, as an interregnum characteristic of transitions from one great principle of economic organization to another. Mass production demonstrated its efficiency advantages over certain kinds of craft production in the last third of the nineteenth century. Yet it took decades before the mass production corporation was consolidated as an institution (to say nothing of the consolidation of the macroeconomic policies on which the stability of that corporation was based). Seen this way, the present is a similar time betwixt and between: after the first convincing demonstrations of the advantages of collaborative production in volatile markets, yet before the consolidation of the mechanisms by which such collaboration can effectively police itself.[9] In any event, the fact that the Russians, too, are without answers to these questions should not be counted as a reason to be especially skeptical of their results.

But it is also possible that we are looking too hard for a new answer to an old question whose significance has dwindled with the passing of the world in which it arose. The more firms monitor one another in collaborative production, the less necessary traditional forms of monitoring by "outside" governance structures may be. That is speculative. What is beyond doubt is

---

[9] A speculative interpretation of key episodes of restructuring in, for example, the United States and Germany is that outside directors or their equivalent are reducing the power of the managers at the head of the corporate hierarchy to encourage decentralization. Keeping track of the reorganization that ensues plainly absorbs the monitors' attention. But eventually they will be pressed to address the problem of how to monitor the new entity whose creation they are superintending; it would be surprising if the same governance institutions that are good at decapitating hierarchies proved adept at supervising the operation of decentralized institutions.

that such mutual monitoring has become more extensively formalized; that under these conditions, prices become boundary conditions on cooperation; and that actual coordination is conducted in the disciplined language of discursive standards. These are the next and final themes of our contrast between the worlds of stable and volatile production.

Target Prices and Discursive Standards

Recall that with long production runs suppliers' bids to produce a given part at a particular price provide sufficient criteria for selection because the customer, who provides the design, can easily judge performance, and short-falls within wide limits are tolerable. But when designs are, in contrast, fixed only after exchanges among different design specialists and between them and manufacturing facilities, prices become boundary conditions for trans-actions, not a sufficient mechanism for selecting partners. Prices still matter because if the selling price of a particular class of final good exceeds certain limits, the good becomes effectively unsalable in its usual market, regardless of performance characteristics. To avoid this, firms in the fluctuating economy estimate the optimal sale price of planned products – the target price – and then set further subtarget prices for individual modules in relation to the overall ceiling. Violation of these limits plainly puts the planned project at risk (Asanuma 1989; Sako and Helper 1994; Smitka 1991).

But just as plainly, offers to provide designs, modules, or components at or below the target prices are, by themselves, simply not informative enough to allow the customers to choose among competing suppliers. The bid alone tells the customer only that the supplier can probably provide a product that meets the initial minimum performance specifications at the proposed price. What the customers need to know in addition is how likely the supplier is to develop and realize more ambitious designs or more efficient production setups in collaboration with others, and how timely and reliable the supplier's performance will be. As the bid is effectively a promise to do something the supplier has never done before in that precise form, and which the customer alone cannot do or even fully define, the bid, so long as it meets the target price, is meaningless unless accompanied by a reliable assessment of the supplier's capacity to do as promised.

Here is where discursive standards now sweeping through the world economy come in. Conventional standards specify and thus permit measure-ment of various combinations of two types of performance characteristics. The first are attributes of products: the tensile strength of various grades of steel, the weight per unit length of yarn, the dimensions of paper, or the number of instructions executed per second by a microprocessor. Such standards allow buyers and sellers to know they are talking about the same thing when they conclude a transaction for a particular product. The Deutsche Industrie Normen provide countless examples of such specifications. Other standards put greater emphasis on the attributes of production processes by specifying by what procedures a particular operation is to be conducted or how the results of particular operations are to be certified or both. Welds completed in compliance with such standards, for example, will have been executed using methods fixed according to the alloys concerned and the environment to which they will be exposed, then tested for conformity with requirements; and the results of these tests will be documented as further specified by the standards. Such, for example, are the standards maintained by the American Petroleum Institute; they assure not only that buyer and seller are referring to the same things in their negotiations, but that the buyer can expect the seller to have diligently verified the accuracy of all representations and to be able to trace, with the help of obligatory documentation, the origin of defects that escaped detection.

Judged against such conventional certification procedures, the new discursive standards appear thin, even vacuous. They specify neither the characteristics of products nor features of production processes – nor do they even prescribe methods for documenting the latter. What they do instead is establish procedures by which firms can be certified as competent to assess, and in that sense warranted to make claims regarding their capability to perform as promised.

Under the most comprehensive and widely acknowledged of these standards, the ISO 9000 series maintained by the International Office of Standards (ISO) in Geneva, Switzerland, a production facility is certified as capable of designing and delivering products and services to customers' requirements in all areas of economic endeavor (Clements 1993; Lamprecht 1993; Peach 1992).[10] To obtain certification, a firm must convince a registrar (whose authority derives from association with the standard-maintaining body) that it can respond systematically to systematic challenges to its assertions of competence. Typically, therefore, the registrar will raise such

---

[10] The ISO 9000 series originated in standards developed by the British government during World War II to assure quality in munitions production. The rapid conversion of civilian firms inexperienced in munitions manufacture to military production, combined with wartime shortages of skilled workers, made quality problems almost unavoidable. As the enemy could not be expected to report the performance of munitions fired against them, methods were devised by which firms could secure the quality of their products by monitoring their production processes, and inspectors could evaluate the reliability of their self-monitoring (Clements 1993, pp. 6–7).

questions as: how does the firm know that it understands its customers' expectations? How does it assure itself that it can deliver the designs and products it promises to provide in accordance with those expectations? How would the firm detect and correct shortfalls in performance? Answers are judged correct to the extent that they reflect both a good fit between firms' organization, technology, and procedures and the environment of expectations within which these operate, and an understanding by the firm of how it would have to adjust to variations in that environment. In theory, therefore, the ISO standards do not require firms to adopt any particular technology, form of organization, or procedures at all, although in practice some ends can be obtained by such a limited range of means that to pursue them does entail particular operational choices. What certification under the standards does do, as we noted at the outset, is qualify a firm as a reliable interlocutor in eventual discussion about its performance capacities. As you will have already noticed, it is precisely such warranted information about performance in relation to promises that customers in the new, volatile economy need to supplement price bids in choosing collaborators. Certification does not, of course, replace detailed discussion of projects and assessments of the chances of their realization, but it does establish that the collaborators are likely to understand particular assertions by the other because both can assume a common understanding of criteria by which such assertions can be justified. ISO certification and the many self-monitoring disciplines to which it is related provide, rather, the dialects of the language in which such discussions are conducted.

The Central Significance of Change at the Margin

As our argument regarding the significance of the new conditions of competition is an all-or-nothing proposition – either the new disciplines are influential everywhere, or else from the vantage point of remote corners of the world economy, they might as well be influential nowhere – we must address, briefly, the questions: how widespread is the new system? How influential does it give signs of becoming? Evidently the bufferless production systems and collaborative supply arrangements have been diffusing to the United States, Great Britain, and Southeast Asia from Japan via transplants since the mid-1980s, and from the United States to the rest of Western Europe and much of Latin America more recently. How far have they gone?

The most reliable surveys of the speed of the new methods in the United States, as measured by the diffusion of clusters of organizational innovations such as quality circles and work teams that organize the flow of production themselves, suggest apparently modest results. About 10 percent of American industrial firms are operating by the principles set out above.[11] This estimate is supported by the repeated observation by those with expert knowledge that almost every local economy in the United States has a few – but only a few – examples of firms succeeding by the new methods. But with regard to the propagation of any radical innovation – and the shift from mass to inventoryless production is certainly that – diffusion to 10 percent of potential adopters is more progress than it seems. Before the 10 percent threshold is reached, firms hesitate to adopt the innovation for fear of paying a penalty for pioneering; after the threshold has been crossed, they are prompted to introduce it for fear of paying a penalty for lagging.

That the situation is shifting from experimental to routine deployment of these methods in the United States is further corroborated by a look at the margin of development defined by new investment in plants and equipment. It has now become standard practice in undertaking such investment in automotive engine, semiconductor, or petrochemical plant to review the performance of technologies and organizations in the most efficient comparable facilities worldwide and to apply the results of these benchmarks to design choices in the investment project. Investment plans prepared in this way, therefore, constitute surveys of the universe of best practice plants of their type. An examination of a half dozen documents of this type from diverse sectors in the last several years makes it clear that, without exception, major new projects are conceived with some version of the new principles in mind, both with regard to the organization of production within the planned facility and its relation to suppliers.[12] All of this is accompanied, the

---

[11] Osterman (1994) finds that some 30 percent of firms surveyed had introduced at least one such innovation. Assuming that some of these firms consider such measures as experimental, but that there is little incentive to multiply unpromising experiments, it is reasonable to raise the bar and count companies as having adopted the new model of organization only if they have in place at least three of the programs by which it operates. Only 10 percent of the firms in Osterman's survey meet that test (Teixeira and Mishel 1993).

[12] See, for example, "Midwest Motor" Company (1991a; 1991b) on file with the author. A composite of reports from the trade press and academic sources illustrates these developments in almost every industry. The most "innovative" of the big three U.S. automobile makers, for example, now signs four-year contracts with its suppliers, with whom it also codevelops modules and systems in just the way described (Helper 1994; Raia 1994). According to the vice president for procurement and supply and general manager of large car operations at Chrysler, suppliers "have seats at the table on every new car and truck project we undertake – and they're aboard from day one. . . . More than 300 supplier personnel now have offices inside our Technical center. . . ." (Raia 1994, p. 45). A Coopers and Lybrand survey found, as such increased participation would require, that "Midwest auto suppliers are adding engineering support in overwhelming numbers to meet auto makers' design demands" (Barkholz 1994). German auto makers establishing U.S. subsidiaries are hiring executives from Japanese trans-

foregoing would suggest, by acceleration in the growth of interest in the new discursive standards.[13] Discussions of reorganization under way in the advanced regional economies of Western Europe, such as Baden-Württemberg, point in the same direction (Kern 1994; Kern and Sabel 1994).

Spread of the methods to developing countries is likewise explosive. The most recent survey of the deployment of computer numerical control equipment in Brazil, Mexico, India, Turkey, and Venezuela shows that use of such equipment is growing at rates far above those estimated in the mid-1980s. Less than a decade ago knowledgeable observers in these countries knew firsthand of almost all the relevant machines in the domestic economy (Edquist and Jacobsson 1988); today they have trouble keeping count of new installations (Alam 1994; Ansal 1994; de Quadros Carvalho 1994; Dominguez and Brown 1994; Tamayo, Cartaya, and Alonso 1994).

From the point of view of our argument, it is particularly revealing that firms in all these countries give as their principal reasons for adopting these machines the need to meet the current, demanding quality standards of their customers. Their use is typically accompanied by the same kinds of changes in organization that accompany introduction of the fluctuating world model in the advanced countries. And in combination the new technologies and organizations do allow the firms to increase their flexibility substantially. The set-up times for the machines are reduced from hours to minutes and the distribution of output by lot size shifts dramatically to shorter production runs – just the results observed in advanced countries that have mastered the use of the new methods, often after several expensive tries. Firms using new technologies, moreover, tend to increase exports as a share of their output to levels that exceed the average share of exports of industrial goods in the national economy. In Venezuela, to take an extreme case, virtually the *only* metalworking firms exporting their goods appear to be those using the CNC

---

plants and pursuing the same forms of collaboration with suppliers in an explicit effort to experiment with forms of organization that can then be applied in Germany (Lowell 1994); and so on.

[13] For example, despite widespread skepticism of their ability to act in concert (Zuckerman 1994), General Motors, Ford, and Chrysler, working through the Automotive Industry Action Group, have also agreed to standardize their supplier audits in conformance with the ISO standard. For example, second- and third-tier suppliers that pass muster in one firm's audit will not be reaudited by the others for at least two years (Plumb 1993). Two questions regarding management's responsibility in the maintenance of quality systems taken from the evaluation form provided to suppliers in anticipation of audits suggest the organizational criteria underlying the standard: "Is a multi-disciplinary approach used in the design process with direct input in decision making? Is company level data focusing on competitors and/or appropriate benchmarks used for improving quality, productivity, and operation efficiency?" (General Motors 1994, pp. 8–9).

technologies (Tamayo, Cartaya, and Alonso 1994). Finally, although the new machines cost more than the equipment they replaced, their greater flexibility and precision made it possible to deploy them more intensively at a greater range of tasks, and there was no evidence in the survey that increasing capital costs, absolutely or per unit of output, creates barriers to entry. Indeed, some of the most successful firms in the survey were newly founded small companies that started off by using CNC technology.[14] The most recent general work on production organization in the developing economies captures nicely this movement in its title: "Easternisation" (Kaplinsky 1994).[15]

Case studies confirm and deepen those impressions. A report on a Mexican automobile assembly plant, the subsidiary of a U.S.-Japanese joint venture, describes an experimental system of team work and job rotation so effective at encouraging acquisition of skill and the resolution of problems by production workers that the plant matches the quality levels of the best performers in the parent corporations without the need for a distant cadre of craft workers specialized in setup or maintenance (Shaiken 1990). A case study of the Malaysian textile industry revels a breathtakingly rapid shift to extremely sophisticated production technology as labor markets tighten and recent vintage Japanese equipment comes onto the secondhand market (Rasiah 1993). What gives these reports particular weight is the authors' surprise, verging on amazement, at their own findings. The author of the automobile study is a former skilled tradesman with long experience in the U.S. auto industry. The idea that production workers – in Mexico – can learn to do almost all the tradesmen's work without benefit of apprenticeship plainly intrigues and disconcerts him. The author of the Malaysian textile industry study was not searching for rapid productivity gains. Rather, he was drawn to the case by the puzzling finding that wages in that industry were rising rapidly despite a political regime inimical to unions and dedicated more generally to keeping wages low to safeguard competitiveness. In social science, as in science in general, unexpected findings have the truest ring.

On this evidence the opening of markets and the fall of communism have indeed unified the economic world; but the one world that is emerging has little place for the forms of industrial apprenticeship supposed in the commonsense account of the conversion from plan to market economies. However much this circumstance has escaped attention in official and

---

[14] The explosion of interest in certification under the ISO standard in developing countries is news. ISO certifications of Brazilian companies have increased from 18 to 410 in the last three years; government projections are that 5,500 firms will be certified by the end of 1997 (Brooke 1994). There are frequent references to ISO in the trade press as a "*de facto* minimum requirement for those wishing to compete globally" (Sprow 1992, p. 77).

[15] See also generally, Humphrey (1995).

academic discussion in the advanced countries, it is well known and of decisive importance to firms from the former plan economies trying to enter world markets, as we shall see next in our discussion of industrial adjustment in the Urals.

Reorganization amid Instability: The Sverdlovsk Region

The Sverdlovsk region in the Northern and Middle Urals, centered on Ekaterinburg, its capital, is well situated to test our beliefs about the global reach and orienting influence of the new discursive conditions of competition. It is far enough from Moscow – 889 miles and two and a half hours by air – to be at the margins of the intrigues of the central elite, and far enough, too, from borders with the advanced countries (Berlin is roughly 2,000 miles to the west, Tokyo about 3,800 miles to the east) to discourage dreams of economic salvation through amalgamation with a prosperous neighbor. Flights of desperate fancy aside, firms here know they are on their own. At the same time the region is a major industrial center, with a proud history of repeatedly mastering demanding technologies rapidly and effectively. Its 4.7 million inhabitants (3.2 percent of Russia's population) produce 14.5 percent of Russia's ferrous metals, 17.3 percent of nonferrous metals, 4.3 percent of construction materials, and 3.8 percent of metal-working and machine-building products (Regional State Property Fund 1993, #1457).

The core of the modern economy grows out of the mining and metallurgy firms established at the beginning of the eighteenth century in connection with Peter the Great's drive to industrialize Russia. By the end of the century, the Urals heavy industry produced two-thirds of Russia's iron and 90 percent of its copper. The region boomed in the early years of the nineteenth century upon discovery of new deposits of gold, platinum, and precious stones. After a bust in the mid-nineteenth century, the arrival of the railroad in the 1880s led the way to further industrial development. Sverdlovsk became a major supplier to Asiatic Russia and the Orient of pig iron, rolled metals, gold, platinum, copper, timber, grain, meat, butter, and flax. It became a major armaments producer during World War II, when approximately 200 industrial plants were evacuated there from European Russia. According to unofficial estimates, in 1990 more than one-third of the work force of the region was employed in defense-related enterprises. Pipelines laid in the Soviet period made Sverdlovsk a distribution hub for oil and natural gas produced in the surrounding regions of Perm, Orenburg, Tyumen, and Komi; much of the large machine-building industry in the region makes the capital goods needed to keep these resources flowing. Forty-three percent of industrial employment is concentrated in this sector, although it accounts for less than 1 percent of regional exports, which are dominated by ferrous and nonferrous metals and other raw materials.

Sverdlovsk is only the largest of the seven regions that together constitute the Urals. Similarly dependent on heavy and defense industry and increasingly convinced of their distinct subnational (though not ethnic) identity, these regions have begun to create common political and economic institutions. One of the first, and probably the most influential, is the intergovernmental Association for the Development of the Urals Region. Its Economic Committee, which connects several networks of industrial managers, financiers, government officials, and scientists, acts as the discussion forum and lobby for much of the generation of enterprise managers that came of age under the old order but is trying to adjust to the new. There is also talk of creating a Urals bank and regional television network.

By design we concentrated our attention on the metalworking and electromechanical sectors rather than metallurgy. The differential between (low) Russian and (high) world market prices for copper, aluminum, platinum, and other metals has, at least until recently, created arbitrage opportunities so great that domestic metals producers with export licenses could enrich themselves without giving a thought to restructuring. For our purposes the firms of interest were those that cannot survive by arbitrage, are too detached from Moscow ministries to count on substantial subsidies, and recognize that the inferior quality of their products makes them unsalable even in developing countries. They realize, therefore, that they must reorganize to produce marketable products or go bankrupt. Almost all the larger manufacturing firms in the Urals are in that situation. Several of our interlocutors told us early in discussions that one of the most humiliating experiences of their lives was the discovery that goods they once proudly made were now disdained by former customers in Turkey (or India or Syria) who had come to expect better things. We investigated a group of firms generally held to be typical of those squarely facing the resulting choices.

By commonsense standards the whole region should have come to a standstill. Inflation – which hovered over 25 percent per month for most of 1992 and 1993, and averaged 7 to 8 percent per month for the first half of 1994 – resulted in interest rates so high that industrial firms could seldom get credit from local banks even on usurious terms (Federal Information Systems 1994, #1333). Even leaving aside the unavailability of credit, it is hard to say whether firms are operating in a price regime of any kind, let alone a regime of world market prices. Most firms are indebted to their suppliers, in arrears to their employees, and owed money by their customers; their liabilities and assets are so hard to evaluate that it is almost meaningless to attempt any conventional financial evaluation of the companies. Payment for current sales and current purchases, furthermore, is often delayed, or settled by barter, so that it is difficult to arrive at a reliable assessment of costs and revenues. A new tax system imposes what enterprises regard as a confiscatory levy on profits – by some estimates it reaches 90 percent. In any case the system is so complex that a company's tax burden depends crucially on how successive operations are reported to the tax authorities and how the authorities interpret the reports. A procession of substantial assessments for underpayment of taxes and legal suits – many of them successful – to overturn those claims demonstrates, in any case, the potentially ruinous ambiguities of the situation. Under these conditions firms should be unable to know what they are looking for by way of products, and still less how to begin making them.

If the absence of a price regime should have been as a commonsense proposition disorienting, so the amorphous property regime in the Urals should have been demotivating. Most of the industrial firms in the region have been privatized in recent years under the second of the three provisions of the Privatization Program of 1992, which allowed current employees to acquire 51 percent of their company's initial stock for a nominal price reflecting the firm's pre-inflation book value. (The few exceptions were firms whose products were deemed essential to national defense or public health by their respective ministries or which had acted under earlier laws to establish themselves as lease enterprises or cooperatives.) This form of privatization certainly freed the firms from control by the state. But rather than concentrate property in the hands of a residual owner, privatization diffused and collected it within the firm in a way that – again as a commonsense proposition – should have paralyzed reorganization.

Because of their connection to military production and because of features of the plan economy we will take up in a moment, most of the firms are obviously active in areas of production that will not be sustainable under market conditions. Because of the general inefficiency of Soviet production, moreover, even firms that are engaged exclusively in potentially viable activities currently employ far too many workers by international standards. In either case, therefore, reorganizations will mean substantial layoffs. Since only a few managers and workers can be sure of their indispensability, and the great majority will be, at best, unsure of their prospects, diffusion of ownership to the collective of incumbent employees should lead to paralysis: every investment plan should reasonably be vetoed by a majority fearful that the minority associated with it will divert the benefits to itself and socialize costs. The result would be a stalemate in which the new private owners can only agree on the need to secure new state subsidies.

These expectations to the contrary, the firms we saw were extraordinarily purposeful and deliberate in restructuring.[16] They are learning to select investment projects that allow for the piece-by-piece reorganization of the firm, produce financial returns, and suggest further projects, often in association with outsiders. The broad orientation of these efforts results almost directly from the general desolation of the post-Soviet economy. The entire industrial infrastructure of Russia – the pipelines, the power transmission and switching equipment, and so on – will have to be substantially improved if domestic firms are to produce the range of goods typical of advanced economies. Firms that can supply replacements that are compatible with the installed capital base and can, therefore, link these and components made to international standards will have large markets, as will a second group of firms supplying capital goods, also compatible with Russian and international standards, to the replacement-supplying group. The surprise, for which you are prepared, is that the property regime, despite its diffusions, does not hinder reorganization and that discursive standards help guide that reorganization in the absence of informative prices. We consider each in turn.

The property regime allows reorganization precisely because, as increasingly in the advanced countries, it operates as a mechanism for regulating the distribution of the gains and costs of adjustment, not as a device for establishing an exclusive locus of control over resources. The key to the arrangement is a widespread, if usually implicit, bargain in which employees – workers and managers alike – obtain such security as is obtainable in return for letting experimental reorganization proceed. Diffusion of ownership among employees means that shifting coalitions of workers and managers can discipline decision-makers of whom they disapprove by threatening to sell, or actually selling, their shares to outsiders who will replace the incumbents or, upon obtaining more than 25 percent of the outstanding stock, secure the power to veto their decisions. In most cities, not to mention isolated company towns, the threat of riot further deters unpopular decisions.

---

[16] In a recent interview, Russian Deputy Prime Minister Aleksandr Shokhin confirmed the emergence of dynamic groups of firms throughout the Russian economy: "It is only today, in the fall of 1994, that we can say that the crisis is indeed beginning to acquire a structural character. What does that mean? In every industry, even in those which have fallen on very hard times, such as the textiles and the defense complex, there have emerged stable groups of leading enterprises which have not simply adapted themselves to the new, market circumstances, but which are quickly asserting themselves on the market, beating their rivals and showing vigorous growth . . . [these] groups of leaders each include 10, 15, or even 20 percent of all enterprises, depending on the individual industry" (Shokhin 1994).

To be sure, managers as a group own a disproportionate and probably growing share of stock in their own companies; and it might seem that they were free to pursue their distinct interests at the expense of restructuring.[17] But within very broad limits, the size of the managerial share has indeterminate effects on reorganization. Managers in restructuring firms are not a cohesive group; they stand to gain or lose proportionately as much as or more than other employees from the – unpredictable – results of the experimental use of assets. Peering into the future from behind this veil of ignorance, they acquiesce in reorganization on more favorable terms but for reasons like those of other employees.

Under these conditions, employees can correctly assume that decision-makers will do whatever possible to protect the well-being of the work force, including continued payment of wages at the highest level consistent with the survival of the company and maintenance of the social welfare institutions traditionally operated by large Soviet firms. All this is tantamount to, and is taken by managers themselves to be, a guarantee to distribute the proceeds from current and future ventures to the employees in accordance with local, mutually understood standards of equity. In return for this guarantee, the employees allow the firm to form new entities that it owns in whole or in part and by means of which it can undertake reorganization or new ventures with or without the participation of outsiders, domestic or foreign. Individual employees thus expect to get something from all the new projects and reckon that the sum of these somethings will be worth more than what they would get by exercising their veto rights and liquidating the firm, even if they do not draw a place in a successful venture.

But although it is widely understood that these entities must enjoy substantial autonomy from central management if they are ever to contribute to the firm's well-being, there is little agreement on the optimal institutional design for securing such autonomy, and arrangements concerning the distribution of equity. The determination of transfer prices between the unit and others in the firm vary substantially even within a single company depending on opportunities and the accumulation of experience. Reorganization along these lines is, moreover, still marginal in the twofold sense that together these entities account for only a small fraction of employment and production, and one by one they are fragile and at the mercy of events. Nonetheless, this type of reorganization is proliferating rapidly and is increasingly regarded as the response of choice to the problem of reorganizing large firms.

---

[17] Estimation of that share is, in any case, difficult because surreptitious concentration of property has continued after privatization. See Blasi (1994); Pistor (1994).

As an example of such efforts at decentralization, also displaying their institutional diversity, consider the Ekaterinburg Mechanical Factory (EMF), a military enterprise producing missile-related hardware that began experimenting in 1985 with reorganization in connection with state-sponsored efforts to promote conversion to civilian production. By 1990 a small shop (with about 30 workers) was incorporated into a joint venture with Philips to assemble video players; when the central government funds used to purchase the parts stopped flowing to the venture, production stopped too. In the same period the firm established more robust and apparently self-sustaining joint ventures with the Yugoslav-German firm "Kostyer," the British firm "Brown," and a Russian firm in Nizhniy Vartovsk. In all four of these, 40 percent of shares were held by EMF as a whole, 40 percent by the outside partner, and 20 percent by the employees of the joint venture itself. Contemporaneously, subdivisions began transforming themselves into independent profit centers (filially) and EMF itself formed a series of wholly owned small enterprises. By summer 1994 there were 10 profit centers within the factory, and five small enterprises. New facilities have been built for some of the profit centers/subsidiaries, so that they can be easily separated from the main plant and thus made more attractive to potential joint-venture partners.

The profit centers, small enterprises, and joint ventures are relatively small; the largest employ only about 70 workers each. At most, therefore, they employ 1,350 people, which would be almost half of the 3,000 employees engaged in civilian work but not quite 20 percent of the total work force of 7,000. Opinions about the prospects of these units vary widely. One high-level manager in the company told us that many were doing well and would probably survive, but the director of what that same official told us was one of the best projects asserted that, with the exception of his unit, few of the new entities would succeed. Regardless of their assessments of individual units, both managers expressed their general approval of the strategy and emphasized the indispensability of pursuing it.

To assess just how pervasive and compelling the strategy of experimental decentralization is, we tried to determine why the few large firms known to reject it did so. To that end we investigated one of the largest local advocates of centrally directed reorganization, Urals Heavy Machinery. The company began as a producer of equipment for the gold-mining industry in the early 1800s, then turned out drilling equipment for the oil industry until it was converted to military use in the 1930s and began to produce artillery pieces. Although conversion began in 1990, as of mid-1994, 70 percent of its production was still military related. It employed approximately 8,000 workers in 1994.

The firm's current strategy is to find several high-volume products whose production requirements match their stock of capital equipment as replacements for the artillery pieces, thus allowing preservation of Urals Heavy Machinery as a whole. Its best bet appears to be specialized pumps for the oil industry, output of which accounted for 40 percent of total production in mid-1994. Pump production could then be supplemented by diversification into consumer goods and transportation equipment, if possible with the help of foreign joint-venture partners.

High-level managers were forthright in explaining this strategy as compelled by the firm's high degree of vertical integration and the physical layout of its production equipment, both of which resulted from adaptation to the Soviet plan environment. In general, operation under the plan system encouraged an extreme form of the vertical integration characteristic of Western mass producers before the onset of instability. Large industrial firms in the Soviet-type economies could sell everything they could make, and the more they protected themselves by in-house production against disruption in supply on the part of suppliers who did control their own input, the more they could produce.

This was particularly true in the case of a firm like Urals Heavy Machinery, whose military customers were extremely reliable and well financed and whose products require constantly changing combinations of a wide range of manufacturing technologies. Thus, guided by the motto "Vse sdelai sam" (Do everything yourself), the firm became a microcosm of the metalworking industry as a whole, building up a huge machine park in which tools were grouped by type: lathes in one shop, milling machines in another. This guaranteed the company maximum flexibility so long as there was an assured market for complex mechanical products that could be made with the entire ensemble of machines.

But the same setup looks prohibitively cumbersome given changing markets for small runs of different products, each built with a different combination of machine tools. The managers at Urals Heavy Machinery were well aware that the company could, in theory, build any of many mechanical products likely to be demanded on Russian markets. But by their calculations the cost of removing the machines required for any such product from their respective shops and mounting them in a production line, plus the cost of disrupting operations in the areas from which they were taken, made reorganization by product line unworkable. Hence the decision to seek substitutes for the artillery pieces that did not require dismantling the old shop structure. But this strategy was clearly regarded as a desperate measure, and even those who supported it plainly wished they had other choices. Some operating managers just below the peak of the firm, moreover, were convinced that the centralized strategy would fail and that Urals Heavy Machinery would eventually have to decentralize authority for product development and production to the workshops, whose capacity for adjustment was in their view demonstrated by the success of such reorganization at another local firm previously organized on the principles of "Vse sdelai sam." Thus, the exception, whether it remains one or not, proves the rule that Sverdlovsk firms see decentralization through formation of substantially autonomous undertakings as the precondition to reorganization and regeneration.

The cumulative result is a pattern of reconstruction that in its defining features resembles the reconstruction of large Western firms adjusting from stable markets to instability. First, like Western firms – such as IBM, General Motors, or Volkswagen – the Urals firms are using learning-by-monitoring institutions to create profit centers, subsidiaries, and joint ventures with the autonomy and incentives to learn through experimental use of their resources while keeping the parent sufficiently informed of their progress so that the latter can provide aid or cut losses in the case of distress. The parent agrees on a project and an initial budget with the new entity, and it makes periodic demonstration of progress toward the agreed end a condition for refinancing. Obligatory, periodic evaluation of results forces the new venture to act decisively to make good on its promises, allows both parties to redefine their joint goals if they like, and allows the parent to redeploy its capital if the old goals seem unreachable and their redefinition implausible. The continual, evaluative discussion that results from this discipline is the analogy in relations between business units to those established between production stations by the removal of inventory buffers. The parties learn from what is not working what needs to be improved, and whether it can be.

Second, like Western firms in the midst of restructuring, the Urals' firms secure the consent of the work force, workers and managers alike, by guaranteeing it as much security as possible – but only that much. This pattern is, if anything, clearer in the West than in the firms we visited, but the bargain was fundamentally the same. Thus first General Motors, then Volkswagen, to continue with familiar examples, have offered their employees periodic guarantees of employment security for limited periods, then used those periods to define new organizational structures in which it is possible to determine which employee can be productively employed in the next round. This is also the open secret of reorganization in the Urals. As revealed by behavior, employees' calculations of the best returns to the bargaining power they acquire through incumbency, however defined formally, are the same as in the West.

Third, as in the West, internal reorganization and decentralization blur the boundaries of the firm and create collaborative production arrangements that fly in the face of the notion of property as exclusive control. We saw that Western firms must increasingly design and produce products in collaboration with independent partners who achieve economies of scope in learning to meet the demands of different customers. Willy-nilly, firms in the Sverdlovsk region are moving in the same direction. The new entities that we have seen are designing their products and production processes with the help of one or more research institutes in the region or elsewhere and with the cooperation of their (usual industrial) customers and suppliers. But the entities are also calling for, and receiving, help from various laboratories and production infrastructure services within the parent company. The more complex each of these groupings becomes and the more each partner, in seeking economies of scope and reducing the effects of any one failure, enters into similar relations in other settings, the harder it will be ever to draw firm institutional boundaries around the parties to even the largest projects. And the more likely it will be that the collaborators regulate relations among themselves by defining how gains are to be shared project by project, as increasingly is the case in the U.S. biomedical and semiconductor and related industries.

Fourth, there is no more certainty in the Urals than in the advanced countries (Japan included) as to how, precisely, to institutionalize these collaborative arrangements – but arguably there is no less certainty in the firms we saw, either. Design teams in the advanced countries are routinely under pressure to develop components with internal units having some claim to the required expertise rather than with outside suppliers. Production units are likewise under pressure to use internal process design staff, maintenance services, tool and die shops, or equipment builders rather than to work with outside vendors or take responsibility for such tasks themselves. There are plainly such pressures within the Sverdlovsk firms. Managing directors were well aware that they could leash decentralized entities by raising the transfer costs of the enterprise services these entities still needed or by stopping reinvestment of revenues generated by the new ventures. Bargaining over such matters would strike managers in the advanced countries as familiar. If there is some hidden but systematic and insurmountable obstacle to collaboration of this type, we in the advanced countries will have an inkling of it long before news of failures in the Urals arrives. But, to anticipate a theme to which we will return in the conclusion, if there is no such flaw, it is hard to see why an innovative advance in institutionalizing the new form of cooperation might not as easily come from Russia as from, say, Brazil, Mexico, or Thailand. Many of the organizational barriers to collaboration in the advanced countries come from the resistance of strong organizations that stand to lose by the changes. Why exclude the possibility that, as so often before in world history, innovation will occur in the guise of imitation in those countries where the old organizations are dramatically weakened and reconstruction (naively?) takes for granted the viability of structures that are still suspiciously novel in advanced countries?

The role of discursive standards, as you will again already have surmised, is to allow the Sverdlovsk firms to define and refine the internal structure of the reorganizing entities even in the absence of ongoing relations with demanding customers. In the advanced countries, we saw, the standards evolve as a language for discussion between customer and supplier. Starting at the boundary defined by what each expects of the other, they encourage detection and correction of procedures that lead to misunderstandings and shortfalls. In that process they help define or articulate the responsibilities and connections among internal work groups in both.

Contrast this with the Urals where the quality laboratory, as keeper of the new standards, temporarily substitutes for and prepares the internal units for eventual exchanges with potential demanding customers whom they must eventually satisfy if they are to enter world markets. To do this the quality laboratory evaluates current production and the organizations that guided it by standards potential customers will use to assess whether the company can credibly make the promises expected of collaborators. So long as the highest-level managers support such evaluation, it produces just the kinds of pressure for self-reevaluation common in advanced country firms, while also accelerating certification under the standard that allows the already qualified firms to recognize others like them.

As a paradigmatic instance of this kind of anticipatory reorganization, consider the case of the Katerina Pipe Factory, a large maker of pipes, primarily for the petrochemical industry. Katerina was started in the early 1960s as part of a program of modernization and expansion of Soviet industry. It currently employs 11,500 workers. Although the firm is well situated, for reasons discussed earlier, to benefit from the modernization of the decayed Soviet industrial infrastructure, it quickly realized that its prospects for survival depended crucially on the ability to meet the DIN, American Petroleum Institute, and ISO 9000 standards. Large-scale reconstruction of domestic pipelines will likely involve participation of foreign companies or consortia, which will take compliance with those standards for granted. And "even" such developing countries as Turkey, India, and Syria, to which Katerina might reasonably expect to export its products, the managers told us with chagrined bewilderment, had become equally demanding.

Hence, we see the current effort to obtain certification and the continuous discussions of quality – convened by specialists from the quality laboratories or informed by information they provide – at all levels of the firm. Laboratory specialists meet with each production shop weekly. The firm's technical director gathers all of the shop heads together to compare performance and discuss quality once a month. Moreover, quality information is combined with financial data in daily meetings where the general director and his deputies gauge each subdivision's overall performance and allocate current revenues.

In light of these developments several monitoring institutions, developed in the Soviet economy to overcome its own inefficiency and stagnation, may paradoxically prove useful in the transition to market conditions. The first are the many institutes built as observatories to track and assess developments in the capitalist countries. It has long been recognized by many Eastern European and Soviet economists that the plan economies compensated for the lack of internal incentives to innovate by observing innovations in the West and adapting them to Soviet conditions once they had matured into standard designs. In that sense the Soviet economy was a copy of its competitors; one of the reasons it fell out of the race after 1975 is precisely because it was unable to adjust to a world so turbulent that designs never stabilized enough to be copied.

But now that the advanced countries, partially in response to the disruptive effects of that very turbulence, are learning to render the information necessary for design coordination in a way independent of particular products and processes, institutionalized observatories skilled in scanning the world for design information and with well-established relations to a wide range of firms suddenly look like institutions every economy will need, not bric-a-brac from a failed economic experiment.

Judging by our experience in the Urals, Russian firms may indeed have an unexpected asset. The traditional Soviet institutional arrangement for new product introduction brought the design and engineering departments of enterprises into continual contact and collaboration with a range of external organizations, such as industrial research institutions, the Academy of Sciences, science and production associations (NPOs), interbranch scientific technical complexes (MNTKs), and universities. Different stages of product development were often divided among the different organizations. Foreign models were consciously used as yardsticks for new product and equipment design (Lawrence and Vlachoutsicos 1990). Of course, in the absence of strong external imperatives to improve product quality, the successive iterations of prototypes and documentation and their mandatory approval by multiple interministerial commissions led to excruciatingly long product-introduction cycles. But the close institutional links forged during the Soviet period may well prove adaptable to the new conditions.

Everywhere one looks, they are being utilized by dynamic firms with clear ideas of how (and how quickly) they need to bring production up to international standards. For example, look at a Urals pharmaceutical company planning the total reconstruction of its plant with the objective of installing special clean rooms for the manufacture of medical products. Before even securing financing for the project, the company had reached agreement on the technical side of the reconstruction with design institutes from Bashkiria and Moscow.

Similarly, the various systems of Soviet quality control that grew out of the horrifying discovery of how little of quality the plan economy produces may serve as the scaffolding, if not the foundation, for building new institutions for certifying firms under international standards. The system of quality management that in many variations became the most widespread among Soviet manufacturing enterprises from all branches, the KSUKP system of Comprehensive Management of the Quality of Output, had two features that may help prepare the way for the introduction of new standards in Russian firms.

First, KSUKP exhibited some of the discursive characteristics of ISO 9000 standards. The system called for enterprises to generate their own product standards in discussion with customers and suppliers and, in the best cases, to assist the latter in raising and systematizing their quality standards. Relations between scientific research and design organizations and the enterprise were deemed of critical importance. In theory at least, discoveries of defects at the level of the individual work station were used as the occasion to open ongoing communications between workers and foremen that cut across the boundaries of groups, shops, and divisions (Parfenovskiy and Lukashin 1986; Prokhorenko and Kurulev 1977).

Second, benchmarking of foreign products and practices was an integral part of the KSUKP system, which was intended to work in concert with the system of state product attestation. After 1965, with the introduction of the "Mark of Quality" award, the Soviet government made a conscious attempt to compensate for the lack of market pressures by granting this award to products that were considered to meet the same requirements as analogous products sold by non-Soviet manufacturers on the world market. Estimates from 1979 put the share of Mark of Quality certified output at 30 percent to 45 percent for most group A, or heavy industry, branches. That these numbers were not pure fiction is suggested by the palpably correct official figures given for building materials and light industry: 3.7 percent and 4.4 percent, respectively (Hill and McKay 1988; Lapusta 1980).

These points of contact aside, however, the KSUKP did differ in crucial ways from the discursive ISO 9000 standards. Despite the rhetorical call for personal responsibility and accountability on the part of each employee for the results of their work, actual measurement and verification of quality were carried out in each factory by teams of full-time "controllers" whose judgment of conformance was ultimately highly subjective. In many accounts, this led to resentment and resistance by workers and bribery of controllers. To the extent that KSUKP became just another way for upper-level managers to monitor, from afar, the honesty and industriousness of shop floor workers, it stopped short of institutionalizing continuous discussions between subunits that would have allowed for joint formulation of expectations and their flexible revision as circumstances changed. In this regard, however, it had as many affinities with earlier, failed waves of quality reform in large Western firms as with the disasters of the Soviet economy. Nonetheless, and despite these shortcomings, in the best firms that we saw, managers indicated that their experience with the KSUKP system had provided points of reference with the aid of which they were able to introduce modern ISO-compatible practices more quickly, if not less painfully.

What Competition Creates

The fall of the Soviet-type economies and the success of their market competitors show, if anything can, the superiority of an economic "pluriverse" of independent actors over an economic universe in which the risks of each become the responsibility of all. Where the former encourages, even compels the experimentalism that leads to new products, processes, and institutions, the latter stifles it. Yet in the commonsense view of the transition, this experimentalism stops short of the building blocks of the market: the firms and the relations among them. Competition, it seems, creates unlimited new possibilities, but not the possibility of creating new forms of competition. For this reason the timeless, textbook version of capitalism, in which the agents are firms controlled by residual owners and coordination among them is principally by price, is not a blueprint for the construction of new market economies.

But set in the firmament of late twentieth-century thought, this is a darkling assumption indeed. It is, after all, a central tenant of that thought that every conceptual scheme – particularly all those of the natural sciences – must be rethought given the answers to the very questions that it itself poses. Conversely, it has proved impossible to find categories of investigative conceptualization that did not themselves have to be reconceptualized in the light of investigation (Davidson 1985; Kuhn 1970; Putnam 1994). Would it not be wondrous if the categories of practical economic investigation as embodied in the precise definition of autonomous economic agents and the relations among them alone rested on unchanging foundations?[18]

If the ideas presented here are right, then this assumption is not wondrous but wrong. For our central claim is precisely that market experimentalism has produced actors and market relations that call into question standard notions of ownership, control, and coordination by price. We claim further that the new forms of collaboration diffusing rapidly through the world economy are in some ways as unsettling to the advanced countries as to transition economies; or, put another way, the transition economies are trying to find their way to market economies that are trying to find themselves.

If these findings are credited at all, they counsel at the least prudence in the dispensation of counsel and greater circumspection still in the authoritative imposition of economic institutions on transition economies. At a minimum the advanced countries should not establish organizational forms and patterns of competition in the transition economies that are being disavowed at home, nor correlatively, should they dismiss every feature of the transition economies that deviates from the textbook notion of competition as a vestigial but potentially lethal attachment to the former central planning.

Victory intoxicates. The fate of victorious generals who fight the last war is well known. History has not been kinder to victors who draw the terms imposed on the vanquished from their own war propaganda or who neglect to learn the lessons of the successes and failures of their own wartime economies.

---

[18] For the view that the foundations of the market economy, once determined by experiment, are for practical purposes unchanging, see Hayek (1973).

References

Alam, Ghayur. 1994. *Impact of NCMTs on Economies of Scale and Scope: The Case of India*. Maastricht, Netherlands: Institute for New Technologies, United Nations University.

Amsden, Alice H. 1989. *Asia's Next Giant: South Korea and Late Industrialization*. New York: Oxford University Press.

Ansal, Hacer. 1994. *The Impact of New Technology on Economies of Scale and Scope: Evidences from Turkish Case Study*. Maastricht, Netherlands: Institute for New Technologies, United Nations University.

Aoki, Masahiko. 1988. *Information, Incentives, and Bargaining in the Japanese Economy*. Cambridge: Cambridge University Press.

Asanuma, Banri. 1989. "Manufacturer–Supplier Relationships in Japan and the Concept of Relation-Specific Skill." *Journal of the Japanese and International Economies* 3, no. 1: 1–30.

Barkholz, David. 1994. "Suppliers Add Engineers to Meet Maker's Demand." *Automotive News,* 28 February, 20.

Blanchard, Olivier, Rudiger Dornbusch, Paul Krugman, Richard Layard, and Lawrence Summers. 1990. *Reform in Eastern Europe.* Cambridge, Mass.: Massachusetts Institute of Technology (MIT) Press.

Blasi, Joseph. 1994. "Russia: Take Another Look, Privatization Is Working." *International Herald Tribune,* 1 July.

Boyer, Robert, ed. 1986. *La Flexibilité du travail en Europe: une étude comparative des transformations du rapport salarial dans sept pays de 1973 à 1985.* Paris: Editions La Découverte.

Brooke, James. 1994. "A New Quality in Brazil's Exports." *New York Times,* 21 October, D1, D6.

Clark, Kim B., Takahiro Fujimoto, and W. Bruce Chew. 1987. "Product Development in the World Auto Industry." Brookings Papers on Economic Activity no. 3: 729–76. The Brookings Institution, Washington, D.C.

Clements, Richard Barrett. 1993. *Quality Manager's Complete Guide to ISO 9000.* Englewood Cliffs, New Jersey: Prentice Hall.

Coffee, John C., Jr., Ronald J. Gilson, and Louis Lowenstein, eds. 1995. *Relational Investing.* New York: Oxford University Press, forthcoming.

Davidson, Donald. 1985. "On the Very Idea of a Conceptual Scheme." In *Post-Analytic Philosophy,* edited by John Rajchman and Cornel West. pp. 5–20. New York: Columbia University Press.

de Quadros Carvalho, Ruy. 1994. *Coping with Change in the Economy: New Technologies, Organisational Innovation and Economies of Scale and Scope in the Brazilian Engineering Industry.* Maastricht, Netherlands: Institute for New Technologies, United Nations University.

Dominguez, Lilia, and Flor Brown. 1994. *The Impact of New Technologies on Scale and Scope in Manufacturing Industry: The Case of Mexico.* Maastricht, Netherlands: Institute for New Technologies, United Nations University.

Dore, Ronald. 1983. "Goodwill and the Spirit of Market Capitalism." *British Journal of Sociology* 34: 459–82.

Dornbusch, Rudiger. 1991. *Money, Trade, and Debt: Reform Options for the Soviet Union.* Cambridge, Mass.: Massachusetts Institute of Technology.

Edquist, Charles, and Staffan Jacobsson. 1988. *Flexible Automation: The Global Diffusion of New Technology in the Engineering Industry.* New York: Basil Blackwell Inc.

Edwards, J.S.S., and Klaus Fischer. 1991. "Banks, Finance and Investment in West Germany Since 1970." Center for Economic Policy Research, CEPR Discussion Paper (update): 497.

Esser, John. 1993. "The Changing Form of Contract Law." Working Paper presented to the Social Science History Association, Baltimore, Maryland, 4–7 November.

Federal Information Systems. 1994. Press conference with Credit Suisse, September 8.

Gao, Bai. 1994. "Japanese Management Reconsidered: The Historical Contingency of an Institution." Department of Sociology, Duke University.

General Motors (GM). 1994. "Quality System Assessment." Chrysler Corporation, Ford

Motor Company, and General Motors Corporation Report.

Gerschenkron, Alexander. 1962. "Economic Backwardness in Historical Perspective." In *Economic Backwardness in Historical Perspective,* edited by Alexander Gerschenkron. pp. 5–30. Cambridge, Mass.: Harvard University Press.

Gilson, Ronald J., and Reinier Kraakman. 1991. "Reinventing the Outside Director: An Agenda for Institutional Investors." *Stanford Law Review* 43: 863–906.

Hansmann, Henry. 1988. "Ownership of the Firm." *Journal of Law, Economics and Organization* 4, no. 2: 267–304.

Hart, Oliver. 1988. "Incomplete Contracts and the Theory of the Firm." *Journal of Law, Economics & Organization* 4, no. 1: 119–39.

——. 1989. "An Economist's Perspective on the Theory of the Firm." *Columbia Law Review* 89, no. 7: 1757–74.

Hayek, Friedrich A. von. 1973. *Law, Legislation and Liberty: A New Statement of the Liberal Principles of Justice and Political Economy.* Vol. 1 of *Rules and Order.* Chicago: University of Chicago Press.

Helper, Susan R. 1994. "Three Steps Forward, Two Steps Back in Automotive Supplier Relations." *Technovation* 14, no. 10.

Hill, Malcolm R., and Richard McKay. 1988. *Soviet Product Quality.* London: Macmillan Press.

Humphrey, John, ed. 1995. "Industrial Organization and Manufacturing Competitiveness in Developing Countries." Special Issue of *World Politics* 23, no. 1 (January).

Johnson, Chalmers A. 1982. *MITI and the Japanese Miracle: The Growth of Industrial Policy, 1925-1975.* Stanford, Calif.: Stanford University Press.

Kaplan, Robert S., and David P. Norton. 1992. "The Balanced Scorecard – Measures That Drive Performance." *Harvard Business Review.* pp. 71–9 (January–February).

——. 1993. "Putting the Balanced Scorecard to Work." *Harvard Business Review,* (September–October) pp. 134–47.

Kaplinsky, Raphael. 1994. *Easternization: The Spread of Japanese Manufacturing Techniques to LDCs.* London: Frank Cass.

Kern, Horst. 1994. "Intelligente Regulierung: Gewerkschaftliche Beiträge in Ost und West zur Erneuerung des deutschen Produktionsmodells." *Soziale Welt* 1: 33–59.

Kern, Horst, and Charles F. Sabel. 1994. "Verblaßte Tugenden. Zur Krise des deutschen Produktionsmodells." In *Umbrüche gesellschaftlicher Arbeit* (special issue 9, *Soziale Welt*), edited by Niels Beckenbach and Werner van Treeck. pp. 605–24. Göttingen: Verlag Otto Schwartz & Co.

Koike, Kazuo. 1988. *Understanding Industrial Relations in Modern Japan.* New York: St. Martin's Press.

Kolb, Deborah M. 1983. *The Mediators.* Cambridge, Mass.: MIT Press.

Kuhn, Thomas S. 1970. *The Structure of Scientific Revolutions.* 2d ed. Chicago, Ill.: University of Chicago Press.

Lamprecht, James L. 1993. "Implementing the ISO 9000 Series." In *Quality and Reliability,* edited by Edward G. Schilling. New York: Marcel Dekker, Inc.

Lapusta, M.G. 1980. *Kachestvo Produktsii: Mekhanizm Upravleniya.* Moscow: Ekonomika.

Lawrence, Paul R., and Charalambos Vlachoutsicos. 1990. *Behind the Factory Walls: Decision Making in Soviet and US Enterprises.* Boston, Mass.: Harvard Business School Press.

Lipton, David, and Jeffrey Sachs. 1990. "Creating a Market Economy in Eastern Europe:

The Case of Poland." Brookings Papers on Economic Activity no. 1: 75–147. The Brookings Institution, Washington, D.C.

Lowell, Jon. 1994. "Dixie Deutschland: BMW, Mercedes Line Up Suppliers Down Yonder." *Ward's Auto World,* July, 54–7.

"Midwest Motor" Company. 1991a. Engine Plant No. 2 60 Degree V6 Engine Program: Organization Design Review. "Midwest Motor" Company, document on file with the author.

——. 1991b. "Welcome To 'Midwest City' V6 Program: Best In Class." "Midwest Motor" Company, document on file with the author.

Nishiguchi, Toshihiro. 1989. "Strategic Dualism: An Alternative in Industrial Societies." Ph.D. dissertation, Subfaculty of Sociology, Nuffield College, Oxford.

——. 1994. *Strategic Industrial Sourcing: The Japanese Advantage.* New York: Oxford University Press.

Nuti, Domenico Mario. 1991. "Stabilization and Sequencing in the Reform of Socialist Economies." In *Managing Inflation in Socialist Economies in Transition,* edited by Simon Commander. Washington, DC: World Bank.

Osterman, Paul. 1994. "How Common Is Workplace Transformation and Who Adopts It." *Industrial & Labor Relations Review* 47, no. 2: 173–88.

Parfenovskiy, Aleksei Borisovich, and Aleksandr Yakovlevich Lukashin. 1986. *Upravlenie Kachestvom Produktsii: Organizatsionno-Ekonomicheskie Problemy.* Moscow: Ekonomika.

Peach, Robert W., ed. 1992. *The ISO 9000 Handbook.* Fairfax, VA: CEEM Information Services.

Piore, Michael J., and Charles F. Sabel. 1984. *The Second Industrial Divide: Possibilities for Prosperity.* New York: Basic Books.

Pistor, Katharina. 1994. "Privatization and Corporate Governance in Russia: An Empirical Study." In *Privatization, Conversion and Enterprise Reform in Russia,* edited by Michael McFaul and Tova Perlmutter. Stanford, Calif.: Center for International Security and Arms Control, Stanford University.

Plumb, Stephen E. 1993. "Big Three Team Up On Quality." *WARD's Auto World,* November, 45.

Porter, Michael E. 1990. *The Competitive Advantage of Nations.* New York: Free Press.

Prokhorenko, V.A., and A. P. Kurulev. 1977. *Upravlenie Kachestvom Produktsii v Nauchno-Proizvodstvennom Ob"edinenii.* Minsk, Belarus.

Putnam, Hillary. 1994. *Words and Life.* Cambridge, Mass.: Harvard University Press.

Raia, Ernest. 1994. "Teaming in Detroit." *Purchasing,* 3 March: 40–5.

Ramseyer, J. Mark. 1991. "Legal Rules in Repeated Deals: Banking in the Shadow of Defection in Japan." *Journal of Legal Studies* 20: 91–117.

Rasiah, Rajah. 1993. "Competition and Governance: Work in Malaysia's Textile and Garment Industries." *Journal of Contemporary Asia* 23, no. 1: 3–24.

Regional State Property Fund, Yekaterinburg. 1993. *The Yekaterinburg Guide for Foreign Investors.*

Rostow, Walt Whitman. 1960. *The Stages of Economic Growth.* New York: Cambridge University Press.

Sabel, Charles F. 1994. "Learning by Monitoring: The Institutions of Economic Development." In *Handbook of Economic Sociology,* edited by Neil Smelser and Richard Swedberg. pp. 137–65. Princeton, NJ: Princeton-Sage.

——. 1995. "Bootstrapping Reform: Rebuilding Firms, the Welfare State and Unions." *Politics and Society* 23, no. 1: 5–48.

Sabel, Charles F., John R. Griffin, and Richard E. Deeg. 1994. "Making Money Talk: Towards a New Debtor-Creditor Relation in German Banking." In *Relational Investing*, edited by John C. Coffee, Ronald J. Gilson, and Louis Lownstein. New York: Oxford University Press.

Sako, Mari, and Susan R. Helper. 1994. "Determinants of 'Trust' in Supplier Relations: Evidence From the Automotive Industry in Japan and the USA." 23rd International Congress of Applied Psychology.

Shaiken, Harley. 1990. *Mexico in the Global Economy*. Monograph Series, 33, Center for U.S.-Mexican Studies, University of California, San Diego, Calif.

Shimokawa, Koichi. 1993. "From the Ford System to the Just-in-Time Production System." *Japanese Yearbook on Business History* 10: 83–105.

Shingo, Shigeo. 1989. *A Study of the Toyota Production System from an Industrial Engineering Viewpoint*. Translated by Andrew P. Dillon. Cambridge, Mass.: Productivity Press.

Shokhin, Aleksandr. 1994. "Interview with Russian Deputy Prime Minister Aleksandr Shokhin." *Federal Information Systems Corporation*, September 14.

Smitka, Michael J. 1991. *Competitive Ties: Subcontracting in the Japanese Automobile Industry*. New York: Columbia University Press.

Sprow, Eugene. 1992. "Insights Into ISO 9000." *Manufacturing Engineering*, September: 73–7.

Stern, Daniel N. 1994. "The Sense of a Verbal Self." In *The Women & Language Debate: A Sourcebook*, edited by Camille Roman, Suzanne Juhasz, and Cristanne Miller. pp. 199–215. New Brunswick, NJ: Rutgers University Press.

Tai, Hung-chao, ed. 1989. *Confucianism and Economic Development: An Oriental Alternative?* Washington, D.C.: The Washington Institute Press.

Tamayo, Francisco, Vanessa Cartaya, and Osvaldo Alonso. 1994. *Nuevas Tecnologias en la Industria Metalmecanica: El Caso Venezolano*. Maastricht, Netherlands: Institute for New Technologies, United Nations University.

Teixeira, Ruy A., and Lawrence Mishel. 1993. "Whose Skills Shortage – Workers or Management?" *Issues in Science and Technology* 9, no. 4: 69–74.

Wada, Kazuo. 1991. "The Development of Tiered Inter-firm Relationships in the Automobile Industry: A Case Study of Toyota Motor Corporation." In *Japanese Yearbook on Business History*, pp. 23–47.

Wade, Robert. 1990. *Governing the Market: Economic Theory and the Role of Government in East Asian Industrialization*. Princeton, NJ: Princeton University Press.

Williamson, Oliver E. 1986. *Economic Organization: Firms, Markets and Policy Control*. New York: New York University Press.

Zuckerman, Amy. 1994. "Caution: ISO 9000 Ahead." *American Machinist*, June: 50–3.

6

COPING WITH HYDRA – STATE OWNERSHIP AFTER PRIVATIZATION
A Comparative Study of the Czech Republic, Hungary, and Russia

KATHARINA PISTOR and JOEL TURKEWITZ

We gratefully acknowledge the essential contributions of our friends and colleagues in the Czech Republic, Hungary, and Russia. A partial list of the individuals who were instrumental in supporting and shaping our work includes Jan Mladek, Oldrich Macak, Gabriella Pal, Laszlo Urban, Olga M. Kisselova, and Alexei N. Makeshin. Comments by John Nellis, Mitchell Orenstein, and Gerald McDermott pointed out several useful modifications in our thinking, and Michaela Popescu provided valuable assistance with data analysis. Finally, we wish to thank Roman Frydman and Andrzej Rapaczynski for their continual intellectual challenges and support in this work. Despite this long list of accomplices, the usual disclaimers apply.

Introduction

Five years after the tumultuous events of the winter of 1989, when the "realities" of the world seemed to change before our eyes, observers have learned to be more cautious in their expectations for the future. Gone are the confident predictions of rapid change from state-controlled economies to efficient systems based on private property, having been replaced by a grudging acceptance that "privatization" in Eastern Europe has little in common with a large garage sale or some other process of distribution. In 1995 participants and observers speak of privatization as a contingent process, replete with complexities both theoretical and technical.[1]

[1] Indeed, commentators on privatization have noted a general slowdown or complete stalemate of privatization programs in many countries in 1994. See the report "Amnesia of

Perhaps it is not surprising that given the speed with which analytical frameworks have had to develop to keep pace with changes in the region, it is still possible to come upon large areas where the ideas of those early days have not yet been revised to encompass a more sophisticated conceptualization. Thus, while the debates that have raged about the dynamics of the process (i.e. whether fast-track privatization or a more deliberate process is most appropriate) have become ever more nuanced, the nature of the process has been regarded definitional. For the most part, the debate about privatization has assumed that at the end of the process assets have been made "private," that is, moved out of the state sector into private hands. The state in this model controls the speed of asset outflow, directs the outflow to particular parties, and is involved, to a greater or lesser extent, in the post-privatization activities of nonstate parties.

In fact the experience of privatization has revealed that the end point of privatization programs is not a state sector separated from a private sector. Instead, the results of the privatization procedures that have reached completion to date have been that assets in the economy are distributed between a set of wholly state-owned companies or enterprises, a set of firms owned by nonstate parties free of the presence of the state as an owner, and a middle group of assets owned by state and nonstate parties. In all countries in the region, the state continues to be the largest single owner of firms subject to privatization, and the majority of assets that have been "privatized" are held jointly by the state and nonstate parties. Thus, privatization does not serve to terminate the role of the state as an owner in the economy overall or even of most individual assets, but rather signals an alteration in the relation between state and nonstate parties regarding ownership rights to assets. Redefinition of the end point of privatization has strong implications for how the entire privatization process is situated. As long as privatization was seen to draw the curtain on state ownership, how the state functioned as an owner before its last curtain call was of merely historic concern, primarily of interest to those people who took the concept of path dependency seriously. Once privatization is acknowledged not as a terminal point for state ownership, but rather as the creation of a new relationship along a state-nonstate ownership continuum, appreciating the size of retained state holdings and understanding how the state functions as an owner are transformed from objects of historic study to topics of immediate relevance for the development of postcommunist economies.

Inclusion of the state as a significant postprivatization owner suggests a

Reform" by the Adam Smith Institute (1994), and *The Economist*, January 21–29 1995, p.61, "Tired of capitalism? So soon?"

need for theoretical and empirical work devoted to working out the implications of state ownership within the transition process. At the theoretical level, there existed only a trivial need for privatization analysts to develop a model or framework for understanding the dynamics of the redefinition of the role, function, and identity of the "state" during transition when the state was seen as an ephemeral actor, withering away as it divested itself of assets. Empirically, it is important to note that the state functions as an owner not as a theoretical construct, but in real time and space. The meaning of state ownership will depend, at least in part, on the nature and extent of each individual state's holdings and the manner in which each state practices its ownership rights.

This chapter takes the existence of state ownership in postprivatization contexts seriously and suggests a framework for analyzing the existing structure of state ownership and the dynamics of change. This analytical approach is used to explore the pattern and practice of state ownership in three countries in the region that have pursued extensive and sharply different privatization mechanics: the highly centralized Czech program that combines monetary and nonmonetary-based asset transfers; the decentralized, sale-based Hungarian efforts; and the decentralized Russian method based on nonmonetary auctions combined with extensive insider participation. The chapter is divided into five parts. The first part quantifies the extent of state holdings in the Czech Republic, Hungary, and Russia. The second discusses the potential dangers of state ownership in the transition economies. The third develops a framework for analyzing the types of state holdings that remain after privatization and the implications of these different classes of holdings for state activism. The fourth focuses on the different ways in which states manage and control retained assets. The fifth part presents some conclusions of this analysis and discusses the policy implications of our findings.

State Ownership after Privatization – The Evidence

Even after privatization state holdings can be extensive, as we shall see in the Czech Republic, Hungary, and Russia. State holdings[2] that exist at the end of

---

[2] The term "state holding" is defined expansively to include assets owned by either the central government or by a ministry or government agency, such as federal or regional property funds, branch ministries, or administrations. Assets owned by local governments are not treated as state property. In addition, we have excluded state holdings in smaller firms from our analysis. For a detailed treatment of state holdings in the trade and service sector in the Czech Republic and Hungary, see Earle, Frydman, Rapaczynski, and Turkewitz (1994).

privatization programs are derived from two primary sources: firms and assets excluded from privatization; and firms, or portions of firms, included in the privatization process that have not been sold or transferred. In addition the state can own assets directly or indirectly through the ownership of a firm that, in turn, has an ownership stake in another company. In the following section we quantify the size of direct and indirect equity holdings of the Czech, Hungarian, and Russian states.

The Czech Republic

The basic structure of the privatization of large economic entities in Czechoslovakia (and later the Czech Republic) is relatively simple. A list of enterprises to be privatized was compiled in July 1991, including roughly 70 percent of all firms in Czechoslovakia, with a total value estimated at CSK 1,200 billion ($30 billion).[3] The listed firms were divided into two groups, to be privatized in two successive "waves".[4] Managers of enterprises included in the first wave were required to submit to their founding ministry plans for the privatization of their firms by 31 October 1991.[5] Competing plans for all or part of any first wave firm could be submitted until the middle of January 1992. Projects were evaluated first by the branch ministries, which had the authority to recommend a particular project but were required to pass on all submitted proposals. The authority to approve a privatization project was vested in the Ministry of Privatization, a task the ministry performed in close consultation with the Ministry of Finance. Upon approval of a plan, firms were commercialized, and ownership was transferred to the Fund of National Property (FNP) for execution of the program.[6]

---

[3] It is difficult to provide a meaningful figure for the number of enterprises involved in the program since enterprises are frequently separated into several smaller pieces at various points in the process. Official figures maintain that over 4,500 enterprises to date have been involved in large privatization, with that number certain to increase as more enterprises have their privatization plans approved. See Ceska (1993, 2), for official data on the privatization process. See Kotrba (1994) for a detailed analysis of the enterprises included in the Czech privatization program.

[4] The voucher auction component of the second wave concluded at the end of 1994, with distribution of shares completed in the spring of 1995. Since, as of this writing, the results of the second wave are still inconclusive, our analyses are based primarily on the results of the first wave.

[5] Managers of enterprises scheduled for the second wave were required to submit similar proposals by 16 August 1992.

[6] The framework for the privatization program was set out in Act No. 92/1991 "On Conditions and Terms Governing the Transfer of State Property to Other Persons."

Mass Privatization

Privatization plans were not required to include any particular privatization mechanism since the Large-Scale Privatization Law allowed for a variety of privatization mechanics, including traditional sale and tender methods, as well as new and untested techniques of basically free mass distribution. Although the law provided no priority ordering of techniques, the influential group around then federal Finance Minister Vaclav Klaus, a group deeply involved in the process of approving privatization plans, openly supported a strong reliance on "voucher auctions" to privatize first-wave firms. The ideological commitment of the leading forces of the Czech bureaucracy to reducing state ownership at the greatest possible speed has been one of the defining features of Czech privatization.

Of similar significance for the emerging ownership structure of the economy was the gradual movement away from privatizing all firms exclusively through the use of vouchers. If all assets were slated for distribution through auctions, then total divestiture of state ownership would have become merely a technical matter of ensuring that the system for registering the demand for assets was properly calibrated to ensure that the market would clear. The decision to develop strategies that did not include a dominant role for voucher privatization was not in all cases a decision to retain ownership, but it was a decision to accept a much higher level of uncertainty about the rate and extent of the shrinkage of state holdings.

First-Wave Privatization

In the end, 988 approved privatization plans called for some portion of a firm's shares to be contributed to the mass privatization program, with slightly over 60 percent of the total value of enterprises included in the first wave. The first wave has proven to be both successful and incomplete. State ownership was drastically reduced in over 60 percent of first-wave firms, and in more than half of these firms the state retained only an insignificant (under 10 percent) number of shares. At the same time, state ownership was barely reduced in more than 20 percent of firms designated for privatization. The FNP continued to own over 28 percent of the first tranche of privatized firms. Table 6.1 provides an overall picture of the degree to which the first wave has succeeded in transferring assets out of state ownership.

The extent of retained state ownership in the core firms of first-wave privatization is closely related to the degree to which a particular enterprise's shares were dedicated to voucher privatization. Systematic differences among subsectors in the proportionate use of voucher mechanisms have resulted in concentrations of state ownership in particular areas of the economy, most

Table 6.1 Extent of Privatization of First-Wave Firms, August 1994

Percentage of shares privatized	Number of firms
0 – 20	268
20.1 – 50	75
50.1 – 70	130
70.1 – 90	334
90.1 – 100	463

Source: Fund of National Property Database, August 1994

Table 6.2 Retained State Ownership in First-Wave Firms Involved in Voucher Privatization (in percentages)

Economic subsector	Proportion of state ownership
Finance & insurance	42.9
Agriculture, forestry & water treatment	28.6
Heavy industry	21.5
Light industry	19.0
Trade & supply	16.0
Research & development	15.3
Consumer & social services	12.3
Construction	8.3
Transportation & communication	7.1

Source: FNP database, August 1993.

notably in the vital financial and heavy industry sectors. Table 6.2 provides a subsector breakdown of the size of retained state ownership in first-wave voucher privatization firms. Pockets of particularly concentrated state ownership exist within these sectoral classifications, peaking at 78.4 percent in the seven iron and steel firms partially privatized by vouchers, with banks (47.2 percent) and engineering firms (29.5 percent) also recording an extraordinary incidence of state ownership.[7] In those instances where the state has retained a significant number of shares, it is frequently either the largest or the second largest shareholder.[8]

---

[7] Data compiled from unpublished 1993 FNP data. All computations concerning the 1993 FNP data are based on data analyses by John S. Earle.

[8] Recent data from 908 companies at least partially privatized using voucher auctions in the first wave reveal that the FNP remains a significant stakeholder (10% or more) in 406 firms. In 108 cases the fund is the single largest owner, while in 252 cases it is among the top two equity holders. Database created by the Privatization Project of Central European University based on company disclosure statements on file at the Center for Securities.

Financial Intermediaries and State Control

While the heavy concentration of retained state ownership in banks and other financial institutions is important, its significance in the economy is multiplied because of the particular dynamics of the Czech voucher process. In a spontaneous development, the vast majority of citizens who participated in voucher privatization elected to place their voucher points at the disposal of intermediate investment organizations. Investment Privatization Funds (IPFs) obtained 71.8 percent of all available voucher points and used them to acquire shares in almost all firms included in voucher privatization (see Mladek 1994, 21). Analyzed by the proportionate ownership of shares made available in voucher auction, investment funds are most significant in the financial and light and heavy industry subsectors (see Table 6.3).

Although over 400 investment funds received some points, the largest seven IPFs[9] dominated the market, collecting 64 percent of the points given to IPFs and 46 percent of all points in the first wave. The largest single fund, created by the Ceska Sporitelna Bank, obtained 950 million of the 8,540 million voucher points (over 11 percent) distributed in the Czech Republic (see Brom and Orenstein 1993). The size of these seven giant firms and the portfolio rules under which investment funds were required to operate

Table 6.3 Investment Fund Ownership of Shares Distributed via Voucher Auctions (in percentages)

Economic subsector	Proportion of investment fund ownership
Finance & insurance	82
Light industry	76
Heavy industry	65
Trade & supply	65
Transportation & communication	60
Research & development	59
Consumer & social services	58
Construction	56
Agriculture, forestry, & water treatment	55

Source: FNP database, August 1993.

[9] It is technically more accurate to speak of "investment groups" than "investment funds" since many of the most important investment companies created multiple funds. Investicni Bank, for example, created 12 different funds for the first wave. In the following data, we aggregate all points and shares held by all the funds established by a single founder.

combine to ensure that one or more of these funds are present in almost all of the 988 firms privatized through vouchers.[10] The implication of this concentration of ownership is a topic for another paper, but what is important for our purposes is the control of these giant IPFs.[11] With the exception of the Harvard Group, all the top seven funds are controlled by Czech or Slovak financial institutions.[12] The state, by virtue of its bank holdings, continues to be present as an indirect owner in almost all firms privatized in the first wave (although that ownership exists three times removed (i.e. the state owns a portion of the banks, which control the investment funds, which control voucher privatized firms). When the data from Tables 6.2 and 6.3 are read together, it becomes clear that many of the sectors where direct state ownership is prevalent also have a high incidence of indirect state ownership. This correlation is particularly robust in heavy industry and the financial sector.

State Ownership of Nonprivatized Assets

While the state has retained ownership of a significant portion of especially important assets included in privatization, it also continues to operate the relatively small number of the pre-1989 enterprises that has fallen outside of the boundaries of the privatization program. While it is not possible to count their exact number, knowledgeable sources place the number of firms not slated for either liquidation or privatization at no more than 500. These enterprises are distributed among various founding ministries: Agriculture, Industry and Trade, Economy, and Telecommunications and Transport, with the Ministry of Industry and Trade holding by far the largest remaining portfolio. As of March 1994, the ministry maintained 316 enterprises in 13 subsectors (three-digit subsector code level) throughout the economy, ranging from mining to internal trade. Ministry enterprises employed 106,787 persons (out of a work force of approximately 5 million), with an average employment per enterprise of 337.[13] The Ministry of Industry and

[10] At the end of the first wave, IPFs were the largest owners in 73 instances, the second largest owner in 518, and the third largest owner in 703. We make the simplifying assumption that a proportionate number of these positions were taken by the top seven IPFs.

[11] The relation between founders and investment funds is more attenuated than we describe. Investment funds were set up by investment companies, which were usually created by subsidiaries of the banks, not by the banks directly, a structure created to circumvent the injunction preventing bank funds from owning shares in other bank funds. Only the Ceska Sporitelna Bank directly established its fund.

[12] Slovenska IB and Vseobecna Uverova are both Slovak financial institutions.

[13] More than 55 of the enterprises have a work force of over 500, with 23 employing over 1,000 workers. The largest single enterprise, a uranium mining firm employs over 7,000 people.

Trade also continues to own 349 enterprises scheduled for termination. These "residual enterprises" employ over 17,000 people.[14]

Hungary

The state in Hungary continues to control many companies through a complicated system of direct and indirect ownership. Quantifying the extent of direct state ownership presents few problems, but only an approximation of the total state holdings of the Hungarian government can be presented because of a lack of available data.

Web of Private and State Ownership

The passage of the Company Law in 1988 resulted in a wave of manager-initiated organizational restructuring of enterprise assets. Seeking to increase the independence of state firms without changing the underlying ownership structure, Hungarian officials in the late 1980s gave increasing power to enterprise managers. The final move was to give managers the right to reorganize all or part of their enterprise into a limited liability company or a joint stock company. Managers cashed in on the opportunity to separate out the best of the enterprise assets in commercial companies and proceeded to distribute shares in these companies. They constructed webs of interlocking company ownerships, some of which included private parties (for details, see Stark 1990; 1995). The end result of this process was that Hungary entered the 1990s with a large proportion of its most valuable productive assets situated in networks of commercial companies that mingled private and state ownership. While the Hungarian government was the owner of a large portion of these assets, state officials had almost completely lost control of the process and were unable to keep track of the ownership structures put in place by their managers.

The advent of the State Property Agency (SPA) put a stop to this chaotic period of company creation and share shuffling, but the government has not been able to roll back ownership structures or disentangle the bramble of property relations. Government officials have been unable to construct comprehensive records on the holdings of each state company, and to some degree, the Hungarian government does not know what it owns.[15] Data

[14] Many of these firms are empty shells whose assets have been removed through various privatization mechanics. There are, however, several firms that retain sizable staffs (8 firms have over 500 employees, with the largest having over 3,000 employees), which are likely to be more difficult to liquidate (unpublished data, Ministry of Industry and Trade, April 1994).

[15] According to one knowledgeable participant in the process, when selling an enterprise, the SPA frequently relies on the bids of private parties to inform it of the assets owned by the firm.

Table 6.4 State Ownership of Firms in Hungary, December 1992

State ownership (in percentages)	Number of firms	Percentage of large firms
100	1,564	16.6
75 – 99.9	626	6.7
50 – 74.9	285	3.0
25 – 49.9	340	3.6
.01 – 24.9	406	4.3
Total	3,221	34.2

Source: 1992 Hungarian Tax Database

included in tax records provide a crude picture of the size and distribution of aggregate state holdings (see Table 6.4).

State Property Agency

In 1989 out of the approximately 2,000 medium and large enterprises and wholly state-owned commercial companies in Hungary, 1,876 firms (with a book value of Ft 1,637.4 billion) were transferred to the State Property Agency.[16] By January 1994, the State Property Agency was the sole owner of only 534 commercialized companies, the majority owner in 38 companies, and a minority owner in 148 firms. In addition to its commercial company holdings, the SPA was also the designated owner of approximately 100 enterprises.[17] The value of the SPA holdings at the beginning of 1994 was listed at Ft 396.30 billion.

The 76 percent decrease in value of the SPA holdings and the 56 percent decrease in the number of firms in the SPA portfolio since 1989 are only partially explained by successful privatization efforts. Through a variety of sale programs, the SPA has succeeded in selling off 438 firms completely and 186 firms partially. The Ft 191.2 billion of assets sold in these proceedings are, however, only slightly more than 11 percent of the value of the original portfolio. The bankruptcy or liquidation of firms (439 firms, valued at Ft 194 billion) and the transfer of firms to other state agencies (236 firms, valued at Ft 1,453.5 billion) account for a much larger part of the decrease in the SPA portfolio.

[16] The transfer was made in accordance with Law No. VII/1990, On the State Property Agency, and Law No. VIII/1990, On the Management of State Property in State Enterprises.

[17] SPA Privatization Monitor, January 1994, p. 1. These numbers differ significantly from those found in the November 1993 Monitor, which lists the SPA as the owner for 209 noncommercialized state enterprises and the sole or partial owner of 760 commercialized firms. According to the November Monitor, the SPA had sold 273 firms outright.

State Holding Company

Most of the assets transferred by the SPA have been given to the State Holding Company (Av. Rt.), created in 1992 in accordance with Law No. LIII/1992 on the Management and Utilization of Property Permanently Remaining in State Ownership. As the title of the law suggests, the equity stakes transferred to the holding company are intended to remain in state hands indefinitely. Given the opportunity in 1992 to designate a portion of the existing state assets as long-term holdings, the government elected to switch the vast bulk of assets to the newly established State Holding Company. The value of the Av. Rt. portfolio exceeded Ft 1,300 billion, distributed among 169 companies, compared with the less than Ft 500 billion assets under the control of the SPA. The portfolio is concentrated in the energy, manufacturing, and financial subsectors with the greatest value in firms in which the holding company is the sole shareholder.[18]

Just over half of the assets transferred to the Av. Rt. had to be kept as permanent holdings (Ft 669 billion); the remainder were eligible for privatization. In the long-term plan for the Av. Rt., the company was to have retained total control of only seven firms, majority or supermajority control of 70 companies, strong minority ownership of 81 other cases, and a relatively small holding in the final 11 firms.[19] The actual portfolio is structured much differently; almost all firms are owned exclusively or in large part by the Av. Rt.

While the data on the direct ownership of the Hungarian state have indicated that little progress has been made in transferring assets to nonstate parties, they have given the impression that state ownership is a relatively discrete phenomenon, primarily including two agencies and fewer than 1,000 firms. In fact, 1992 tax data suggest that the state had a direct or indirect ownership presence in over 3,220 Hungarian firms, or roughly one-third of all Hungarian joint stock companies.[20] This greater than three-fold increase in the number of firms fully or partially owned by the Hungarian state is largely a legacy of the wave of manager-initiated organizational

[18] In 129 companies, the Av. Rt. is the sole shareholder, and in another 24 firms the Av. Rt. has an equity stake of between 50 and 95 %; 96 % of the value of the company's portfolio is located in these firms (see "This Is the Av. Rt." information booklet, 1994).

[19] See "This Is the Av. Rt.," 1994.

[20] Part of the information requested by tax authorities is a breakdown of firm ownership. There is reason to believe that state holdings are systematically under-reported in the database in that many firms list their owners as "domestic legal persons" irrespective of the extent to which these companies are owned by state bodies. All tax data analysis is based on research conducted by Istvan Janos Toth (1994).

restructuring of enterprise assets that commenced with the passage of the Company Law in 1988.

An image of indirect state ownership is illuminated by 1994 data on two subpopulations in the Av. Rt. portfolio.[21] The level of company–company ownership is suggested by the ownership positions held by five randomly selected manufacturing firms owned by the Av. Rt.[22] These firms held shares directly in 49 commercial companies, of which 35 were limited liability companies. In 12 cases the Av. Rt. firm held a majority position, and in 8 cases it was an equal co-owner. Of the 28 minority positions, 18 were under the 25 percent needed to block important corporate actions under Hungarian corporate law. A far more extensive group of ownership positions are maintained by six commercial banks owned by the Av. Rt.[23] The combined holdings of these banks exist in 229 firms, and the equity position of the bank is equal to or more than 25 percent in 145 instances. The number of firms connected by ownership to the Av. Rt. would be further enlarged if it were possible to view the holdings of these 278 first-order companies.

In sum, Hungarian state ownership is both extensive and diffuse. The state continues to own directly most of the assets it held in 1990, and its indirect holdings extend the tentacles of state ownership throughout the economy. In most cases in which the state retains some ownership, it is the majority owner.

Russia

In Russia state holdings are also extensive and widely decentralized. A large proportion of current state ownership relates to assets that were permanently or temporarily excluded from the mass privatization scheme. However, mass privatization in most cases did not lead to full privatization of enterprises, and the state remains an owner in the majority of companies after the completion of voucher privatization.

Mass Privatization

Russia completed its voucher privatization program in June 1994. Between January 1993 and June 1994, an estimated 14,000 to 15,000 companies were

---

[21] We are indebted to George Grunfeld for his assistance in making available data concerning the Av. Rt. portfolio.

[22] This group of firms is a nonrepresentative sample.

[23] The portion of equity owned by the Av. Rt. in these banks ranges from 11% to over 91%. In those banks where the Av. Rt. position is relatively insignificant, the Ministry of Finance owns a large stake. In only one bank does the total combined government ownership dip under 50%, and in this case the Av. Rt. holds a 49.3% position.

sold in voucher auctions, in which on average 18 percent of a company's shares were sold.[24] The remaining shares were offered to insiders or temporarily retained by the state for future sales through cash auctions, investment tenders, or additional voucher auctions. Despite the relatively small proportion of companies' shares privatized by this method, voucher privatization has been important, because a significant portion of Russia's large enterprises were mandated to be privatized under this program.[25] Privatization regulations required companies with more than 1,000 employees and a book value of at least 50 million rubles to set up a privatization plan and initiate their corporatization by submitting this plan to the State Committee on the Management of State Property (GKI). As it turned out, the average charter capital of companies that completed voucher auctions was 69 million rubles with roughly half of all firms being well below the 50 million threshold.[26]

Because little data have been published, a true evaluation of the success of voucher privatization, including total asset value privatized and a breakdown of retained state ownership stakes, is impossible. Data published by the GKI give a breakdown only of the number of companies in various sectors of the economy.[27] According to these data, by June 1994, 101,575 out of 145,638 (or 70 percent) of all former state enterprises had completed privatization.[28] Of these privatized companies, 18,963 [29] (or 18.67 percent) were corporatized and their shares were subsequently sold. An additional 19,199 companies are leased companies, including those with a buyout option. Privatization methods and the extent of privatization for the remaining 64,413 companies are not revealed.

[24] For details on the results of voucher auctions, see Boycko, Shleifer, and Vishny (1995, table 5.1). According to the authors, the total number of voucher auctions (15,779) somewhat overstates the number of companies privatized through voucher auctions, because numerous companies went through more than one voucher auction.

[25] See Presidential Decree No. 721, 1 July 1992, On the Commercialization of State and Municipal Enterprises.

[26] Of those companies that were privatized, 7,647 had an average charter capital of only 12 million rubles (see data published in *Kommersant Weekly* No. 25, 12 July 1994). The relatively high mean is mostly due to the high charter capital of companies in the oil and gas sector, which reached an average of 3,945 million rubles (see ibid.).

[27] The subsectors listed are light industry, food industry, construction, construction materials, agriculture, vehicles, retail trade, wholesale trade, consumer goods, consumer services, unfinished construction objects, and other; the latter comprising the largest group, namely 10.8% of all companies (*Panorama Privatizatsii* No. 13, 40, July 1994, Statistics: Privatization in Numbers).

[28] In this data base, completing privatization, is synonymous with the completion of a particular privatization procedure, not with being privatized 100%.

[29] The number is higher than the number of companies sold through voucher auctions, suggesting that some of these companies were sold by other means.

Insiders and State Ownership

Voucher auctions took place only after insiders had secured a substantial proportion of the shares for themselves under one of the options offered in the privatization program. In roughly two-thirds of all cases, insiders acquired 51 percent of their company's shares in a closed subscription at 1.7 times book value (calculated as of 1 January 1992, unadjusted for inflation). These shares were bought with vouchers, personal cash, or enterprise funds made available to employees in special privatization funds. Those shares that had not been distributed to insiders or sold through voucher auctions were to be transferred via cash auctions, tenders, or other means from the state property funds to nonstate parties.

Privatization arithmetic, based on privatization options and the average amount of shares sold at voucher auctions, suggests that between 15 and 31 percent of the shares remain in the hands of privatization agencies for further sales following the completion of voucher auctions.[30] The extent of this pool of assets is unclear, since there has been no centralized attempt to track dynamic change in postvoucher auction ownership levels. However, state ownership tends to be higher in companies where the state made use of its right to retain a controlling block of shares. This affected mostly companies in high value sectors, such as oil and gas.[31] With respect to all other companies, policies pursued by the regional property funds appear to have played a major role in either downsizing or retaining state holdings. Table 6.5 indicates the extent of state holdings in seven regional property funds.[32]

---

[30] The equation goes as follows: Two-thirds of all companies adopted privatization option 2, according to which 51% of all shares are sold to insiders only. In the majority of option 2 cases, an additional 29% of shares were distributed via a voucher auction, leaving 20% of the shares in the hands of the property fund. For companies privatized under option 1 (which accounts for roughly the remaining one-third, since only very few companies adopted privatization option 3), 40% of the shares were transferred to insiders (25% nonvoting, 10% voting to nonmanagerial workers, and 5% voting to top management), 29% were given into voucher auction, leaving 31% with the property funds. In option 1 and 2 firms, a further 5–10% of total shares could be transferred to a fund for employee shares of the company (FARP), an institution similar to an ESOP, if the privatization plan of the company so provided.

[31] The average number of shares of these companies offered at voucher auctions is below the mean for all companies and amounts to only 15.5% for oil and gas extraction companies, 12.1% for companies in the electro-energy sector, and 10.3% in the oil processing sector (see *Kommersant Weekly* No. 25, 12 July 1994).

[32] The Privatization Project Regional Property Fund Survey was conducted as a letter survey addressed to 70 regional funds in summer 1994.

Table 6.5 Retained State Ownership in Seven Russian Regions, August 1994

Regions*	Number of state holdings by percentage of state ownership						Total
	0	0.1–5	5.1–10	10.01–15	15.01–20	>20	
A	13	14	18	43	26	92	206
B	6	12	13	4	5	27	67
C	122	3	15	0	15	4	159
D	65	5	30	48	52	78	278
E	129	23	22	25	21	155	375
F	14	43	21	3	11	19	111
G	140	21	4	6	5	27	203
Total	489	121	123	129	135	402	1,399
%	34.9	8.6	8.7	9.2	9.6	28.7	100

Source: Privatization Project Regional Fund Survey, summer 1994.
* The names of the regions are kept confidential by request of the interviewees.

The data reveal significant variance in property funds' activity.[33] They show that in the seven regions the state no longer holds any shares in 34.9 percent of the privatized enterprises, but it does hold shares in the remaining 65 percent. In 537 companies, or 38 percent, the state holds more than 15 percent of the shares. Given the normal distribution of shares that results from the various privatization methods,[34] it is highly probable that in these companies the state is the largest single block holder. The postvoucher privatization program, issued by presidential decree in July 1994, mandated complete divestiture of regional fund holdings by 1 January 1995.[35] However, clear signs that this mandate was being followed were visible[36] only in the

[33] These data are obviously not representative but allow at least a glimpse at the size of state holdings after privatization. The findings are generally in accord with ownership data obtained in other studies. See e.g. Blasi and Shleifer (in this volume) whose data reveal that in only 42% of companies has state ownership been reduced to zero. Similarly, results from a survey on Russian voucher funds reveal that the state is represented on companies' boards in 48% of all companies, which suggests that the actual presence of the state as an owner is even higher, see Frydman, Pistor, Rapaczynski (in volume 1).

[34] See Blasi and Shleifer (in this volume); Pistor (1995); Boycko, Shleifer and Vishny (1993), referring also to earlier data collected by Joseph Blasi.

[35] Postvoucher privatization program adopted by Presidential Decree No. 1535, 22 July 1994, published in *Kommersant Weekly* No. 28/2, 2 August 1994, p. 54, continued in No. 29, 9 August 1994, p. 54.

[36] Lists of enterprises subjected to privatization in the second stage of privatization were published by GKI in Rossiiskaya Gazeta starting 14 April 1995. Unfortunately, there is no indication as to how many shares of these companies are to be sold and whether they had already been partially privatized. By 26 April, a list of over 2,300 companies in seven subsectors, including agro-industrial complex, light industry, timber industry, material technical supply, metallurgy, science, education and social sphere, had been published, with the list continuing.

spring of 1995, after the replacement of Vladimir Polevanov (the immediate successor to Anatolii Chubais), who had even suggested the renationalization of parts of the privatized enterprises.

Indirect State Ownership

Indirect state ownership was heavily restricted by Russian privatization legislation. The state, including state-run associations and organizations and firms in which the state still owned 25 percent or more of all shares, was not permitted to buy company shares during privatization. The same restrictions apply to potential founders of voucher investment funds or the management companies of these funds; these prevented the emergence of indirect state ownership through state-controlled financial intermediaries, as happened in the Czech case. However, these restrictions apply only to purchasing shares in the privatization process, not to purchasing shares on secondary markets. Whether state-controlled entities have (re)purchased shares on the secondary market is not known, but proposals aimed at restocking state portfolios continue to be actively generated.[37]

In addition to the block of shares retained by the state in firms included in the mandatory portion of the Russian privatization effort, the state remains a full or partial owner in firms through various other mechanisms. First, Russian privatization legislation excludes a host of assets from privatization.[38] These assets have remained largely under the control of the old branch ministries, usually the founding organs. Second, another category of assets was included in the privatization program at the discretion of the Russian government or GKI[39] or, on the regional state property level, of regional state agencies.[40] In instances where the Russian government or GKI elected to include discretionary firms in the privatization process, it could

[37] Possible options that have been discussed are equity transfers to the state in return for credits (a proposal apparently put forward by the Ministry of Economics) or the creation of state investment funds that would acquire shares in poorly performing companies either on the secondary market or from voucher funds that wanted to clean their portfolio of shares in nonperforming companies. See *Kommersant Weekly* No. 13, 12 April 1994, p. 2, which reports that this was a joint proposal by the Ministry of Economics and one voucher investment fund.

[38] This includes most natural resources, military facilities, atomic reactors, rail and water transport, and the like. See the privatization program for 1994. For a detailed discussion based on the privatization program for 1992, see Frydman, Rapaczynski, Earle, *et al.* (1993b).

[39] The types of enterprises and assets to which these rules apply include, but are not limited to, enterprises in the energy and financial sectors, and enterprises with a charter capital exceeding 1 billion rubles (as of January 1992) irrespective of their industry sector, as well as liqueur companies (under the control of GKI).

[40] This group of enterprises was limited to those necessary for the local infrastructure, including local transport facilities; sewage; pharmacies; and cultural, sport, and educational facilities.

still decide to withhold a controlling block of 25, 38, or 51 percent of the firm's shares from transfer, or issue golden shares.[41] In general, companies that were made subject to controlling state ownership were organized into holding companies,[42] in which control rights were shared between state bodies and management. Only a small proportion of shares in the parent company and the subsidiaries were offered at voucher auctions to the public, and block holding especially by foreign investors was heavily restricted.[43]

Enterprise Associations

In addition to assets retained by official state bodies, quasi-state organizations continue to shape the Russian ownership structure. These organizations are a product of the spontaneous privatization of former ministries or state committees, which now appear in the new clothes of enterprise associations (see Johnson and Kroll 1991; Frydman, Rapaczynski, Earle *et al.* 1993). Their main task is to make themselves indispensable, and their major strategy, therefore, is to regain power by establishing holding companies, obtaining control rights over shares from regional property funds, and lobbying forcefully in Moscow for companies under their umbrella.[44]

Regional Property Funds

Finally, regional administrations, including the regional branches of the federal privatization agencies, have played a role in retaining state assets. Both GKI and the property fund rely on their regional branches for the implementation of privatization. In Russia, true to the age-old principle that "Russia is big and the tsar is far," regions differ substantially from each other in the implementation of privatization, observance of policy guidelines, and usurpation of power. Exceeding their authority, regional GKIs or regional property funds have frequently decided to retain a controlling block or issue

---

[41] Under Russian legislation, a golden share which may be issued only in favor of the state, gives its holder the right to veto some key decisions, including changes in the company's bylaws; reorganizing and liquidating the company; acquiring equity holdings in other entities; and pledging, leasing, or selling assets that are included in the privatization plan of the company. A golden share is initially issued for a period of three years (see Presidential Decree No. 1392, 16 November 1992).

[42] This is particularly true for the oil, gas, and coal sectors.

[43] One of the four oil holding companies adopted a government approved charter providing that any acquisition of shares amounting to more than 1% of all outstanding shares requires approval by the board of directors, and aggregate holdings of all foreign investors may not exceed 5%. See Decree No. 271 of the Russian government, 19 March 1993.

[44] As evidence from field research shows, a representative of such an association can be an attractive candidate for the board of directors, especially when running on a platform of easy access to state credits (unpublished protocol of shareholder meeting attended in Vologda oblast, 25 January 1994).

a golden share. This practice forced the national GKI to adopt a special resolution that explicitly prohibited such activity.[45] A common practice, confirmed by the letter survey of regional property funds, is the transfer of voting rights over shares under the control of property funds to other state structures. This is another instance in which property funds violate if not the letter of the law, clearly its spirit.[46] Privatization legislation provides that proxies may be given to potential buyers of assets to be privatized, excluding state structures. It explicitly rules that the act of registering a company as a joint stock company severs all forms of state control by ministries and federal or regional state administration.[47] Despite this legislation, a coalition of regional privatization agencies and either federal or regional ministries or associations might regain control over parts of residual state assets.[48]

These categories of state holdings encompass only one portion of the Russian state's portfolio of commercially important assets. Beyond ownership of shares in companies, the state has remained a monopolist owner of both agricultural and commercial real estate. Russia's new constitution allows private ownership of land[49] and the postvoucher privatization program reinforces and elaborates a procedure of land privatization laid out in previous presidential decrees.[50] But, as of now, none of these measures has succeeded.

Dangers of State Ownership

The outcome of East European privatization strategies to date, from sale procedures to radical free distribution programs, has been that the state continues to be the largest single owner of privatized assets. We now lay out the potential adverse developmental implications associated with high levels

[45] GKI Regulation No. 1563, 8 September 1993.

[46] Three out of seven property funds reported the transfer of voting rights in numerous companies, particularly in large companies. Note that property funds are legally prevented from transferring title of these shares to the state or state controlled structures. This presumably is why they are transferring proxy rights, not full title.

[47] Section 10.3 of the Regulation, On Commercialization of State Enterprises, adopted by Presidential Decree No. 721, 1 July 1992, and section 6 of the decree itself. In addition, property funds were encouraged to transfer shares that were not sold immediately to potential owners. According to the 1992 privatization law this explicitly excludes any type of state or state controlled structure.

[48] For the role of regional property funds and regional governments, see also Slider (1994).

[49] See Art. 9 of the Constitution.

[50] See e.g. Decree No. 301, 25 March 1992, On Selling Land to Physical and Juridical Persons upon Privatizing State and Municipal Enterprises; and Decree No. 631, 14 June 1992, On the Procedure for Selling Land Plots upon Privatization of State and Municipal Enterprises.

of state ownership in transition states. This analysis is not an argument that state ownership is *per se* bad or that the optimal ownership structure would include no state-owned assets. Rather, we focus on understanding the unique issues raised by existing levels of state ownership in Eastern Europe. This conceptualization includes differentiating the state from all other types of owners in the transition environment and distinguishing state ownership in postcommunist states from state ownership in other regions of the world or in other times.

Ownership is often analyzed as if it involved a unidirectional relationship wherein owners direct managerial conduct. Factoring in the other dimensions of ownership, such as the effect of ownership on shaping the owner or the relationship among owners, is relatively unimportant in market economies, since organizational development and the interaction of owners take place within well-defined institutional confines.

To take a simple example, there is doubtless some impact on the internal dedication of resources when a Western bank becomes an owner of a particular asset, but this resource reallocation is unlikely to have severe consequences for the functioning of the bank, given its organizational history, and the vast array of rules and expectations that define its operations and functions. When we move our bank to Eastern Europe, however, the situation changes dramatically. Here, with little if any organizational history to rely upon or effective regulatory control, the definition of the term "bank" is an open matter, and the impact of the bank as an owner of assets is likely to have significant repercussions both on the way banks will evolve and on a host of economic developmental issues relating to the functioning of capital markets.

The need to consider the multiple dimensions of ownership in Eastern Europe is even more pronounced when dealing with state ownership, since the redefinition of the role of the state is at the heart of the transition process. Our analysis of the potential implications of state ownership focuses on two relationships: that between state ownership and political development and that between state ownership and economic development.

State Ownership and Political Development

While how the state acts as an owner, in Eastern Europe and throughout the world, has been the subject of an extensive body of theoretical and empirical literature (and is a subject we will address below), the influence of state ownership on the development of postcommunist governments has been relatively ignored. This neglect is perhaps due to the inability of most current analysis to provide a theoretical rationale for why state involvement in the economy is particularly problematic. The analysis of the state's transformation from owner to regulator has frequently been within a debate about the relative efficiencies of state regulation versus state ownership – a debate whose premise that regulation and ownership are in large part substitutes necessarily fails to appreciate the distinction between these two types of state involvement.

Ownership versus Regulation

From a legal perspective, state ownership and regulation are, in principle, diametric opposites. The essence of ownership, be it private or state, is its discretionary character. Ownership has been defined as the residual control over rights that have not been contracted out, or over rights that have not been (and often cannot be) made explicit (Grossmann and Hart 1986). While it is possible for governments to develop rules prescribing a process for making decisions, the nature of ownership prevents an *ex ante* determination of how state ownership should be practiced. Challenges to the exercise of state ownership are, therefore, severely limited, open only to those parties with sufficient access to the decision-making process to police compliance with procedural requirements. Regulatory control in contrast is rule based, founded on objectives laid out in specific legislative acts, and limited to the jurisdiction and competencies enunciated in the law. For the most part, regulations are subject to legal challenge based on their content and the manner of their enforcement.

It is certainly true that the sharp contrast in principle that we have drawn between discretionary ownership and rule-based regulation is not always so clear in practice. Decades of experience with attempts to regulate modern market economies and the insights gained from the work of regulatory economists have made us aware of the range of departures possible from the rule-based nature of regulation and of the ways in which the transparency of regulation setting can be obscured. At the same time, governments have experimented with structures and procedures to decrease the discretion afforded to parties entrusted with state ownership rights. These refinements, however, only deflect attention from the fundamental divide that separates regulatory activity from ownership control: regulation follows the principle embedded in modern democracies that acts of government require a legislative basis, while state ownership does not.

Thus, the move from owner to regulator is synonymous with the acceptance by the state of constitutional or legal restrictions on its ability to act, a self-limitation of state power that is implied when governments are said to operate in accordance with the "rule of law." The point here is not that state ownership of economic assets is incommensurate with the rule of law, a position that would imply that no existing state adheres to such principles, but to suggest the critical developmental issues that are raised by the existing high level of state ownership in postcommunist states. Governments throughout Eastern Europe remain owners of large portions of their economies, necessitating broad exercise of discretionary authority, at a time when it is essential for them to renounce the arbitrary and unrestricted use of power that characterized the communist period. At the very least, state ownership in the region increases the complexity of creating credible commitments to abide by legal restraint of state power. At most, high levels of state ownership may make it impossible for governments to credibly commit to distancing themselves sufficiently from the discretionary nature of their Communist predecessors.

In addition, cost considerations may encourage governments to hold on to ownership. Due to the volume of legislation necessary for effective regulation and the range of possible legal challenges to rule setting and application, state action via regulation is a particularly expensive undertaking, especially when compared with the costs of policy implementation through ownership decisions.[51] Moreover, extensive retained ownership may discourage financially and administratively poor governments from dedicating resources to building up regulatory capabilities. State ownership may, therefore, forestall the time-consuming and labor-intensive process of establishing regulatory structures, an inhibitory effect that has implications for the future willingness of governments to abandon their current holdings. In a perverse feedback loop, the weakness of alternative control mechanisms can be used to defend the necessity of state ownership. This reasoning further suppresses the creation of regulatory machinery and results in a deeper entrenchment of state ownership.[52] Such a lock-in effect was part of the dynamic operating in many developing countries in the 1950s and 1960s, when they found it increasingly difficult to give up ownership, a position initially justified by the regulatory weakness of the state (see World Bank 1991, 130).

Nonstate Owners

While there are many reasons to be concerned about the impediment state ownership poses to reconstructing the basis of state action, the aspect most germane to the current study is the consequence for the development of

---

[51] See Sappington and Stiglitz (1987) for a detailed discussion of the transaction costs associated with government involvement in the public and private provision of commodities, along with comments on the relative costs in regulated industries.

[52] The lack of a regulatory structure was specifically cited by a government official as the reason for retention of the state holding in the largest Czech energy company. Notes of interview with CEZ official, on file with the authors.

nonstate owners. When the state reveals a lack of commitment to respect the constraints imposed by the rule of law, nonstate parties may be deterred from investing in the economy. They may fear the possibility of the state diminishing their property rights not only through directs confiscation, but also through indirect appropriation by arbitrary interference (for example, by taxation).

Economic Development

Multiple Objective Functions

Unlike private firms that generally come into existence to exploit profit-making opportunities, the rationales for the creation or continued operation of a state-owned firm can be as varied as the interests that the state pursues. State firms may be established to pursue economic gains, but they may also be created to guarantee the provision of certain services, to coordinate the efforts of competitors who would otherwise not cooperate, to create jobs, or even to increase the popularity of the government or certain politicians. Most state firms are organized for a combination of these and other reasons, with different rationales coming to the fore throughout the life of the firm. These competing and fluctuating objectives complicate tremendously the construction of a criterion for evaluating portfolio performance; whether or not a state firm should be evaluated on its profitability, its contribution to regional employment or training, or its contribution to getting a politician re-elected are political, not economic, questions.[53]

Unable to create an overarching set of rules on how to balance competing social objectives, many governments cede the task of directing and monitoring state ownership to the same portion of the state apparatus responsible for "owning" the state's assets, frequently with only the vague direction that state ownership should serve the "public interest." In the absence of clear objectives, state parties responsible for ownership have wide latitude to create their own measurement criteria.[54] Not surprisingly,

---

[53] Our characterization of the mixed objectives of state ownership and our subsequent discussion of the behavior of state firms have a significant and important counter-example: the Chinese village and township enterprises that have been a key part in the recent Chinese economic boom. See Walder (1994) for an examination of their core features. The performance of these state-owned firms may in part be due to some private-like aspects of government at the cadre level. See Nee (1989) on the "openness" of the organizational boundaries of the government bureaucracy in Chinese rural communities, derived from the agrarian roots of the Chinese Communist Party.

[54] As Niskanen (1973, 39) writes, "It is impossible for any one bureaucrat to act in the public interest, because of the limits on his information and the conflicting interests of others, regardless of his personal motivations."

ownership objectives are often set to maximize the budget for the skills and interests of the participating bureaucrats (Niskanen 1973). The multitude of official and nonofficial functions governing state assets limits both the ability to clarify the management of state assets and the possibility of effective public oversight of state agencies entrusted with ownership responsibilities.

A good example of the tendency for state ownership to be practiced in an equivocal manner may be taken from the international experience with sophisticated state holding companies. The reasons for establishing these companies usually include rationalizing governmental control of its assets, increasing managerial autonomy from political interference, and creating opportunities for greater exposure to market forces. This triad illustrates that the organizational innovation is expected to readjust the relationship between owners and managers in state-owned firms so that they approximate those found in private companies, with subsequent benefits in productive and financial efficiencies.[55] Some state holding structures have been created for particular purposes, such as restructuring (e.g. IRI in Italy) or privatization (e.g. Treuhandanstalt in Germany). The data of studies analyzing state holding companies in various parts of the world indicate that although significant differences exist in the performance of holding companies, they are united in that once they are created, they, or the enterprises they are entrusted with, are rarely liquidated.[56] The longevity of both the holding companies and the underlying enterprises is partially due to the continual flow of government subsidies to these structures.[57]

Insurance Function of State Ownership

Regardless of the opportunities for value creation or enhanced economic efficiencies that can be derived from enterprise bust-ups, the political dynamics of state ownership encourage organizational conservation, even

[55] See Kumar (1992) for an extensive discussion of the organizational rationales for state holding companies.

[56] The finest example of the tendency for state holding companies to avoid liquidation is IRI, the Italian company that today owns stakes in many core Italian firms despite its original charter that called for it to cease to exist five years after it was formed in 1934. An example of a state holding company that has been liquidated after completing its tasks is the German Treuhandanstalt.

[57] See Kumar (1992); at the same time, Kumar somewhat puzzledly concludes that historical experience (particularly in Italy and Germany) shows that when properly organized, state holding companies are effective at restructuring firms and performing other tasks that require strong decision-making. For a detailed analysis of the structure and functioning of the Treuhandanstalt and the degree to which West Germans dominated the organization, as decision-makers, purchasers, and subsidizers, see von Thadden (1994). This "foreign" domination raises significant questions as to whether the Treuhandanstalt offers a meaningful point of comparison for domestic state holding companies in the West or the East.

when the maintenance of existing enterprises requires large direct or indirect grants. The workings of this "state insurance umbrella" can be observed in Eastern Europe where despite the well documented noncompetitiveness of much of the communist-built state sector, the combination of such factors as direct state subsidies, loan forgiveness programs, and noncollection of liabilities owed to the state has been sufficient to allow all but a small number of state firms to continue operation. Even in Poland, the country usually singled out as the place where hard budget constraints have been imposed most rigorously on the state sector, while liquidation procedures have been initiated in over 1,000 nonagricultural state enterprises, only 172 enterprises had actually been liquidated as of 31 December 1993.[58]

Analysts often note the conservative nature of state ownership and the strong powers assembled by enterprise managers during the last years of the communist period and conclude that ownership in Eastern Europe gives state officials little or no power to influence the workings of individual firms. It is clear that over the last 20 years state ownership in the socialist countries has been mostly characterized by a greater or lesser degree of loss of control over assets. This process accelerated during the last years of Communist rule and has only been slightly altered in the postsocialist period. As we will discuss further below, structures to oversee or to define objectives for state asset management have been largely absent in the transition economies. However, the assumption that state officials are of only marginal importance to the firms in state portfolios is too strong. The limited willingness of state authorities to close down enterprises is not synonymous with passive ownership any more than vesting extensive control rights in the hands of enterprise managers implies that the interests of state authorities are not taken into consideration.

Faced with unclear and competing objectives, state ownership is characterized by both neglect and conflictive intervention. Both are problematic. Reliance on neglect has led managers and other insiders to create procedural and structural relations that allow them to capture profits while saddling the state with liabilities – a separation of assets and liabilities that leads to perverse economic development as well as locking-in the need for a continual flow of subsidies. Concern about state intervention, which frequently serves to interject noneconomic concerns into the workings of the firm, leads managers to pursue equivocal business strategies, resulting in sub-optimal results. Furthermore, the combination of state officials' interest

---

[58] Report on Privatization in 1993, Ministry of Ownership Transformation (1994). These numbers do not include completed projects of enterprises involved in the leased buyout program confusingly termed "privatization by liquidation." The slow pace of enterprise liquidation may signal procedural difficulties, as well as significant variance in the interests of parties who initiate liquidation and the state parties running the liquidation process.

to retain the power of ownership and private parties' interest to rid themselves of liabilities creates strong incentives for extensive intermingling of private and state ownership.

Empirical Evidence

The conduct of state firms in Eastern Europe has been the topic of a large and growing number of empirical studies,[59] and has attracted the attention of scholars seeking to model firm behavior under a range of conditions.[60] These studies reveal an array of firm responses to new conditions, as well as the inclination of state managers to pursue restructuring efforts that limit threats to the position of firm insiders.[61] Documented improvements in the economic performance of state firms appear to be as much examples of skillful exploitation of special market conditions as of successful restructuring in such areas as new product development or product mix.[62] Moreover, they may capture only the immediate response to macroeconomic pressures and cannot reveal the long-term sustainability of firms, especially once the expectation fades that firms will be privatized and the control structure be altered at the micro level.

State Firms and Private Firms

The conduct of state ownership also has consequences for private firms. Recognizing the insurance consequences of state ownership, private creditors may decide that they are best served by lending to state firms or those firms

[59] See Carlin, van Reenen, and Wolfe (1994) for a review and synthesis of the findings of all case studies of Eastern European firms reported as of early 1994. The large majority of these studies has been conducted on state-owned enterprises. The study that was probably most influential in shaping the discussion on the potential of state-owned firms to adjust to economic pressure is Pinto, Belka, and Krajewski (1993).

[60] See e.g. Aghion, Blanchard, and Burgess (1993), for a model that explores improvements in managerial behavior that can be expected when managers can effectively signal their competency through successful restructuring, and the government establishes a credible commitment to privatization – conditions that may be hard to find in Eastern Europe.

[61] See Carlin, van Reenen, and Wolfe (1994), regarding a marked tendency for state firms to adopt relatively passive adaptive strategies. But see Commander and Coricelli (1995) for comparative country studies on labor policy in the state and private sectors in several Eastern European nations, revealing near universal voluntary and involuntary shedding of labor in the state sector.

[62] See Pinto, Belka, and Krajewski (1993) reporting improved economic performance in a group of Polish state enterprises that the authors link to a variety of changes in firm behavior. See, however, Pinto and van Wijnbergen (1994) for data that show that 91% of the exports of the chemical and metallurgical firms that dominate the category of profitable firms identified in the earlier paper are identical to products sold in domestic and CMEA markets prior to 1989; and Carlin, van Reenen, and Wolfe (1994) for comments on the special features of the Polish chemical market.

where the state holds a significant equity stake. Data from Western economies indicate a private creditor lending bias in favor of state-owned companies, as a result of which state enterprises tend to finance a higher percentage of their investment through lending than private competitors with otherwise identical features (see Jenkins 1985). Given the limited amounts of capital available in most transition economies, preferential treatment of firms with state ownership may crowd out private borrowers.

In addition to creditors, private and privatized companies, pursuing shelter from uncertainty, may build close relations with those firms whose ownership structure provides them with a state-granted insurance guarantee. Western economic history is filled with examples of the negative economic consequences that occur when private firms in particular sectors or regions become highly dependent as suppliers, purchasers, or collaborators in R&D projects on firms thought to be insured by the state.[63]

Finally, the very size of existing state holdings encourages private forces to dedicate resources to influencing state conduct, rather than investing in more productive activity. The potential return derived from changes in state ownership policy when state ownership is extensive may dwarf the more risky returns to be gained from successfully competing in product markets.[64] Those private and state parties able to profit from influencing ownership practices will have strong incentives to press for the continued existence of the source of their revenues, which is state ownership (see North 1990, 99).

Retained State Ownership in Transition Economies – A Framework for Analysis

Listing ways in which state ownership could negatively affect economic and political development in Eastern Europe does not directly translate into an analysis of the impact state ownership has had in the countries of the region. As a first step toward linking our theoretical critique of state ownership with the portfolios of state assets we previously detailed, we assume a limited

---

[63] See Grabher's study (1991) on the Ruhr valley: when the decline of the heavily subsidized coal and steel sector finally could not be prevented anymore, it was not only the coal and steel industry in the region that crashed, but a whole range of supplier, processing, and R&D firms that had built too close ties with the subsidized industries.

[64] As Douglass North (1990, 87) writes, "To the degree that there are large pay offs to influencing the rules and their enforcement, it will pay to create intermediary organizations between economic organizations and political bodies to realize the potential gains of political change. The larger the percentage of society's resources influenced by governmental decisions (directly or via regulation), the more resources will be devoted to such offensive and defensive organizations."

number of basic conditions: that the existence of state ownership has some developmental consequences for all countries; that these effects vary widely along multiple dimensions; and that the influence of state ownership is impossible to measure directly since this would require the ability to compare existing circumstances with the political and economic development that would have existed but for the presence of state ownership – a counterfactual test best reserved for laboratory settings or for relatively simple phenomena.[65]

Our analysis of the dangers of state ownership has indicated that the level of state involvement in firm activities on the one hand and the commitment of the government to ensuring the continued existence of state firms on the other hand are key aspects in the development of state holdings. Yet many standard ways of analyzing portfolios reveal little about these elements. Divisions of state holdings along sectoral lines or according to the size or value of the state position are traditional classification principles, but their limitations for our purposes are readily apparent. The level of state involvement in the working of two state-owned assets in the same sector, for example, may bear few similarities because of the differences in the rates of unemployment where the firms are located, the composition of the regional economies in these locations, or the political strength of the two managers, to name just a few variables. Merely increasing the number of explanatory factors to classify assets and try to extrapolate behavioral implications leads to the construction of a matrix only slightly less complicated than the phenomena being categorized. Moreover, even such a complex matrix is bound to remain a static description of existing state ownership with no hints as to the course of future developments.

To capture the dynamics of state ownership in the transition process, it is important to determine the rationale for the retention of assets, along with identifying the state structures that dominate decision-making about asset management. Only by combining these elements is it possible to capture the essence of the evolving nature of state ownership in Eastern Europe, because only together do they bring into focus the interests of the state structures and the implications for the way in which assets will be managed.

---

[65] It is possible to examine partially the influence of state ownership on firm development by comparing the performance of firms where the state continues to be present as an owner and those where the state is absent. See Commander and Coricelli (1995) for data revealing differential labor policies pursued by state, private, and privatized firms in countries throughout Eastern Europe. The authors are involved in an ongoing CEU Privatization Project–World Bank research project that examines connections between ownership, corporate governance, and performance.

Residual and Elected State Holdings

Unlike other classes of owners, state ownership in transition states is characterized by the retention of assets, not their acquisition. The preservation of ownership is ambiguous, because it is uncertain whether the perpetuation of the relationship was based on an official allegiance to ownership or occurred for other reasons, such as the absence of interested buyers or the lack of interest by the state party designated as the seller to conclude the transfer. These differences in the basis for ownership have strong implications for the manner in which the state will act as an owner.

The most direct link between a justification for state ownership and a behavioral expectation exists for those assets that the government has already offered for sale or otherwise made available for transfer. The mechanical problems in divestiture which have resulted in states retaining "residual holdings"[66] come in many different forms, from the difficulty in creating an auction process calibrated to ensure that the market clears, to failed sale offers where failure is closely associated with resistance by state authorities to part with equity. Despite these differences in the nature of the technical trouble, residual holdings share the feature that official government policy has renounced an interest in keeping them as part of the portfolio. Residual assets, therefore, are likely to be maintained on a temporary basis. Consequently, the dedication of official resources to these firms and the level of sanctioned involvement in their activities should be minimal.

On the opposite side of the spectrum, we find assets the state elected to retain permanently or temporarily. Different rationales govern the decision usually made at the outset of privatization to retain assets in state ownership. As a result, the state is likely to pursue a host of different policies in these companies. For example, most transition governments and many analysts are convinced that a group of firms exist that are potentially viable but are in drastic need of restructuring. In their current form these firms are unlikely to find investors who can credibly commit to devote the necessary time, resources, and skills to the risky task of restructuring.[67] Governments retain these assets due to conditions specifically connected to the transition period.

---

[66] The term "residual holding" is used in this chapter exclusively to refer to assets that remain in state hands despite having already been made available for transfer. All other state holdings exist due to an affirmative act on the part of the government or other state actors.

[67] Even if outside investors appear, the state faces a significant moral hazard problem given that many of these firms are very large, and the state's commitment to letting market forces determine the fate of the firm is of questionable credibility. To the extent that investors believe that the state will ultimately come in to bail out the firm if it proves necessary, investors have incentives to engage in outright fraud or excessively risky behavior.

For this set of assets, the government has committed itself to an activist ownership stance for an interim period, including active monitoring of management, if not the day-to-day running of the firm. A different type of ownership management can be expected when ownership has been retained because of particular features of assets, such as their scale (in the case of power generation facilities) or their perceived importance to a cultural heritage (PICK sausages or Herend porcelain). Since the rationale for preserving these holdings is neither temporally nor developmentally contingent, the commitment to retaining these assets is long term, while the level of involvement in firm activities is much less definite.

Acquisition of Control Rights

The landscape of observable state holdings is, of course, not as clear cut, as the distinction between residual and elected state holdings suggests. During the privatization process, the government or other state structures may decide to withdraw assets from privatization or to delay, if not indefinitely postpone, the transfer of assets in selected enterprises. Again, the rationales for these measures may vary. Governments may decide that rather than subjecting themselves to a giveaway of potentially valuable assets, they should hold on to shares for future sales that might generate revenue for the state budget. Alternatively, other state structures may realize that the retention of state holdings is the only justification for their own existence and, therefore, be reluctant to support rapid privatization, which is bound to undermine their own future. Finally, even where the central government remains committed to a wholesale transfer of state assets to nonstate parties, regional governments can derail privatization efforts and lobby for an active state policy that secures employment or protects an industry sector that is concentrated in the region.

Lock-in Effects

Even in cases where reform governments maintain an interest in decreasing the size of their portfolios, they may find that the choices they have made at the beginning of the privatization process, the intragovernmental struggles over the management of assets, and the actions of private parties increase the difficulties of disposing of the remaining state holdings. Thus, when governments elect to become actively involved in the restructuring of firms, they may find it difficult to extricate themselves from ownership. If the government is able to successfully manage the restructuring effort, there is little reason to give up ownership. If, on the other hand, the restructuring effort fails and the firm remains in desperate need of subsidization, the government is unlikely to find a private buyer and may be able to renounce its ownership only by closing down the firm, which decision is, of course, the one the government declined to make earlier in the transition process. The more transition governments have become associated with the management of firms, the more problematic they are likely to find the transfer of assets retained at the beginning of the privatization process.

Governments may also find themselves locked into their current ownership positions due to the activity of nonstate parties. We have discussed the incentive private groups have to associate themselves with state holdings so that they can dispose of their liabilities. While private–state links have taken different forms, many include arrangements that mix together state and private ownership in the same firm. Any action the state now takes to promote the sale of remaining state holdings directly impacts on the value of these private equity positions. The value of private holdings may decrease in the eyes of current shareholders with the removal of the state insurance umbrella. However, the value of private holdings may also increase, as the transfer of assets to private parties may increase liquidity and market valuation of shares free from state interference. To the extent private shareholders oppose a sale, because they see greater value in continuous state ownership, the state may find itself in a private lock-in. Finally, where private shareholders attempt to benefit from future sales, political pressure may prevent the state from carrying out transactions that appear to benefit only a minority. As a result, the sale of retained state assets could remain a highly politicized issue.

Multiple Rationales

The preceding examples by no means exhaust the possible explanations for the continued existence of retained state ownership. However, they indicate that the nature of state holdings and the way in which the state expects to manage them may differ considerably even in a single country. As rationales are not exclusive either for a single enterprise (i.e. multiple policy rationales for holding onto a single firm) or for general policies (i.e. a policy reason for holding onto an asset does not preclude a fiscal reason), multiple explanations can be expected for most state holdings. Moreover, governmental decisions concerning the management of ownership will alter the initial rationales. We are, therefore, faced with an evolutionary process whose outcome is not easily predictable.

Control and Management of Retained State Assets

The governments of the Czech Republic, Hungary, and Russia have only belatedly realized the new challenges posed by the existence of extensive state holdings after the completion of privatization programs. The immediate response has often been an attempt to create new control structures for the management of these assets or to reallocate control rights to different state structures. As we have seen, the (reform) government is not necessarily the only player in this game. In each country we can observe different patterns of policy goals pursued by various actors, as well as a wide variance of effects for the companies concerned. By applying our analytical framework to the Czech Republic, Hungary, and Russia, we can draw some preliminary conclusions about the importance of the presence of the state as an owner.

The Czech Republic

Residual and Elected Holdings

The aggregate Czech holdings we have documented can be neatly divided into relatively distinct subpopulations. Czech holdings are separated into a small number of positions retained due to the importance of these assets to the economy, a larger number of transitional industrial policy holdings and stakes held for fiscal reasons, and finally, a large but diminishing number of equity positions derived from the mechanical failures associated with shares that remained at the end of the first wave. The largest class of temporary holdings, selected mainly for fiscal reasons, is a 3 percent stake in every company that was subject to privatization; this stake was transferred to the Restitution Investment Fund (RIF). The purpose of this fund is to cover payment to persons deemed to be owed cash restitution for the acts of the previous regime.[68]

The importance of involuntarily retained assets in the overall portfolio is

[68] The Restitution Investment Fund (RIF) was created in accordance with Law No. 403/1990, Mitigation of Property Related Injustices, to provide a central fund for the compensation of recognized victims of the communist regime. Individuals who are judged to be owed compensation are awarded RIF shares if it is not possible to return lost property; or compensation for nonproperty related injustices. RIF was initially capitalized by receiving 3 percent of the shares of each firm privatized in the first wave of privatization, and has recently received an infusion of new shares from each company privatized in the Second Wave. While a small number of shares have been distributed to individuals for compensation, nearly 60 percent of the 3.7 billion RIF shares are owned by the FNP, and over 70 percent of the voting shares are held by it. No requirements mandate that RIF maintain shares in all firms, but in spring 1994, RIF still held shares in over 1,000 first wave firms. Prior to the transfer of second wave shares, the value of the fund stood at CSK 11 bln. Interview with Arnost Dobsa, on file with the authors.

relatively minor. Residual positions exist because of under-subscription to shares in voucher auctions or the failure to complete a direct sale. As sales played a relatively insignificant role in Czech privatization plans,[69] the 6 percent of shares that remained at the end of the first wave make up the majority of these stakes. The Ministry of Privatization has moved aggressively and successfully to sell off these positions via share offerings in the stock market, and by including firms that failed to sell a large number of their shares in the first wave into the second wave.

While the current portfolio has been largely elected, Czech official policy has renounced an interest in the long-term maintenance of this level of ownership. A combined total of 41 permanent stakes were reserved for the state in the firms that were included in the first and second waves.[70] Most of these holdings were distributed throughout the economy, but as we have seen, a concentrated set of long-term stakes were created in the banking sector, where almost 20 percent of the asset value of the four banks privatized in the first wave were reserved for the state.[71] The cluster of long-term holdings of the Czech state is enlarged by the estimated 500 enterprises that have been excluded from the privatization process.[72]

The remaining temporary positions can be divided into two unequal groups. Approximately 400 stakes are slated to be transferred primarily through sale tenders or auctions; the primary rationale for their creation is seemingly a fiscal one – the desire to sell these large block holdings for a price that would generate some revenue for the state budget. The final group of 45 temporary holdings, encompassing majority stakes in many of the largest industrial firms in the nation,[73] is planned to be extensively restructured by the state prior to eventual transfer.

[69] Approved privatization plans for the first wave called for transfers based on direct sales, auctions, or tenders to account for approximately 4% of the value of assets to be privatized. The relative importance of sale procedures increased slightly in the second wave. The combined number of approved privatization plans that designated shares for sale in the first and second waves does not exceed 250, and approximately 90% of these sales have been completed (FNP data base, November 1994).

[70] Czech privatization plans include a separate category of shares designated "shares to be held permanently by the FNP." Twenty-eight permanent stakes were set aside in the first wave, with an additional 13 permanent positions created in the second wave.

[71] The second largest concentration of permanent stakes was created in the basic research sector, where 5% of the shares were reserved for the state. In contrast, less than 0.05% of the shares offered in first wave light or heavy industrial firms were designated as permanent holdings (see 1993 FNP database).

[72] The extent of the state's commitment to maintain these enterprises is, in fact, relatively uncertain. An inventory of remaining enterprises is now being undertaken, and there have been some rumors that a third wave of privatization is a possibility.

[73] Of the 45 firms, 17 are involved in electrical or gas production and distribution. The

Acquisition of Control Rights

The Czech privatization program has been highly centralized with little to no discretion left to branch ministries or local governments. This has minimized the struggle within the state apparatus for holding control rights to parts of the state portfolio. Nevertheless, at the end of the first wave control rights in 45 companies[74] were reallocated from the FNP, the body in charge of selling state assets, to the Ministry of Industry and Trade, the legal successor of numerous branch ministries. The purpose of this transfer was to restructure these companies extensively before eventual transfer. Whether restructuring will be successful and the sale of assets eventually completed are still open questions. A time frame for the completion of this transitional industrial policy task has not been set. The original plans for the restructuring of only one set of firms among these 45 companies envisioned a five-year process.

Management of State Holdings

At the outset of privatization, the goal to privatize as many assets as quickly as possible shaped the government's policy of managing state assets during the interim period. Assets not marked for privatization were mostly left with the founding ministries. For residual or elected state holdings, allocation of control rights and the development of management structures were decided mostly on an *ad hoc* basis, with a limited number of central actors participating.

The government is most passive toward its restitution fund holdings. RIF is managed by a private investment company selected by the Fund of National Property.[75] Although the FNP is the owner of more than two-thirds of RIF's shares, the FNP's oversight of the RIF is limited to one individual who serves on the four-member management board. In addition to the FNP, the Czech Land Fund, a bank, and an independent lawyer are on the board. No clear rules appear to govern the manner in which the RIF portfolio is to be managed, and the management contract, which was concluded for an indefinite period, contains no standards to measure contractual compliance. The most important action the board has taken is to prevent concentration

---

remaining 28 firms are concentrated in mining and heavy industry. The importance of these transferred firms to the national economy is suggested by the fact that among the companies involved are 14 of the top 25 nonfinancial firms in the country in terms of revenue. For listing of Czech firms based on 1993 revenues, see *Central European Economic Review*, Summer 1994, p. 12.

[74] Originally, the ministry had requested over 70 companies.

[75] The investment company, Prvni Investicni, is associated with the Investicni Banka.

of the portfolio, thus ensuring that RIF will be the most passive of portfolio investors.

Minimal monitoring also generally characterizes government manage-ment of its residual stakes. Held and managed exclusively by the Fund of National Property, an agency that officially disclaimed any responsibility for corporate governance matters, residual stakes are only infrequently the subject of serious governmental concern. The internal rules of the FNP do not require it to be represented on either the supervisory or management board in companies where its stake is under 25 percent. The fund is also not required to attend shareholder meetings in cases where its share is under 20 percent. As a result, residual holdings below these thresholds are left un-monitored by the FNP.[76]

Active monitoring with strong conservative tendencies is the hallmark of FNP activity in the 400 firms in which it manages sizable temporary stakes. Since temporary stakes exceeded 20 percent in over 200 cases, the FNP is represented on the supervisory board and/or management board in a large number of these firms, and FNP representatives take part in shareholder meetings. No legislation defines the manner in which the FNP is to act as an owner, but a set of internal rules has been crafted to guide FNP representa-tives at shareholder and board meetings. Czech law requires that all directors serve as individuals, not as representatives of legal entities. Therefore, individuals nominated by the FNP to sit on boards owe a duty of loyalty not to the government, but to the company. Reflecting the assumption that temporary holdings will be retained only until a suitable sales contract is concluded, FNP officials maintain that when controversial issues arise at the board level, their representatives are supposed to protect the interests of the future owners, a rather vague instruction given the uncertainty as to the identity of the future parties. The role of custodian for future owners has been translated to mean that government representatives have generally voted against fundamental restructuring of firms, and particularly against the sale of valuable firm assets.[77] At the shareholder level, individuals desig-nated by the FNP to exercise voting rights at the annual meetings are given guidelines. How to vote on issues on the agenda is usually decided after consultation with FNP divisional chiefs.[78]

[76] Anecdotal evidence from several interviews with company managers supports the claim that the government is mainly an absentee owner in involuntarily-held firms. In those firms in which the FNP was under 20%, managers uniformly reported that no FNP representative participated in any corporate governance activity.

[77] In several interviews, managers complained about their limited ability to deal with finan-cial distress due to the FNP's unwillingness to consider selling off parts of the firm.

[78] The FNP is empowered to vote its shares without consulting with other government agencies except in three cases, enumerated in Law No. 171/1991, where the FNP is required to

The ownership strategy of the government is considerably more activist in firms that the government has deemed to be too important to allow to fail.[79] While the shares in these core financial and industrial firms are "owned" by the FNP, separate management structures have been constructed for each different type of asset. Thus, the 30–35 percent stake that the government retains in each of the major banks is managed by a committee comprised of the chairman of the Fund of National Property, the minister of privatization, and the general director of the Czech National Bank. Although few details concerning the government's actions as an owner are available, close monitoring of bank activities takes place, and the government is reported to have used its ownership position on several occasions to intrude in bank behavior.[80] Few Czech observers, however, believe that the government actively uses its bank ownership positions to intrude into the activities of the bank-dominated funds, or through them, into those of the firms held by the funds.

A greater level of state involvement exists in firms that are held for fiscal and industrial policy reasons and that the government is attempting to restructure through a nonstate party. In these firms (best represented by the large heavy manufacturing firm Skoda koncern Pilzen, a.s.) management of the government's holding is handled by an ill-defined group of officials from the FNP, the Ministry of Industry and Trade, and the Ministry of Finance. They engage not only in close monitoring of managerial behavior, but also are active in locating necessary financing and interacting with other stakeholders.[81] The apex of activist government involvement is reached in those firms where the government is leading the restructuring efforts. This group of firms, comprised of the 45 firms whose management was transferred to the Ministry of Industry in Trade, operate with the day-to-day involvement

consult with the Ministry of Privatization prior to voting on: change of the property structure affecting more than 20% of the firm's assets; leasing of assets affecting more than 20 percent of the capital; and an increase in the firm's capital of over 20%. Failure to comply with the law can result in criminal sanctions.

[79] It is not possible to identify with any precision the identity of firms in this category, although some suggestion concerning their numbers is given by the government's maintenance of blocking or majority positions in over 20 of the 25 largest firms in the nation as of mid-1994, and its significant presence in most of remaining key heavy manufacturing firms.

[80] The most sensational instance of this behavior reportedly occurred when, at the insistence of the Klaus government, the editor of a bank-owned newspaper highly critical of the government was fired. The widely reported governmental involvement in the lending policies of the large banks is probably of much greater importance to the economy but has been much harder to verify.

[81] For a detailed examination of government behavior in this group of firms, see Hayri and McDermott (1994) and McDermott (1994).

of government officials.[82] In conducting its management of these firms, the ministry is subject to little oversight. Transfer of managerial authority over the firms was effectuated by a private contract between the chairman of the FNP and the minister of industry and trade, a document that neither required nor received legislative scrutiny.

Lock-in Effects

The Czech government is subject to lock-in pressures in its holdings in both the financial and heavy manufacturing sectors. The original justification for retaining large stakes in banks was for the state to provide a minimum degree of economic stability. But whether the Czech government will be able to transfer remaining stakes in banks to private hands in the short to medium term is questionable. The first announcements of proposals to sell off a portion of the state position were resisted by current shareholders, which, as we have already noted, are primarily investment funds associated with "rival" banks. The lack of interest in the banking community for a sell-off of the state's holdings would seem to be a classic example of an ownership lock-in brought about by private interests. A different set of ownership dynamics operate in the heavy manufacturing sector, where the Czech government may find its exit options constrained by its activist ownership stance. The fact that ownership in the heavy industrial sector is strongly dominated by the FNP in conjunction with bank-dominated investment funds suggests that concerns over the role of the state as an owner in the Czech Republic will be focused on the sector that lies at the core of the Czech economy.

Hungary

Residual and Elected Holdings

The nature of the Hungarian privatization process precludes any attempt to match various types of state holdings with state bodies or to trace the many indirect links between state enterprises, which provide only a shell for a host of private activities, and their founding organs, regional governments, or other parts of the state administration. The classification presented here is, therefore, only a rough approximation and mostly incomplete, as only direct state holdings can be captured. Nevertheless, it gives some insights into the division of power over state assets within the Hungarian government.

---

[82] In one of the firms given to the Ministry of Industry and Trade, the supervisory board has met over 20 times in the last 12 months, giving some indication of the degree of involvement in company activities. In this firm, the role of the supervisory board had been enhanced so that no important decision could be taken prior to receiving board approval.

Four principal groups of state owners manage the Hungarian direct holdings. (1) The SPA owns all of the residual holdings, a total of approximately 700 firms. (2) The Av. Rt. owns temporary and permanent shares in 169 firms, with some component of the holdings in each firm designated as permanent stakes (although temporary stakes make up roughly three-quarters of the Av. Rt. total). (3) Branch ministries directly own a few significant assets, such as the Hungarian railroads and portions of the largest banks (holding over 70 percent of the shares in two of the largest banks). (4) The Treasury Asset Management Organization (KVSZ) owns a variety of assets, with a primary focus on real estate.

Unlike the Czech Republic, where it is possible to match subgroups of temporary and permanent holdings with different policy or fiscal objectives, crisp distinctions do not seem applicable to the Hungarian portfolio of elected holdings. The rationale for placing assets under the authority of the Av. Rt. is stated in section 2 of the Hungarian law On the Management and Utilization of Entrepreneurial Assets Permanently Remaining in State Ownership (No. LIII/1992). According to this law, they shall include assets of "economic-strategic, national economy, or other important interests." Holdings can also be transferred to the Av. Rt. because they serve national public service purposes; because economies of scale require the unified integration of research, production, and distribution; or because the sale of the firm is expected to entail a lengthy process. The ultimate decision to transfer assets to the Av. Rt. and thereby withdraw them from immediate privatization, was vested in the Hungarian government. As has been documented already, the Av. Rt. ended up with some of the largest and most valuable firms in the country, many of which it owns completely. The six subcategories into which the Av. Rt. has organized its portfolio give a glimpse of the industry sectors dominated by this state agency: energy and infrastructure, industry, agriculture and forestry, research and development, culture, and financial institutions.

State assets under the control of the SPA are subject to privatization, indicating that the SPA is only a temporary owner of state assets. The temporary status of these assets has not prevented the SPA from attempting to be actively engaged in selecting a buyer, setting the sales price, and establishing the conditions under which the new owners must utilize their property.[83] The SPA's efforts at designing the Hungarian economy have repeatedly been frustrated by the lack of interest of investors, which has

---

[83] The SPA has repeatedly attempted to establish extensive conditions in their tender offers, including employment floors and investment commitments, as well as limitations on changes in the postprivatization ownership structure.

reduced SPA leverage in negotiating with the employee or managerial-led groups that have dominated privatization sales in the last few years. The block of shares that the SPA frequently retains after selling a portion of its shares to a buyer and its position as sole owner in the firms that have yet to be privatized at all give the SPA the chance to actively manage a wide range of residual assets.[84] However, the sheer size of the SPA portfolio has worked against an active management strategy, and the bonus structure of SPA staff and enterprise managers has always focused attention on privatization and not firm performance.[85]

Acquisition of Control Rights

The acquisition of control rights over state assets took place, for the most part, prior to the establishment of either the SPA or the Av. Rt., with enterprise management having been the main beneficiary. The devolution of authority to enterprise managers did not prevent fierce battles among state bodies for the authority to control the state's remaining property rights. As legislative guidelines concerning the types of assets to be retained by the state on a permanent basis were vague, the outcome was ultimately left to the relative power of various state bodies, with some assets shifted two or three times due to alterations in the balance of power. Most of the state banks, for example, were first owned by the SPA, later transferred to the Av. Rt., and are currently shared by the Av. Rt. and the Ministry of Finance. The constant theme in the allocation of ownership authority between 1990 and 1994 is that the government continued to move firms into those structures over which it had the greatest control.[86]

The desire to capitalize a newly created pension and health fund with assets from privatized companies only served to complicate the state infighting over the fate of state property, as did the distribution by the first postcommunist government of a vast sum of compensation notes to be redeemed by the sale of state properties.[87] Determination of how assets

---

[84] In the early years of the SPA, official policy was to sell a 49% block to an investor with an option to purchase another portion of the firm at a later date. Since 1993, the SPA has made a practice of retaining a sizable minority position in most of the firms it has sold, with the residual SPA position reserved for eventual transfer to the state social insurance fund.

[85] SPA managers can receive bonuses of up to 120 percent of their base salary. Proceeds from privatization are weighted twice as strongly as company performance in determining the size of the bonus. SPA staff payments are tied even more closely to proceeds in privatization.

[86] The latest step in the reallocation of control rights over state assets has been a merger of the SPA and the Av. Rt. into the State Privatization and Asset Management Company pursuant to the adoption of a new privatization law on 9 May 1995.

[87] The Hungarian government has distributed compensation coupons worth over Ft 220 billion. to victims of the Communist regime in accordance with Law No. 33/1991, On Partial

should be apportioned to meet the state's commitments was left to a committee comprised of the representatives of all the major interested groups. It is not surprising that the result has been a great deal of acrimony and very little progress on determining the ultimate allocation of firms.

In addition, there are some indications that even when control rights have been securely vested in one of the many competing agencies, the agencies are unable to establish their authority. As we will discuss below, both the SPA and the Av. Rt. have concluded that they cannot rely on their board nominees to protect their interests. At the same time, appointments of state directors by the SPA or the Av. Rt. to corporate boards, especially in large and valuable companies, have been highly politicized. Different state bodies often tried to place "their" people on such boards, which may well have given them increased leverage in those companies.

Management of State Holdings

As in the Czech Republic, management of state assets is mostly decentralized, and the rules governing state agents' activities in these companies are established separately by different state bodies. However, in contrast to the Czech Republic, it is difficult to trace any clear difference in the way assets are managed either to the purpose of their retention or the state agency in charge.[88] Companies under the SPA or the Av. Rt. are corporatized, and both agencies have had to learn how to deal with the problem of monitoring within the framework provided by corporate law. Completely understaffed for the tasks of overseeing the management of state assets,[89] the state agencies were forced to rely on outside representatives for active monitoring. Given that the

Compensation for Damages Unlawfully Caused by the State to Properties Owned by Citizens in the Interest of Settling Ownership Relations. These coupons can only be used to purchase state property. One measure of the level of public confidence in the government's commitment to make sufficient property available to redeem the coupons is the sharp discount (of up to 80%) at which the coupons are traded.

[88] The ownership behavior of these agencies was expected to exhibit dramatically different levels of activism, an expectation clearly revealed in both the titles of the laws creating the respective competencies of the agencies, and the content of these laws. Law No. 53/92, On the Management and Utilization of Entrepreneurial Assets Permanently Remaining in State Ownership, contains the following provision concerning ownership rights: "The shareholder's rights in the [State Holding Company] are personally exercised by the Minister appointed by the Government as the representative of the State." In contrast, section 70 of Law No. 54/1992 on Sale, Utilization, and Protection of Assets Temporarily Owned by the State states, "The Property Agency is entitled to manage the state property only exceptionally and temporarily. The opinion of the minister of the relevant portfolio shall be obtained in order to make a decision about the management of state property."

[89] The level of staffing at the SPA is indicated by the total of 15 case officers assigned to a division of the SPA with responsibility for over 250 firms (interview with Mr. Atilla Lascsik, State Property Agency, June 1994).

process of appointing board members soon became an intensely political process, both the SPA and the Av. Rt. determined that their organizational interests were not sufficiently protected by their nominees, and both agencies have moved to disempower management and supervisory boards in order to centralize key control decisions. As part of this process, the SPA and the Av. Rt. have frequently changed the corporate bylaws of companies in their portfolios to vest shareholder meetings with the right to set managerial compensation and to hire and fire the chief executive officer. The decision to remove power from management and supervisory boards requires that control and monitoring of management is limited to at best a few sessions a year and to the most egregious cases of asset stripping or management failure; all other cases are likely to escape the eyes of state representatives.[90]

Still, board representation in at least partially state-owned companies appears to be an attractive position for former managers of state enterprises and state officials, who together comprise the largest pool of applicants for these positions.[91] However, the fees paid to management and supervisory board members could account for this, rather than a desire to strengthen control rights.[92]

These results suggest that the Hungarian state has limited impact at the company level, irrespective of the length of time assets are expected to be held by the state or the reason that justified their retention in the first place. Nevertheless, this does not mean that the state is uniformly passive or of marginal importance. The presence of the state as an owner has given it some leverage in influencing certain decisions, such as energy prices or the closure of factories in regions with high unemployment. Moreover, it has granted enterprise management access to the powerful network of state officials who are still closely involved in directing the flow of revenues and contracts within the economy, including credit contracts with state-owned banks.[93] Thus, for all the diffusion of direct state control, the web of state

[90] Even outright asset stripping has been brought to the attention of Av. Rt. only through newspaper reports; interviewee with Av. Rt. employee, 23 June 1994.

[91] Av. Rt. held a competitive tender in the fall of 1993 for supervisory and management board positions in companies in its portfolio, and representatives of the agency reported that these were the people mostly represented.

[92] Depending on the placement of a company in terms of its size and economic importance, in companies owned by Av. Rt., supervisory board members may receive remuneration of between Ft 15,000 and 80,000 per month, and management board members between Ft 20,000 and 100,000. The respective fee structure at SPA ranges from Ft 14,000 to 40,000 for supervisory board members and Ft 20,000 to 50,000 for management board members.

[93] The chairman of the supervisory board of one state company interviewed suggested that rather than applying to state-owned banks directly for credits, they spoke to the Av. Rt. individual responsible for their sector, and that this person in turn contacted the Av. Rt. individual in charge of the banking sector.

ownership is more than a powerless relic of early spontaneous privatization. At least for large and valuable companies, it provides an important network for decision-making and economic governance.

Lock-in Effects

The potential lock-in of existing state ownership is an endemic problem throughout the Hungarian portfolio. As we have documented, private parties in Hungary have been able to intertwine themselves with state firms in a dizzying array of organizational relationships. While these arrangements were initiated prior to 1990, the postcommunist governments have been largely unable to disaggregate firms or affect the level of company–company ownership. The disintegration of firm boundaries has reached extraordinary dimensions.[94]

The fluidity of organizational arrangements presents severe barriers to the sale of state assets. Since the boundaries of firms are so vague, it is difficult to know what property is owned by a particular firm, much less what rights are acquired with ownership. It is, therefore, not surprising that outside investors have shown little interest in many parts of the state portfolio, and the only parties that are convinced that they can profit from ownership are the same enterprise managers who were instrumental in creating the current confusion of property rights. Even the enterprise managers and employee groups that have dominated privatization sales during the last two years have been willing to enter into purchase only with extraordinarily high levels of state guaranteed and subsidized loans.[95]

The interwoven nature of the Hungarian economy not only diminishes the ability to find buyers for state property, but also increases the risk for the government of parting with ownership. The failure of one large firm has the potential to have disastrous repercussions throughout the economy, a fact that is obvious to state and private parties alike. Given the choice of being held hostage by private parties threatening to close down a firm unless they are provided with sufficient subsidization, or the retention of these assets in state hands, the Hungarian government may determine that maintaining ownership is the least unpleasant alternative.

---

[94] See the contribution of David Stark in this volume for a particularly clear picture of the organization of economic activity in Hungary.

[95] Data from a sample of 17 cases of employee buyouts in Hungary from 1991 through 1993 found that 11 of the firms financed more than 70% of their purchase with loans (see Karsai and Wright 1994). For a detailed analysis of employee buyouts in Hungary, see Earle and Estrin, in this volume.

Russia

Residual and Elected Holdings

As we have seen, Russian privatization programs divided all state assets into those that were to be retained by the state, for which privatization depended on a decision by GKI or the whole government, those for which privatization was mandatory, and those that should be privatized only by regional privatization programs. But these categories are only a rough indication of the type of assets the state may have elected to retain. Various state structures have managed to either retain or regain control rights over state assets, often in coalition with the enterprise management.

The major trademarks of the Russian privatization program had been both its vagueness and its reliance on voluntary compliance by interest groups in companies and bureaucratic structures. This combination has left ample room for special privatization arrangements, particularly in companies formally excluded from privatization, as well as in companies where the state retained a controlling block. For example, the exclusion of television and broadcasting services from privatization has not prevented their privatization but has rather exempted these assets from the application of general privatization rules. This in turn has opened the back door for spontaneous privatization of some of these companies, and for special privatization regimes for others, which benefit mostly a handful of selected banks, some spin-offs of the state-owned parent companies, and various state structures.[96] Likewise, because the Russian government could control privatization of the gas and oil sectors and retain controlling blocks in these companies at least temporarily, only small blocks of shares were offered to the public (usually in a fashion that would ensure widely dispersed share holdings and thus little governance), with the greater part remaining in the control of a coalition of inside management and state bureaucrats.[97] Thus, many of the seemingly elected holdings were not necessarily selected for

[96] The privatization of mass media was part of the major power struggle between Yeltsin and the Supreme Soviet in 1993. Subsequently, various privatization regimes were drafted and redrafted, and finally, a new holding structure "ORT" created, in which the state holds 51% of the shares and a selected number of banks the remaining 49% (see *Kommersant Weekly* No. 11, 28 March 1995, p. 12).

[97] The privatization procedure of Gazprom and some of the largest oil holding companies in fact ridiculed the official purposes of voucher privatization, which were to enable the participation of the population (see *Kommersant Weekly* No. 3, 1 February 1994, p. 33). Note also that a new coalition of government officials and banks has emerged and government plans exist to transfer management of shares in many of the most valuable firms to these banks in return for credits provided by them to the state budget (see report in *Financial Times*, 26 April 1995, p. 2, "Banks eye Russian companies").

public purposes, either fiscal or policy oriented, but were selected for more private purposes.

In other cases, a more justifiable public rationale for retaining assets in state ownership can be identified. GKI has used a golden share at times to exert better control over companies that had attempted to escape the privatization scheme set forward by the agency. Moreover, for many types of assets subject to special government approval and continued state ownership, rationales for their retention may also be deduced from the nature of the asset, such as the desire to protect scientific and cultural facilities or to control natural monopolies, including utility companies.

The initial categorization of various types of assets in the privatization program has proved to be crucial for the fate of these assets. While the privatization program gives the Russian government or GKI only an option to retain a controlling block or issue golden shares in a portion of firms subject to privatization, hardly any of these companies were placed within the general privatization regime. This suggests that the placement of a company in a category other than mandatory privatization shifted the struggle for control over assets in favor of forces that were antagonistic to speedy privatization, and in fact, left little room for the relevant state structures to decide otherwise. Whether this reflects simply a weakness on the part of the state or the exploitation of maneuvering room by a state–management coalition is difficult to say, and may have varied from case to case.

Placing a company or an entire industry sector under a special privatization regime also gave bureaucrats and management employed in these sectors considerable influence in structuring the state holding to preserve their interests. Numerous state holding companies, including those created under the auspices of GKI, are simply reorganizations of former state ministries. One such example is Rosugol', the state holding company for the coal industry, which has managed to preserve practically all of its employees within the new structure, including the administrative body seated in Moscow.[98]

Unlike the Czech example, the Russian voucher auction system provided no room for residual state holdings as a consequence of share offerings that remained under-subscribed. Shares were fully distributed after one round of bidding with the number of submitted vouchers divided simply by the number of shares. Where necessary, a share split occurred.[99] Consequently,

---

[98] Interview with Sergey I. Shoumkov, general director of the Scientific & Technical Mining Association, 8 June 1994.

[99] In only a few cases could shares not be fully distributed (i.e. if the number of shares after a share split could not be fully allocated), which usually resulted in a cash auction where the remainder was sold.

the stakes the property funds controlled after completion of voucher auctions were elected, not residual, holdings. They are the result not of a mechanical failure to distribute all shares, but of the design of the privatization program, which earmarked only a relatively small portion of shares for voucher auctions.[100] This vagueness enabled interested state structures to move in and fill the gap.

Acquisition of Control Rights

Property funds in different regions emerged as one of the most important state structures with a special interest in retaining control over assets. As we have pointed out, the regional branches of the Federal Property Fund pursued widely diverging policies. The federal fund in Moscow has not been capable of monitoring their activities and does not even have access to data on postvoucher privatizations conducted by them.[101] In principle, regional property funds were obliged to sell the remaining shares in cash auctions or tenders. But in many cases the property funds have only slowly, if at all, proceeded with additional privatization. The reason is apparently not a failure to find buyers,[102] but rather a reluctance to attempt additional sales. Since complete privatization leads to the closure of these funds, they have strong incentives to retain assets as a justification for their own existence.

Regional property funds are often supported or even supplanted in acquiring control over assets by regional governments, which attempt to enhance their power by usurping control rights over state holdings within their jurisdictions. The most pronounced case of open opposition by a regional government to federal privatization policies has been the case of Moscow city.[103] Just before the completion of voucher auctions, the Moscow government refused to register state companies as joint stock companies, a necessary first step to accomplish privatization,[104] thereby threatening to undermine the attempt to bring voucher privatization to a successful end.

[100] To a great extent this was the result of a political battle over how many shares should be privatized through vouchers. Yeltsin's attempts to allocate at least 29% of total shares to voucher auctions were vetoed twice by the Supreme Soviet in 1993 (see Presidential Decrees No. 640, 8 May 1993, and No. 1108, 26 July 1993, as well as the Regulation of the Supreme Soviet No. 5609-1, 6 August 1993).

[101] Interview conducted with Iurii A. Zverev, one of the deputy chairmen of the Federal Property Fund, 6 June 1994.

[102] According to the results of the letter survey about property funds, in only a few cases was the property fund unable to find buyers (see above).

[103] For a systematic overview of privatization policies pursued by various regional funds based on primary and secondary sources, see Slider (1994).

[104] *Kommersant Weekly* No. 20, 7 June 1994, p. 29, "Konflikt Chubais–Luzhkov."

And in early 1995, the mayor of Moscow, Iurii Luzhkov, went so far as to issue a regulation empowering the city to renationalize enterprises within its jurisdiction.[105]

Management of State Holdings

Over all, Russian state holdings appear to be even more diffuse and less traceable than the direct state holdings of the Hungarian state. Control structures are often naively based on the assumption that the state would actually exercise control in the interest of the company and/or its future owners. Moreover, regulations have fallen short of designing a workable monitoring system. For example, every state enterprise that was corporatized before subsequent privatization was mandated to have a representative of the property fund and a representative of the local state authorities on its corporate board.[106] How these state representatives were appointed, what their role should be, and how their behavior was to be monitored remained essentially open questions. In contrast to both the Czech Republic and Hungary, Russian privatization legislation thus ensured that the state could legally play a more active role in privatized companies if the relevant state structure so desired,[107] but it did not provide a framework for monitoring these activities.

Nevertheless, the role of state representatives as active shareholders in these companies should not be overstated. The sheer number of companies that require oversight and the essentially passive role the state played before privatization make active intervention in the day-to-day affairs of the majority of companies an unlikely scenario. However, state representatives are likely to play a crucial role in supporting different groups of shareholders. Results from a survey of Russian voucher investment funds suggest that state representatives tend to side with the current management (see Frydman, Pistor, and Rapaczynski in volume 1), a tendency that is likely to further undermine the already weak control rights outside investors have. The Federal Property Fund has countered the activities of regional funds by issuing guidelines similar to the ones used by the Czech FNP, namely that assets should be managed "in the interest of the future owners."[108] The interpretation of this vague guideline is likely to vary depending on the perception of those reading

[105] *Financial Times*, 8 February 1995, p. 5, "Moscow grants itself the power to renationalize."

[106] See Art. 8.1 of the Model Statute for Corporatized Companies Confirmed by Presidential Decree No. 721, 1 July 1992.

[107] State representatives could be replaced at shareholder meetings, but many companies may in fact have had an interest in keeping them on board (see Pistor 1995).

[108] Interview Iurii A. Zverev, deputy chairman of the Federal Property Fund conducted by the authors, 6 June 1994.

it about who these owners should be and what interests they ought to have.[109]

In an attempt by the federal government to regain the upper hand in controlling and monitoring state assets, President Yeltsin issued a decree in the summer of 1994 entitled On Some Measures to Ensure State Management of the Economy (Presidential Decree No. 1200, 10 June 1994). The purpose of this decree is to regulate the appointment, qualifications, and supervision of state representatives in fully or partially state-owned companies. The major weakness of the decree is, once again, its ambiguity. The state structures in charge of making appointments are simply listed; there is no matching of asset control rights with the right to make appointments or providing mechanisms to solve potential disputes between various state structures. Thus, the right to appoint state representatives is granted to the Russian government, to other branches of the executive, or to the property fund. When civil servants rather than ordinary citizens are to be appointed, the decision shall be taken by the Russian president, the Russian government, other branches of the executive, or the property fund. The likely outcome of this ambiguity is that the state structure with the strongest *de facto* control rights in a particular company will dominate these decisions without any further oversight.

In contrast to Hungary and the Czech Republic, in Russia the relevant legislation provides a much tighter control structure for state representatives. They have to disclose their voting intentions, and for a number of decisions taken at shareholder meetings, they need to obtain prior approval from the state organ that appointed them.[110] In addition, the Russian government has the right to adopt standards on voting behavior for state appointees beyond the issues listed in this decree. Violations of rules established in the decree or of implementing administrative regulations are sanctioned with disciplinary measures against state appointees. Other shareholders, or the company itself, have recourse against state officials only to the extent a company's charter so provides.

Companies that have not been privatized or corporatized remain under the control of branch ministries or state committees. The decree on

---

[109] The interviewee at the Federal Property Fund pointed out himself that there is a distinction between "real owners" and "speculators," the former including current management, the latter referring to voucher investment funds.

[110] These decisions include changes in the articles of incorporation, changes in the charter capital, appointment or election of representatives to corporate organs or important management positions, decisions to obtain credits in the amount exceeding 10% of the net actives of the company, the sale of immovables, the creation of subsidiaries, and the participation in other companies (see Presidential Decree No. 1200, 10 June 1994).

managing state assets, in line with already existing legislation,[111] regulates that the principal control device for these assets is management contracts to be concluded between the relevant state body and the company's top management.

The impact of these rules on company management is difficult to gauge. The attempt to provide a central regulatory framework for overseeing state appointees clearly differs from the Czech or the Hungarian examples, where the formulation of such guidelines was left to different state agencies. However, rather than suggesting excessive control by the central government, it reflects a desperate attempt by the Russian government to bring some order into the struggle over asset control, which in Russia appears to have taken far more severe forms than in the other countries.

Lock-in Effects

As we have seen, in Russia state ownership after completion of voucher privatization is not only extensive, but also backed by strong interests of various state structures, which retain control rights over assets. This suggests that Russia is likely to face an intrastate lock-in as the country embarks on the second stage of privatization. Experiences from voucher auctions can serve as a proxy for the kind of defense strategies that may be invoked, including physically restricting access to auctions by unwanted buyers, selling shares only in small portions, conducting numerous auctions, or simply delaying and finally stalling the privatization process.[112] Private lock-ins are less likely, although companies that still benefit from continuous soft credits or tax exemptions resulting from state ownership might resist forgoing them. However, these benefits have become less frequent for most sectors. Absent such an insurance umbrella, private parties are likely to gain, rather than lose, from further privatization. A lock-in situation caused by public protest appears to be much less likely. With the important exception of land privatization, which continues to be a highly emotional subject, earlier feelings about privatization have for the most part given way to a more cynical perception of the process.

Conclusion

This chapter has attempted to draw attention to state ownership in transition economies as a postprivatization phenomenon in Eastern Europe. The data

---

[111] See the RSFSR Law on Enterprises and Entrepreneurial Activities, 25 December 1990.

[112] Results of unpublished pilot study on the role of voucher investment funds in privatized firms conducted by the CEU privatization project, January 1994.

that has been presented calls for recognizing the persistence of state ownership, even in countries where extensive privatization programs have been
concluded. At the same time, comparisons of the distribution of state
holdings, and the organizational structures that have been created to manage
these holdings have indicated that state ownership is by no means a unitary
phenomenon, but one that is strongly contingent on the design of privatization programs, the level of cohesion of the state bureaucracy, and the
strength of nonstate forces in the economy.

Given the differences in privatization policies, bureaucratic traditions, and
the importance of private forces that distinguish the Czech Republic,
Hungary, and Russia, it is not surprising that the current structure of state
holdings and the issues raised by state ownership in each of these countries
are, in many respects, country specific. However, state ownership in all three
countries creates dynamics that tend to entrench the postprivatization
ownership structure. It is our appreciation of the enduring nature of state
ownership and its capacity for self-generation that has led us to characterize
state holdings as a modern day hydra, which, like its ancient Greek mytho-
logical namesake, has the ability not merely to withstand attacks, but to take
ever more threatening forms.

Our conclusion that state ownership continues to be at the center of the
economies of Eastern Europe, irrespective of the privatization strategy
governments have pursued, has analytical as well as policy-related implications. Analysts have frequently treated the degree to which private
economic forces contribute to the creation of gross domestic product
(GDP) as a proxy for the extent to which transition economies have moved
away from their communist past. Implicit in this formulation is a division
of the economy into state and private sectors. The ownership arrangements
that we have detailed, including the intermingling of state and nonstate
elements, suggest that this analytical construction is unsound. While the
diminishing role of the state sector in generating wealth clearly shows that
the state's monopoly over economic activity belongs to the past, the mixed
private and state holdings that dominate the Czech, Hungarian, and
Russian environments indicate that the relationship between the shrinking
of the "state sector" and the importance of state ownership in the economy
is not a direct one. Insight into the actual significance of state ownership
can only be obtained by carefully tracking the extent and structure of state
holdings and the dynamics of private–state interactions – a study requiring
the close, fact-rich scrutiny of developments within the region. We wish to
emphasize that given the ubiquitous existence of state ownership
throughout transition economies and the disintegration of boundaries
between state and private holdings that has occurred in the past years, the

study of ownership in the region is inseparable from the study of state ownership.

Recognition of the central importance of state ownership in the postprivatization context also creates a pressing need to devise mechanisms for managing state holdings. This creative task is complicated by the multiple objectives that any successful management structure must consider, including increasing the ability of the state to monitor the management of holdings, decreasing the risk of the intrusion of politics into the micro-aspects of firm activities, and assisting governments in achieving their desired portfolio through facilitating the successful divestiture of residual and temporary assets. The attention to the question of postcommunist state ownership management has focused on the first two of these tasks, with policy suggestions generally aimed at introducing private corporate governance procedures into state asset management. Eastern European governments have been advised to clarify property rights and rationalize the management of state holdings. This translates into regaining the powers traditionally associated with ownership, transforming state firms into joint stock companies, and finally, concentrating ownership rights in state agencies organized as holding companies. Concurrent with the reform of the structure of assets and the structure of ownership has been an attempt to increase the professionalism of responsible officials by dedicating resources to train government agents in the fundamentals of modern portfolio management.

Increasing the effectiveness of state ownership management is obviously important, but our discussion of the essential nature of state ownership suggests that efforts to improve the performance of state holdings should be approached with some skepticism. There already exists a long history of attempts to make state holdings function just like private firms, and the economic results that have been achieved to date should temper projections of the gains to be realized through rationalization strategies. More importantly, our critique of postprivatization state ownership signals our belief that the relevant issues relating to state ownership in Eastern Europe extend well beyond the confines of the relationship between owners and assets. Once the dimension of state ownership for the development of the state itself is considered, the effort to structure state holdings to mimic private arrangements becomes increasingly problematic. Thus, the establishment of state holding companies or similar structures organized on the basis of private corporate law creates unique problems for the establishment of the rule of law in the region. Using private law to incorporate state activity signals that state action is treated as if it were synonymous with private activity. However, it is precisely this equivalence that is renounced when governments agree to abide by constitutional restraints on power. When state holding companies were envisioned as short-lived institutions within stable democracies, their threat to the definition of state power could be largely ignored. In comparison, in the context of Eastern Europe, where these institutions are likely to become enduring fixtures and democratic traditions are considerably less well established, discounting the possible ramifications of these structures for political development appears to be ill-advised.

The problems posed by attempts to organize state ownership as if the state were analogous to a private party are compounded by the negative consequences such steps have for the ability to monitor or effectively challenge the discretionary use of state power. The task of monitoring a corporatized state firm or a state holding company is vested with internal corporate structures, including shareholder meetings and management and supervisory boards, even more than in purely private firms, as state shareholding provides a buffer for external stock market control.

We have already discussed the difficulty of monitoring state firms due to the multiple objectives of the government. This general public policy issue translates into complex monitoring problems in corporations with mixed ownership. Even where private law offers shareholders the chance to challenge decisions taken by the company's management or supervisory board[113] (i.e. where directors were faced with a conflict of interest), these rights are difficult to enforce where the target of shareholder actions is decisions taken by state representatives.

In mixed companies, it is not so much that conflict of interest issues arise from particular transactions, but that a constant conflict of interest exists given that the state has economic, social, and political interests that are, at least to some extent, antagonistic to the interests of their private shareholding partners. The threat of civil liability cannot be expected to bring the objectives of state directors in line with private concerns. Moreover, given the multiplicity of state objectives, shareholders face almost insurmountable problems in proving a conflict of interest or causation between damages to them or the company and a decision taken despite a conflict of interest. In the end, because the state is not analogous to a private party, private commercial law is insufficient to discipline the behavior of state agents.

We conclude not that corporatization of state firms is in principle ill-advised or that the creation of state holding companies should necessarily be avoided, but rather that comprehensive management schemes must

---

[113] Note, however, that the corporate laws of the countries in question do not provide for derivative suits. Even direct actions by shareholders to defend their own interests are difficult to construct and enter unknown legal territory.

acknowledge the full range of issues that are unique to state ownership in Eastern Europe. Therefore, the construction of state ownership management policies should be dual-track, with one helping the state create effective institutions that are in line with rule-based limitations on state power, and the other directed at aiding private owners to develop effective private property rights. Designing management and monitoring systems that work to increase the cost of ownership for the state, while decreasing that cost for private parties, is the most effective way for policymakers to create clear definitions of state power, increase the regulatory capacity of the government, and facilitate the shrinking of state portfolios. Structural innovations may well be a part of such thoughtfully designed reform programs, provided that these innovations are accompanied by measures to augment the state's ability to regulate conduct. In their corporate laws, reform programs should also consider including special standards of conduct for state agents or allowing claimants to bring class action or derivative shareholder suits against those agents. Alternative legal reforms might limit the ability of state bodies to vote their shares except in certain cases. While programs to change the manner in which state ownership is controlled in Eastern Europe may be made up of several different components, their sum effect should be focused on encouraging the government to function more like a government, not less so.

References

Aghion, Philippe, Olivier Blanchard, and Robin Burgess. 1993. "The Behavior of State Firms in Eastern Europe: Pre-Privatization." EBRD Working Paper No. 12 (October).

Boycko, Maxim, Andrei Shleifer, and Robert W. Vishny. 1993. "Privatizing Russia." Brookings Papers on Economic Activity 2: 139–181. The Brookings Institution, Washington, D.C.

——. 1995. *Privatizing Russia.* Cambridge, Mass.: Massachusetts Institute of Technology (MIT) Press.

Brom, Karla, and Mitchell Orenstein. 1993. "The 'Privatized' Sector in the Czech Republic: Government and Bank Control in a Transitional Economy." *Europe-Asia Studies* 46, no. 6: 889.

Carlin, Wendy, John van Reenen, and Toby Wolfe. 1994. "Enterprise Restructuring in the Transition: An Analytical Survey of the Case Study Evidence from Central and Eastern Europe." EBRD Working Paper, No. 14 (July).

Ceska, Roman. 1993. "Results of Privatization through 1993 – Part I." *Privatization Newsletter* of the Czech Republic and Slovakia, 20, March.

Commander, Simon, and Fabrizio Coricelli. 1995. *Unemployment, Restructuring, and the Labor Market in Eastern Europe and Russia.* Washington, D.C.: World Bank.

Earle, John, Roman Frydman, Andrzej Rapaczynski, and Joel Turkewitz. 1994. *Small Privatization: The Transformation of Retail Trade and Consumer Services in the Czech Republic, Hungary, and Poland.* Budapest: Central European University (CEU) Press.

Frydman, Roman, Andrzej Rapaczynski, John Earle *et al.* 1993. *The Privatization Process in Russia, Ukraine, and the Baltic States.* Budapest: CEU Press.

Grabher, Gernot. 1991. "The Weakness of Strong Ties." In *The Embedded Firm: On the Socioeconomics of Industrial Networks,* edited by Grabher Gernot. London: Routledge.

Grossman, Sanford J., and Oliver D. Hart. 1986. "The Costs and Benefits of Ownership: A Theory of Vertical and Lateral Integration." *Journal of Political Economy* 94, no. 4 : 691–719.

Hayri, Aydin, Gerald A. McDermott. 1994. "Restructuring in the Czech Republic – Beyond Ownership and Bankruptcy," unpublished manuscript.

Johnson, Simon, and Heidi Kroll. 1991. "Managerial Strategies for Spontaneous Privatization." *Soviet Economy* 7, no. 4: 281–316; comment by Jeffrey Sachs 317–21.

Karsai, Judit, and Mike Wright. 1994. "Accountability, Governance and Finance in Hungarian Buy-outs." *Europe Asia Studies* 46, no. 6: 997–1016.

Kotrba, Josef. 1994. "Czech Privatization: Players and Winners." CERGE-EI Working Paper Series, No. 58.

Kumar, Anjalie. 1992. "The State Holding Company, Issues and Options." World Bank Discussion Papers No. 187, World Bank, Washington D.C.

McDermott, Gerald A. 1994. "Renegotiating the Ties That Bind: The Limits of Privatization in the Czech Republic." Discussion Paper FS I 94–101, Wissenschaftszentrum Berlin für Sozialforschung.

Mladek, Jan. 1994. "Czech Privatization Process: Time for Corporate Governance." Paper prepared for IIASA conference, Output Decline in Eastern Europe – Prospects for Recovery?

Nee, Victor. 1989. "Peasant Entrepreneurship and the Politics of Regulation in China." In *Remaking the Economic Institutions of Socialism: China and Eastern Europe,* edited by Victor Nee and David Stark. Stanford, Calif.: Stanford University Press.

Niskanen, William A. 1973. *Bureaucracy and Representative Government.* Chicago: Aldine Atherthon.

North, Douglass C. 1990. *Institutions, Institutional Change and Economic Performance.* Cambridge, Eng.: Cambridge University Press.

Pinto, Brian, and Sweder van Wijnbergen. 1994. "Ownership and Corporate Control in Poland: Why State Firms Defied the Odds," unpublished manuscript.

Pinto, Brian, Marek Belka, and Stefan Krajewski. 1993. "Transforming State Enterprises in Poland: Evidence on Adjustment by Manufacturing Firms." Brookings Papers on Economic Activity, No.1: 213–55.

Pistor, Katharina. 1995. "Privatization and Corporate Governance in Russia: An Empirical Study." In *Privatization, Conversion and Enterprise Reform in Russia,* edited by Michael McFaul and Tova Perlmutter. Boulder , Colo.: Westview Press.

Sappington, David E. M., Joseph E. Stiglitz. 1987. "Privatization, Information and Incentives." *Journal of Policy Analysis and Management* 6, no. 4: 567–82.

Slider, Darrell. 1994. "Privatization in Russia's Regions." *Post-Soviet Affairs* 10, no. 4: 367.

Stark, David. 1990. "Privatization in Hungary: From Plan to Market or From Plan to Clan?" *East European Politics and Societies* 4: 351–92.

Toth, Istvan Janos. 1994. "Ownership and Performance in Hungary, 1990–1993," unpublished manuscript.

von Thadden, Ernst L. 1994. "Centralized Decentralization: Corporate Governance in the

East German Economic Transition." EDI Working Paper, pp. 94–50, World Bank, Washington, D.C.

Walder, Andrew G. 1994. "The Varieties of Public Enterprise in China: An Institutional Analysis." Paper written for the project The Changing Role of the State: Strategies for Reforming Public Enterprise, Policy Research Department, World Bank, Washington DC.

World Bank 1991. *The Challenge of Development*, World Bank, Washington D.C.

7

CORPORATE LAW FROM SCRATCH

BERNARD BLACK, REINIER KRAAKMAN, and
JONATHAN HAY

Acknowledgments should go first to the many people who participated in the effort to develop Russian company law that provided the genesis and many of the ideas for this article. The participants include Alexander Abramov, Ian Ayres, J. Robert Brown, Catherine Dixon, Elena Kabatova, Louis Kaplow, Claudia Morgenstern, Melinda Rishkofski, Howard Sherman, Anna Stanislavovna Tarasova (the principal drafter of the Russian text of the draft law), Victoria Pavlovna Volkova, and John Wilcox. We thank John Coffee, Ronald Gilson, Bruce Kogut, Mancur Olson, Ibrahim Shihata, Douglas Webb, and participants in the University of Toronto Law and Economics Workshop for helpful comments on earlier drafts. We also thank Joseph Blasi, Andrei Alexandrovich Volgin, Rolf Skog, and Daniel Wolfe for their comments on the draft law on which this article was based. Reinier Kraakman received support from the Harvard Program for Law and Economics, which is funded by the John M. Olin Foundation.

For more expanded discussion of the theoretical underpinnings of the self-enforcing model of corporate law presented here, and lessons that can be drawn from the self-enforcement approach for the supposed efficiency of developed country corporate laws, see Bernard Black, Reinier Kraakman, and Jonathan Hay, "A Self-Enforcing Model of Corporate Law," forthcoming in Harvard Law Review, vol. 109 (1996).

Introduction

What model of corporate law should govern publicly owned companies in newly privatizing or emerging capitalist economies? Although the corporate form plays a key role in the privatization of formerly Communist countries and the development of other emerging market economies, this question has no ready answer. Newly privatizing or developing countries should not simply copy the corporate laws of developed Western economies. The corporate laws of developed countries depend upon highly evolved market, legal, and governmental institutions,[1] and upon cultural norms that often do not

---

[1] We use the term "institution" here in a broad sense to include private organizational structures such as stock trading systems and securities registrars; public organizational structures such as securities regulators, skilled commercial courts, and a reliable mail system; and

exist in emerging economies. And even if these laws could be exported to emerging markets without modification, there would be a case for not doing so before first taking a hard look, since these laws are likely to be as much the product of idiosyncratic historical developments in their countries of origin as of purely functional imperatives.

We believe that the principal goal of corporate law should be similar in developed and emerging economies – succinctly stated, corporate law should maximize the value of corporate enterprises to investors, thus reducing the cost of capital. But the differences in institutions between developed and emerging economies require different means for achieving this goal. Moreover, in many emerging markets, corporate law must serve a second goal: to foster public confidence in capitalism and in private ownership of large firms.

If corporate law is to work within the infrastructure that is available in an emerging market, it must be designed substantially from scratch. Fortunately, this can be politically feasible. Existing law is often rudimentary, and interest groups are often less organized than in developed economies. Thus, the bias toward the status quo that limits departure from existing legal rules in developed countries is often weaker in emerging economies. One can rethink from first principles what corporate law *ought* to look like and what related legal and financial institutions it *ought* to rely on and promote.

In an important sense, no law can be designed completely from scratch. Emerging economies have *some* legal and market institutions, *some* norms of behavior, *some* distribution of share ownership, and *some* financial institutions. Corporate law must reflect existing institutions and encourage the development of missing or weak beneficial institutions. For example, if employees are an important class of shareholders as a result of mass privatization, company law must adapt to this background fact. Company law must also limit the influence of existing bad institutions, such as widespread official corruption.

This chapter sketches the basic elements of a model corporate law for emergent economies through a case study: an effort, in which we participated, to develop corporate law for Russia. As this book went to press (December 1995), a draft law based on our work has been passed by the Russian legislature and has been sent to President Yeltsin for his signature. We begin with three central claims. The first is that the elements of an effective corporate law depend on time, place, and culture. The law that works in the United States, Britain, Germany, or Japan (our principal developed country prototypes) will not satisfactorily resolve the basic problems that corporate law must address in an emerging market. It will not achieve a

mixed public-private structures such as self-regulatory organizations, an accounting profession, and sophisticated financial accounting rules.

sensible balance among company managers' need for flexibility to meet rapidly changing business conditions, companies' need for low-transaction-cost access to capital markets, large investors' need to monitor what the managers do with investors' money, and small investors' need for protection against self-dealing by managers and large investors. The defects in the law will increase the cost of capital and reduce its availability.

In developed countries, corporate law is only one of a number of legal, institutional, and cultural constraints on the discretion of corporate managers and controlling shareholders that together achieve a satisfactory balance among these sometimes competing needs. As Ronald Gilson (1981) has argued, where other constraints work more effectively, corporate law should play only a minor role. In emerging economies, nonlegal constraints are weak or absent. Thus, corporate law is central in the effort to give the participants in the company incentives to create social value and prevent them from transferring wealth from others to themselves. When these market institutions are absent, the "market" cannot fill the regulatory gaps that an enabling-type corporate law leaves behind.

Moreover, corporate law in developed countries has evolved together with legal institutions that make the law work. For example, the United States relies heavily on expert judges to assess the fairness of transactions where managers have a conflict of interest, as well as the reasonableness of takeover defenses. These judges can make decisions literally overnight when necessary, so that judicial delay does not kill a challenged transaction. In emerging markets, weak legal institutions often further limit the available regulatory options. In Russia, for example, courts function slowly if at all. Many judges are holdovers from the Soviet era who do not understand business and are disinclined to learn. Some are simply corrupt. One can hope for better courts, but only over a period measured in decades. In the meantime, corporate law must rely on courts as little as possible.

Our second central claim is that despite the context-specificity of corporate law, there is a large class of "emergent capitalist economies" (including formerly Communist countries) that are sufficiently similar to permit useful generalization about the features of corporate law that will be useful for them. For example, Russia is perhaps extreme, but hardly alone, in having malfunctioning courts, weak and sometimes corrupt regulators, and ill-developed capital markets.

As we argue below, four aspects of national context are critical to the design of corporate law: (1) the background factors that shape the goals of corporate law, such as the ownership structure of public companies (most Russian companies today have majority control by managers and employees, but only limited residual state ownership); (2) the sophistication and reliability of the legal system; (3) the sophistication of capital markets and related market institutions; and (4) the cultural expectations of managers, shareholders, and the general public (in Russia Sergei Mavrodi can run a pyramid scheme, put tens of millions of dollars into his own pocket, and after the pyramid collapses be elected to public office).[2]

Emerging capitalist economies are less developed than Western economies on each of these dimensions. Russia serves as a useful prototype of an emergent economy both because of its size and intrinsic importance and because it is at the far end of the continuum from developed economies on all of the key dimensions that are critical to the design of a corporate law. Thus, it can illustrate with special clarity the ways in which corporate law for emergent economies differ from corporate law for developed economies.

Our third claim is that it is possible, despite the constraints of weak markets and weak legal infrastructure, to design corporate law that will work tolerably well: that will vest substantial decision-making power in the hands of those with incentives to make good decisions; that will reduce, though it cannot eliminate, fraud and self-dealing by corporate insiders; that will give managers and controlling shareholders incentives to obey the rules, even where they could probably get away with ignoring them; that will reinforce desirable cultural attitudes about proper managerial behavior; and that will still leave managers with the flexibility they need to take risks and make quick decisions. Indeed, good law – corporate or otherwise – is enormously important in emerging economies precisely *because* related institutions are weak. In developed countries, corporate law often plays a minor, even "trivial", role in an overall system of corporate governance (see, e.g. Black 1990; Roe 1993). A good law can add far greater relative value in developing economies.

Every corporate governance system yet devised fails with uncomfortable frequency in the often volatile circumstances faced by companies in emerging markets.[3] Thus, corporate governance will often fail in emerging economies. Yet precisely because occasions for governance failure are common in emerging markets, the marginal value of good company law will be significant if it can prevent even a fraction of the failures that might otherwise occur.

The central features of the company law that we develop below for the Russian context are:

[2] See, e.g., Rosett (1994); Liesman (1994). Mavrodi was elected to Parliament, and his stated reason for running was to obtain legislative immunity from prosecution for tax fraud.

[3] For a sample of recent scholarship on comparative corporate governance, see Roe (1994); Gilson and Kraakman (1993); Gilson and Roe (1993); Black and Coffee (1994); Charkham (1994).

1. Reliance on self-enforcing mechanisms for shareholder protection to the extent possible. By self-enforcement, we mean that the law relies for its success on actions by direct participants in the corporate enterprise (shareholders, directors, managers), rather than indirect participants (judges, regulators, legal and accounting professionals, financial press). In particular the law relies as little as possible on formal enforcement by judges and regulators. The principal mechanisms are: shareholder approval, including in some cases supermajority approval or approval by a majority of outside shareholders, for broad classes of major transactions and self-interested transactions; approval by a majority of outside directors of self-interested transactions; cumulative voting for directors, which gives large minority shareholders the power to select minority directors (protected with requirements for one common share, one vote; minimum board size; and no staggering of board terms); a unitary ballot, on which both managers and large shareholders can nominate directors; and pass-through of voting power from nominee holders to beneficial owners. The honesty of the vote is protected through confidential voting and independent vote tabulation.

2. A higher degree of protection of outside shareholders than is common in developed economies, to respond to the combination of a high incidence of insider-controlled companies; the weakness of other constraints on self-dealing by managers and controlling shareholders; a distribution system for shares (voucher privatization) that did not let investors insist on contractual protections as a condition of investing; and the need to control fraud to strengthen the political credibility of a market economy. The protection comes through a combination of the self-enforcement mechanisms discussed above, preemption rights when the company issues new shares, and appraisal rights for shareholders who do not approve major transactions (enforceable either in court or through arbitration).

3. Reliance, for the most part, on procedural protections, especially transaction approval by independent directors, independent shareholders, or both, rather than on flat prohibitions of categories of transactions. The reliance on procedural protections balances the need for shareholder protection against the need for business flexibility.

4. An overall effort to build legal norms that participants in the corporate enterprise will see as reasonable, and comply with voluntarily. The need to induce voluntary compliance reinforces our preference for procedural rather than substantive protections. For example, managers are more likely to evade a flat ban on self-interested transactions than a procedural requirement for shareholder approval, if they think that they can obtain the approval. Yet, once they decide to obtain shareholder approval, they

may voluntarily make the transaction more favorable to the company, to be certain of approval and to avoid embarrassment.[4]

5. Apart from major transactions and self-interested transactions, giving the board of directors broad power to set dividends; establish company policy; and hire, fire, and compensate the chief executive. The default rule is a unitary board, but a two-tier board as in Germany is a permissible alternative.

6. Takeover rules adapted largely from the British City Code on Takeovers and Mergers, which require notice to the company and the public when a shareholder exceeds 15 percent ownership; a delay period before a change-of-control transaction (30 percent ownership is our proxy for control) to provide a market check on the fairness of the price; a requirement that a shareholder who acquires a 30 percent stake offer to buy all other shares at the same price unless other shareholders waive this requirement; and a ban on defensive actions that could frustrate a takeover bid unless the actions are approved by the target's shareholders.

7. Shareholder protection against dilutive share issuances through a requirement that shares be issued only at market value, as determined by the board of directors; shareholder approval for issuances to insiders (under the self-interested transaction rules); shareholder approval for large issuances; and preemptive rights.

8. Safeguards for the rights of employee shareholders, to prevent managers from controlling the voting of employee shares. These rules reflect the importance of employee ownership for Russian firms that went through voucher privatization.[5] The principal safeguards are a ban on manager control of trusts and other entities formed to hold employee shares, opt-out rights and a maximum two-year life for any such trusts, individual decisions on whether to sell shares, and confidential voting.

9. Strong legal remedies, *on paper,* for failure to follow required corporate procedures, to encourage corporate actors to comply with the rules rather than risk strong penalties for ignoring procedures. For example, a shareholder who acquires a 30 percent interest without giving the required advance notice, or without offering to buy all remaining shares, loses voting rights for *all* shares, although voting rights can be restored

---

[4] In the economic literature, "self-enforcement" is sometimes given only this narrower meaning – a contract is said to be self-enforcing if it induces voluntary compliance. See, e.g., Telser (1980). Inducing voluntary compliance is an important element of our approach to company law, but it captures only part of what we mean by a "self-enforcing" law.

[5] See the chapter by Blasi and Shleifer in this volume (survey of 200 privatized Russian companies shows mean employee ownership of 65% and median ownership of 60%). For background on Russia's voucher privatization, see Boyko, Shleifer, and Vishny (1994).

by majority vote of the other shareholders. Strong remedies compensate, in part, for the low likelihood that remedies will be exercisable in fact.

10. Where possible, use of bright line rules, rather than standards, to define proper and improper behavior. Bright line rules can be understood by those who must comply with them and have a better chance of being enforced. Standards, in contrast, require judicial interpretation, which is unavailable, and presuppose a shared cultural understanding of the policy underlying the rule, which is also largely nonexistent.

The combination of easily understood rules and strong sanctions for noncompliance can potentially initiate a virtuous cycle, in which cultural norms of proper behavior by corporate managers, now weak or absent, are reinforced as some managers comply voluntarily with the new rules, others comply to avoid legal risk, still others comply because they have strong shareholders who can punish deviation, and all managers observe how other managers behave.

There are limits to what a self-enforcing corporate law can accomplish. For example, cumulative voting will not directly help a small shareholder who owns five shares. Nor will a small shareholder who opposes a merger find it worthwhile to exercise appraisal rights. Thus, small shareholders remain vulnerable to expropriation of their wealth by managers and controlling shareholders. A self-enforcing law can *partially* protect small shareholders in three principal ways. First, rules such as cumulative voting that strengthen the influence of *large* outside shareholders encourage outside investors to buy large stakes and become active monitors. These large investors' actions will often benefit all outside investors. Second, the effort to build independent boards and vest key decisions in independent board members will sometimes protect small shareholders. Third, all shareholders benefit when managers are induced to follow the law.

We sketch the basic requirements that a corporate law for emergent economies must satisfy, and our approach to drafting such a law, as follows. First, we outline the alternative drafting strategies open to emergent economies and introduce our own preferred strategy: one designed to yield a "structural" or "self-enforcing" corporate law. Second, we describe the primary components of a self-enforcing corporate law in the context of the Russian Federation. Third, we address remedies, an area of special concern if legal institutions are weak. Fourth, we consider how corporate law can address the abilities or disabilities of particular classes of participants in the corporate enterprise, including creditors, employee-shareholders, venture capitalists (often including foreign investors), and the state (which is an important residual shareholder in many newly privatized economies).

This chapter focuses on large companies where some shareholders do not work in the business. We do not, for the most part, consider the special problems of close corporations. The law, however, must carefully attend to the needs of small companies. The procedural protections that are appropriate for a company with 10,000 shareholders would be ludicrous and crippling for a tiny company with five shareholders who all work in the business.

We focus also on *company law*, conventionally understood: that is, the law that articulates company structure and regulates relationships among shareholders, as well as between the shareholders and corporate managers. American corporate law, for our purposes, includes state corporation statutes; the common law of fiduciary obligation; the provisions of the securities laws that regulate corporate voting, control contests, and other fundamentally internal matters of corporate governance and structure; and stock exchange listing standards that impose corporate governance requirements on listed companies. Similarly, British company law includes statutory company law, the common law of fiduciary duty, the listing standards and guidelines of the London Stock Exchange, and the British City Code, which regulates control transactions with the effective force of law, although it is administered by a self-regulatory organization. By contrast, issues bearing on the relationships between workers and companies, such as whether to mandate union selection of a portion of the board along the lines of German codetermination or to encourage employee ownership through tax benefits or other means, as in American employee stock ownership plans, are beyond the scope of this chapter.

The Available Drafting Strategies

The Enabling Model and Its Limitations

In developed countries, corporate law is understood to provide a convenient set of rules (usually default that can be varied in the corporate charter) to encourage profit-maximizing business decisions, provide professional managers with adequate discretion and authority, and protect shareholders (and to some extent creditors) against opportunism by corporate insiders including entrenched managers. But no one assumes that the corporate law of developed markets accomplishes these objectives alone. In the enabling market paradigm, a competitive product market, an efficient capital market, and a market for corporate control all exert strong pressures on corporate managers to enhance shareholder value. Elaborate disclosure and antifraud provisions assure shareholders of reliable information about company performance. And sophisticated courts and administrative agencies keep sharp eyes out for corporate skullduggery.

These multiple investor protections let the corporate law itself tilt far toward enhancing transactional flexibility. For example, the Delaware corporation statute is a highly discretionary enabling law, many of whose major provisions are default rules. The statute is accompanied by fiduciary doctrines that give the Delaware courts wide latitude to review for opportunistic behavior *ex post*, but the courts punish only egregious instances of self-dealing or recklessness. All else is left to private institutions and the market.

In emergent economies the efficiency goal of encouraging production in the corporate form dictates a more protective corporate law for several reasons. Corporate insiders are likely to exercise voting control over the great majority of public companies. Because this ownership structure presents a clear risk of opportunism by insiders toward public shareholders, encouraging outside investment in companies requires strong minority protections.

Of course, appropriate contractual protections for minority public shareholders would result automatically in a world of perfect contracting without informational asymmetries or naive investors. The assumption that financial markets in developed countries can approximate the conditions necessary for efficient corporate contracting is a central theoretical underpinning for the enabling model. But this assumption clearly fails in emerging economies where informational asymmetries are severe, markets are inefficient, market participants are less experienced, and the economy itself is likely to be in flux. Each of these factors allows opportunism that the participants in the corporate enterprise may be unable or unwilling to avoid by contract.

In addition, in privatizing economies, such as Russia, the entire initial structure of private relationships among participants in companies is the product of government fiat rather than private contract. The ownership structure of a privatized Russian company was imposed by the privatization program, its initial charter was prescribed by the privatization ministry, and the company's principal bank lenders were often selected before privatization began. These relationships were not negotiated by the relevant parties with an eye toward their own self-protection.

Beyond these efficiency justifications for protective corporate law, political goals support minority shareholder protection in emergent economies. Egregious opportunism or scandals may erode the political legitimacy of corporate ownership in emergent countries, or even erode support for the market economy generally.[6]   The political risk of a destructive public reaction to scandal is a negative externality of insider discretion that law in an emergent market must take very seriously. And even if corporate scandal does not trigger a political maelstrom of populist reaction, it may significantly damage investor confidence in environments where disclosure is minimal.

Even as the economic and political goals of corporate law in emergent economies favor a strong protective function, limitations on enforcement resources constrain how this protective function is discharged. The most significant legal limitation is weak or ineffectual judicial enforcement. The substantive legal remedies available to judges may be ill defined or inadequate. Judicial procedures may be cumbersome, or the court system overtaxed. And the judiciary itself is likely to be ill-trained and may sometimes be simply corrupt.

Emergent markets are also unlikely to have administrative agencies that can handle corporate law matters, such as disclosure policy, which benefit from detailed rulemaking and administrative enforcement. Moreover, they lack the nonlegal enforcement resources found in developed economies, including self-regulatory institutions (such as the New York or London Stock Exchanges and the British Takeover Panel) and private firms that protect clients against abuse and reduce informational asymmetries (such as investment banking, law, and accounting firms). Disclosure, in particular, is an important constraint on management behavior in developed economies that is often weak or absent in emerging economies. Disclosure of management self-dealing can lead to formal enforcement or, at a minimum, public embarrassment. Disclosure of self-dealing or business problems can also lead to market sanctions, such as a lower stock price, reduced availability of credit, or difficulty in hiring employees.

A final reason why developed countries can make do with relatively weak formal constraints on manager and large shareholder opportunism is that managers and large shareholders are embedded in a culture that discourages opportunism. Few American corporate managers doubt that they work for the shareholders, even if they and their shareholders sometimes have different ideas about what this concept means. Moreover, developed country managers are accustomed to routinely following laws of all kinds and to thinking of themselves as law-abiding.

Russia offers a marked contrast. Russian enterprise managers cannot

---

[6] Thus, elements of the Russian right, including former Speaker of the Russian Parliament Ruslan Khasbulatov, attack the entire privatization program as a mafia scheme (see Blasi and Shleifer in this volume).

follow the law or accurately disclose their financial results and stay in business. They must lie about their income to the tax authorities (and, therefore, to investors also); bribe the tax inspector, the customs inspector, the local police, and many other government officials; pay off the local mafia; and so on. It is not surprising that these managers often see corporate law as merely another obstacle to be gotten around in any way possible. Some have declared their charter, or the stock ownership of their top management, to be "commercial secrets." Some simply lock unwanted shareholders out of the shareholder meeting, conduct a shareholder vote by show of hands (dominated, of course, by employees), or refuse to transfer shares if they don't approve of the new owner. Misconduct so basic is rare in developed markets, precisely because it would be instantly condemned as making hash out of the ground rules of the corporate form.

The Prohibitive Model

Having surveyed the constraints under which corporate law in emerging markets must operate and the concomitant limitations on the usefulness of the enabling model, we turn to the question: what form should such a law take? Some aspects of corporate law for emergent markets follow easily from the protective function that it must discharge and the limited tools available to enforce it. To the extent possible, the law should consist of relatively simple rules that can be easily understood and applied even by unsophisticated corporate participants and judges. In addition, the core rules should often be mandatory, rather than default provisions changeable by shareholder vote, given the weakness of market checks on corporate insiders and the prevalence of controlled companies.

There are two general approaches that satisfy these general requirements. One we term the "prohibitive model": a statute that bars suspect classes of corporate behavior in considerable detail. The second we term the "self-enforcing model": a law that creates corporate decision-making *processes* that allow minority shareholders to protect themselves by their own voting decisions.

The prohibitive model is familiar from nineteenth century corporation statutes in the United States and Great Britain, and to some extent from European corporate codes today. These codes simply bar many kind of corporate behavior that are open to potential abuse, such as self-dealing transactions and cashout mergers. Such prohibitive statutes were adopted in market circumstances that resemble in some respects those of emergent economies such as Russia. One plausible approach to corporate law for emergent economies is to return to the restrictive drafting strategy of the past.

That developed economies have evolved away from the prohibitive model toward an enabling model – far away in the United States and Great Britain, less far in Continental Europe – does not mean that the prohibitive model is inappropriate for emergent markets. Enabling statutes would predictably fare far worse in emergent economies where controlled firms are the norm and nonlegal restraints on controlling insiders are weak.

But prohibitive statutes have severe drawbacks, even in emergent markets. First, they impose major costs on companies by mechanically limiting the discretion of corporate managers to pursue legitimate business decisions. By most accounts, the driving force behind the rise of enabling statutes in developed markets was the value of flexibility to transactional planners, corporate managers, and ultimately to shareholders (see, for example, Romano 1993). The inflexibility of substantive prohibitions can be (and in Continental Europe often is) reduced by creative judicial interpretation, but this requires creative and knowledgeable judges.

Morever, many formal constraints become ineffective as practitioners discover how to avoid them. The classic example in the Anglo-American context is the demise of the protective function of legal capital following the introduction of low-par stock. In addition, prohibitive statutes require significant judicial or administrative involvement. Disputes about rules governing specific corporate behaviors are inevitable, not least because transaction planners will look for ways to comply with the letter of the statute but not its spirit. These disputes, in turn, require knowledgeable judges who can resolve the disputes in sensible ways.

The Self-Enforcing Model

A central claim of this chapter is that in emerging markets a self-enforcing model of corporate law – in which mandatory procedural and structural rules empower outside directors and large minority shareholders to protect themselves against opportunism by controlling insiders – dominates both the prohibitory model and the enabling model. The self-enforcing model greatly reduces the need to rely on courts and administrative agencies for enforcement. Thus, it is robust even when these resources are weak. And it combines much, though not all, of the flexibility of the enabling model with a degree of investor protection that the enabling model cannot match, and perhaps the prohibitory model cannot match either.

The structural constraints that define the self-enforcing approach to corporate law operate both at the shareholder level and at the level of the board of directors. At the shareholder level, these constraints typically assume the form of shareholder voting requirements. For example, a statute might require supermajority shareholder approval for a central business decision, rather than the simple majority approval that characterizes the enabling approach. It might require a shareholder vote for a broader range of corporate actions than an enabling statute, including decisions to issue significant amounts of new equity or purchase major assets.[7]   A self-enforcing statute can police related-party transactions with approval by independent directors, a majority of noninterested shareholders, or both. The voting decisions of shareholders with their own money at stake, if obtained through fair procedures and full disclosure, provide a way to distinguish between good and bad transactions that is more fine grained than formal prohibitions could possibly be.

To enhance the value of the voting mechanism, the self-enforcing statute can include a universal ballot that large shareholders can use to place director nominations on the voting agenda, including independent vote tabulation, to ensure honest vote counting. Other structural constraints on the shareholder level can include appraisal rights for shareholders who oppose key business transactions and preemptive rights when companies make significant new issues of stock.

At the level of the board of directors, the statute can mandate that a certain proportion of the directors on company boards must be independent and vest approval of some decisions, such as decisions involving related party transactions, exclusively in the hands of these independent directors. The statute can create board structures, such as an audit committee composed of independent directors, that hold authority in defined areas.

An important feature of a self-enforcing statute, we believe, is a voting rule for election of directors that allows outside shareholders to elect a fraction of the board, such as a cumulative voting rule. Such a voting rule links decision-making constraints at the shareholder and the board levels by assuring that large outside shareholders can elect a fraction of the board to protect their interests. Outside representation makes it harder for insiders to ignore or deceive minority shareholders. And over the long run, cumulative voting, by making possible the election of some directors who truly represent shareholders, can influence how all directors come to understand their role in the corporate enterprise.

---

[7] To the extent that an enabling statute contains *any* mandates for shareholder votes on particular types of transactions, it partakes of the self-enforcement approach. The differences are ones of degree. The self-enforcing approach contains more and stricter mandates because it places greater weight on the goal of protecting outside investors against insider opportunism, and lesser weight on maximizing business flexibility.

Governance Structure and Voting Rules

The self-enforcing approach to corporate law constrains the discretion of managers and majority shareholders by granting voice and sometimes veto rights over important corporate actions to outside directors, noncontrolling shareholders, or both, in the expectation that these directors and shareholders can police whether the proposed corporate action is value increasing for the enterprise as a whole or merely a wealth transfer. These constraints can be described by the level on which they operate, that is, shareholder or board. They can also be characterized by the actions they affect: the voting procedure by which shareholders elect directors, the mechanism by which the board or the shareholders appoint and dismiss top management, the transactions that require special approval procedures, and the rules that constrain decisions, by shareholders or managers, to buy and sell control in corporations.

The self-enforcing model relies heavily on board and shareholder voting mechanisms. Thus, it requires careful specification of governance structure and shareholder voting rules. To avoid manipulation, governance structure must be simple, and malleable only within narrow limits. Some of the enabling model's flexibility over governance, voting processes, and capital structure is sacrificed to preserve flexibility over the range of substantive decisions that the corporation is permitted to take.

This and the next two parts of this chapter describe in greater detail the self-enforcing model with particular reference to a proposed approach to a Russian statute. We will justify the structural rules we favor as concrete examples of the theoretical framework for a self-enforcing law developed above.

Allocation of Management Powers

There are two basic options in choosing a review process for corporate actions: representative democracy, in which shareholders act through elected representatives (the board of directors); and direct democracy, in which shareholders vote directly for or against particular actions. Representative democracy alone is often unsatisfactory because boards can too easily become lazy or captured by management. Thus, the company law of every developed country provides for direct shareholder review of selected corporate actions such as mergers. Conversely, however, direct democracy is far too slow and costly for most decision-making in large companies. Moreover, because small shareholders must act on limited information and face severe collective action problems, direct democracy can quickly deteriorate in widely held companies into total manager control.

We mediate between the weaknesses of each approach with a simple hierarchical governance structure that allocates managerial power to a board of directors, subject to shareholder review for particular actions. The shareholders elect the board; the board chooses the managers (subject to shareholder review of its choice of top manager); the board (sometimes a defined subset of the board) approves particular types of actions, including those that require shareholder approval; for all other actions, the board decides when the managers can act unilaterally and when they need board approval.

This governance structure has multiple advantages. First, it assures a measure of accountability: shareholders know whom to blame if things go wrong, and the structure provides double review by both board and shareholders of important or suspect transactions. Second, it provides the board with reasonable though not total flexibility. The board decides within broad limits how best to use its own limited time, but a conscientious board must meet often enough and take enough business decisions to make it unlikely to descend into ill-informed irrelevancy – a strong risk in the German two-tier board model, where the supervisory board meets rarely and does little other than choose management.[8]   Third, this structure does not require more of shareholders than they can deliver. Apart from choosing the board, shareholders do not make decisions unilaterally. Instead, shareholders review actions that have already been approved by the board, which accords with the limited information available to small shareholders and ensures that managers cannot circumvent the board by appealing directly to shareholders for support.

While the governance structure we describe gives broad power to the board of directors, this power is constrained, in turn, by granting shareholders broad power over the board's constituency: for example, by requiring directors to be elected annually through cumulative voting and permitting shareholders to remove the board without cause.[9]   The path

---

[8] The structure has enough flexibility to allow a company largely to replicate the two-tier management structure, if the board so chooses. The "board of directors" can hire a "board of managers," and delegate to it all day-to-day management responsibility, subject only to whatever limited oversight the board of directors chooses to exercise. However, the board of directors remains responsible to the shareholders for the consequences of this choice; it cannot blame a legal structure that limits the board's power over management.

[9] For mechanical reasons, a system with cumulative voting must allow shareholders to remove the entire board, but *not* individual directors. If directors could be removed individually, a majority shareholder could vote to remove a director elected cumulatively by a minority shareholder and thus nullify the effect of cumulative voting. Compare Del. Gen. Corp. L. §141(k)(i) (cumulatively elected directors may not be removed if votes against removal would be sufficient to elect).

toward effective shareholder use of these tools to increase company value is smoothed in various ways, which include restricting companies to a single class of voting securities that also carry a residual economic interest in the company's profits and facilitating shareholder nomination of director candidates and free shareholder choice from among all nominees.

Allocation of Voting Power: One Share, One Vote

Shareholder voting rules for the election of directors must resolve two basic issues: how votes are allocated among investors and how votes are tabulated to select directors. The goal of a self-enforcing statute is to resolve these issues in a fashion that increases the likelihood that corporate actions will maximize corporate value. The natural resolution of the first issue is to match, as closely as possible, voting power to economic interest: that is, to mandate a single class of voting common stock that has a residual interest in corporate profits and votes according to the one share, one vote principle.[10] The one share, one vote principle is widely accepted across jurisdictions. It is the dominant rule in the United States, Great Britain, and Japan. Moreover, nonvoting or low-voting stock is under strong criticism from large investors in countries like Germany where it has been common.[11]

The case for the one share, one vote rule turns primarily on its value in matching economic incentives with voting power and in preserving the market for corporate control as a check on bad management.[12] By contrast, the case for permitting companies to deviate from a one share, one vote rule in developed economies turns on (1) the usual claim that informed parties will choose optimal arrangements on their own; and (2) the existence of an efficient market, in which company founders will realize a lower price if they make an inefficient decision to sell lower-voting shares. But these arguments against the standard rule lose much of their force in emerging markets. First, public offerings are unlikely to be priced with a high degree of efficiency. Second, in privatized economies, including Russia, there were no true

[10] In practical terms this means limiting the voting rights of securities (preferred stock and debt) that are senior to a company's common stock and limiting the company's ability to issue securities, principally options to purchase common stock, that are equivalent to or junior to common stock.

[11] In the United States a one share, one vote rule is maintained by agreement among the principal stock exchanges, rather than by company law. In Britain, one share, one vote is essentially universal because of strong support from institutional investors, who refuse to buy the shares of a company that has a different rule (see Black and Coffee (1994, 2024).

[12] For pieces of the extended debate over one share, one vote in the United States, see Gilson (1987); Lowenstein (1989); Easterbrook and Fischel (1992, 63–5); Gordon (1988); Seligman (1986).

founders who could make an economic decision whether to sell control rights as well as economic rights. Instead, one faces the much more troubling prospect of midstream charter changes, proposed and perhaps coerced in various ways by managers who plan to gain control without risking significant economic value.[13] Third, there is simply more need for investor protection against egregious self-dealing by company managers in emerging markets than in the United States or the United Kingdom, where the Victor Posners, Donald Trumps, and Robert Maxwells are seeming aberrations. For example, in Russia stories abound like that of the managers of a natural resources company who sell most of its output to another company and never collect the accounts receivable, while not paying the company's rent, taxes, utilities, or even employees for months or years – presumably, one suspects, in exchange for payments made to these managers' overseas bank accounts.[14] Voting common shares are no panacea for this behavior, but at least they can help.

Put another way, multiple-class voting structures create incentives to abuse control. Control (like other assets) tends to move to those who value it most. But since those who abuse control may value it more than those who do not, bad owners can often outbid and thus drive out good owners. In developed economies, market and cultural constraints will usually be strong enough to overcome this effect and keep abuse at manageable levels (although even this is uncertain). In emerging markets, abuse will proliferate without a one share, one vote rule.

Indeed, a mandatory one share, one vote rule protects shareholders in emerging economies even if their companies would otherwise initially issue only one class of voting stock by assuring investors there will be no subsequent change of rules in midstream. The rule can thus lift the value of all shares. To analogize to ordinary product markets, whenever product quality is difficult for buyers to measure (the "lemons" situation), minimum quality rules can be welfare enhancing. The case for quality rules in securities markets is especially strong because of the risk in securities markets (largely unique to securities markets) that the quality of what one has bought will be changed after the date of purchase and the strong incentive for unscrupulous investors to profit by doing precisely that.

[13] For discussion of the special problems created by midstream charter changes, see, e.g. Bebchuk (1989); Gordon (1989, 1573–85); Black (1990, 566–70).
[14] See, e.g., "Russian capitalism," *The Economist,* 8 October 1994, pp. 21, 23.

Voting for Directors: Cumulative Voting

The one share, one vote rule is conventional in many jurisdictions and has easily understood virtues. Our approach to how votes are to be tabulated in selecting directors relies on a less common solution, whose advantages are also more subtle: mandatory cumulative voting, related requirements for minimum board size (a seven-director minimum ensures that a 15 percent shareholder can elect one director), and annual election of directors (staggered board terms, by reducing the number of directors elected at one time, have the same effect as small board size in diluting the effectiveness of cumulative voting).

Cumulative voting addresses several problems at once. First, it serves the obvious function of giving large minority shareholders a voice in board actions, though not a controlling voice. Second, a seat on the board provides access to information about the company's affairs. Thus, for large or organized shareholders board seats won through cumulative voting can substitute for disclosure that is provided in developed economies in a variety of more direct ways: through financial disclosure rules; market analyst and financial press reports; market price signals; and, especially in Germany and Japan, nonpublic financial reports to the company's lead bank.

Third, cumulative voting increases the likelihood that at least a minority of directors is truly independent of management, and – what is also important though often neglected in the United States – that these directors will owe affirmative loyalty to shareholders who elect them (see Gilson and Kraakman 1991). Director independence takes on special significance for us because it interacts with rules, discussed below, that vest in outside directors the power to review transactions in which managers have a personal financial stake. This review by independent directors is especially important because of the weakness of fiduciary rules and cultural constraints as checks on self-dealing. In addition, the influence of a minority of outside directors can be extended beyond disclosed self-dealing transactions if in large companies the law requires an audit committee composed of independent directors to choose the company's auditors, outside registrar, and "counting commission" (i.e. persons who will count shareholder votes).

Fourth, cumulative voting reinforces the principle that directors owe their loyalty to shareholders, not to the company's officers. As such, it forms a piece of a broader effort in the corporate law to develop and reinforce voluntary compliance with behavioral norms that have served developed countries well. For example, a presidential decree mandating cumulative voting for privatized firms already seems to have triggered this norm-reinforcing effect in Russia over the past year. Almost no firms had outside directors before the decree, but today they typically have outside directors in rough proportion to the holdings of outside blockholders (see Blasi and Shleifer in this volume). Many firms have ignored the decree on the surface by not implementing cumulative voting. Nevertheless, in those firms where investors would have had the power under cumulative voting to elect a director or two, investors have often achieved the same result without an open election contest – exactly the result one hopes for. Similarly, as some Russian firms appoint outside directors, it is becoming the norm, so we hear, for others to do so. We do not claim that these voluntarily appointed "outside" directors are always truly independent. But some are, and before long, norms of behavior for outside directors will develop that will encourage others to be more independent, perhaps, than the managers who chose them initially expected.

Precisely because cumulative voting serves these multiple purposes, it is a central element of our effort to develop a self-enforcing corporate law. It will not ensure truly independent directors, or directors accountable to shareholders, at all companies. Moreover, we are not so sanguine as to rely on the board of directors, or even on nominally independent directors, as the sole protection of outside shareholder interests – we also contemplate a relatively broad range of transactions, including self-interested transactions, for which shareholders have veto power or other protections. But cumulative voting will strengthen the boards of at least some companies, and that will help.

The fact that cumulative voting is optional in most developed countries, and many companies do not adopt it, does not detract from its value as a cornerstone of a self-enforcing law. In most of these other countries, market, legal, and cultural forces combine to achieve the goals that only cumulative voting can help to achieve in developing markets.

Consider outside shareholder representation on the board of directors. In the United States, large outside shareholders often obtain representation on the board of directors in rough proportion to their ownership interest. Management might be able to defeat the large shareholder's nominees in an election contest. But this is not certain, and company managers would rather allow a large shareholder to have a couple of board seats than risk losing the election contest, which would probably mean losing their jobs. Or a company will give an large investor representation on the board to get the investor to invest. Or the company will, simply because it is normal to do so, appoint independent directors – often, an absolute majority of the board – who can perform much of the oversight that would be undertaken by directors chosen by large shareholders under cumulative voting.

In addition, developed countries that do not rely heavily on outside directors have similar oversight mechanisms. For example, although outside shareholders in Great Britain often lack direct board representation, British managers know that a modest number of institutional investors can combine forces to oust the board if the need arises. And even with this protection, large British institutional investors are now pressing for independent boards to supplement the crisis-oriented oversight that they now exercise for themselves. Similarly, in Japan large shareholders can act through the main bank to force a change in management, much as American shareholders might act through an independent board of directors.

The principal argument raised against cumulative voting as a mechanism of shareholder oversight is that it creates the possibility of a divided board, which might be less effective than a board elected on a winner-take-all basis. But the available evidence suggests that this is not a large risk in practice. The experience of developed countries with proportional representation of large shareholders on the board, whether this arises from cumulative voting or from agreement with management, is that proportional representation usually works well. Indeed, large shareholders often insist on proportional representation of the type that they would receive with cumulative voting even when it is not required by statute. Moreover, the argument that cumulative voting is divisive is also suspect on theoretical grounds. It is rarely in the interests of a large shareholder to try to interfere with the smooth functioning of the board of directors. And when a large shareholder does attempt to interfere, it is often a sign of some other pathology, for which cumulative voting might be an incomplete cure but still perhaps better than the alternative, which might be a unified board stolidly supporting management as it marches the company toward disaster (see generally, Gordon 1994).

Empirical studies in developed countries suggest that shareholders benefit from the availability of cumulative voting (see Bhagat and Brickley 1984). For emerging markets, where other sources of shareholder protection are weak, we believe that the likely benefits of cumulative voting for minority shareholders greatly outweigh its potential costs.

Voting Procedures: Universal Ballot and Independent Tabulation

Of course cumulative voting is only part of the architecture of a voting system. Ancillary rules are necessary to articulate procedures and safeguard the distribution of voting power that is implicit in the cumulative voting rule. In particular the voting regime must provide rules to govern the form of shareholder proxies (or ballots), the nomination of candidates for election to the board, the introduction of proposals for shareholder votes, and the tabulation of shareholder votes. Also, voting regimes for companies in emerging economies must take special precautions against efforts to subvert shareholder voting through coercion or fraud.

We endorse the so-called "universal ballot," or consolidated proxy, both as the form of the shareholder proxy and as the framework for nominating directorial candidates and introducing shareholder proposals. Where the voting regimes of conventional company laws typically require each faction in a proxy contest to distribute its own proxy, the universal ballot lists the qualified candidates of all factions on a single consolidated proxy, which is prepared at company expense and made available to shareholders well in advance of the shareholder meeting. Under this regime, the incumbent board and all shareholder groups exceeding a threshold size may nominate candidates on the company's ballot. In addition, shareholder groups exceeding the same threshold size may list one or more proposals (in the Russian statute, two) for a shareholder vote at general meetings with no restrictions on subject matter.

Like cumulative voting itself, these liberal provisions for including shareholder nominations and proposals on the company's ballot permit relatively small aggregations of shares to participate in shaping the company's voting agenda. Of course, the precise size at which shareholder groups ought to receive the right to list board candidates on the company's ballot is a matter of judgment. On the one hand, a very low threshold invites abuse by shareholders with little incentive to take the company's interests seriously. On the other hand, allowing shareholders to nominate even when they could not elect a director under the cumulative voting rule encourages activists to organize and represent larger groups of otherwise disaggregated shareholders with common interests. The Russian statute balances these competing concerns by setting the size threshold that permits shareholder groups to place board nominations and shareholder proposals on the universal ballot at 2 percent.[15]

The best voting procedures in the world are useless, however, when they are subverted by coercion, vote buying, or fraud – chronic dangers in emerging economies such as Russia. Coercion and vote buying occur when someone, typically a company insider, induces shareholders to vote against

---

[15] By contrast, the statute sets the threshold for petitioning to convene a special shareholders meeting (as distinct from the annual regular meeting to elect directors) at 10% of qualified voting shares. This higher threshold reflects not only the considerable expense of holding a shareholders meeting but also the fact that most decisions such a meeting might take would require at least a majority vote – as opposed to the 10%–15% necessary to elect a director under the cumulative voting rule. In the face of opposition from an incumbent board, majority approval is unlikely unless a proposal has widespread or large-block backing from the outset.

their investment interests by threatening to punish "wrong" votes, reward "right" votes, or both. In the Russian case, coerced voting is a particular danger because management is in a position to exercise its workplace authority to command the votes of the large blocks of stock held by employee shareholders. Although this problem merits specialized regulation (see section, Protection of Employee Shareholders, below), the first defense against the coercion of workers' votes is equally appropriate to all forms of coercion and illicit vote buying: namely, placing a mandatory rule of confidential voting in the company law. Insiders who cannot monitor shareholder votes lose the power to manipulate votes through rewards or sanctions.

In contrast to coerced voting, voting fraud occurs when outsiders cannot monitor insiders – or, more specifically, when outsiders cannot monitor the insiders who have the power to alter or miscount ballots in the service of their own agenda. Moreover, voting fraud is a particular concern when controlled companies operate under cumulative voting, because relatively small changes in vote tallies can importantly affect minority representation on the board.

The obvious way to protect against fraud and to secure the confidentiality of voting is to take the functions of collecting, tabulating, and storing shareholder ballots out of management's hands insofar as possible. The Russian statute accomplishes this separation in two ways. For large companies (of more than 1,000 shareholders), it vests the tabulation function in an independent share registrar that large companies are required to maintain for the different purpose of reliably recording share transactions. For smaller companies unable to afford such a share registrar, the tabulating function is vested in a separate commission of outsiders that cannot include directors or company officers (although these commissioners are approved by the board of directors). While such a board-appointed commission is less protective than an independent share registrar, voting fraud may also be easier to detect in small companies where shareholders often know firsthand who supports whom in contested elections.

But even if such statutory protections against manipulated voting are effective, a last troubling question about cumulative voting remains: how much will it really matter, given that insiders generally control the board in Russian companies and presumably in the companies of emerging economies generally? We have already discussed how cumulative voting *can* matter in controlled companies, provided that outside blockholders make use of it. Minority board representation serves as a device for monitoring insiders and for leveraging the authority of outsiders to pass on suspect transactions through the committee structure of the board. A concern that cumulative voting might not matter, then, must be a concern that minority blockholders will fail to take advantage of it, presumably because the costs of formally seeking board representation outweigh the benefits. But here the preliminary Russian data are encouraging because they suggest that large outside blockholders expect to have representation on the board in controlled companies (see Blasi and Shleifer in this volume). Moreover, even when formal cumulative voting is not used and management's slate is the only one, the option of cumulative voting may well have an effect. Most obviously, it may determine whom management invites on its slate; less obviously, it may deter management from actions that could provoke an outsider's slate to enter the race. Thus, the important question, ultimately, is not how often shareholders will avail themselves of cumulative voting, but whether cumulative voting is available when someone tries to use it and whether minority shareholders find that the threat to resort to cumulative voting has significant deterrent and bargaining values.

The Costs of the Self-Enforcement Approach

Self-enforcement introduces costs as well as potential benefits for the corporate enterprise. First, shareholder votes or other shareholder remedies, such as preemption rights for new stock issuances, introduce administrative cost and delay. Thus, while *how much* more common mandated shareholder votes and other procedures should be in emerging than in developed markets requires balancing the expected costs and benefits of expanding a particular protection, in some instances full shareholder protection will be less economic than partial protection. For example, one advantage of cumulative voting is that it creates a more shareholder-loyal board, which in turn permits the law to vest more decisions exclusively in the board and to require a shareholder vote less often. Although these board decisions provide less shareholder protection than a shareholder vote, they will also be faster and less costly.

A further cost of self-enforcement protections is a subtle loss of flexibility in designing the business enterprise. The self-enforcement model controls the structure within which corporate decisions are made, while leaving freedom over the substantive decisions. But a single decision-making structure will not fit all companies. To some extent, the law can allow for this by providing different rules for companies of different sizes and by dictating structure only when there seems strong need to do so. But we cannot anticipate in advance all the ways in which companies might want for good reason to depart from the prescribed structure. In theoretical terms, we cannot fully escape the usual expanded choice argument for an enabling law.

Again, judgment is needed on when to provide different rules for differently situated companies. The *direction* of difference of a self-enforcing law from an enabling law is clear: more of the structure must be prescribed. The *extent* of the difference will increase with firm size. More elaborate procedures, such as independent registrars or separate audit committees, will only be appropriate for larger companies. Which procedures are appropriate for which firms is an exercise in balancing.

Structural Constraints on Particular Corporate Transactions

In any corporate law the basic governance structure and voting rules are the sole legal backdrop only for routine business transactions. Very large, unusual, suspect, or potentially transformative transactions are often subject to more specialized regulation to protect outside investors from unusual risks of abuse. Since these key transactions are particularly risky for investors, they are logically accorded special treatment. Moreover, in keeping with the project of a self-regulatory corporate law, the special treatment we prescribe takes the form of structural constraints rather than prohibitions for four categories: mergers and similar major transactions, self-interested transactions, transactions in shares, and control transactions.

Mergers and Other Major Transactions

Mergers, large sales of assets, large acquisitions of assets (whether directly or indirectly through a subsidiary), reorganizations, and liquidations are essential tools for restructuring companies. However, they can also radically alter the nature of a shareholder's investment, and they have historically been a common means by which insiders can loot the company's assets. To respond to this danger, major transactions commonly require the approval of at least a majority of shareholders, even under the enabling laws of developed economies. Enabling statutes also frequently provide a second, individualized mechanism of shareholder protection in the form of appraisal rights that permit shareholders to demand payment of the fair value of their shares, as determined by a court, instead of accepting the consequences of the transaction.

The list of transactions that require shareholder approval in developed countries, and the required size of the shareholder vote, should form a floor for the statute of an emerging economy. The key decisions are (1) whether to require a tougher shareholder vote than majority approval; (2) what additional transactions should require a shareholder vote; (3) what appraisal rights shareholders ought to have if the company completes a transaction that they oppose.

Shareholder Vote Requirement

Setting a shareholder approval threshold for major transactions requires analysis of the typical ownership structure of public companies and of the most likely forms of potential abuse.[16] For Russia the typical ownership structure of privatized enterprises leads us to propose approval by two-thirds of the outstanding shares.[17]

The shareholder vote requirement should be high enough so that managers and employees cannot reach it too easily without support from outside shareholders. In Russia this means a supermajority vote because most companies have majority ownership by managers and employees. But the vote requirement must not be so high that the company cannot complete a beneficial transaction because the necessary shareholder vote cannot be obtained. For example, managers might propose a merger that will increase productivity at the merged firm but also lead to layoffs. If the vote requirement is too high, opposition by employee shareholders could block the transaction. The two-thirds rule strikes a balance between the costs and benefits of a supermajority vote requirement.

Requiring supermajority votes to approve certain decisions involves the usual costs and risks of departing from a majority vote rule. A large outside shareholder will have holdup power and may be able to obtain personal benefits by threatening to use this power to block a value-increasing transaction. Or the rational apathy of small shareholders may make it hard for the company to obtain approval of a value-increasing transaction. The two concerns interact: the rational apathy of some shareholders increases the holdup power of other shareholders. Suppose, for example, that a company's managers wish to sell a significant fraction of its shares to another company in return for new investment that will preserve value for investors but cost jobs today; a high shareholder approval requirement will increase the risk that employee shareholders can block this value-enhancing transaction.

For Russia, given roughly 60 percent manager and employee ownership,

[16] These approval requirements are in addition to the rules for self-interested transactions, discussed below, that will apply in some cases, as when a parent company merges with a controlled, partly-owned daughter company or when managers of the target company are offered an opportunity, not given to other target shareholders, to invest in the acquiring firm.

[17] For Russia we also propose an exception for investment funds, which (1) typically have a huge number of tiny shareholders and (2) lack the substantial employee ownership that characterizes privatized firms. The first factor makes a two-thirds vote harder to achieve, the second makes it less important as a protection against management overreaching. Here, we think a simple majority of outstanding shares should suffice.

relatively concentrated outside ownership of most firms, and modest residual state ownership, approval of key corporate actions such as mergers by two-thirds of the outstanding shares strikes a rough balance between setting an approval threshold high enough to make shareholder protection meaningful and limiting the holdup power of outsiders. For share issuances, we think that a simple majority of outstanding shares should suffice. But a different ownership structure could lead to a different judgment.

Transactions Requiring a Shareholder Vote

Deciding which transactions should require a shareholder vote also requires lawmakers to strike a balance between flexibility and the protection of minority shareholders. A shareholder vote to approve a transaction is costly in time and money: managers must either call a special shareholder meeting or wait until the next regular shareholder meeting to ask for approval of the transaction by the shareholders. This cost and delay will increase the cost of completing transactions and will deter beneficial transactions entirely. Thus, the shareholder vote requirement should only apply to transactions that transform the nature of the company or involve a substantial risk of abuse: that is, where the value of protecting shareholders clearly outweighs the costs of a mandatory vote.[18]

For Russia, the transactions that we believe should require a shareholder vote are:

1. a merger or other business combination involving the company and one or more other companies;
2. a liquidation of the company;
3. a transformation of the company into a legal entity of another type, such as a partnership;
4. a sale of assets, directly or through subsidiaries, equal to 50 percent of the book value of the company's assets;[19]

[18] Significant transactions must also be approved by the board of directors of the company, but this offers little protection of outside investor interests when the company's managers control the board.

[19] There should be a normal course of business exception to handle the special case of a trading company that regularly makes large purchases and sales of goods, on a thin equity base. The definition of asset sales should not include a pledge of assets to secure a loan. Such a pledge, followed by intentional default on the loan, can be used as an indirect way to sell assets without a shareholder vote. But most pledges are likely to be legitimate, and often a default under one loan agreement will have adverse consequences under other loan agreements, because of cross-default provisions. On balance, we believe that the lost flexibility from treating a pledge of security for a loan in the same manner as a sale exceeds the gain in additional protection of shareholders against sales for less than fair value.

5. a purchase of assets or other transaction that will result in the company owning, directly or through subsidiaries, additional assets equal to at least 50 percent of the book value of the company's assets.

The first three items on this list need little comment. The requirement of a shareholder vote for mergers and liquidations is standard in most company laws. Only the fourth and fifth requirements, dealing with sales and purchases of assets, are relatively strict in comparison to developed countries.[20] The rationale for lower voting thresholds in Russia is simply that transactions in the 50 percent range, that is, very large transactions, can destroy a company with the stroke of a pen if they happen to be self-dealing transactions designed to gut the company on management's behalf. Of course, self-dealing transactions are also subject to voting restrictions, as we will describe shortly. But we cannot be confident that self-dealing transactions will always be disclosed. Therefore, a size-based voting requirement provides a backup constraint on the hidden self-dealing transaction. When so much of a company is at stake, multiple protections are desirable.

For the same reason we also propose a shareholder vote on smaller purchases or sales of assets between 25 percent and 50 percent of a company's value that are not *unanimously* approved by all directors, including outside directors selected through cumulative voting. Finally, for enforceability, accounting values rather than market values should trigger the shareholder vote or unanimous director approval requirements. Although market values might be preferable in theory, they are not administrable in a country like Russia with neither an efficient stock market nor reliable professional appraisers.[21]

Appraisal Rights

Even in enabling-type corporate laws, a shareholder who votes against a major transaction that requires a shareholder vote can typically demand

[20] For example, American corporate law imposes no restrictions on the purchase of assets and only requires a shareholder vote for the sale of "substantially all" assets. See, e.g., Del. Gen. Corp. L. §271 (1992). A sale of more than 75% of balance sheet assets generally requires a shareholder vote under this provision, while similar sales (between 26% and 75%) may trigger a vote on occasion. See Herzel, Sherck, and Colling (1982); Gilson and Black (1995).

[21] On the difficulty of administering a market value test for shareholder votes on sales of assets, see Gilson and Black (1995: 523–4). A balance sheet test serves tolerably well for sales of assets, since balance sheet numbers for the assets to be sold can be compared with the total balance sheet value of the company. In the case of asset purchases, accounting numbers are somewhat less satisfactory; the value of the asset, as it is carried on the books of the seller, must be contrasted with the book value of the buyer. Although this test will lead to some arbitrary outcomes, it is nonetheless preferable to attempts to reconstruct market value.

payment of the fair market value of his shares, as determined by a court. Like most other shareholder protections, this so-called appraisal remedy is far from perfect. On the one hand, it has been sharply criticized for the burdens that it imposes on transacting corporations, including a possible drain on a company's liquidity that may deter value-enhancing transactions (see, e.g., Manning 1962). On the other hand, the capacity of the appraisal remedy to check breaches of fiduciary duty by managers is sharply limited, especially since only large minority shareholders are likely to exercise their appraisal remedy under any circumstances (see, e.g., Brudney and Chirelstein 1974).

The appraisal remedy, which works badly even in developed markets, will surely work worse in emerging markets. Yet there is no obvious alternative. Judicial or regulatory approval of major transactions is neither practicable nor desirable. Hence, one can only try to ameliorate the worst problems associated with appraisal rights in emerging economies. For example, appraisal rights in developed economies typically require a shareholder actively to oppose a transaction; in an emerging market this condition weakens an already weak right. Given poor mail systems, shareholders may not learn of a transaction in time to vote against it or may find that their votes did not reach the company in time. Counting commissions or outside auditors that tally the votes in large companies will presumably count "no" votes, but smaller companies may simply discard those votes without leaving shareholders any proof of having voted. Therefore, we propose that shareholders who do not vote *for* a major transaction should be able, promptly after the transaction is completed, to obtain payment of the fair value of their shares measured before the transaction took place.

Company law must also be alert to the potential misuse of the appraisal remedy. For example, minority shareholders might sabotage a beneficial transaction by demanding that the company buy back their shares at a time when it is strapped for cash. One way to balance the need for shareholder protection against the company's need for flexibility is to give shareholders only a short period after the transaction is completed to seek to have the company buy back their shares. Otherwise the right to sell one's shares back to the company will be a valuable put option that can be exercised if the value of the company's shares declines after the transaction, even if the decline is unrelated to the transaction itself.[22]

---

[22] More generally, a put option is inherent in any system of appraisal rights. This creates a collective action problem: a shareholder who seeks appraisal rights for a stock-for-stock merger can, at modest cost, obtain a significant time window in which to decide whether to pursue the appraisal rights or abandon them and receive the merger consideration. Granting this option is costly to the other shareholders. If mails are reliable, it is appropriate to limit access to this free option by requiring that a shareholder must vote against the merger, not

A further problem that arises with special force in emerging markets is the valuation issue of how to determine the fair market value of shares. This is important not only for appraisal, but also for other procedural protections, including those accompanying major transactions and repurchases by the company of its own shares. Even developed economies have trouble defining fair market value in a consistent fashion. In an emerging market, a simple statement that shareholders should be paid the fair market value of their shares will fail of its intended effect, merely because no one will know how to determine fair market value. Further definition of an intrinsically difficult concept is needed. We offer a possible approach below, with no claim that it is the only available one.

Fair Market Value

The market value of property, including the common stock or other securities of a company, shall mean a price at which a seller, who is fully informed about the value of the property and is not obligated to sell the property, would be willing to sell, and at which a buyer, who is fully informed about the value of the property and is not obligated to buy the property, would be willing to buy.

Fair market value shall be determined by the board of directors, unless in a particular case the decision as to fair market value is vested by this law in the founders of a company or a court or an arbitration tribunal. If some but less than all directors are interested directors as to the transaction or transactions that require the determination of fair market value, the determination of fair market value shall be made by the noninterested directors. In the case of a public company, the determination of fair market value shall be made by the noninterested independent directors.

The person (persons) making the decision on the fair market value of property may rely on the advice of auditors or other independent valuation experts. If the property to be valued is a publicly traded security, the person (persons) making the decision shall consider, in making their decision, market price over a period of no less than two weeks before the date of the decision as to fair market value, but only to the extent that market price is a reliable measure of the security's value. If the property to be valued is common stock of a company, the "value" of a share shall be understood as a pro rata claim on the underlying value of corporate assets, as these are

---

simply (as in our proposal) fail to vote, by imposing tight time limits for exercising the appraisal right (which reduce the option's value) and perhaps by limiting the corporate actions that give rise to appraisal rights. This is an example of a situation where a rule that is appropriate for emerging markets should change as a background institution changes – in this case, the mail system.

presently organized and managed. In setting a price for this value, the person (persons) making the decision may also consider the shareholder capital of the company, the price that a willing, fully informed buyer would be willing to pay for all of the company's common shares, and other factors that they consider important.

Self-Interested Transactions

Transactions by a company that personally benefit directors, managers, or large shareholders are inherently suspect, because the director, manager, or large shareholder (whom we will call an "insider," recognizing that the description may not be accurate for a large shareholder) may be able to cause the company to enter into the transaction on unfair terms. Yet we cannot simply return to the broad prohibitory approach to these transactions that characterized U.S. law in the early twentieth century, because sometimes these transactions are advantageous to the company – this is, after all, the underlying reason why broad prohibitions disappeared. Outright prohibition, therefore, is justified only in exceptional cases where there is little business justification for an interested transaction and the risk of abuse is particularly high. We suggest only two such cases: loans by the company to insiders and payments (kickbacks) by another person paid to an insider in connection with a transaction between the company and the other person. Elsewhere, the self-enforcement approach to the regulation of interested transactions relies on an especially rigorous set of procedural protections to reduce the incidence of illicit self-dealing.

The principal procedural protections are (1) a vote by noninterested directors or for large companies a vote by noninterested *independent* directors, and (2) a vote by noninterested shareholders. The level of procedural protection appropriate to a self-interested transaction depends on balancing the risk that additional protections will prevent good transactions against the likelihood that they will deter bad transactions. Since approval by noninterested directors is relatively easy to obtain, it should be required before the company can enter into *any* self-interested transaction. But since shareholder approval is costly and time-consuming to obtain, it should be required only for large transactions.

We do not pretend that this approach will prevent all self-dealing. Sometimes insiders will hide their interest in a transaction – but then the prohibitory approach will fail as well. Sometimes directors will not act independently of the managers. But company law can reduce the frequency of abuse. In some transactions, the insiders' interests cannot be concealed, and in others the insiders will decide to obtain an honest vote to protect the transaction against later attack in the courts. Also, managers who think of themselves as honest will voluntarily follow the rules. When self-interested transactions are disclosed, shareholders or noninterested directors can vote down the worst transactions, and the requirement of a vote can make self-dealing more difficult and therefore less common. The requirement that transactions be disclosed to shareholders can also deter some self-interested transactions.

The value of a requirement that self-interested transactions be approved by independent directors will be meaningful only if the directors are truly independent. There is no way to guarantee the independence of outside directors who are chosen by management. But many firms will have some directors who were elected by outside shareholders through cumulative voting. Since these directors are likely to be truly independent, their approval ought to be required for self-interested transactions in larger companies. Thus, the cumulative voting rules interact importantly with the rules on self-interested transactions.

Transactions in Shares

A third class of special transactions that merit structural protections is share issues and repurchases. Company sales and repurchases of shares not only have the potential of shifting company value from outside investors to company insiders (as do sales of company assets), but issuances and repurchases of shares also have the potential to shift voting power among classes of shareholders. However, nothing may be more critical to the survival and growth of a company than its ability to raise new capital as the need or opportunity arises without time-consuming procedural obstacles. Among developed countries, corporate law (as distinct from securities law) generally poses no requirements on issuances of shares below a critical threshold such as 20 percent.[23] By contrast the regulation of share repurchases is more diverse, ranging from almost no regulation in the United States to a near-prohibition until recently of share repurchases in Japan.

Issuance of Shares

There is a deceptively simple way to protect shareholders against a company's managers selling shares for less than fair value: forbid the company from having authorized but unissued shares. Then the managers must come to the

[23] In the United States, New York Stock Exchange rules rather than state corporate law require a shareholder vote for share issues greater than 18.5% of outstanding shares (*N.Y.S.E. Listed Company Manual*, §703.08A).

shareholders whenever they want to issue shares. We reject this approach because either it is so strict that raising capital becomes too difficult, or paradoxically, it will come to mean nothing at all. If literally every issue of new shares required a separate shareholder authorization, managers simply could not issue shares rapidly to exploit unexpected financing and investment opportunities. Moreover, the shareholder vote requirement would preclude the use of equity consideration in small transactions and greatly complicate option-based incentive compensation plans. Given these drawbacks of barring authorized but unissued shares, however, managers would undoubtedly search for a way around the ban. Most likely they would ask shareholders for blank check authorization of share issuances at every annual meeting. Yet if this ploy were successful, the draconian restraint on share issues would collapse into an empty formality, leaving shareholders with no protections at all.

Shareholder approval.   In lieu of a ban on authorized but unissued shares, the self-enforcing approach to corporate law offers instead a more complex series of mechanisms to balance shareholder protection against the costs of regulation. The goal is to provide reasonable protection to shareholders against issuance of shares for less than fair market value or issuance to alter the ownership and, therefore, the control of a company without unduly burdening the share issuance process.[24]

To make it easier for companies to issue shares, shareholders should be able to authorize shares that will be issued by the company only at a later date. The board of directors will decide when and if to issue these authorized but unissued shares. Of course the shareholders can refuse to authorize shares if they do not trust the managers to sell the shares at a fair price, but we expect that this will be rare. The general requirement of approval by two-thirds of the outstanding shares to amend the charter will give outside shareholders some control over the company's ability to increase its authorized shares.

The concern that shareholders' interests will be diluted by a sale of stock for less than market value is especially strong if the stock is sold to directors, managers, or large shareholders. The proposed law addresses this concern in several ways. First, a sale of stock by the company to a director, manager, or 20 percent shareholder is a self-interested transaction that requires approval by noninterested directors and by noninterested shareholders. Second, a sale

[24] These rules focus on the interests of the company's *existing* shareholders. It is the job of securities law to protect the interests of the purchasers of shares when shares are sold to the general public.

by a company of shares equal to 25 percent or more of its previously outstanding shares should require approval by a majority of outstanding shares, excluding shares held by the acquirer of the new shares. In the usual case where the acquirer is not already a large shareholder, this is less strict than the two-thirds vote for mergers and other major transactions. This is appropriate because shareholders, other than those who are acquiring the new shares, share a common interest in selling the new shares at a high price. Third, the preemptive and participation rights described below apply even for sales of stock that do not otherwise require a shareholder vote.

Preemption rights.   We propose that in any issuance of shares, with only limited exceptions, the company must offer shareholders preemptive rights, which are common in Britain and Europe. Preemptive rights require the company to either offer any shares pro-rata to existing shareholders or obtain a shareholder vote waiving preemptive rights in a particular case. This protects shareholders against issuances for less than fair value.

Preemptive rights impose a substantial cost – a preemptive rights offering is costly for a company with many small shareholders and is relatively slow. Thus, any preemptive rights requirement must allow for waiver, including routine waiver at an annual meeting, when no particular offering is planned. Yet the waiver procedure revives the risk that shareholder interests may be diluted by below-market sales of stock. To combat this risk, we contemplate that shareholders who do not vote to waive their preemptive rights will receive *participation rights*, which operate after the offering and give shareholders rights to buy the same number of shares at the offering price they could have bought had preemptive rights been available.

If the shares are sold at a fair price, shareholders will have little reason to exercise participation rights, and an offering without preemptive rights will take place much as in Britain and Europe, where a waiver binds all shareholders. And if some shareholders exercise participation rights, this will typically be a good outcome for the company because more capital is raised.

If the company sells shares for substantially below fair value, which is the situation where investor protection is needed, shareholders who have participation rights will rush to buy additional shares at a bargain price. This will let these shareholders recoup most of the dilution caused by the below-market issuance. It will also embarrass the managers by making the underpricing obvious to all shareholders and make it more difficult for the managers to convince shareholders to again waive preemptive rights. Conversely, shareholders should be more willing to waive preemptive rights if they know that the discipline of participation rights, albeit exercised by others, makes it less likely that managers will issue shares too cheaply.

Participation rights pose a subtle but important risk to the viability of preemptive rights waivers. Shareholders who do not vote to waive preemptive rights retain participation rights; shareholders who vote to waive preemption rights do not. The participation right is an option, exercisable for a limited period after the company sells shares, to buy shares at the same price. Like any option, it has value. Even if all shareholders are better off if preemptive rights are waived, each individual shareholder is better off if others waive the preemptive rights, but the individual does not, thereby keeping this valuable option.

To make participation rights viable, one must limit the value of this option. Limits can arise in several ways. First, the time period for exercising participation rights should be as short as is practical, given communication systems, to reduce the pure time value of the option, assuming a sale of shares at market value. Second, there will be a built-in lag between the time that the rights can be exercised and the time that additional shares are received, again determined by communications technology. This will complicate risk-free arbitrage, where a shareholder buys shares at one price using participation rights and immediately resells the shares at a higher price in the market. Third, and most critically, an emerging market is characterized by high bid-asked spreads – and often by intervals where the market does not clear – where one cannot sell one's stake at *any* reasonable price. These attributes of emerging markets, which create the need for participation rights as a check on managers' power to sell shares below fair value, also greatly shrink the option value of participation rights for a fairly valued offering.

Our judgment is that, if shareholders trust the company's management, the value of the participation rights option will be small enough so that preemptive rights waivers will be routinely granted by shareholders at annual meetings. But the participation rights proposal should be seen as frankly experimental and in need of revisiting if waivers become unduly difficult. One simple alternative is to give all shareholders participation rights, whether or not they waive preemptive rights.

Repurchase and Redemption of Shares

A company can reacquire its shares in a number of ways that raise different concerns. First, it can *repurchase* its own shares for cash or other property, including its own securities, in a voluntary transaction where the selling shareholder is not obligated to sell. Second, the company can *redeem* its shares in a transaction that is obligatory for at least one party. For example, preferred stock is often redeemable. These transactions can be either pro-rata (open on equal terms to all shareholders) or nonpro-rata. We consider here issues of fairness to holders of common stock in repurchases and, for preferred stock, fairness to holders of the class being repurchased or redeemed. Stock repurchases involve conveying corporate assets to shareholders, often common shareholders, and thus also can involve wealth transfer to holders of junior securities, especially common stock, at the expense of holders of debt or preferred stock. We discuss protection of these classes of investors below.

Pro-rata offer to repurchase common stock for cash.   The simplest transaction is an offer by the company to repurchase its stock for cash. An offer to repurchase made pro-rata to all shareholders is basically the same as a dividend. Such a repurchase, if made at fair market value, is merely a way for the company to distribute cash to shareholders. Because repurchases of this type are a valuable corporate tool, especially if (as in Russia) they are tax favored compared with dividends, they should be permitted absent any restrictions in the company's charter. A pro-rata repurchase offer to all shareholders does not raise significant fairness concerns and should not require special approval by shareholders.

The law should require, however, that even a pro-rata repurchase offer be made at fair market value unless a different purchase price was agreed on by contract between the company and the shareholder at the time that the shares were acquired. The decision as to fair market value should be made by the directors of the company who are not interested in the transaction. For a public company, the decision as to fair market value should be made by the independent directors who are not interested in the transaction. This is because insiders, who are usually large shareholders, always have an indirect interest in a repurchase of shares. If they are not themselves sellers, they will want the company to buy shares for as low a price as possible. The sellers may be willing to sell because they do not know the true value of the shares.

If stock markets were well developed, it would be desirable to treat a repurchase of shares by a public company on the open market at the market price in the same manner as a pro-rata repurchase, since all shareholders will have a reasonably equal opportunity to sell their shares at that price in the market. But, in a highly illiquid stock market of the type that characterizes many emerging markets, a repurchase, supposedly made on the open market at the market price, may be used as a way to repurchase shares from insiders at a favorable price. The insiders will know when the company will be buying shares and will sell at that time at a high price. After the company finishes buying these shares, the price will drop again.

Nonpro-rata offer to repurchase shares of common stock.   An offer to repurchase shares made only to some shareholders and not others raises a concern that insider shares will be repurchased at more than fair market value, or that the company will use its power to repurchase shares to buy out a troublesome shareholder at a high price. We propose that a nonpro-rata repurchase of shares must be made at fair market value, as discussed above, and must also be approved by a majority vote of all shares qualified to vote. If the identity of the shareholders whose shares are to be repurchased is known, they should be disqualified from voting their shares. If the identity of these shareholders is not known, as in the case of a repurchase in the open market, then all shares can vote.

Finally, a nonpro-rata offer to repurchase shares from insiders should be treated like any other self-interested transaction: it should require (1) approval by a majority of noninterested directors or, for public companies, by a majority of independent noninterested directors; and (2) approval by a majority of noninterested shares.

Offer to repurchase preferred stock for cash.   The law should permit a company to repurchase its preferred stock for cash, subject to any restrictions in the charter. A repurchase offer for preferred stock raises few fairness concerns for holders of common stock or for holders of preferred stock as long as it is pro-rata. Thus, the law should not require special approval for pro-rata offers, but only that they proceed at fair market value unless shareholders agreed to a different purchase price at the time the shares were sold. Of course, if the preferred stock is junior to another class of preferred stock, the company's net assets must be sufficient to cover the liquidation preference of the more senior preferred stock after the repurchase. In addition, nonpro-rata repurchases should first require approval from the holders of the class of preferred stock to be repurchased in the same manner as for nonpro-rata offers to repurchase common stock.[25]

Offer to purchase stock for securities or other property.   Unless the charter provides otherwise, a company should be able to repurchase its shares for securities or other noncash property. The same rules should apply to offers to repurchase shares whether the consideration is cash or property, including other securities of the company. For noncash consideration, the fair market value of the property delivered by the company must be determined by the board of directors or for a public company by the independent directors, excluding any directors with a personal interest in the transaction.

---

[25] The rules on nonpro-rata repurchases should also apply to offers to purchase a company's stock by its subsidiaries.

Redemption of shares at option of company. A redemption of shares is a transaction in which the shareholder is required under the company's charter to sell his shares back to the company. Because the shareholder cannot choose not to sell, the principal risk is that the price offered by the company will be too low. To respond to this risk, we believe that a company should be able to redeem stock only pro-rata or by lot to the extent necessary to avoid redemption of fractional shares. A pro-rata mandatory redemption of common stock is the same in substance as a dividend, except for the possibility of different tax consequences.

For common stock, there is no special need to permit nonpro-rata redemption. Nonpro-rata redemption is too easy a way for managers to buy out unwanted shareholders, probably at a low price. For preferred stock, redemption should be at the redemption price specified in the charter or, if no price is specified, at fair market value. The same rules for protection of creditors and holders of preferred stock that apply to repurchases should apply to redemptions. With these protections in place, redemption of preferred stock should be permitted, subject to any restrictions in the company's charter.

Mandatory redemption. It should be permissible for the charter to require the company to redeem its preferred stock or to give the holders of preferred stock the right to demand redemption of the preferred stock at a specified date or on the occurrence of a specified event or events. The company's obligation to redeem shares would be subject to the limits on any repurchase or redemption established for protection of creditors. In addition, the board of directors should not be obligated to redeem stock if the company lacks sufficient funds to do so. This is the central difference between stock and debt – debtholders have a contractual right to be repaid and can force the company into bankruptcy if they are not paid, while stockholders cannot.

The holders of common stock should not have the right to demand redemption of their shares. This is equivalent to the right to demand payment of a dividend. The decision on whether to pay dividends on common stock should be left in the hands of the board of directors.

Reverse stock split. A reverse stock split, in which small holdings become fractions of a new share and are cashed out, is a form of mandatory repurchase of common stock. Since it is nonpro-rata, it should require approval by a majority of outstanding shares, and the price paid for fractional shares should be fair market value. Because of the potential for repurchase through a reverse stock split at an unfair price, shareholders whose shares are cashed out should be able to obtain a judicial or arbitral valuation of the shares, just as for a merger or other major transaction.

Control Transactions

Control transactions are transactions in which a controlling shareholder purchases (or aggregates) a controlling block of stock in the company. Such transactions can assume a wide variety of forms, ranging from open market purchases and tender offers to large issues of shares by companies directly in the course of financing or merger transactions. But whatever its form, the transfer of control in our view merits regulation in its own right – notwithstanding the fact that many control transactions will also be regulated by the rules governing reorganizations, major transactions, or self-interested transactions.

Control transactions receive disparate treatment under the statutes of developed economies. They are unregulated in the most important U.S. jurisdictions or regulated principally with a view to discouraging them but are widely regulated elsewhere including (as we discuss below) in Great Britain. Beneath this divergent treatment lies a familiar policy dilemma. On the one hand, control transactions are frequently engines for efficient restructuring. In a friendly sale of control, the control shareholder who pays a premium price for a control block often does so because the shareholder expects to improve the efficiency of the company in ways that will benefit all shareholders (see, e.g., Barclay and Holderness 1992). Equally important, the ability of an outside investor to aggregate a controlling block of a company's stock without the consent of the company's managers is an important constraint on bad management. Thus, there are powerful efficiency reasons to avoid overregulating both friendly and hostile control transactions. On the other hand, control transactions may also occur for bad reasons: the new controlling shareholder may plan to loot the company or use control to manipulate share prices and acquire minority shares at a price far below their true value.[26]

Whatever the optimal regulation of control transactions in developed economies, we believe that the dangers of looting that cannot be otherwise deterred require basic regulation of control transactions in the Russian context. Fortunately, the British City Code on Takeovers and Mergers and the proposed European Community 13th Directive on Company Law offer a self-regulatory solution that is easily adapted to the Russian statute. Our proposed law protects minority shareholders in control transactions by

---

[26] For a systematic development of these points, see Bebchuk (1993).

requiring that a shareholder who acquires a 30 percent interest in a company buy all remaining shares at the highest price paid for any shares in the 30 percent control block within the previous six months. In effect, minority shareholders receive a "put" option to sell their shares to the new controlling shareholder. The 30 percent threshold that triggers the put option is simply a bright-line approximation of the share ownership needed to convey effective control of the company.

This City Code rule, as it is sometimes termed, is a powerful deterrent to inefficient control transactions, since even poorly informed minority shareholders will presumably exercise their put options upon receiving any indication of possible looting or suspect management by a new controller. It is equally clear, however, that the City Code rule deters some efficient control transactions. For example, if a controlling shareholder already extracts large private returns from a company, a new and more efficient acquirer may not be able to afford the controller's demand for a premium price for the company's shares if the would-be acquirer must also pay the same high price to minority shareholders. Alternatively, in the underdeveloped Russian capital market, a would-be acquirer of a control block simply may not be able to finance a put option for minority shareholders. These costs of the City Code rule can be mitigated (although not eliminated) by our further proposal to permit minority shareholders by majority vote to opt out of the requirement that an acquirer of control must offer them a put option. Thus, where the purchaser of a control block can persuade minority shareholders that the transaction is in their interest as well, the purchaser can avoid the costs of an offer to repurchase minority shares.

A second concern associated with control transactions is the danger that disaggregated shareholders can be induced to sell control too cheaply. This may happen if an acquirer secretly accumulates control through numerous open market transactions, although shareholders would have demanded higher prices had they known of a control interest and other potential acquirers might have been prepared to offer higher prices as well. To prevent such secret acquisitions of control, the proposed law requires that shareholders who acquire 15 percent or more of a company's stock publicly disclose their identity, shareholdings, and plans and then wait 30 days before buying more shares. This gives the company's managers time to respond to the secret acquisition by seeking a higher bidder, proposing an alternative transaction that is more favorable to the shareholders, or convincing shareholders that their shares are worth more than the acquirer is offering to pay. Similarly, a person who plans to acquire 30 percent of more of a company's shares should also publicly announce this plan at least 30 days before completing the acquisition. This allows a competing bidder to make a higher offer, even when the original transaction was approved by the company's managers.

Together these provisions help to ensure that changes in control occur at fair prices. They encourage auctions of companies undergoing a change of control by providing a time period during which the managers of the company can find an outside bidder who will offer a higher price, or an outside bidder can offer to pay a price that is higher than the price to be paid in a transaction supported by management. Thus, these delay and notice provisions protect both management against secret takeovers and shareholders against low-priced takeovers supported by management.

Finally, the prospect that managers might ignore shareholder interests raises a third key concern associated with control transactions: that is, the risk that managers may block changes of control to preserve their own jobs. This danger arises in hostile takeover bids, when managers typically argue that they need to wield the power to reject bids in the interests of shareholders. We are skeptical of this argument in developed economies, where it has enjoyed a good deal of success. We are even more skeptical in the Russian context, where managers are already heavily entrenched through a combination of share ownership and effective control over the voting power of employee shares.

In response to a hostile bid for control, managers should be allowed a reasonable period of time to find a higher bidder or to persuade shareholders not to sell their shares. They should not be permitted additional power to defeat hostile takeover bids by deploying preclusive defensive tactics such as "poison pills." Experience in the United States and European countries teaches that managers' claims to use these devices in the interests of shareholders are often false. Whatever managers say, when jobs and power are at stake, they often act to preserve their positions, even at great cost to shareholders. Moreover, even independent directors often act to favor the managers' interests. Thus, we believe strongly that *shareholders*, not managers or directors, should decide whether a control change occurs or not by selling (or not) their shares. U.S. directors with the power to do so have often turned down takeover offers priced at twice the previous market value of shares on the supposed grounds that shareholders will do even better if the takeover is defeated. The managers who make these claims rarely offer to resign when, as usually happens, their optimistic predictions do not come true.

Circular Voting Structures

One particular defensive tactic, circular voting structures among affiliated companies, raises difficult line-drawing problems that merit separate consideration. Circular voting structures commonly turn on a parent company's power to direct the voting of large blocks of its own stock held by its own subsidiaries. By voting such stock, parent company managers can entrench themselves with their own company's resources. Yet, barring subsidiary cross-ownership would be an impractical response to circular voting, since subsidiaries often hold their parents' stock for good reason, as when parents acquire target companies in reverse triangular mergers.[27] Rather, a more sensible response is merely to bar the cross-voting of parent stock held by subsidiaries, since cross-voting carries obvious risks but few clear benefits.

The real complication in barring cross-voting of a subsidiary's shares lies in setting the threshold size of the *parent's* holdings in the subsidiary that triggers the prohibition. In Delaware, as in U.S. jurisdictions generally, only majority-owned subsidiaries are barred from voting parents' stock.[28] But this rule is far too narrow. Although the managers of parent companies clearly control majority-owned subsidiaries, they may also exercise working control at far lower ownership thresholds. Thus, the model Russian statute would bar the voting of "parent" stock when parents hold 30 percent or more of their subsidiary's voting stock – the same threshold for working control that triggers minority shareholders' put rights under the acquisition provisions. Needless to say, legal entities such as trusts and partnerships in which a company holds more than 30 percent of ownership or control rights must also be barred from voting shares in their parents.

To be sure, such a ban on cross-voting subsidiary-held shares can prevent only egregious entrenchment schemes because it allows cross-voting at parent ownership levels below the 30 percent threshold and thus permits groups of companies to tie up control internally through cross-holdings. For example, the rule would not bar a Japanese-style *keiretsu*, in which a dozen companies held 5 percent stakes in one another, even though such a structure would preclude any control challenge to the management of a member company that was not sanctioned by the group.[29] But there are reasons for permitting such structures. They may serve benign as well as defensive purposes: for example, cross-ownership may encourage mutual monitoring or help to enforce relational contracts in the product market.[30] In addition, entrenchment seems a less pressing threat when controlling shares reside in a

---

[27] In a reverse triangular merger, a parent company acquires a target by merging a subsidiary into the target. The consideration for the acquisition is parent stock held by the subsidiary, which is exchanged for the stock of the target company. The advantage of the transaction is that it does not disturb the corporate identity or contractual relationships of the target

[28] See, e.g. Del. Gen. Corp. L. § 160(c).

[29] See Gilson and Roe (1993) (describing cross-ownership in *keiretsu* structures).

[30] See Gilson and Roe (1993) (arguing that cross ownership in vertical *keiretsu* may serve in part to enforce and stabilize intragroup contracting).

286 Black, Kraakman, and Hay

larger group of companies, as distinct from a single parent company whose managers have a powerful interest in their own incumbency.

Indeed, there is one circumstance in which even the 30 percent trigger for prohibiting cross-voting must be relaxed: a target company in a hostile takeover cannot be permitted to strip an acquirer of the right to vote target stock by purchasing a 30 percent stake in the acquirer as a defensive measure. In mirror-image acquisitions of controlling blocks of stock, the rule must be that the first buyer (the acquirer) retains its voting rights regardless of the target's response, as long as the statutory acquisition rules are observed.

Remedies

A defining feature of the self-enforcement model is a strong effort to economize on enforcement resources. This leads, for reasons already discussed, to a preference for bright-line rules – barring the few cases where general standards are used for their value in shaping voluntary behavior over the long term, despite their unenforceability in the near term. A related feature should be an attempt to define clearly the remedies for violations of the rules, rather than to leave their development to the courts. This will not always be possible, but some common violations can be anticipated and their consequences elaborated, rather than be left to the uncertain wisdom of judges to determine. For remedies, as for the underlying legal norms, simplicity will often trump fine-grained tailoring of the remedy to a concrete situation.

Remedies should generally take the form of rights running to shareholders directly, rather than of rights mediated by the corporation (acting on behalf of all shareholders) or by regulators. Thus, the cumbersome device of the derivative suit – a suit by the shareholder in the name of the corporation – has little place in an emerging economy because it requires painstaking judicial oversight of when the board should have the right to control the suit. Instead, shareholders should be given direct rights to recover damages from managers or large shareholders if they discover a previously undisclosed self-interested transaction. In the spirit of a self-enforcing statute, moreover, shareholders can sometimes be left to determine the content of a remedy. One example is our proposal that a shareholder who improperly crosses 30 percent ownership should lose voting rights unless they are restored by majority vote of the other shareholders; a second example is our proposal that a shareholder vote must be retaken to remedy improper voting procedures, thus permitting shareholders to decide how to react to the misfeasance of the managers the first time around.

A key question is how strict the penalties for violation of the rules should be. Here two factors argue in favor of strict penalties, while two others argue in favor of limiting the severity of the sanctions. The relative force of the different factors will vary depending on context, which makes it difficult to generalize about the optimal severity of sanctions. We describe the factors that bear on the choice of sanction below and offer examples that illustrate our own balancing judgment.

The first factor arguing for strict sanctions is the need to motivate for proper conduct when actors know that the probability of enforcement is low (see Becker 1968). Consider, for example, violations of the requirement that self-interested transactions receive the approval of disinterested shareholders. We propose that managers, directors, and 10 percent shareholders who violate this requirement by failing to disclose an interested transaction must return all profit from the transaction to the company. Contrary to the majority rule in the United States, we reject a defense based on transactional fairness, as well as *ex post* shareholder ratification as a defense to liability in self-dealing transactions, because these defenses weaken incentive to obtain the shareholder vote *ex ante*. Managers will be tempted to ignore the procedures *in advance* if the remedy for failing to follow them is a mere reprise of the required procedures. If one asks, where is the harm as long as shareholders approve an action *ex post*, the answer is the loss of the prophylactic value of *ex ante* approval and *ex ante* disclosure. Not every transaction that would be approved *ex post* will be proposed *ex ante*; not every transaction that would be disapproved will be challenged.

The second factor calling for strict sanctions is an offshoot of the use of bright-line rules. When actors cannot be certain if their conduct is lawful, severe sanctions can chill legitimate behavior. In the corporate sphere, for example, a major justification for the business judgment rule – which protects directors from liability even for demonstrably stupid decisions – is the fear of chilling risk-taking in a world where we often want managers to take gambles, sometimes long-shot gambles, on limited information. Other things equal, the more the law uses bright-line norms, the less a severe sanction will chill desirable activity.

For example, we propose that the remedy for crossing the 30 percent ownership threshold for the control transaction rules without prior notice or without offering to buy all remaining shares should be loss of voting power *as to all shares* held by the 30 percent shareholder and his affiliates, unless other shareholders vote to restore voting rights, or the shareholder acquires at least 90 percent of the outstanding shares. A severe sanction is appropriate here not only because violations may be difficult to detect (acquirers may hide ownership by buying through undisclosed affiliates) but also because a clear rule means that inadvertent violation should be rare.

Other factors cut against severe sanctions. One cannot assume that corporate managers will know the rules. Especially for rules that apply to small companies, strong sanctions may seem unacceptably harsh for inadvertent violators. A related factor is that the law must be seen to be fair if it is to serve its goal of inducing voluntary obedience and, ideally, the conformity of culture to the new law. The need for perceived fairness means that sanctions will fall well short of the economist's simple prescription that the sanction equal the gain from improper conduct divided by the probability of detection. These considerations explain why, for example, we do not propose double or triple damages for undisclosed self-interested transactions.

Sometimes, no remedy may be better than a remedy that is apt to be misapplied by inexpert courts. For example, we propose that directors should *never* be liable for actions taken without self-interest. That is, we close off the narrow recklessness/gross negligence exception to the business judgment rule, because we have no confidence in the ability of courts to decide when conduct is sufficiently outrageous to warrant imposition of personal liability.

Finally, there are cases where there is no ideal remedy. Suppose that a company fails to use cumulative voting. One cannot invalidate the actions of the improperly elected board without imposing an unrealistic burden on others having contractual dealings with the company to investigate its governance. The violation is clear enough so that one can imagine imposing personal liability on board members for loss to the company from actions approved by an improperly elected board. Yet we hesitate to do so, partly because small companies may unwittingly fail to comply with the cumulative voting rules and partly because the directors who would resign to avoid this liability may be the best of a bad lot. We are left with the weak sanction of running a new election – which will at least allow shareholders to vote again, knowing how their directors have behaved in the past.

What If Courts Do Not Function at All?

Are strong remedies enough to make the self-enforcing model work if judicial enforcement is as weak, corruption as widespread, and organized crime as strong as is currently the case in Russia? To what extent can it be self-enforcing not only in the sense of empowering outside shareholders but also in the basic sense of eliciting compliance without relying on consistent official enforcement? To explore this question, let us imagine, counterfactually, a world with *no* official enforcement: that is, no official organ to enforce corporate law rules. If the self-enforcing approach can work there – in the sense of setting standards that are often complied with – then it can only work better if official enforcement is merely weak, rather than absent, as is the case in Russia.

The concept of rules without enforcement is not entirely new. Robert Ellickson (1991), in particular, has explored situations in which norms of conduct emerge when no official enforcement is possible, as for fishing vessels in international waters, or when official rules are out of touch with practical needs and a consensus develops around different norms. Here, we consider the potential for law without official enforcement in the specific context of corporate law. For example, suppose that company directors can ignore all corporate law, voting rules without fear of official intervention. What recourse is open to a 20 percent shareholder who wants a seat on the board if the company erases him from the shareholder register, refuses to provide cumulative voting, or conveniently loses his ballot?

One answer is that the question has been posed too starkly. Even without official sanctions, most companies will not resort to such tactics. Some will comply with the written law simply because it is both written and reasonable. Some managers will comply because otherwise they risk embarrassing news stories or being looked down on by their more law-abiding friends. Some will comply because this is how their peers behave. Companies that want to raise capital will have to comply with the rules, so as to build a reputation for honest behavior. Companies that want long-term contractual relations with others also must pay some attention to their reputation for honesty and fair dealing.

In addition, there may be harsher penalties for breaking the rules. A world without official enforcement will surely have unofficial enforcement. Suppose, quite plausibly in Russia, that some shareholders will resort to violence if what they see as their rights are violated, but company directors are not sure who will and who will not react this way. No shareholder is likely to shoot a director merely for making a bad business decision. That would be foolish on the shareholder's part: unlikely to encourage better business decisions in the future and likely to encourage retaliation in kind. But the situation is different if the directors break a clear rule. A wrong has been committed; if some shareholders feel they must respond, a director faces personal liability of a tangible kind. It follows that few directors will act in blatant disregard of the written law. At the very least, the directors will take the demand of a 20 percent shareholder for board representation seriously. They will weigh the costs against the benefits, much as they would do if official enforcement were one possible cost.

To be sure, private enforcers need not enforce only the written rules. But private enforcement will often develop this way. Moreover, it is not necessary that all shareholders be willing to act extralegally or even be capable of doing so. It is enough that a few can. Fear of these few can cause directors to behave properly toward all shareholders. Directors will anticipate that the more blatantly shareholder rights are violated, the more likely it is that some shareholder will take extralegal action, and thus the greater the expected sanction associated with the violation will be. For example, wiping a shareholder off the register is more likely to provoke a violent response than refusing to use the required procedures for approving a related-party transaction. In this case, the corporate law will be, quite literally, a set of default rules that the participants in the corporate enterprise can depart from jointly or unilaterally. As with any set of default rules, it will be costly to ignore them or contract around them; indeed, contracting around will be especially difficult in precisely the assumed situation of no official enforcement.

We do not suggest that such a world is anything near ideal. Some directors will be shot for imagined wrongs. Shareholders, too, are at risk if they buy shares in the wrong company and then complain when the company is looted. Large shareholders will often succeed in obtaining private benefits from the company, especially if these can be hidden from other shareholders. But on the whole, those with guns will often be polite to each other, especially if, as will be the typical case for corporate enterprises, they expect to meet again. Repeated interaction magnifies the importance of reputation and the risk of retaliation for misbehavior. A corporate law that defines norms of politeness in ways that the participants perceive as reasonable can be effective in the absence of any official enforcement.

Once we introduce the possibility of some recourse to courts, even to corrupt courts or courts whose decisions can be ignored because the loser can bribe the enforcer, the effectiveness of corporate law quickly increases. A corrupt judge can twist a reasonableness standard to reach the decision he was paid to reach. He cannot so easily twist a requirement that the company provide cumulative voting. If he finds an exception on some spurious grounds, it will be obvious to all. The judge will lose face in the community – few corrupt officials want to admit their corruption in public. And such a judge will risk personal retaliation, much as corporate managers do.

Over the longer term, blatant violation of norms can also create a constituency for enforcement. Shareholders will bring political pressure to strengthen enforcement capability. They will have obvious abuses to point to. News stories will highlight the scandals, bringing further pressure for enforcement. Test cases, even if they fail in corrupt courts, will form a base for public opinion, and there will be repeat players in financial markets who are willing to underwrite the cost of a test case.

Finally, even if official enforcement is weak today, it may be stronger tomorrow. Corporate actors will be reluctant to rely on nonenforcement if the downside risk from violating the rules extends far enough into the future so that future enforcement is possible. This will be doubly true if corporate rules are designed with a long tail and with severe enough sanctions if enforcement takes place. For example, managers may prefer to seek share-holder approval of a self-interested transaction if they judge that approval is reasonably likely, rather than risk having the transaction unwound sometime in the future.

In short, corporate law can be reasonably effective even under conditions of weak official enforcement. And law can do much to shape private behavior even without official enforcement.

Regulation of Special Classes of Participants

Beyond regulating particular classes of transactions, company law for emerging economies must also recognize the needs, vulnerabilities, and limitations of particular classes of financial participants in public companies. In the case of Russia, two classes of participants require status-based protec-tion in the company law: creditors and shareholding employees. Creditors require protection against efforts by shareholders or managers to extract wealth from a firm, leaving creditors to collect from an empty shell. Employee shareholders require protection against management efforts to use power over employment as a lever to control the voting of employee shares, to the detriment of both employees and outside shareholders generally. By contrast, a third class of shareholder, the state, may need to have its powers as a shareholder restricted if they are likely to be exercised for corrupt or extra-corporate reasons, as when officials who control state shareholdings trade their votes for personal favors that managers can supply. Finally, the law should attend to the interests of large, active investors, domestic or foreign, who demand influence or even control in exchange for large infusions of capital. Here the worry is whether the self-enforcing model is overprotective: do its mandatory rules, such as one share, one vote, prevent these investors from structuring financial arrangements with the companies in which they invest in mutually beneficial ways?

Protecting Creditors and Preferred Shareholders

In developed and emerging economies alike, contract is the principal instru-ment of self-protection for creditors and preferred shareholders. Banks can take security interests in company assets; bondholders can demand covenants that restrict distributions of corporate assets; trade creditors can provide only short-term credit, thus limiting their loss in the event of default; and preferred shareholders can seek the power to elect the board of directors if dividends are missed. But experience also suggests a role for legal limits on distributions even in developed economies. In the United States, for example, contractual limits on corporate distributions are supplemented by company law, which bars dividends by an insolvent company, by "look-back" provisions of bankruptcy law that allow recapture of prebankruptcy distributions, and by fraudulent conveyance law.

In an emerging market, the need to protect creditors is even greater because they are often less sophisticated; because contracts may not be readily enforceable; and because credit market institutions may be absent, such as financing factors to monitor borrowers on behalf of small trade creditors and information services to report on credit histories and financial strength. But despite the greater need for protection, the available legal tools for protecting creditors are very limited. In Russia bankruptcy law does not function at all, let alone contain sophisticated look-back provisions; secured lending is crippled by a Civil Code provision that gives secured lenders third priority in insolvency proceedings, after personal injury claims and employee claims (Russian Civil Code art. 64); courts cannot interpret sensibly a Delaware-like rule that looks to market value, rather than book value, to determine whether a company was insolvent after paying a dividend.

To respond to the limitations of contract law and bankruptcy law, we believe that corporate law in emerging markets should include two types of protections for creditors: (1) a limit on dividends and stock repurchases that requires companies to have a positive *book and market* value after the dividend or repurchase; and (2) a fairly standard fraudulent conveyance provision that, although fuzzy, provides some additional protection against transactions that diminish the company's assets.

Limits on Dividends and Stock Repurchases

The simplest ways for a company to distribute assets to shareholders, leaving less for creditors, are through dividends (cash, stock, or other property) and stock repurchases. These are identical transactions from a creditor's perspective and should be regulated in the same manner. The law should permit dividends or repurchases only if after payment the company will (1) have assets greater than liabilities, whether assets and liabilities are measured at book or at market value; and (2) can reasonably expect to be able to pay its bills as they come due. The first test is an asset test for solvency of the company; the second test is a liquidity test for solvency.[31] (For repurchases

---

[31] In the United States, a third solvency test is also used: after the transaction, the company

the requirement that the company repurchase stock at fair market value also provides some protection for creditors since if the company is close to insolvency, its shares will have little value.) Similarly, to protect preferred stockholders, the law should allow dividends on or repurchases of common stock only if after payment the company's assets minus its liabilities exceed the liquidation preference that the preferred stock would enjoy if the company were to be liquidated immediately.[32]

We recommend asset tests based on both book value and market values to regulate company distributions. Book value may be a totally unrealistic measure of value in any economy with high inflation, and especially in Russia where many intercompany debts that will never be paid are still listed as assets. However, the alternative of a market value test alone is very difficult to apply because the market prices of assets are hard to determine. By contrast, the liquidity test may have real bite in Russia. A company that has positive book value only because it has not written off uncollectible intercompany debts – a common situation in Russia – will have trouble convincing any business actor that it met this test if it pays a big dividend one month and defaults on the next. Indeed, the mere statement of this rule may dissuade some borrowers from clear violations, particularly in Russia where banks are reputed to employ Mafia hit men to encourage repayment of debts.

Finally, we propose to protect creditors and preferred shareholders by compelling companies to disclose large dividends or repurchases that may affect company creditworthiness. By statute companies must notify creditors promptly about dividends or stock repurchases that decrease book value by more than 25 percent. This lets the creditors avail themselves of contractual rights and evaluate whether and on what terms to extend new credit. Large creditors can, of course, insist on notice of dividend restrictions by contract, but trade creditors may not be able to, or think to, and often lack other sources of information about changes in a borrower's financial condition.

---

must not have an unreasonably small amount of capital left with which to conduct its business (National Conference of Commissioners on Uniform State Laws, *Uniform Fraudulent Transfer Act* § 4(b)(i)). But this extremely vague test is rarely used in practice. In keeping with our preference for defining requirements as clearly as we can to guide both directors and judges, we do not consider this third standard to be useful in an emerging market.

[32] If there is more than one class of preferred stock, a similar restriction would apply to dividends or repurchases of a junior class of preferred stock. The dividend or repurchase would be permitted only if, after the dividend or repurchase, the company's net assets were sufficient to pay the liquidation preference of the more senior preferred stock.

Fraudulent Conveyances

Although dividends and stock repurchases are particularly suspect as asset distributions, any corporate transaction can be a vehicle for extracting assets from the company to the detriment of creditors and often shareholders as well. The challenge is how to block such bogus transactions without impeding ordinary business dealings. Here we can do no better than the vague standard, familiar from fraudulent conveyance law, that a transaction is improper if (1) the company does not receive reasonably equivalent value, and (2) the company fails an asset-based or liquidity-based solvency test after the transaction. The standard of reasonably equivalent value is vague, but it can at least reach the egregious cases where a company transfers all of its remaining assets to third parties for nominal consideration in order to evade its legitimate creditors. For example, a typical Russian situation involves a raw materials company selling its product at a fraction of market value to another company controlled by its managers, who then resell at the market price. A creditor, irate shareholder, or even a judge should be able to spot a sale at a bargain price followed by prompt resale at a far higher price. And, as this example suggests, many fraudulent conveyance transactions are self-interested, which also enlists the self-interested transaction rules in protecting creditors and those shareholders who do not share in the company's largess.

A Methodological Note

In framing these creditor protection rules, we may appear to have moved beyond the self-enforcing model of procedural protection to that of substantive prohibition. In part, we have. Prohibitive restrictions on dividends and stock repurchases are justified by the strong incentives of shareholders and managers to grab what they can from a sinking ship; the dearth of legitimate reasons for a company near insolvency to pay dividends; and the difficulty of attacking this problem in another way, since a company's relationships with creditors are too complex to permit a voting solution. The justification for prohibiting fraudulent conveyances outright is even stronger. Apart from payments to shareholders through dividends and stock repurchases, companies should never enter into transactions without receiving reasonably equivalent consideration in return.

In part, however, the appearance of substantive prohibition is deceiving. A company with genuine business need to pay a dividend that the book value test would otherwise prohibit can do so by first raising new equity capital to pay off its old creditors. The company can even recreate its old capital structure if lenders can be found. In effect statutory distribution restrictions mean that the company must give creditors a chance to vote with their feet. Evading the distribution restrictions by recapitalizing debt has substantial transaction costs, which is why these restrictions are appropriately limited to the extreme cases in which companies would have no net book or market value after distribution payments. Yet the possibility of a recapitalization softens the harshness of the book value test in an inflationary environment where book value is a poor measure of actual value.

Protection of Employee Shareholders

In many Russian companies, he who controls the votes of employee shares controls the company. This is not lost on company managers, who have quickly developed ways to ensure that they decide how employee shares are voted. In part the corporate law can respond, as is discussed above, by diffusing power within the corporation to larger minority shareholders, and thus weakening the absolute control of holders of 51 percent of the votes. But the law can also act directly to protect employees by securing their rights to vote and transfer shares without coercion. Confidential voting and independent tabulation help – managers who do not know how an employee has voted cannot threaten reprisal for a vote against management. But more is needed, lest managers resort to other coercive techniques. For example, some Russian managers already have caused/forced/convinced employees to transfer their shares to a long-term trust, voted by the managers, from which shares cannot be withdrawn.

The problem is familiar in developed countries in the guise of statutory time and other limits on voting trusts and similar arrangements that separate the economic interest in stock from voting power. It is acute for employees who may not be fully aware of what they gave up when they agreed to join a trust. And it is doubly acute in Russia because there is no trust law to limit managers' control over trusts and because most employees either cannot make an *informed* choice about joining a trust or are given no choice – they are told to put their shares into a trust managed on behalf of the "labor collective."

A ban on all employee trusts and similar devices for pooling employee shares would respond to the problem of manager domination, but it would also foreclose the possibility of a labor union-controlled trust that might serve as a valuable counterweight to management. Our judgment for Russia was that this solution is too extreme. Instead, we proposed several related rules to regulate employee trusts. First, managers should not be permitted to control any trust formed primarily to hold employee shares (employee trust). Second, employees should have the right, at any time, to sell shares or withdraw them from an employee trust. Third, the maximum duration of any such trust should be short, say two years, to give employees a frequent option to opt out of participating. Fourth, company managers should neither ask an employee how he has voted or whether he has sold or plans to sell his shares, nor retaliate against an employee because of how the employee has voted (or whether the employee has sold) his shares. Enforcement of these rules would be difficult, but some managers would honor them voluntarily (now, they often believe that defending the company by locking up employee votes is proper). Moreover, if the principle is established, the press would explore clear violations and assist even weak labor unions in protecting their members against overt retaliation.

The State as Part-Owner

The state is frequently an important equity holder in emerging economies – especially in the privatizing economies of Central and Eastern Europe. In Russia, for example, the best available data for mid-1994 (after completion of voucher privatization, but before cash privatization) suggest that regional property funds in Russia retain some equity in the majority of privatized companies and hold stakes of 20 percent or more in perhaps one-third of all companies.[33] Thus, regional property funds are not infrequently the largest single shareholders in Russian companies, although their holdings are generally smaller than the combined insider holdings of managers and employees.

The issue raised by large state holdings of voting stock is whether state organs should be restricted in the exercise of voting rights over the shares that they control – perhaps along the lines of the American rule that requires federal employee pension funds to vote in proportion to other shareholders. Several concerns are raised. Most generally, government officials will not behave like private shareholders who bear the economic consequences of company decisions. More specifically, officials may form alliances with managers at the expense of shareholders, competitive markets, or both and may influence company policies in inefficient directions to accomplish public ends (such as preserving employment in a particular region). But, state officials could serve as a counterweight to insider domination of Russian companies, particularly if a regional property authority were planning to sell its shares in the near future.

In Russia we are not sure how likely local officials are to behave like real shareholders. For this reason, we favor neutralizing government shares in the

[33] These estimates are from a nonrepresentative survey of a handful of regional property funds (see Pistor and Turkewitz in this volume).

election of boards of directors. State bodies should neither nominate nor vote for candidates for the board of directors, although they should retain authority to vote on company issues, such as mergers, charter amendments, and the like. Of course, convincing government authorities to adopt such a policy of strict neutrality may be a difficult matter – officials who are likely to abuse their voting power are unlikely to support limits on that power.

Venture Capital

The fourth class of nonstandard investors are those whom we term "venture capitalists": large, active equity investors, foreign or domestic, who demand influence or even control as the price of their investment. Just as venture capitalists are primary suppliers of equity capital to high-risk start-up companies in developed economies, venture capitalists are likely to be important sources of equity capital in emerging economies, where most companies are highly risky because of a rapidly changing economic environment, whatever their size or prior track record.

Venture capitalists in developed economies exploit the enabling model's flexibility laws to tailor elaborate control arrangements for their own protection. One might ask, then, whether the mandatory procedures of the self-enforcing model will prevent arrangements that these investors might otherwise prefer. At first glance it might seem that two features of our proposal are especially likely to interfere with venture capital investments: (1) the requirement that each company have a single class of voting common stock, and (2) the obligation, triggered by a purchase of over 30 percent of a company's common stock, to offer to buy all remaining shares at a commensurate price. But in fact these provisions will not block the control arrangements that venture capitalists traditionally demand, but only make them modestly more complicated to create. Suppose, for example, that a venture capitalist wants to buy directly from a company newly issued shares that will represent a 40 percent interest in the firm. Our control transaction rules permit the firm's current shareholders to waive their "put" rights to sell their own shares to the venture capitalist after such a transaction by a simple majority vote. Obtaining such a waiver would impose virtually no added cost on the company, since shareholders must vote to authorize a 40 percent share issuance in any event. By contrast, if the venture capitalist wished to buy a 40 percent stake from existing shareholders, rather than from the company, then a vote on waiver would entail some transaction costs and delay, but our judgment is that these costs are justified by the protection that the buyout rule accords minority shareholders.

A more difficult but still soluble problem arises if the venture capitalist wishes to make a minority investment while retaining veto rights over critical transactions. Under the enabling model, such a transaction is often structured by creating a second class of voting stock that gives the investor both general voting rights and – perhaps through a class vote – the particular veto rights that are desired. Under the self-enforcing model statute that we propose, the same control structure can be created by combining partial ownership of a single class of common stock with creation of a class of preferred stock equipped with voting rights limited to issues of particular concern to the venture capitalist. Indeed, virtually the only rights that a venture capitalist could not demand under our proposed statute are (1) voting rights for directors disproportionate to its total equity investment or (2) voting rights for directors attached to preferred rather than common stock. And even these restraints could be finessed for particular investment opportunities through a joint venture contract that allocated management power as the participants saw fit.

Conclusion: Self-Enforcing Law in Emerging Economies

In this chapter we have argued that the best model for company law for an emerging economy is neither the enabling model that characterizes developed economies today nor the prohibitive model that characterized corporate law a century ago, but instead a self-enforcing model. The core of this model is an effort to harness the incentives of participants in the corporate enterprise to provide meaningful shareholder protection despite the absence of the multiple private and public enforcement resources of developed economies. Minority and outside shareholders require more legal protection from insiders in emerging markets because the market controls that provide such protection in developed economies are weak. Yet, because public enforcement is also weak, company law in emerging markets cannot simply substitute formal law enforcement for the missing market controls.

To operate effectively in the difficult environment of emerging markets, company law must be self-enforcing in a double sense. First, it must provide procedural mechanisms that replace absent mechanisms for formal enforcement and allow outside and minority shareholders and directors to police the opportunism of managers and controlling shareholders. These constraints should be procedural, rather than substantive as in the prohibitive model, to preserve the great value of flexibility in corporate decision-making.

Second, because self-enforcement in this first sense is also difficult and costly, the company law must elicit a substantial measure of voluntary compliance from managers and controlling shareholders. Toward this end, the statute must articulate bright-line and easily understood rules and must provide terms that corporate actors recognize as appropriate to their business circumstances. Thus, although the model is intended in part to substitute private enforcement for the government enforcement mechanisms of developed economies, it also rests in part on self-enforcement of a different kind: the inherent organizing force of clear and legitimate law in an otherwise chaotic business environment.

The drafting strategy implicit in this self-enforcing model reaches almost every aspect of company law. At the most basic level, our model statute structures the company's voting system to increase the influence of minority blockholders. It mandates a single class of voting common stock, a one share, one vote rule, and a cumulative voting rule for the election of directors. In addition it provides for a universal ballot, by which large shareholders can nominate board candidates.

Similarly, the model statute relies on process constraints to regulate classes of suspect transactions. Significant self-dealing transactions must be authorized by majority votes of both disinterested directors and disinterested shareholders. Mergers, liquidations, and large purchases and sales of assets require an authorizing vote of two-thirds of outstanding shares – a high threshold necessary to ensure that the management–worker coalitions that control most Russian companies must enlist at least some support from outside investors to complete these transactions. New issues of shares are subject to preemption rights. These can be collectively waived by a shareholder vote, but shareholders who do not approve the waiver receive *ex post* participation rights, much as shareholders who do not approve a merger receive appraisal rights. The acquisition of control stakes carries the obligation to offer to purchase minority shares, and defensive measures that might prevent shareholders from selling out to would-be acquirers are prohibited.

These and other features of the self-enforcing approach produce a company law that is novel in the aggregate, even if many of its individual provisions (such as mandatory cumulative voting) are familiar. The model flatly prohibits almost nothing except efforts to opt out of its process requirements. Nonetheless, it significantly constrains managing insiders and controlling shareholders by allocating to large-block minority shareholders (i.e. those shareholders with sufficient holdings or support to win board representation under a cumulative voting rule) considerable power to influence corporate decision-making.

It is inherent in our model that corporate law should evolve as an economy evolves. As compared with the enabling model, the self-enforcing model gives greater power to outside investors but at the cost of greater rigidity in the basic structure of corporate governance. As market constraints and a sophisticated judiciary develop to constrain opportunism by managers and large shareholders, the comparative merit of the enabling model will increase. In 10 or 20 years, perhaps, mandatory cumulative voting, or a mandatory one share, one vote rule, will have outlived its usefulness and can be relaxed.

Perhaps too, as the liquidity of shareholdings increases, institutional shareholders will tend to reduce their percentage stakes in companies so as to make the exit option more viable.[34] If large investors choose exit over voice, the voice-enhancing benefits of the self-enforcing model will shrink, while the costs of voice will remain. Corporate law then should, and probably will, evolve toward fewer voice-promoting rules.

But evolution toward the enabling model is not a foregone conclusion. Given the mutual interaction between the law and the evolution of companies and financial institutions, in which strong protections for large outside investors encourage large percentage investments, the self-enforcing statute may prove substantially stable. These large shareholders could also provide the political constituency to preserve the self-enforcing model against the attacks of managers seeking greater autonomy. The result would be a different model of a mature company law: one that relied much more on internal decision-making processes and shareholder authorization, and much less on *ex post* litigation, than is currently the practice in the United States.

[34] For development of the argument that financial institutions will often choose exit over voice if both options are available, see Coffee (1991); Black and Coffee (1994) (empirical study of behavior of financial institutions in Great Britain).

References

American Law Institute (ALI). 1994. *Principles of Corporate Governance: Analysis and Recommendations.*

Banerjee, Neela. 1995. "Russian oil company tries a stock split in the Soviet style." *Wall Street Journal,* 15 February, A14.

Barclay, Michael, and Clifford Holderness. 1992. "The Law and Large-Block Trades." *Journal of Law & Economics* 35: 265.

Bebchuk, Lucian. 1989. "Limiting Contractual Freedom in Corporate Law: The Desirable Constraints on Charter Amendments." *Harvard Law Review* 102:1820.

—— 1993. "Efficient and Inefficient Sales of Corporate Control." Working Paper, Harvard Law School Program in Law and Economics.

Becker, Gary. 1968. "Crime and Punishment: An Economic Approach." *Journal of Political Economy* 76: 169.

Bhagat, Sanjai, and James Brickley. 1984. "Cumulative Voting: The Value of Minority Shareholder Voting Rights." *Journal of Law & Economics* 27: 339.

Black, Bernard S. 1990. "Is Corporate Law Trivial?: A Political and Economic Analysis." *Northwestern University Law Review* 84: 542.

Black, Bernard S., and John C. Coffee, Jr. 1994. "Hail Britannia? Institutional Investor Behavior under Limited Regulation." *Michigan Law Review* 92: 1997.

Blasi, Joseph. 1994. "Russian Privatization: Ownership, Governance, and Structuring," unpublished report.

Boyko, Maxim, Andrei Shleifer, and Robert Vishny. 1994. "Voucher Privatization." *Journal of Financial Economics* 35: 249.

Brudney, Victor, and Marvin Chirelstein. 1974. "Fair Shares in Mergers and Take-Overs." *Harvard Law Review* 88: 297, 304–7.

Charkham, Jonathan. 1994. *Keeping Good Company: A Study of Corporate Governance in Five Countries.* Oxford: Clarendon Press.

Clark, Robert. 1986. *Corporate Law.* Boston: Little, Brown & Co.

Coffee, John C., Jr. 1991. "Liquidity versus Control: The Institutional Investor as Corporate Monitor." *Columbia Law Review* 91: 1277.

Easterbrook, Frank, and Daniel Fischel. 1992. *The Economic Structure of Corporate Law.* Cambridge, Mass.: Harvard University Press.

Ellickson, Robert. 1991. *Order Without Law.* Cambridge, Mass.: Harvard University Press.

Gilson, Ronald J. 1981. "A Structural Approach to Corporations: The Case against Defensive Tactics in Tender Offers." *Stanford Law Review* 33: 819.

—— 1987. "Dual-Class Common Stock: The Relevance of Substitutes." *Virginia Law Review* 73: 807.

Gilson, Ronald J., and Bernard S. Black. 1995. *The Law and Finance of Corporate Acquisitions.* 2d ed. Westbury, New York: Foundation Press.

Gilson, Ronald J., and Reinier Kraakman. 1984. "The Mechanisms of Market Efficiency." *Virginia Law Review* 70: 549.

—— 1991. "Reinventing the Outside Director: An Agenda for Institutional Investors." *Stanford Law Review* 43: 863.

—— 1993. "Investment Companies as Guardian Shareholders: The Place of the MSIC in the Corporate Governance Debate." *Stanford Law Review* 45: 985.

Gilson, Ronald J., and Mark J. Roe. 1993. "Understanding the Japanese Keiretsu: Overlaps Between Corporate Governance and Industrial Organization." *Yale Law Journal* 102: 871.

Gordon, Jeffrey. 1988. "Ties that Bond: Dual Class Common Stock and the Problem of Shareholder Choice." *California Law Review* 76: 1.

—— 1989. "The Mandatory Structure of Corporate Law." *Columbia Law Review* 89: 1549.

—— 1994. "Institutions as Relational Investors: A New Look at Cumulative Voting." *Columbia Law Review* 94: 124.

Herzel, Leo, Timothy Sherck and Dale Colling. 1982. "Sales and Acquisitions of Divisions." *Corporation Law Review* 5: 3, 25.

Liesman, Steve. 1994. "A Moscow promoter goes from jail cell to Parliament seat." *Wall Street Journal,* 1 November, 16

Lowenstein, Louis. 1989. "Shareholder Voting Rights: A Response to SEC Rule 19C-4 and to Professor Gilson." *Columbia Law Review* 89: 979.

Manning, Bayless. 1962. "The Shareholder's Appraisal Remedy: An Essay for Frank Coker." *Yale Law Journal* 72: 223.

Roe, Mark. 1993. "Some Differences in Corporate Structure in Germany, Japan, and the United States." *Yale Law Journal* 102: 1927.

—— 1994. *Strong Managers, Weak Owners: The Political Roots of American Corporate Finance.* Princeton, New Jersey: Princeton University Press.

Romano, Roberta. 1993. *The Genius of American Corporate Law.* Washington, D.C.: American Enterprise Institute Press.

Rosenstein, Stuart, and David Rush. 1990. "The Stock Return Performance of Corporations That Are Partially Owned By Other Corporations." *Journal of Financial Research* 13: 39.

Rosett, Claudia. 1994. "P.T. Barnum missed a marvelous thing: Russian investments." *Wall Street Journal,* 27 September, A1.

Seligman, Joel. 1986. "Equal Protection in Shareholder Voting Rights: The One Common Share, One Vote Controversy." *George Washington Law Review* 54: 687.

Telser, Lester. 1980. "A Theory of Self-Enforcing Agreements." *Journal of Business* 53: 27.

INDEX